The Bible, Sexuality, *and* Culture

"*The Bible, Sexuality, and Culture*, written by Brian Peterson, is a book worth reading. Why? Peterson addresses moral issues that the church will have to answer. In his book, Peterson gives a clear and solid explanation of the issues, identifies the historical teaching of the church and applies it to the issues, and supports his explanation with a wealth of resources that provide readers with additional sources."

—**DONALD G. BENNETT**
USA coordinator, Division of Education, Church of God

"Brian Peterson's book is like 'cold water to a thirsty soul.' Grounded in accurate hermeneutics and orthodox theology, the book covers relevant topics such as marriage, sexuality, and morality. Peterson's knowledge of history combined with his insights into the present cultural decline make this book a must for anyone who wants to understand how far down the proverbial slope we have come. Thankfully, Peterson invites us to return to the ways of God, the truth of Scripture, and the indwelling of the Holy Spirit who will lead us to 'model what true and authentic sexuality looks like.'"

—**TIBERIUS RATA**
Professor and associate dean, Grace College and Theological Seminary

"The radical reimaging of the biblical narrative regarding sex, marriage, family, and culture has moved our nation to the precipice of an ethical collapse. Although Christian tradition has for centuries held strong dogma in these areas, our generation is witnessing a profound weakening of them and there has been very little serious academic engagement regarding the matter. Thankfully, Dr. Brian Neil Peterson has written an incredible scholarly and biblically sound book, which I highly recommend for any pastor, church leader, parent, or grandparent who wishes to help this generation navigate between biblical truth and cultural pressures."

—**LAMAR VEST**
Former chairman, National Association of Evangelicals

"With today's all-out attack on biblical norms for marriage, sexuality, and family, Peterson's book demonstrates that God's design for marriage, family, and sexuality is best. It must be defended and celebrated. This study, grounded in the Word and sound theology, will help you take a stand."

—**MICHAEL L. BROWN**
Host, Line of Fire broadcast

The Bible, Sexuality, *and* Culture

Raising a Family in a Postmodern
and Post-Christian World

Brian Neil Peterson

RESOURCE *Publications* · Eugene, Oregon

THE BIBLE, SEXUALITY, AND CULTURE
Raising a Family in a Postmodern and Post-Christian World

Copyright © 2021 Brian Neil Peterson. All rights reserved. Except for brief quotations in critical publications or reviews, no part of this book may be reproduced in any manner without prior written permission from the publisher. Write: Permissions, Wipf and Stock Publishers, 199 W. 8th Ave., Suite 3, Eugene, OR 97401.

Resource Publications
An Imprint of Wipf and Stock Publishers
199 W. 8th Ave., Suite 3
Eugene, OR 97401

www.wipfandstock.com

PAPERBACK ISBN: 978-1-7252-9245-1
HARDCOVER ISBN: 978-1-7252-9246-8
EBOOK ISBN: 978-1-7252-9247-5

05/24/21

This book is dedicated to my youngest child, Cassie, who is my third daughter and fifth child. Cassie, you were born during my time writing this book and specifically as I was writing my chapter on procreation. Although only a few months old, you have been a blessing to our family already. We are now living in a brave new world where children are regularly seen as a burden. Western culture has forgotten the value of children and have rejected the foundational Genesis mandate of procreation. My prayer for you Cassie is that you will become a true follower of God and a faithful adherent to the Genesis mandates.

Contents

Preface | ix
Abbreviations | xvii

1 The Genesis Mandates and the Problem of the Fall | 1
2 Postmodernism's Influence on Culture | 15
3 God as Sovereign Creator | 34
4 The Marriage Mandate Part 1 | 53
   Biblical Marriage and Sexuality
5 The Marriage Mandate Part 2 | 69
   Marriage Redefined
6 The Mandate of Family and Procreation Part 1 | 88
   Family
7 The Mandate of Family and Procreation Part 2 | 112
   Procreation—Abortion and Culture
8 The Mandate of Family and Procreation Part 3 | 133
   Procreation—Abortion and the Bible
9 The Mandate of Gender Distinctions Part 1 | 155
   A Biblical Introduction
10 The Mandate of Gender Distinctions Part 2 | 175
   Homosexuality and Culture
11 The Mandate of Gender Distinctions Part 3 | 203
   Homosexuality, the Church, and the Bible
12 The Mandate of Gender Distinctions Part 4 | 228
   The Transsexual Revolution

13 The Mandate of Species Distinctions | 248
14 The Influence of Politics on Morality and Evangelicals | 264
15 Conclusion | 282

Bibliography | 293
Scripture Index | 319

Preface

"Something is rotten in the state of Denmark," and it is only getting more odious as the years go by.[1] Marcellus's words from Shakespeare's Hamlet in the first half of the above sentence sums up well the state of Western culture vis-à-vis biblical sexual standards and morals. Indeed, culturally, America is like the rotting fish alluded to in the above quotation. The America of the past five decades would be a foreign country to the founding fathers. Women screaming for their "right" to kill their unborn children; men and women marching for their "right" to marry whomever they choose of the same gender; people petitioning for their "right" to become whatever gender they desire and to use whatever restroom they feel inclined towards while the rest of society bows to their demands; a presidential contender, who if he had succeeded in his bid, would possibly have been the first president with his *husband* serving as the first "gentleman" of the White House; and environmentalists placing creature and creation above humanity. I am certainly not the first to notice this chaos. Recently I saw a meme on social media from Elizabeth Johnston, aka, the "Activist Mommy," which read, "We live in a society where homosexuals lecture us on morals, transgenders lecture us on human biology, baby killers lecture us on human rights and socialists lecture us on economics."

I am sure that the founding fathers would roll over in their graves if they knew what postmodern politicians and activist judges have done to their founding document, which was rooted in Judeo-Christian principles.[2] To be sure, our culture and governmental agencies have uprooted the biblical moorings of a bygone era.[3] Activist justices sitting

---

1. I owe the recollection of this line to Guinness, *Impossible People*, 73.
2. See also Grudem, *Politics*, 64–65.
3. See Ashford, "Christian Politics," 446–47.

on the highest court in the country have declared that these types of societal "advancements" were all part of the intent of the founding fathers when they drafted and ratified the Constitution of the United States of America.[4] And when states have referendums on social issues such as gay-marriage, and the populace votes to limit social change for moral reasons, the courts step in and override the will of the people repeatedly. Their reasoning? They insist that the majority cannot impose religion (i.e., biblical morality) upon the minority, while often invoking the misused phrase "separation of church and state."[5] If you are anything like me, as a father of five children all under the age of ten, you may be wondering how we got here and how do we make things better? I want to assure you that you are normal if you are concerned with the state of our country and what this means for our children and grandchildren. I certainly am.

While it is true that governments cannot save us—for that is the role of Christ's shed blood—they are important for establishing what is morally right and good for the purpose of societal flourishing. We elect people to represent us and they in turn make laws and appoint judges, many of whom have lifetime appointments. When we elect politicians, who pass legislation legalizing unbiblical acts like abortion, same-sex marriage, no-fault divorce, special rights for trans people, or any other morally questionable act, we in essence are telling our kids that this type of activity is acceptable because our government has legally sanctioned these sinful actions.[6] In short order, the central ideas of these laws and legal rulings are condoned and then taught in public schools as being normal and moral.[7]

It should not surprise us, then, when the next generation, and those that follow, have a relaxed or transformed morality that is antithetical to all that is godly and God-ordained. When we boil down most of these attacks against godly morality, we find they are an undermining of God's moral mandates as established in the opening two chapters of Genesis; what I have called the Genesis mandates. These mandates include: God as sovereign lawgiver, the separation of species and dominion of humans over the created order, the establishment of binary gender, the giving of marriage for the purpose of procreation, and the establishment of families

---

4. See also Grudem, *Politics*, 29–36, 131–54.
5. Grudem, *Politics*, 32–33.
6. Grudem, *Politics*, 97–99.
7. See Grudem, *Politics*, 98n15.

as the foundation of society. Today most of these, especially those related to sexual morality, are mocked and marginalized as being irrelevant to a progressive society. That is why, as I will point out throughout this book, as evangelical believers it is our responsibility to teach our kids right and wrong and to stand against agendas and people—elected or otherwise—who seek to erode our moral foundation through legislative actions that are against the wellbeing of a moral society as established by God.

Some might already be thinking, "What can Christians do to stem the tidal wave of immorality?" Recently I read an excellent article by Michael Brown who addresses this very issue by pointing out the dangers of Christian complacency and defeatism when it comes to fighting the culture wars. Many Christians—evangelicals in particular—take the stance that if God is going to return at any moment, why bother? Let the culture implode.[8] We simply cannot take such a stance. Jesus, in the parable of the talents, warned his servants to remain active until he returned (Luke 19:13). We need to emulate the great reformers of the past who brought about cultural change to end the moral scourge of slavery, racism, inequality, and the like. This is the reason why I am writing this book: to help students, pastors, educators, parents, and grandparents understand the issues going on around them. I want to impart solid biblical instruction on how to combat culture wars in any period. Will the world get worse? Most likely. Can we do something about it? Absolutely! We can educate our kids. We can stand firm for what the Bible teaches. We can get involved in the transformation of culture and the political process. We *can* make a difference.

This book is geared toward evangelical believers, although theological and social conservatives within mainline churches and the Catholic tradition will hopefully find my arguments helpful as well, especially if they are concerned about what is happening in Western culture and the church. At the same time, I recognize that those outside of the church or those who have already accepted cultural shifts as "inevitable," may see this book as naïve and uninformed: they would be wrong. I cannot help but hear the words of Paul ringing in my ears, "For the message of the cross is foolishness to those who are perishing, but to us who are being saved it is the power of God" (1 Cor 1:18; NIV). While I am certainly aware that this verse focuses on the *preaching* of the Gospel, it is no less

---

8. Brown, "Multigenerational Perspective."

true when one is *preaching* the truth of the "gospel" related to God's established morality, especially to a lost and rotting culture.

There are a variety of factors which are causing Western culture to race like a speeding freight train towards the proverbial cliff. While certainly not an exhaustive list, these include: the negative influence of media of all types; an increase in college-educated youth who have been trained by radical and left-leaning professors who advocate secular humanism, cultural Marxism, and the deification of self; a rejection of Judeo-Christian principles as the basis of Western cultural ideals; a secularization of the church in general, and the evangelical church specifically; and a rejection of God and the Bible as the foundation for morality. On the latter point, based upon recent trends it is obvious that many denominations are rejecting the long-held biblical teachings on sexual sin and ethics.

Christian books dealing with ethical issues written even a decade ago are in many ways obsolete as Western culture and the church obliterate established norms regarding sexuality, moral issues, and ethical standards. One example immediately comes to mind. In 2010, renowned theologian and Bible scholar Wayne Grudem wrote a 600-page book on politics and the Bible, which was published by Zondervan, a leading distributer of Christian textbooks. In it Grudem handled most of the hot-button social and moral issues in America as of the first decade of the twenty-first century.[9] Yet, in one decade, several of his warnings have come to fruition as Western society plows forward tearing down moral and ethical fences at a record pace. The instruction offered by Grudem has been ignored by most people perhaps because it was primarily geared towards an academic audience. Whatever the case may be, his warnings have been rejected not just by the culture but also by many so-called professing Christians.

A good portion of the blame can be laid at the feet of Christians who continue to elect people to political and church offices who openly espouse values contrary to a biblical model. For a political example, in the span of a decade, the Obama administration removed the "don't ask don't tell" policy so that openly gay men and women could serve in the military (ca. 2010). By 2013, gay couples could adopt, and by 2015 the Supreme Court of the United States, in *Obergefell v. Hodges*, legalized same-sex marriage. From a cultural perspective, the Boy Scouts of America, after

---

9. Grudem, *Politics According to the Bible* (Zondervan, 2010).

winning a narrow 5–4 Supreme Court decision in 2000 (*Boy Scouts of America et al. v. Dale*) to keep homosexuals out of leadership positions, broke under pressure from LGBTQ groups and in 2013 allowed openly homosexual participants. By 2015, the new president of the Boy Scouts, Robert Gates, the former Defense Secretary under President Obama, pushed the organization to accept openly homosexual individuals to serve as scout leaders.[10] By 2017 the group preemptively opened its doors for transgender participants.[11] Finally, from an ecclesial perspective, it goes without saying that sexual ethics have been at the heart of most of the denominational splits in the past decade. In 2020, Pope Francis became the first Catholic pope to endorse same-sex civil unions—a move that is sure to confuse many conservative Catholic believers.

How did we get here so fast? Our culture has rejected God and Judeo-Christian ideals and replaced them with secular humanistic ideals, which, according to Paul, are directly influenced by demonic spirits that currently have control over nations (Eph 2:2; cf. Dan 10:13, 20).[12] In this context, today's Western culture is fertile ground for every kind of sexual and moral deviance and a rejection of God's plan for society.[13] We should not be surprised to see our culture exhibiting the depravity reflective of its fallenness. When people do what they say is "natural" for them, no matter how sinful, in a way they are correct: in a fallen state, it is natural for people to reject God and to practice sin.[14] Nevertheless, that does not mean we, as a society, should accept such practices. Is God in control? Absolutely! A problem arises, however, when the church also begins to reflect the evil influences typical of the world. When it gets to this point, something needs to be done. Pastors, educators, parents, and caregivers of children must take an active role in combatting these influences in their children's lives.

On the parental level, one of the ways some combat this onslaught is through Christian private schools or homeschooling (as my wife and I have chosen to do). By doing so, children are sheltered—in a good way—from a post-Christian society until they are equipped to effect change. In this regard, I struggle with those who willingly throw their children to the

---

10. Lee, "Boy Scouts."
11. Lee, "Boy Scouts."
12. Dallas, *Gay Gospel*, 219–20.
13. Watkins, *New Absolutes*, 239–40.
14. See Satinover, *Homosexuality*, 146–67.

proverbial "wolves" without doing their due diligence to counterbalance the secular perspectives and postmodern "diet" they are fed every day for twelve or more years. Again, when the church itself, the haven of spiritual instruction and communion with God, begins to be encroached upon by these same evil and ungodly influences, what are we to do? When it gets to this point believers must act and stand firm on the Word. We must hold the line and do what the Word says as opposed to what society deems just and appropriate. Jesus warned that false prophets would enter the sheepfold as wolves in sheep's clothing (Matt 7:15).

Personally, I have chosen to respond to the ever-increasing assault on the Word of God and on the ethical standards laid out clearly in God's Word through writing and teaching. Those of us equipped by God to undertake such a task must be willing to speak up and help instruct this spiritually dying generation. God takes seriously how we confront sin in our midst. We cannot allow sexual sin and moral laxness to invade the body of Christ, as though it belonged there because of the mantra "Jesus is loving and accepting of all people." While the latter point is true, the former still needs to be addressed. Sin must find no place among us lest it cause the whole lump of dough to be leavened (1 Cor 5:6–7). We need to draw clearly defined boundaries between faithful teachers and pastors, and those who teach false doctrine and refuse to be corrected (1 Thess 3:6, 14–15) lest God judge the entire church for our failure to do so (Rev 2:20–22).[15] I take this calling and task seriously. As pastors, educators, parents, and grandparents, you, too, have an awesome responsibility to instruct and get your congregation, your children, and your grandchildren in front of sound teachers and pastors, as opposed to those who will tickle their ears.

In this vein, recently I presented at a church on this same topic of the Genesis mandates. After I had finished, I was approached by a woman. She thanked me for my presentation and continued by saying that she had brought her teenage son, who had rejected Christ and the church and had come out as transgendered. She said, "he probably hates you right now, but I am glad he was here to hear what you had to say." The topics in this book are not going to be easy to hear for some people, especially those who are struggling with these types of sexual and moral sins and sexual confusion. Some may have already been told by psychologists or pastors that they are fine, and that God is fine with their present state of

---

15. Dallas, *Gay Gospel*, 220–22.

confusion. Some may have even been told that they are "normal" in their sexually and morally confused state. I am here to declare what the Word of God has to say about it. There is an ethical and moral standard that is not "relative" and unstable like the shifting sand upon which today's cultural foundations are based. God's Word is firm and will always remain so. For me this is encouraging and should be for you as well.

From the outset, it must be stressed that God is no prude when it comes to sexuality.[16] God's opening two commands to humanity were to eat from the fruit of the land and to be fruitful and multiply, that is, have sexual relations (Gen 1:26–28). Sexuality is God's idea but there are boundaries which God has established that are not to be crossed. Yet, younger evangelicals are increasingly moving in an "enculturated" direction by accepting many forms of sexual deviancy as "normal" or acceptable. What does that mean for educators, pastors, parents, and grandparents? It is clear. Whatever category within which you find yourself, it is incumbent upon you to educate the younger generations in the ways of God. Books like this are geared to help you do just that. We cannot wait and hope that someone else will do this. If we do not do it, the world and those with ungodly agendas will step in and fill the void and the ground which we are ceding to them.

Sadly, I have watched evangelicals in the West becoming more and more polarized both ethically and politically. Those who do not agree with the central tenets of the faith tradition on issues of morality and sexual ethics are either jumping ship, or are influencing their individual churches to accept ungodliness. This will have the net effect of evangelicalism having to face the similar plight of the Episcopal, Presbyterian, Methodist, Lutheran and other mainline churches of the recent past who have split into two or more factions. Baptist, Pentecostal, Four Square, you name it, are either now, or will be faced soon, with similar divisive situations over moral and sexual issues if we continue on the same trajectory. It is now that we need to return to the moral standards established by God in the opening chapters of Genesis.

Finally, I want to note that the tone of this book is not meant to be condescending or harsh. It is coming from a place of concern with the church's lack of sound instruction on these issues. It is also coming from a place of relative frustration with evangelical publishers who are unwilling to publish so-called "controversial" material that opposes these agendas.

---

16. See Allender and Longman, *God Loves Sex*, 118 although I strongly disagree with their views on intimacy before marriage (see pp.119–20).

Indeed, I received pressure from two publishers not to write a book in the format which is often framed as the "us vs. them" perspective. And another rejected it outright for similar reasons. Whether out of fear of political and cultural backlash or whether the "them" in the "us vs. them" is in fact the evangelical elites in publishing houses and education, cannot be known for certain. I would like to think it is neither, but I am not that trusting. As a teacher of predominantly young evangelicals, I know firsthand that by the time I stand before first-year undergrads, most have been so influenced by culture that it is virtually impossible to change their minds on these ethical issues. As such, take this book as an impassioned plea to pastors, educators, students, parents, and grandparents to be a part of the solution now before it is too late.

Abbreviations

ACLU	American Civil Liberties Union
AEI	American Enterprise Institute
BBR	*Bulletin for Biblical Research*
BLM	Black Lives Matter
BSac	*Bibliotheca Sacra*
BWHO	*Bulletin of the World Health Organization*
CDC	Centers for Disease Control and Prevention
DSM	Diagnostic and Statistical Manual
ExpTim	*Expository Times*
GLAAD	Gay & Lesbian Alliance Against Defamation
JBMW	*Journal of Biblical Manhood and Womanhood*
JESOT	*Journal for the Evangelical Study of the Old Testament*
JETS	*Journal of the Evangelical Theological Society*
LGBTQ	Lesbian-Gay-Bisexual-Transexual-Questioning
MCPS	Montgomery County Public Schools
NAC	New American Commentary
NPR	National Public Radio
Them	*Themelios*
TynBul	*Tyndale Bulletin*
VT	*Vetus Testamentum*

Chapter 1

The Genesis Mandates and the Problem of the Fall

In 1948 Richard Weaver wrote in his book *Ideas Have Consequences*, "There is ground for declaring that modern man has become a moral idiot." An ominous declaration when you consider that there is more evidence to support that claim today than when he wrote it. We have turned our backs on the institutions and safeguards that have prospered and protected us for centuries. We are paying dearly for this choice. The West is unraveling before our very eyes.[1]

THIS COMMENT BY WILLIAM D. Watkins back in 1996 notes well the serious moral and ethical trouble that Western culture is facing. Watkins wrote his book *The New Absolutes* roughly fifty years after Weaver's comments, and here we are another twenty-five years later, and we have not improved. In fact, Western culture has gotten far worse. The continued downward spiral in the past two decades is frightening if you are a Christian living—or raising children—in this environment. As we will see throughout this book, sexual morality has been thrown out the proverbial window. We have opened a Pandora's Box, and barring another great awakening, Western culture is in serious trouble. From their youngest years, children are being exposed to increasing sexual depravity. For example, the 2020 Super Bowl half-time show highlighted

---

1. Watkins, *New Absolutes*, 235.

the oversexualization of Western society when they presented a sexually charged performance including a striptease show. This is no longer "family-friendly" viewing. Many Christians were outraged while many others responded with a mere shrug of the shoulders and the response: "What's the big deal?" Too many have become numb to the rottenness of our morality. And the increased militancy of the LBGTQ and current radical environmental movements push against all that the Bible teaches about proper sexual and creation ethics. Some will retort, I am certain, with the claim that I am fearmongering and employing the slippery slope argument. But what has happened in the past decade or more to Western culture and our morality is nothing less than staggering. This is not a slippery slope; it is a slippery cliff!

At the heart of the current sexual and moral revolution is the rise of postmodern thought which has inundated every facet of Western society, the church included. Now to be fair, I am not attempting to make postmodernism the boogeyman in the closet. On the contrary, many have noted the benefits of postmodern thought. It appropriately challenged the certainties of modernity's rationalism and its assertion of complete objectivity.[2] Nevertheless, I would argue that the benefits of postmodernism are very limited in scope. Even the concept of objectivity and certainty is relative based upon the area of life and epistemological concepts one is discussing. As I will point out throughout this book, the one area that humanity can be certain of, and the one area that is immutable, is the instruction of morality and ethics as presented in the Genesis mandates. These are laws that are not up for negotiation and subjective reasoning. The mandates of Genesis 1 and 2 establish several categorical imperatives for all people of all times.

That said, the purpose of this introductory chapter is to lay a foundation for the remainder of the book. I will look at three key issues. I will begin by examining what I mean when I speak of the "Genesis" or "creation mandates." Second, I will look at how the fall of humanity is at the heart of our rejection of these mandates. Finally, I will show how the fall has affected everyone's sexuality whether male or female, old or young.

---

2. Kelly and Dew Jr., *Understanding Postmodernism*, 135–36, 158–60.

The Genesis Mandates

In an earlier essay on this topic I note the quotation "Don't ever take down a fence until you know the reason it was put up," which is a paraphrased form of a concept present in a book written by social critic G.K. Chesterton (1874–1936).[3] In that essay, I go on to state that "In the past half century or more, and with ever increasing speed, Western society has been tearing down fences related to sexual ethics and morality in general that had remained firmly fixed for millennia."[4] What are these "fences"? I have chosen to label them the "Genesis mandates" established by God at creation. Dietrich Bonhoeffer opted for similar terminology in his discussion on biblical ethics.[5] Succinctly put, God created the world and all that is in it, "good." At the apex of creation God made man and woman—male and female—and gave them dominion over all of God's creation (Gen 1:26–28). God then commanded the man and woman to procreate and fill the earth which is immediately placed within the context of the covenant of marriage (Gen 2:24). From this union, humans joined God in the creation process to form societies with the family unit as their foundation.[6] Therefore, the mandates for moral and ethical order may be listed as such: species distinctions, which includes proper governance by humanity over both the animals and the environment; the establishment of binary gender—male and female; the importance of procreation—within the context of marriage—for the continuation of the human race; and finally, the establishment of marriage and the family as the bedrock of society. Of course, at the top of this list of mandates is the recognition that God is creator, that he is sovereign over his creation, and that he can mandate these ideals for creation's flourishing.

If God has established this ordering, then the undoing of the Genesis mandates is nothing less than an attack on everything wholesome and "good" first initiated by God himself at creation. While we are told that the ethical and moral advances in Western culture are just, right, and

---

3. Chesterton, *The Thing*, ch. 4, paragraph 1.

4. Peterson, "Genesis Mandates," 125.

5. Bonhoeffer's mandates included work, marriage, government, and church. Bonhoeffer, *Ethics*, 17–22; 388–408. As noted by Gushee, *Changing Our Mind*, 94–95.

6. I could also add the mandate of work as sanctioned by God in 2:15. Today, many in Western societies are advocating a basic income for all people which will kill the incentive to work. God has instilled within us the desire to be productive which in turn helps bring meaning to people's lives.

good, the current trajectory of society—and in some cases the church itself—to undermine these mandates is not of God; this is an attack of the Enemy (1 John 5:19). In recent years in Western culture, there has been a desire by certain activist groups to destroy that which God has created good. As we will see in later chapters, this can be instigated by both political or social-agenda-driven groups and by those who identify as "biblical scholars." In the latter case, the use of the Bible for morality has often been belittled due to its supposed contradictory nature[7] or due to the fact that we live in a fallen world and therefore are prone to sin and fall short of God's ideals. As such, some argue that the Genesis mandates are ideals that can never be attained. To be sure, humanity will fail to meet God's ideals in some cases (e.g., divorce) or we can be affected by the fallen nature of the world (e.g., intersex issues); yet, when it comes to the basic mandates set forth by God for human flourishing, we do not have the freedom to undo, redefine, add to, or reimagine them as some have proposed.[8] Because many are now moving to a default position of blaming the fall for the warping (although they would not use this term) of the Genesis mandates, I will briefly examine how we as believers should understand these mandates in a post-Genesis-3 world.

Sexuality and the Fall

The fall changed everything for humanity, including human sexuality. It is no surprise that after Adam and Eve sinned, they immediately tried to cover their nakedness because of their shame: they recognized they had fallen short of God's ideal. Already, we can learn something about the devastating outcome of sin: breaking God's laws is shameful. It is telling when many in Western culture flaunt their sexual deviance without shame. Despite the fallenness of humanity, our sexuality and morality must be made subservient to the will of God as elucidated in the Bible.

The recent social trends towards evermore deviant behaviors have not left the evangelical world without its casualties in its attempt to navigate the seismic changes to our sexual ethics. One of the ways to get around the clearly defined mandates of Genesis is to center one's sexual

---

7. See for example Knust, *Unprotected Texts*, 344–45; and Collins, *Biblical Values*, 3–19, 216–20.

8. E.g., Achtemeier, *Same-Sex Marriage*, xiii; and DeFranza, "Common Ground," 90, 93.

The Genesis Mandates and the Problem of the Fall

ethics in the post-fall world which Jesus came to redeem. Because most of the movement on sexual ethics in the recent past has focused on LGBTQ concerns, I will use one scholar familiar with these issues to illustrate my point, even though many could be listed. Former evangelical David Gushee[9] once held to the Genesis 2:24 mandate of heterosexual marriage as the only paradigm for coupling and bemoaned the downward spiral of culture in this regard.[10] Recently, he has realigned his thinking with modern cultural trends even though he would insist that it is due to his readjusted interpretation of Scripture. Gushee (see also James Brownson) now suggests that "Christian theology does better leaning forward towards Jesus Christ" and his "new creation" as opposed to leaning "backward" to the creation ethics.[11] Gushee also suggests we have to live in a post-Genesis-3 world where we accept that sexuality is broken as opposed to the ideal of Genesis 1 and 2.[12]

While the effects of the fall are important to keep in mind when dealing with sexual ethics, Gushee and others are wrong in their assertions that allowances must be made for LGBTQ lifestyles. Jesus himself leans "backward" to the creation ethics to teach about marriage, as does Paul in Romans 1 when dealing with sexual pairing. I find it somewhat disingenuous when affirming scholars are more than willing to resort to the pre-fall era when it comes to women's roles in marriage and ministry, that is, the focus on equality in all areas—a valid point to make—but refuse to apply the same hermeneutic for sexuality.[13] It is telling of a bias and/or an agenda when affirming scholars want to move away from the Genesis mandates because of their rigidity. Gushee insists that his new approach is "treating people the way Christ did" (more on this in a minute).[14] He concludes by noting that as with other misinterpretations of key issues, the church will repent and change their position on LGBT

---

9. Gushee originally identified as evangelical but has since moved away from these convictions, one of them being related to sexual ethics. See Gushee, *Still Christian* (2017); and Gushee, *After Evangelicalism* (2020).

10. See Gushee, *Getting Marriage Right*, 33–34.

11. Gushee, *Changing Our Mind*, 96; and Brownson, *Bible, Gender, Sexuality*, 269.

12. Gushee, *Changing Our Mind*, 96–98. See also Evangelical Mark Achtemeier's *Same-Sex Marriage* (2014).

13. See further my comments in Peterson, *Sin of Sodom*, 11.

14. Gushee, *Changing Our Mind*, 116 see also 143.

issues and before we know it, the debate will be over and we will all be wondering "what the fuss was about."[15]

Appealing to the fallen nature of humanity to accept and affirm LGBTQ lifestyles is just one more step in Western societies' cultural death spiral. Many of these types of post-fall arguments related to sexual ethics appeal to experience and emotion as opposed to biblical teaching. Gushee in particular spends much time and space enumerating the harm done to LGBT children in the name of an outdated and harmful Christian teaching against sexual minorities.[16] While I would agree that we should never abuse any person, especially a child (Matt 18:6–7), we must not open the door to the acceptance of alternate sexual ethics and morality simply because of the effects of sin or confusion in a young person's life. What Gushee has pointed out is not necessarily to be blamed on an outdated or wrong Christian and biblical sexual ethic, but rather what happens when sin is allowed to invade our culture and our churches. In many cases, younger and younger children are "coming out" as homosexual or trans simply because of the wide acceptance of these lifestyles in Western culture and the prevalence of LGBTQ-themed media. Why shouldn't one expect sin to proliferate when it is normalized? Yet, this is not how affirming scholars couch it. It is always the church's fault as opposed to recognizing the Enemy's attack against our children (1 Pet 5:8). Acceptance is not going to solve the sin problem; it will only make it worse.

As I will demonstrate moving forward, even though people in the Bible corrupted aspects of the Genesis mandates because of the fallenness of humanity (e.g., polygamy, war brides, divorce) that does not mean that we should do the same. We are held to a higher standard post-cross than those of the Old Testament world (Luke 12:48). Therefore, when it comes to the mandates of Genesis 1 and 2 vis-à-vis the results of the fall in Genesis 3, God's creation mandates are always incumbent upon all peoples in all cultures. It is a truism that the results of the fall created problems for all people in every culture, regardless of what naturalists, atheists, and rationalists might say to the contrary. When it comes to our ability to reason our way through issues like ethics and morality, we will always fail. Therefore, we must abide by the absolutes which are laid out by God in Genesis 1 and 2 if we expect to have cultural harmony and thriving.

---

15. Gushee, *Changing Our Mind*, 145.
16. The Reformation Project, "Gushee"; and Gushee, *Changing Our Mind*, 126–45.

We simply cannot allow culture and its ever-shifting "norms" to dictate our sexual and moral ethics.

I think the clearest presentation of the results of the fall on our sexuality and the overriding of cultural norms is that presented by Jesus during his conversation with the Pharisees regarding divorce (Matt 19 and Mark 10). Culturally, the Pharisees, who followed the Mosaic Law, embraced divorce basically for any reason. Jesus' response was not to go into a detailed discussion of cultural taboos and norms. Instead, Jesus bypasses all these meaningless discussions (at least in the context of establishing the "truth" of God's Word) and immediately goes to the Genesis mandates and points to two of the main ones I am addressing here. First, he notes the division of the genders/sexes into male and female in Genesis 1:27, and then Jesus quotes Genesis 2:24 and the importance of marriage. Both, says Jesus, are ordained by God and not to be superseded by human cultural thinking and proclivities or the "hardness of people's hearts." Therefore, by the very example of Jesus, the elevated and universal status of the Genesis mandates are established as absolute truths. When Gushee accepts the sinful lifestyles of practicing LGBTQ people with the assertion that he is "treating people the way Christ did" he is actually going against Jesus' instruction. Gushee's position would hardly be accepted by Jesus if he refused to cave to the Pharisees on divorce. While divorce was actually allowed in the Torah (Deut 24:1), LGBTQ lifestyles never were. Jesus' firm position on two of the Genesis mandates, despite the results of the fall, obliterates the very basis of the postmodern argument that there are no absolute moral and ethical truths binding upon all cultures for all times (see my next chapter). This is no less true for us as individuals, who must face the fact that our sexuality and moral reasoning are broken as a result of the fall. To be sure, the effects of the fall extend beyond the account of Genesis 3. The remainder of the book of Genesis highlights this point well.

The Brokenness of Humanity on Display in Genesis

In December of 2019, former US President, Barack Obama, commented that the world would be a better place if women were in charge.[17] While I recognize the point he was trying to make, the reality is that due to the fallenness of all humanity, it is clear that we would have troubles whoever

---

17. Outnumbered, "Obama Says."

is in power. The belittling of one gender in favor of the other is not the answer. In today's Western culture, this rejection of masculinity in favor of femininity falls within the discussion of what has been pejoratively labeled: "toxic masculinity." Once considered the fringe in academia, this modern sociological idea is now mainstream. Those holding to this belief are challenging every trait that was once used to define what it meant to be a boy or a man. Rarely, if ever, is a counterargument about possible "toxic femininity" ever offered.[18] The Enemy knew that the wedge that the fall drove between male and female was the best place to start when destroying God's good mandates. I will return to this in Chapter 4.

Many have noted that the fall tainted human sexuality.[19] However, this is not how secular educators and the broader culture have taught our children. Today, many academics use sociobiology, which is heavily influenced by evolutionary thought, to explain the more promiscuous nature of men versus women. The theory goes something like this: as men evolved, the most aggressive and larger males, because they had endless amounts of sperm, sought to spread their genetic material to as many females as possible. Females, on the other hand, were choosier and waited for the more dominant males. Over time, the genetic makeup of males reflected these traits of dominance and promiscuity, which were present in the earlier males within the species, while females evolved to be more choosy with whom they mate.[20] While these theories may serve well our postmodern culture where people do not like to take responsibility for their actions, or where people like to blame nature for their own faults or sin, this is problematic in light of the moral principles of the Bible, especially as taught in Genesis.

Recently, I wrote an extended article dealing with the sexual brokenness of humanity, both male *and* female.[21] Apart from the general patriarchal setting of Genesis when dealing with marriage, I assessed all the cases of sexual exploitation in Genesis and found that the author presents an almost equal number of accounts dealing with sexual exploitation in some form for both men and women. The following list summarizes my findings.[22]

---

18. Murray, *Madness of Crowds*, 102–3.
19. Balswick and Balswick, *Authentic Human Sexuality*, 58, 71.
20. See Balswick and Balswick, *Authentic Human Sexuality*, 323.
21. Peterson, "Sexual Exploitation," 693–703.
22. Peterson, "Sexual Exploitation," 701–2.

The Genesis Mandates and the Problem of the Fall   9

Men against Women

1. Abraham uses Sarah's sexuality twice to save himself (12:10–20; 20:1–7)
2. Lot offers his virgin daughters to the crowd of men for sexual gratification (19:8)*
3. Isaac uses Rebekah's sexuality to save himself (26:6–11)
4. Laban exploits Leah for financial gain (29:23–25)
5. Shechem rapes Dinah (34:2)
6. Reuben takes sexual advantage of Bilhah (35:22)

Men against Men

7. Ham takes sexual advantage of his father, Noah (9:20–25)**
8. The men of Sodom seek a sexual encounter with the visitors/angels (19:4–11)*
9. Ishmael may have committed a sexual act on his younger brother, Isaac[23] (21:9)**

Women against Women

1. Sarah uses Hagar as a womb and abuses her (16:1–4)
2. Leah uses Zilpah as a womb (30:9–10)
3. Rachel uses Bilhah as a womb (30:3–8)

Women against Men

4. Lot's older daughter takes sexual advantage of her drunken father (19:33)
5. Lot's younger daughter takes sexual advantage of her drunken father (19:35)
6. Rachel and Leah barter for Jacob's sexual services (30:14–16)

---

23. Others have noted this as well, see Coogan, *God & Sex*, 77.

7. Tamar seduces her father-in-law to get pregnant (38:14–19)
8. Potiphar's wife tries to seduce Joseph and then falsely accuses him (39:7–20)*

*Unfulfilled or partially fulfilled act
**Interpretation is debated

What this study showed is that both men and women's sexuality and moral judgment are flawed. In this vein, when speaking of the ancestral narratives, Old Testament scholar, John Goldingay, notes, "While the stories pass few explicit moral judgments, they imply that these realities of marriage and family are not the way things are supposed to be. They imply a contrast with the ideal announced in God's words in Genesis 1, echoed in the words of the narrative and of Adam in Genesis 2."[24] To be sure, all have sinned and fallen short of the glory of God (Rom 3:23). Nevertheless, this does not mean that we are not to strive for the ideal, or that we are not accountable to God for our rejection of the Genesis mandates.

What I found interesting about my study is the fact that in Genesis, women were aggressors against women almost as much as against men. What is more, of all the possible historical contexts, in this patriarchal setting women sexually abused or tried to take advantage of men in particularly heinous manners. Lot's daughters took sexual advantage of their father (incest) by getting him drunk, Tamar disguised herself as a prostitute to entrap her father-in-law, and Potiphar's wife pressured a young Joseph daily in his workplace to have sexual relations with her and then falsely accused him leading to his imprisonment.

This brief overview is not meant to downplay male sexual aggressiveness and related sins throughout history, but rather to show that the author of Genesis understands that everyone's sexual morality has been marred by the fall, even those of the female gender. However, this is not always the way it is presented in Western cultures. For example, groups like the #MeToo movement have laid sexual brokenness predominantly at the feet of men. While men are indeed dominant perpetrators of sexual aggression, the brokenness of human sexuality and ethics is on display every day and it affects more than just men, as witnessed by numerous news reports.[25]

---

24. Goldingay, *Old Testament Theology*, 275.
25. McCarthy, "Survivor"; Gearty, "Massachusetts Professor"; and Norman, "British Woman."

Sexual Brokenness is Everywhere

The rejection of the Genesis mandates dealing with sexual ethics has now become more prevalent in Western cultures due to the lowered standards of what we deem to be acceptable sexual behavior. You cannot pervert every aspect of sexuality and not expect it to affect everyone involved, even women, who have often been immune to charges of egregious sexual behavior and exploitation—although see my discussion above. In civilized Western cultures of the recent past, women often represented the good and positive aspects of proper sexual ethics and marriage was a means of "taming" men. Now while some may see this as a sexist statement, I am merely noting what has been traditionally asserted. Since the sexual revolution, this is no longer the case. In fact, as evidenced by any number of recent surveys and news reports, sexual degradation practiced by women is on the rise. For example, sexual addictions are not just male problems: females also struggle with the use of pornography and the like,[26] although males tend to do so in greater numbers.[27] One cannot turn on the television without being faced with headlines noting the sexual exploitation of minors, not just by men, but also by women.[28]

The troubling issue is the double standard when it comes to sexual exploitation and perversion practiced by "consenting" adults. I am in no way trying to say that this is fine, but rather that Western culture has often laid the blame for sexual brokenness at the feet of men, especially heterosexual men, while either turning a blind eye or giving a pass to those who are from a group who have an alternate sexual orientation or proclivity. I will give two examples of the double standard. First, the inappropriate sexual relationships of the US congressional representative from California, Katie Hill, ended in her resignation. However, her actions got passed over by the media and instead were broadcast as an attack by the political "Right" against a strong bi-sexual female. Second, British social commentator, Douglas Murray, points to an event involving Ellen DeGeneres in October 2017, which occurred right around the time of the Harvey Weinstein indictment. In this example, DeGeneres posted a sexually suggestive picture and comment about entertainer, Katy Perry.[29] While the comparison between Weinstein and DeGeneres

---

26. See Isom, *Conversations* (2018) for a discussion on female pornography use.
27. Balswick and Balswick, *Authentic Human Sexuality*, 300.
28. Lapin, "Sports Illustrated"; and Roberto, "Miss Kentucky."
29. Murray, *Madness of Crowds*, 41.

is certainly not on par, it did highlight the reality that DeGeneres's type of sexual "exploitation" was apparently acceptable.

When women in powerful positions, especially those who lobby against oppression, are faced with similar allegations, many times their supporters circle the wagons and defend the accused's actions.[30] Men on the other hand are usually guilty until proven innocent; the debacle during the Supreme Court hearing of Brett Kavanaugh is a case in point. That is not to say that men do not make up the majority of sexual harassment charges.[31] This seems to be rooted in the male sex drive and their more aggressive nature when it comes to going after "sexual conquests."[32] And, as just noted, in America's new period of "wokeness" it is becoming all too common to see women's names and pictures in the headlines when it comes to sexual harassment in and outside of the workplace. In fact, more and more female teachers are being charged with inappropriate sexual contact with their students. This troubling trend is just another side effect of the over sexualization of Western society. Studies have shown that adolescent girls who have been exposed to excessive pop music videos and come from dysfunctional families tend to have an increased tolerance for sexual harassment.[33] While this speaks to those who are acted upon, it is not a stretch to see how such exposure and programming can lead to a female being the abuser.[34] With traditional roles falling by the wayside, the sexual aggressiveness of women is not far behind. When women are determined to be just the same as men in every respect—jobs, power, aggressiveness or what have you—women playing the role of the harasser should not be surprising. After all, why shouldn't powerful women have what powerful men have, namely, whatever or whomever they wrongly desire? Not surprisingly, most harassment against men is perpetrated by a powerful woman under whom they work where "power differentials" are in play.[35]

Social critics are seeing the growing trend of female sexual aggressors.[36] In a section of his book under the sub-heading titled "Make Him

---

30. Murray, *Madness of Crowds*, 58–59.
31. Balswick and Balswick, *Authentic Human Sexuality*, 228.
32. See Balswick and Balswick, *Authentic Human Sexuality*, 224–27.
33. Balswick and Balswick, *Authentic Human Sexuality*, 230.
34. Balswick and Balswick, *Authentic Human Sexuality*, 232–33.
35. Balswick and Balswick, *Authentic Human Sexuality*, 233.
36. Murray, *Madness of Crowds*, 73–75. Note some of his more modern examples.

Drool," Murray describes how the sales and music industry sexualizes females. Murray describes in explicit detail the song of a well-known female pop artist whose music video is so sexually explicit that I will refrain from describing it here. Essentially, the video is one extended sexual tease for a man who is reprimanded at the end of the video for simply responding to what was literally shoved into his face in a sexual manner. At the heart of this issue is the fact that Western culture is teaching girls and women that they are to be sexy but not "sexualized" by men.[37] It was not that long ago that a song like "Wake Up Little Susie" (1957) ran afoul of the censors for merely intimating that a boy and girl spent the night together but now the sexually explicit "song" WAP by Cardi B is a top hit and is praised by the critics. What ever happened to Paul's teaching on not defrauding one's brother or sister in Christ? (note 1 Thess 4:6). This double standard has created much confusion for men in how women are to be treated or what they want. Men are "told" by what they see that it is fine for women to entice and tease, but a man dare not respond for fear of being accused of exploitation. But where did the exploitation begin? I would say in Genesis after the fall. Yet, in our cultural setting, which has sexualized everything from buying a car to buying a pair of shoes, it is clear that we have made sex a commodity. Scholars have picked up on this analogy and have noted that once that commodity has been sold, people quickly want more variety to appease their lusts. This is just one more reason why Western culture is seeing the rise in sexual perversion and a rejection of God's good mandates. If those things that were once viewed as sexually taboo are now too "tame" for an increasingly sexually exploitive culture, how much more will society reject the God-honoring mandates of Genesis 1 and 2?

Conclusion

Whether humanity agrees or not, the Genesis mandates set the standard for human sexual ethics and morality. Yet, in light of the fall, it is clear that we are all sexually broken.[38] Women cannot blame men and men cannot blame women for that brokenness; we are all complicit. What is more, every facet of our being has been affected by the fall. The depravity of humanity, in this regard, is evident throughout history. The difference

---

37. Murray, *Madness of Crowds*, 77–80.
38. See Wilson, *Mere Sexuality*, 140–41.

we are facing today, however, is the compounding of sexual immorality and moral degradation all in the name of progress and "sexual justice." Sexual perversion is no longer on the fringes of society, it is becoming mainstream and enshrined in the laws of the land. In the past, cultures certainly collapsed due to decreased sexual ethics and morality (I will return to this in a later chapter), but never has this happened in situations where nations heavily influenced by Judeo-Christian ideals turned from those ideals at such a stunning and break-neck speed (of course, excluding the nation of Israel; cf. Jer 2:11). Western cultures, and America in particular, which were firmly established upon biblical ethics rooted in the Genesis mandates, are now rejecting those mandates in favor of a new "normal." Sexual deviance of all types is being accepted as normal. In this vein, some propose that abnormal sexual conduct should not be so labelled if all cultures say it is fine: only what is rejected by all cultures should bear the label of abnormal.[39] How did we arrive at such a philosophy of sexual ethics? It began when post-Christian Western cultures adopted a postmodern mindset and rejected absolute moral truths. This is the topic of my next chapter.

---

39. See sources by Balswick and Balswick, *Authentic Human Sexuality*, 59.

Chapter 2

Postmodernism's Influence on Culture

FOR THOSE WHO ARE already familiar with postmodernism, you may want to skip this chapter and move directly to my discussion beginning in Chapter 3. Nevertheless, I would encourage all my readers to read on because there may be important factors that those familiar with this topic have not considered when addressing the crucial topic of sexual ethics and morality. In this chapter I will demonstrate how many of postmodernism's claims are problematic at their core when it comes to the Genesis mandates. I will also show how mainline scholarship has influenced much of the move to marginalize and reject biblical morality.

Postmodernism's Pervasive Influence

On February 14, 2020, a concerned group of individuals within the Southern Baptist Convention (SBC), launched a new effort under the banner of the Conservative Baptist Network to try to thwart the rising trend in the SBC of drifting to the left. This "conservative resurgence" is like the one launched forty years earlier. The main concerns are the growing trends toward postmodern ideology, at least in some parts of the denomination, exemplified in an intolerance for conservative political positions and the passing of Resolution Nine.[1] The latter point focuses on "social justice

---

1. Southern Baptist Convention, "Critical Race Theory." See also the scathing assessment of Critical Race Theory by Peter Boghossian and James Lindsay in their interview, Lindsay and O'Fallon, "Trojan Horse."

concepts of Critical Race Theory and Intersectionality[2] . . . ideologies that have their roots in Neo-Marxist and postmodern worldviews."[3]

Wherever we turn, the effects of postmodernism are visible. Here is just one example coming from America's largest evangelical denomination. Whether we realize it or want to admit it, postmodernism and its assertions are in the church. It is brought into youth groups and young adult classes weekly by those who are attending secular grade schools and universities. It is brought into the pews by everyone influenced by all forms of media. And it is brought to the pulpit by clergy trained in seminaries that have rejected biblical authority, and by extension, the ethical mandates of God. Put simply, postmodernism is here to stay for the foreseeable future so Christians must be ready to take a stand and call it out when it rears its ugly head in the guise of cleverly crafted agendas masquerading under the banner of equality and social justice for all. Do not think that hiding behind the four walls and stain-glassed windows of our churches will protect us. Christians must educate themselves concerning this onslaught or they will be swept along with the godless agendas being driven by equally godless postmodern philosophies. At this point you may be asking the questions: What is postmodernism? Where did it come from? What are its tenets and the philosophies of which I should be so concerned? It is to these questions that I now turn.

Postmodernism Defined

When I speak of postmodernism, I use the term in a broad sense, what philosopher Heath White calls a "mind-set, a worldview, or a family of similar worldviews, a set of perspectives shared by many people who have come of age rather recently."[4] At the heart of postmodern thought is the idea that "truth should be seen as socially constructed, where the truth in question is ultimately the creation of a human community rather than (in some sense) preexisting the efforts of a particular community."[5] The framework within which the "human community" functions or exists is

---

2. Martin, "Heated CRT/I Debate." For more on Critical Race Theory, see Ascol, "Critical Race Theory."
3. Martin, "New Conservative Resurgence."
4. White, *Postmodernism 101*, 11.
5. Kelly and Dew, *Understanding Postmodernism*, 101.

what we call "culture" and it is "to people what water is to fish."⁶ We "swim" in it without even realizing it. What is more, the changing culture affects every facet of our lives for good or bad depending on how one accepts or rejects the cultural shifts, and believe me, we have been seeing cultural shifts. As such, one can appreciate the need for evangelicals to take note of where this cultural "river" is taking us.

Throughout, I will focus on the "moral concern" with these postmodern tenets as opposed to the "evangelistic concern" as outlined by White.⁷ While the latter is certainly important, I will leave that to those who minister weekly within this brave new world. My focus on the moral concern fits well with my expertise in biblical exegesis (i.e., interpretation) and instruction dealing with morality and sexual ethics. This is vital because understanding this part of the effects of postmodernism on culture will inevitably affect how evangelism is done.

At the same time, it is certainly true that postmodernists are not against all truth (e.g., who would disagree that Prince Edward Island in Canada is the setting for Anne of Green Gables?), rather they are against absolute *moral* and *ethical* truths that transcend all cultures.⁸ The challenging of truth is as old as time. The serpent did it with Adam and Eve in the garden when he said, "Did God say . . . ?" (Gen 3:1), and Pilate did it to Jesus—of all people—when he challenged Jesus with the quip, "What is truth?" (John 18:38). But when it comes to the tenets of moral and ethical truth espoused by postmodernists, Christians must push back against them based upon the absolute moral teaching of the Bible (I will return to this below). Paul's words are fitting: "Let God be true and every person a liar" (Rom 3:4; my paraphrase). Yet, at the same time, we need to know as evangelicals what we believe and why. It is not enough to say to our postmodern child or friends, "you are wrong!" without explaining why. Again, the purpose of this book is to help you do just that. That brings us to the next question: How did we end up having to deal with postmodernism in every facet of our lives?

---

6. White, *Postmodernism 101*, 12.

7. White, *Postmodernism 101*, 18, 59–60.

8. White, *Postmodernism 101*, 50, 53.

The Decline of Modernism and the Rise of Postmodernism: A Brief History

Today's rejection of Christian morals based upon the Bible did not happen overnight. On the contrary, long after the rationalistic trends of the Enlightenment (ca. 1660–1789), influential European thinkers already suggested that Christianity—and by extension the teachings of the Bible—was for the "morally weak" (Friedrich Nietzsche—1844–1900), the "psychologically unhealthy" (Sigmund Freud—1856–1939), a "tool of oppression" (Karl Marx—1818–1883), or "was scientifically unsupported" (Charles Darwin—1809–1882).[9] Not surprisingly, all of these thinkers prior to the postmodern era were vitally influential in the fields of philosophy, psychology, sociology, economics, and science. This line of thinking flowed into the universities and eventually grade schools through teachers and administrators. In every case, the belittling of Christianity and its teachings from the Bible helps to explain the natural progression of the undermining of biblical morality in Western culture.

These soft and hard sciences have supplanted Christianity in a variety of ways not the least of which is the removal of the supernatural. There has also been an elevation of what has become known as scientism over religion. Part of the outcome of this shift is the willingness of political forces to impose upon society what they decide is correct thinking regarding many of the social issues that were once dominated and controlled by the church.[10]

I will return to the topic of politics and evangelicalism in Chapter 14, but for now suffice it to say that it is evident that scientism has influenced Western culture for more than two hundred years. Ironically, the same "science" that was used to convince Western culture of the rightness of homosexuality and same-sex marriage is now being rejected when it comes to the trans issue: biology has been set aside in favor of "feelings."

The voices and teachings of the revolutionary thinkers of the past one hundred and fifty years influenced many in Western culture during the twentieth century. Under this influence, later thinkers began to point out the inadequacies of modernism. The death knell of modernism and the rise of postmodern thought in America was thrust onto the stage by a series of events most notably during the 1960s. For those old enough to remember these incidents the chaos that engulfed that time period is

9. Kelly and Dew, *Understanding Postmodernism*, 31, 42.
10. Ashford, "Jordan Peterson," 14.

still memorable. Stewart Kelly and James Dew note that these happenings included: the free speech movement in Berkley in 1960, which challenged mainstream cultural beliefs; the loss of innocence when John F. Kennedy was assassinated; the civil rights movement; race riots throughout America that destabilized communities; the Vietnam War and the ensuing student-led protests; the challenging of establishment values; multi-cultural awareness; a growing awareness of the evils of colonialism and imperialism and a belief in the moral superiority of certain cultures; the questioning of language to capture "reality"; the rise of the political Left; the bedlam of 1968 (the assassinations of Robert Kennedy and Dr. Martin Luther King Jr., the Tet offensive, the Democratic National Convention); and the birth of the women's movement.[11] The unrest caused by these events paved the way for radical shifts in Western culture spearheaded by radical thinkers in the universities. While some of these events were positive (e.g., the civil rights movement), the general chaos of this period of uncertainty and the questioning of established norms opened the door for a hijacking of traditional morality and thinking in America.

Some have attributed the shifting sands within Western culture and academia to the influence of "cultural Marxism." The difference between Marxism and cultural Marxism is the shift from a focus on economic liberation to social and sexual liberation. In the latter case, self is elevated and one's own perspective of reality takes priority over the old restrictive Judeo-Christian sexual ethics and morality.[12] The way the cultural Marxists achieve their goals is through the force of the state.[13] Put simply, they lobby the state to remove the barriers to the true self. This is accomplished by the state passing laws limiting or quashing any resistance from those holding Judeo-Christian ideals within the larger culture. Cultural Marxists then hail these new laws as establishing the environment for the "oppressed" to "flourish." The way the cultural Marxists operate is to divide people into classes (often called "identity politics," which is common within academia[14]) and then pit them against each other.[15] If one group is in anyway not respected at the same level as another, the

---

11. Kelly and Dew, *Understanding Postmodernism*, 49–50.
12. See also Sandlin, "Cultural Marxism."
13. Sandlin, "Cultural Marxism."
14. See Ellis, *Breakdown*, 55–57.
15. See also White, *Postmodernism 101*, 74–75.

state must be used to level the playing field.[16] Cultural commentator, P. Andrew Sandlin points out that in this new system, even how one is created can be deemed repressive and "a barrier to the good life." As an example, he notes the trans movement where one's gender needs to be altered in order for a person to be their "true self."[17] The only way the cultural Marxists, which are also known as progressives, can succeed is through constant conflict—using violence if necessary—all the while removing the oppressive class (whites, Christians, men, etc.) from their positions of power and hegemony while the cultural Marxists rise to the top.[18] Indeed, many in America reeled as the nation was gripped by the George Floyd protests for weeks that were fueled by those who wanted to overthrow all that America was founded upon, namely, the rule of law and order. The leadership in many cities sought to defund and/or abolish police departments—a natural next step to their continued call to "abolish ICE" (Immigration and Customs Enforcement) and the DHS (Department of Homeland Security). Anarchy is the friend of these types of movements. As previously noted, many of these types of cultural shifts begin in the universities and schools with radical educators manipulating impressionable young minds. I follow John M. Ellis's definition of radical when defining these educators: they represent those who are first and foremost political in their focus and reject all debate because their mind is already made up; they also have one goal, to transform society to match their beliefs.[19]

Postmodernism in Education

Many of the radical changes in society have been fostered by left-leaning academics. It should come as no surprise that the educational system in the West, from kindergarten to graduate school, is being influenced by postmodern thought, specifically moral relativism, when it comes to sexual ethics. Instead of the previous generations of professors who mostly believed in absolutes, since the 1970s and 1980s both the professors and the students now embrace moral relativism and its natural outworkings.[20]

16. Sandlin, "Cultural Marxism."
17. Sandlin, "Cultural Marxism."
18. Sandlin, "Cultural Marxism."
19. Ellis, *Breakdown*, 55.
20. Watkins, *New Absolutes*, 23–26.

Sexual proclivities of all types are now normalized and celebrated within the university. Not surprisingly, this has been brewing for some time as university faculties have moved to the Left.

A number of recent books have documented this shift. For example, Murray notes that typical of this shift to the Left is the rise of identity politics and intersectionality, which dominates left-leaning faculty thinking, and is counter to a conservative perspective.[21] The reason for this is the hijacking of academia within the universities, especially the social sciences, by the radical ideologies of the Left, many of whom were the radicals of the 1960s who are now tenured professors and hold leadership positions in universities and colleges.[22] Retired professor, John M. Ellis, notes that in 1969 the ratio of liberals, moderates, and conservatives was 45, 27, and 28 percent respectively.[23] By 1999 Ellis notes that those numbers had shifted radically with the liberal-to-conservative ratio becoming closer to 7 to 1, with English departments showing a staggering 88 to 3 ratio and political science with an 82 to 2 ratio.[24] In a separate 2004 study, the Ivy League schools had even higher ratios at 49 to 1 among the junior ranks of professors, meaning it is not getting better, it is getting worse with liberals packing their departments with like-minded thinkers.[25] Based upon a 2006 study of 927 institutions, the overall ratio reached 8 to 1.[26]

The departments so central to teaching about citizenship and government are now completely dominated by liberal thinkers. Is there any wonder why our children come back from universities with a changed ideology? But this is not even the worst. Murray and Ellis continue by noting that the same 2006 study showed that almost one fifth of social science professors in the US identified as "Marxist" and "activist" with many going so far as to identify as "radical"; the general Humanities did

---

21. Murray, *Madness of Crowds*, 52.

22. See also Peterson, *12 Rules for Life*, 310–11; Watkins, *New Absolutes*, 194–204; and Ashford, "Jordan Peterson," 21.

23. Ellis, *Breakdown*, 25.

24. Ellis, *Breakdown*, 26.

25. Ellis, *Breakdown*, 32–33.

26. Ellis, *Breakdown*, 28. Murray and Ellis both cite the same study of Neil Gross from Harvard and Solon Simmons from George Mason University titled "The Social and Political Views of American Professors," 24 September, 2007. Both professors identify as liberal.

not fare much better.[27] Not surprisingly, a recent study by the American Enterprise Institute from 2016 showed that only five percent of social science professors identify as conservative.[28] The current trends show that these disparate ratios are now bleeding over into other departments—like the sciences—making the future of higher education dim to be sure. Soon there will be no opposing voice anywhere on American university and college campuses. As of 2016, the ratios based on political voting for five main departments (Economics, History, Journalism/Communications, Law, and Psychology) in a forty-campus survey revealed an overall ratio of 11.5 to 1; History and Journalism ranked highest with 33.5 to 1 and 20 to 1 ratios respectively.[29] Since this survey, it has gotten worse with another study now showing the once 8 to 1 ratio in 2006 is now 12 to 1 with 39 percent of the campuses surveyed having no Republican faculty present while the other 61 percent of campuses were close to zero![30] Again, it is important to recognize this shift if we want to understand why Western culture is moving away from Judeo-Christian ideals, especially those of the Genesis mandates. Society is shifting because our younger generations are being indoctrinated to accept anti-biblical principles.

This troubling shift is also present within evangelical schools. In his podcast called *The Briefing* for Friday, Dec 6, 2019, Al Mohler, the current president of the Southern Baptist Theological Seminary, points out this exact issue. He calls those wanting to shift evangelical Christianity towards postmodern tenets as the "Evangelical Left." Mohler notes that the problem is the failure of evangelical administrations to "hire rightly" thus opening the door for these postmodern trends. Mohler continues by noting that a solid and impressive curriculum vita is not the most important thing, it must be the candidate's stance on biblical authority not cultural trends. Also, the forming of LGBTQ clubs on evangelical campuses is just the beginning of the slippery slope. Postmodernism will not allow for this type of "tolerance" only, they want full acceptance and celebration as the next step. You cannot remake Christianity in this

---

27. Murray, *Madness of Crowds*, 52; and Ellis, *Breakdown*, 31–32.
28. See Lawrence, "AEI Panel"; and Irvine, "Marxist Professors."
29. Ellis, *Breakdown*, 34.
30. Ellis, *Breakdown*, 35. Ellis (p.36) notes that among University of California employees, 97.46 percent of all political contributions by faculty went to Democrats in 2017–2018.

regard.³¹ You instead make something other than Christianity; you make a false religion.

No longer is academia used primarily for exploration and advancement, instead the focus has shifted to propaganda and activism.³² This trend is made even more troubling by the fact that many in these fields, Marxist or otherwise, praise the works of radicals and postmodern deconstructionists such as Michel Foucault, Antonio Gramsci, Gilles Deleuze, Paul de Man, and others.³³ Generally speaking, those who operate and view life through this lens are suspicious of the past traditions and values and instead view everything through the "'prism of power.'"³⁴ Of course this begs the questions: Whose power? Whose worldview should be dominant? The underdog's? The radicals'? Whose? They seek to deconstruct everything of value in culture, literature, history, you name it, except, for the current assertions of the academy itself.³⁵

Closely connected to the Marxist bent of many professors is the growing tendency within the Humanities to push "critical social justice." There is also a complete rejection or "canceling" (from which we get the "cancel culture" idiom) of anyone, even if it is their own colleagues, who opposes their group think.³⁶ The place where these "cancerous cells" of division are growing is in the "ever-metastasizing offshoots of the social sciences" (e.g., Queer Studies, Women's Studies, Black Studies etc.).³⁷ Regarding these new areas of academic study, the general approach is to politicize any perceived oppression of these "marginalized" groups for the purpose of pushing a left-leaning agenda while silencing or shaming any dissenting voice in the "dominant class" and "reeducating" the rest.³⁸ Their voices in "scholarly" journals are quoted approvingly by politicians and administrators and then used to formulate policies for schools and governing bodies. The cycle is completed when students at all levels adopt these questionable theories as "fact" and perpetuate the myths associated

---

31. Mohler, *The Briefing* (Friday, Dec 6, 2019).
32. Murray, *Madness of Crowds*, 59.
33. Murray, *Madness of Crowds*, 53; and Watkins, *New Absolutes*, 200–201.
34. Murray, *Madness of Crowds*, 53.
35. Murray, *Madness of Crowds*, 53.
36. See Ellis, *Breakdown*, 13.
37. Ellis, *Breakdown*, 57–61; and Murray, *Madness of Crowds*, 53.
38. Watkins, *New Absolutes*, 197.

with their professors' faulty logic and research.[39] As I noted earlier, evangelicals are not immune to this because our children attend the schools where this rubbish is propagated.[40]

It is no secret among honest—and usually socially conservative—academics and cultural critics (e.g., Jordan Peterson and Douglas Murray) that much of what the cultural Marxists publish is nothing more than gibberish rooted in political and social activism.[41] In an extended online interview, James Lindsay (who self-identifies as "really liberal" and an atheist) tells his story about how he and two of his colleagues (Peter Boghossian and Helen Pluckrose) did an experiment throughout 2017 and 2018 whereby they wrote a series of bogus papers and submitted them to several different peer-reviewed journals in the Humanities.[42] The common denominator was that they focused on topics of social justice particularly centered around the supposed oppression of sexual and social minority groups, what is today often labelled as "identity politics" or "social group status."[43] What made this so egregious was that they began with the conclusion that they knew a specific academic journal would want (e.g., the highlighting of some form of social or sexual oppression). They then padded their papers with all the catch phrases and methodologies prevalent in the Humanities regularly pawned off as scholarship under the guise of critical theory (e.g., Queer Studies, Feminist Studies; Liberation Studies). In one case they reworked Hitler's *Mein Kampf* in feminist jargon without the peer reviewers picking up on the irony. Another paper that was accepted for publication was titled, "Human Reactions to Rape Culture and Queer Performativity at Urban Dog Parks in Oregon." The article purported to prove that the modern social paradigms such as rape culture and queer performativity could be understood by examining the sexual behavior of dogs.[44] This is what many of the educators of our parishioners, kids, and grandkids consider relevant so students can be "woke" to the plight of the oppressed.

---

39. See the example given by D'Souza, *Illiberal Education*, 208–10.

40. So, too, Ellis, *Breakdown*, 153–55.

41. See Murray, *Madness of Crowds*, 60–63. A fine example of such convoluted writing is that exemplified by Butler, *Gender Trouble* (1990/2007).

42. Lindsay, "Deep Dive."

43. This event spawned an entire Wikipedia entry: https://en.wikipedia.org/wiki/Grievance_studies_affair.

44. Neo-atheists assert that wokeness is the death knell of the Christian church. See Lindsay and O'Fallon, "Trojan Horse," at the 67–70-minute mark.

I can attest to this in my own discipline which has been influenced by the social sciences in interpretive approaches to the Bible. I have stopped attending the annual meetings of the Society of Biblical Literature—the putative "leading" organization in biblical studies—simply because many of the presentations lack any solid foundation in the Bible. Most rely on the latest fad or interpretive methods (e.g., queer theory, monster theory, feminist theory, liberation theory etc.). If on the face of it, most of these approaches are blatantly anti-God then one does not have to work too hard to understand why our Western culture is in such a freefall. The worldview of these academics, and by extension their sycophants (i.e., their gullible students), is that the blame game is easier to play than extending forgiveness to others for past faults.[45] To be sure, at times a corrupt system can oppress. And yes, even those from the church can be complicit (e.g., sexual abuse). But what the postmodern cultural Marxists want is complete capitulation and overthrow of the old systems and institutions of which Christianity and the Judeo-Christian worldview are at the top. Those who imbibe these philosophical worldviews refuse to take personal responsibility for their actions. Instead, they embrace what is often labeled a "victim mentality." When something goes wrong at school, at work, or within the education system it is always due to some systemic oppression or racism or the fault of society in general. Left unchecked, this in turn will ultimately create the conditions for the collapse of society.

I will conclude this section by returning to the list of events that shaped the 1960s and brought about the demise of modernism and paved the way for postmodernism. While all of these events of the 1960s were truly life-altering, and for that matter, culture-altering, I am left with the belief that many of these events were orchestrated by the Enemy to create an atmosphere of chaos and anarchy culturally in order to bring about a greater plan to bring down a "Christian" America, or at least a Judeo-Christian-influenced Western culture. Along with the questioning of morality and religious, cultural, and political establishment principles, Christian beliefs and established dogma were placed in a category like all other religions and faiths. This was the goal, I believe, of the Enemy (1 John 5:19). But is Christianity just another religion? Multiculturalists would answer in the affirmative.

---

45. Murray, *Madness of Crowds*, 53.

Postmodernism's Multicultural Push to Marginalize Judeo-Christian Ideals

The myopic drive of multiculturalism and diversity has helped postmodernism to marginalized and relativized Judeo-Christian values and sexual ethics. Now while multiculturalism is good in so far as it should make us aware of other cultures, I am not alone in believing that all cultures, or at least the governing ethical and moral principles of those cultures, are necessarily equally good.[46] I do not adhere to cultural relativism or to the belief that cultures that demean women, or that worship pagan deities, or that oppress the innocent or murder dissenters, are equal to cultures that are rooted in biblical principles.[47]

After returning to my native Canada from the US to start my PhD program, I noticed the pitfalls of multiculturalism with fresh eyes. Canada prides itself on being a "patchwork quilt" whereas the United States has always been likened to a "melting pot." During my first weeks of study I was sitting in the cafeteria and struck up a conversation with a lady about the blessing of salvation. I was used to being around conservative evangelical believers who believed the Bible and held that Jesus was the Way the Truth and the Life and that no person comes to the Father except through him (John 14:6). I was quickly awakened out of my theological and evangelical naivete when she said that Jesus was the way for some but for others (Muslims, Hindus, Sikhs, etc.) there were other means of salvation. I soon realized I was "no longer in Kansas." This was a prime example of the results of not only the multi-culturalist policy of Canada, but of postmodern thinking, namely, that Judeo-Christian values are not superior to other religious ideologies.

I think one of the clearest representations of this leveling of the religious playing field is the moniker "coexist." I have seen this literally on the bumper stickers of "believers'" vehicles, as tattoos on their bodies, and heard it in their conversations. To quote the old ABC detergent commercial, "If there is no difference, why pay more?" Why live according to the principles of the Bible as established by God in Genesis? Indeed, at that point all bets are off and one's governing principles of morality are up for grabs. Unfortunately, today in many circles "multiculturalism" is also code for the inclusion of not just other ethnicities, but of diverse and oppressed groups (e.g., sexual minorities) within our current culture

---

46. So, too, Ellis, *Breakdown*, 98, 133–34.

47. See also Watkins, *New Absolutes*, 197–98.

in the West. In order to bring justice and elevate the oppressed classes, the old systems of Western/European culture based on Judeo-Christian ideals must be destroyed. And as previously noted, the classroom is the perfect place to pit the old values against the much more enlightened and "just" values of this new multiculturalism.[48] There is no true coexistence for those who embrace it.

From a cultural relativistic perspective, because Judeo-Christian ideas, especially from Genesis 1 and 2, were central to establishing sexual ethics for America, the diminishing or marginalization of these principles in Western culture, means that a new morality of ethics needs to take its place. Of course, postmodernists are ready to offer their form of ethical and moral standards as a replacement.

Postmodernism and Its Influence on Sexual Morality

Considering our current trend toward multiculturalism, we must consider how this will affect our sexual ethics. Due to the subjective nature of truth when it is defined based upon a given culture and its context, some have asked: Whose "truth" is to be followed?[49] This is exactly the chaos and ambiguity in which postmodernists revel. Their belief that "there is no reality except what is constructed by one's experience"[50] is the seedbed for the chaos in our modern Western society. Postmodernism rejects a "one-size-fits-all" morality because this is too restrictive. As such, postmodernism allows for a variety of moral systems which in turn opens the door for systems that are problematic because they are unbiblical and, in many cases, anti-God. Scholars have noted that where modernity based its sexual ethics and morality on science and basic naturalistic thinking, often favoring Western cultural Judeo-Christian standards, postmodernism rejects these older evaluative ethical standards of "right" and "wrong" in favor of pretty much any sexual ethic, which is accepted by the wider culture.[51] This ultimately boils down to relativism: the relativism of postmodernity versus the absolutes of the Bible. The sexual revolution found its home in just such a setting.

---

48. Watkins, *New Absolutes*, 194.
49. Watkins, *New Absolutes*, 201.
50. Balswick and Balswick, *Authentic Human Sexuality*, 320.
51. Balswick and Balswick, *Authentic Human Sexuality*, 320–21.

Today, we are living in a postsexual-revolution world where sexual promiscuity and perversion has now been normalized in the media.[52] A culture cannot long stand under such conditions. On this, professor of theology and culture, Bruce Riley Ashford, correctly notes the dangers inherent in the sexual revolution and its rejection of long-standing institutions like the church and the family; under the guise of freedom, sexuality has become commodified and all sexual expression is now acceptable as long as it is between two consenting adults.[53] To be sure, our society is now reaping the moral whirlwind, the effects of which we feel on a daily basis. Even some professing Christian philosophers, ethicists, and theologians are embracing postmodern tenets and arguing that there are no "universal truths that apply to all people in all cultures."[54] The truth is that such an assertion belittles and marginalizes the authority of God's Word as transcending culture and time.[55] National surveys clearly reveal the shifts within all areas of morality in Western society, the church included.

In the early 1990s George Barna conducted a series of national surveys examining the belief in relativism vs. absolutism. The findings were telling of a generation that had been influenced by education and culture. What was most telling is the responses of evangelicals. In the 1994 survey, 42 percent of evangelicals rejected the idea of absolute truth and 40 percent rejected absolute ethical and moral truth.[56] This, of course, flies in the face of biblical instruction. That survey was over 25 years ago. If the church has bought into moral relativism, then how are we to expect the world to reflect anything different? This troubling trend among Christians has only continued. In a July 2015 survey, Barna reported that while 80 percent of Americans are concerned about the moral state of the country, a statistic that was fairly consistent across all age groups with 90 percent of Christians expressing concern, when asked about the basis for morality, 74 percent of Millennials (those born between 1984-1998) said it was what worked best for the individual.[57] When asked about the place of culture

---

52. Balswick and Balswick, *Authentic Human Sexuality*, 324. See also, Mouser, "Report."

53. Ashford, "Jordan Peterson," 14.

54. Kelly and Dew, *Understanding Postmodernism*, 235. Here the authors point to the problematic assertions of Franke and Grenz as found, for example, in their book *Beyond Foundationalism* (2001).

55. Kelly and Dew, *Understanding Postmodernism*, 236–39.

56. Watkins, *New Absolutes*, 27–28.

57. Barna, "End of Absolutes."

in determining what is morally right, 65 percent of all adults agreed one's culture should set the standard.[58] When it came to sexual morality, 69 percent of Americans accepted that consenting adults should decide when something is right or wrong, while 40 percent of Christians accepted this premise.[59] In another survey, Barna found that over 50 percent of Americans, both young and old, agreed that there was no singular correct or right religion and that many religions lead to eternal life. The same survey continued to point out the troubling trend of moral relativism among Generation Z (those born between 1999-2015) which was highlighted by their belief that "sincerely believing something makes it true."[60]

Despite this conclusion, 83 percent of professing Christians strongly or somewhat agreed that the Bible was the absolute truth for morality. What does this tell us? It shows that there is a disconnect with what people say and what they do. It may also reflect the growing trend among many denominations to believe that the Bible condones the sexual ethics embraced by Western culture. As we will see, this is due in large part to the increase in professing Christians, evangelicals included, who are reinterpreting the Bible to endorse such practices as same-sex marriage, transgenderism, unrestricted abortion, rampant divorce, and sex outside of marriage. David Kinnaman, president of the Barna Group, notes that morality based upon "finding yourself" and then pursuing "self-fulfillment" is the new standard quickly replacing biblical morality.[61] What this boils down to is the complete acceptance of self over God and what God has said in the Bible. By rejecting a God-ordered plan for the world, culture, and for human lives, Western cultures are quickly perverting God's good plan for sex, as presented in Genesis 1 and 2, and instead are using sex and all its derivations and deviations to fill the void of the religious desires God placed inside every human. Of course, this will never fill the void of loneliness or bring fulfillment in life. When culture shifts its focus from God and instead glorifies sex and sexual deviations, the demise of a once godly culture and heritage is sure to follow. Sodom and the cities of the plain are a stark reminder of this very reality. Today, many feel like they have been liberated by the sexual revolution and their newfound freedoms to explore and celebrate sexual deviance

58. Barna, "End of Absolutes."
59. Barna, "End of Absolutes."
60. Barna, "Atheism."
61. Barna, "End of Absolutes."

all supported and underpinned by governmental sanction and enshrined by laws. But this is to miss what really is at stake: the heart and soul of our culture as mandated by God. Societies that embrace such behaviors are enslaving themselves.[62] Today's moral and sexual revolution is rooted in an insidious type of relativism in that it is absolutism masquerading as relativism.[63] Thus, what we have in America is a battle between two absolutes, one based upon a biblical model and the other which promotes self as the absolute final authority. While most of those promoting self as the highest good may fall among the average populace, those pushing agendas for a new morality, which undermines the Genesis mandates, tend to be from the Left.[64]

When the Left speaks of "tolerance" this is code for an acceptance of their views alone and an intolerance for anything or any view that is counter to their position. What is being attacked is not all religious absolutes, but rather a certain *type* of absolutism, namely, Christianity and its claim that the Bible is the final arbiter of right and wrong. That is why Islam, Hinduism, and any other world religion are given a pass in Western culture while Christianity is singled out for ridicule and marginalization. This is no less true of Bible-believing Christians, especially evangelicals. We are being marginalized and scapegoated as *the* problem in America because of our "intolerance" to the changing moral and ethical demands of Western culture. We are caricatured for our political stances, for our moral standards, and for our rigidness on important social issues. Unfortunately, this is not just coming from the "radical" Left. The liberal elites of evangelicalism and mainline denominations also are lining up to wag their finger at those who hold these "antiquated" standards. They try to shame conservatives into accepting the new absolutes while patting themselves on the back for being in step with "culture" and for being on the "right side of history" when it comes to the changing tide.

Conclusion: A Final Word about Scholarly Voices

Cultural change is real, especially when one stops to consider that until about fifty years or so ago the sexual ethics of the church and Western

---

62. Ashford, "Jordan Peterson," 14–15. See also Ashford, "Christian Politics," 447.
63. Watkins, *New Absolutes*, 43, 244.
64. See also comments by Carson, *Christ and Culture*, 133.

culture were basically in harmony.⁶⁵ That is, marriage was foundational, children were a blessing, homosexuality was wrong, and trans issues were non-existent. What changed? Postmodernism's influence on every level of society beginning with scholarship. Books on "Christian" or "biblical" sexual ethics are a dime a dozen and come from all perspectives, theological, philosophical, exegetical, sociological, psychological, and so on. One of the common denominators of many of these "biblical" approaches is the rejection of the divine inspiration of Scripture.

When preparing to write this book I was amazed at how many scholars have written books with titles that declare the truthfulness of the given author's theory. Phrases like "What the Bible Really Says" or "The Bible's Contradictions about Sex" betray attempts to "enlighten," many times a biblically illiterate populace, about the so-called specious claims of the Bible concerning sexuality. In many ways, these titles are a statement revealing their authors' hubris. They propound that for over two thousand years of church history, not to mention Jewish history, people have misunderstood what the Bible teaches on sexuality. In some cases, scholars flat out tell their readers that the Bible cannot be used for sexual ethics because of these supposed contradictions.⁶⁶

As a teacher of the Bible, I am always cautious when "the wise" and intellectuals purport to know all about what God is doing and how biblical authors misunderstood God in the area of morality and sexuality. Paul gave a stern warning to the wise of his day about this perspective. He said: "God uses the foolish things to confound the wise and the weak things to confound the strong" (1 Cor 1:27; my paraphrase). After all, God revealed the news of the coming of his son to lowly shepherds as opposed to the elite "scholarly" class in Jerusalem. Put differently, those who read the Bible with conviction can easily understand that the plain teaching of the Bible rejects many of our modern ethical trends.

Nevertheless, mainline scholarship continues to muddy the already murky waters of sexual ethics and morality by producing books challenging the belief that one can use the Bible for hard and fast rules for living. Generally, they conclude that the Bible is conflicting and not univocal on many of the issues facing Western culture today. Those who attempt to use the Bible as a means of moral and ethical instruction are labeled

---

65. Pruss, *One Body*, 2.
66. Knust, *Unprotected Texts*, 344–45.

pejoratively as naïve or "fundamentalists."[67] While it is true that there are troubling teachings in the Bible like slavery and patriarchal oppression, the difference between descriptive (what is informative) and prescriptive (what is required) language is rarely discussed. What is more, when it comes to the issues of sexual ethics, God's ideal is, for the most part, straightforward.

The most troubling issue with modern biblical scholarship is that the authority of the Bible is questioned, and the Bible is often likened to any other text that can be changed or amended as culture changes. Coogan is a case in point when he likens the Bible to the Constitution of the United States and the amendment process.[68] Of course, this is a false dichotomy. While both may be authoritative for a given community (citizens of the US vs. believers), they are not equal. One is inspired and the other is simply a man-made document that will one day pass away. At the same time, there is a move within evangelicalism to downplay the importance of the moral and ethical teaching of the Old Testament Torah,[69] the basis upon which this current book is founded. The over emphasis of the historical contextualization of the Old Testament—and the New Testament as well—has caused a bifurcation between biblical and modern ethics and morality. Fortunately, there are still many who see the applicability of the Old Testament's moral and ethical instruction for today, at least at the level of universal principles.[70] In the chapters that follow, I will interact with several scholars, evangelical or otherwise, as I tackle the Genesis mandates in turn.

So why should you listen to another scholar if so many are biased or misuse the Text? This is a fair question. All I have to offer is my calling to educate God's people. When I was called, God impressed upon my heart Hosea 4:6a: "My people are destroyed from lack of knowledge" (NIV) because the *priests* have not done their jobs. As an OT scholar, the words of Amos ring in my head as well, "I am neither a prophet nor the son of a prophet" (Amos 7:14). Amos did not grasp for the position of spokesman for God he simply delivered the word of God to a lost and dying people. In a way, I resonate with his words. I come from a family of eight children

---

67. A good example of what could be labeled an "elitist" position on this topic is found in Collins's new book *Biblical Values*, 1–19.

68. Coogan, *God & Sex*, 193–96.

69. See for example the recent work of Walton, *The Lost World of the Torah* (2019).

70. See Gane, *Old Testament Law*, 197–218 and Longman, *Bible and the Ballot*, 24–50.

whose parents fell into the category of low income with no university graduates (at least when I was called by God). I was a carpenter until I was thirty and only then reluctantly went to Bible school at God's urging. I was an introvert by nature and did not like speaking to crowds. God called me at this time because he wants me to work for him and deliver a message. Yes, I have the degrees to back up what I say, but I do not boast in those things (Phil 3:3–7), instead I boast in the cross and in the change Jesus made in my life. I love God and God's Word and I hope you will sense that moving forward. Unfortunately, those who reject God and God's existence will naturally reject his mandates. It is to this point that I now turn to begin our study of the specific Genesis mandates.

Chapter 3

God as Sovereign Creator

ONE CANNOT BEGIN TO address the ethical and moral issues facing Western culture today without first pointing out the role that culture's rejection of God has played in these seismic shifts. Western culture is quickly bringing about a clash between the "law" of the West and the "law" of the Bible—the basis for Christian dogma in the church. Whose "law" will win out? For Bible-believing Christians, the answer is simple: God's law will always win out.

The opening two chapters of Genesis establish God as creator and designer of all creation including species distinctions, gender and sexuality, marriage, procreation, and the family unit as the foundation of society. The opening line of the Bible states that God spoke everything into existence as he stood outside of time and creation itself. Throughout the biblical Text it is clear that God has the authority to demand of his creation whatever he feels is appropriate for their flourishing. Later, God used his prophets to call Israel to return to moral, ethical, and righteous living as established by God in his Torah. Amos and Micah are just two examples who speak in terms of social and moral justice. Jesus also stressed both the centrality of the creation mandates for marriage (Matt 19:3–12) and the role that his heavenly Father played in directing his and his followers' lives (Matt 4:3–10; 26:39, 42; John 17; 1 Cor 15:28). Through recitation of the Apostles' and Nicene Creeds, for the past 2000 years of church history, believers have regularly acknowledged that God is at the top of our belief system, and by extension, serves as our Guide and Judge. And since the earliest days of America, the church has played a key role in keeping God central to our belief system, a reality made evident in the wording of the Declaration of Independence. Considering this long church and American tradition of acknowledging the place of God in our lives, exactly how has the rejection of God come about in Western society when Judeo-Christian ideals have played, and continue to play, such a central role in our lives?

To begin, many discussions concerning morality and sexual ethics in our postmodern world revolve around the role of sexual norms of the past and their putative "oppressive" nature for some groups. Part of the problem in Western culture is a rejection of the Creator as sovereign over humanity's sexuality and morality. Science and modernity's philosophical focus on rationalism has created increased scrutiny on what role "God" and a Christian worldview should play in society. God-rejecting educators at all levels, secular humanists, those deifying science and naturalism, neo-atheists and secular philosophers (e.g., Richard Dawkins, Sam Harris, and Christopher Hitchens) along with action groups like the American Atheists have played a crucial role in helping shape current thought processes vis-à-vis a biblical worldview in the West. In this wake, the rise of scientism, atheism, agnosticism, and post-Christian thought in the West have all contributed to the gender and sexuality debates. This is no less the case for the culture wars prevalent in Western culture in the past half century and those being fought even more vociferously in the past two decades.

This secularization of society has not left the church unscathed. Many mainline traditions have already sold out to the new rationalism and "settled science" relating to sexuality and climate change (see Chapter 13) that is dominating Western society. Within evangelical circles, young people are moving away from the faith and authority of God and his Word and adopting these new worldview approaches to faith, reason, sexual ethics, and morality. As such, many young evangelicals are joining the metaphorical *and* literal march for "equality" and "justice" for those who are suffering sexual and gender "oppression" while at the same time moving to the Left politically in order to align with the new "wokeness." For a new generation of evangelicals, God's Word does not hold the same authority as it did a generation or two ago. Parents and grandparents are now faced with this shift within the worldview of their children and grandchildren. In some cases, they find themselves worlds apart. As we will see, based upon a number of research surveys (e.g., Barna, Gallup, and Pew), Millennials (those born between 1984–1998) and Generation Z (those born between 1999–2015) are rejecting the authority of God and God's Word to set boundaries for people's sexual and moral ethics, and in turn, for culture.

In this chapter I will examine, in cursory fashion, how this shift has occurred and the implications it has for the future of the church and Western society if it is not checked with sound, lucid, and persuasive counter arguments from Scripture. Moving forward, I hope to present many of these arguments throughout the following chapters. Christians should also avail themselves of the cogent arguments by evangelical apologists and philosophers such as John Lennox, Al Mohler, William Lane Craig, Paul Copan, Michael Brown, and Hugh Ross (to name a few).

The Shifting Tide

From the very opening lines of Genesis a fundamental truth is established: God created all things and is therefore responsible for the moral standard for all people.[1] And Genesis 3 shows us clearly that when we allow the Enemy to offer an alternate reality apart from God—"Did God really say . . . ?"—God will judge those who reject his commands/mandates. The rejection of God in Western culture has had a detrimental effect on the morality of our culture. While throughout I will be noting *how* Western culture has rejected God, the *why* is still just as important. As we will see, much of the rejection of God is based upon how people view life in general through a scientific lens, or what is often known as naturalism or a secular humanistic philosophical bent. When considering the work of Francis Schaeffer, Bruce Waltke points out the issues with this type of worldview. Waltke says, "A system of thought that cannot provide sure values for man who demands values is inconsistent with reality and does not provide a framework with which he can live consistently. The evangelical, by contrast, turns to the Bible and finds that it speaks with moral certainty, claims to give to dependent man a statement of that which is absolutely good, promotes life, has been verified again and again as historically accurate in those areas capable of being subjected to empirical test, and above all is accompanied by the convincing work of the Holy Spirit."[2] When rationalism dominates one's worldview, it does not take long for a rejection of God to follow. Who needs some "mythical being" in the heavens to

---

1. Grudem, *Politics*, 116–17.
2. Waltke, "Reflections," 5.

answer all our questions when we have science and reason? Thus, society has marginalized God and pushed him to the periphery.

What is telling, however, is that statistics show that compared to the average person, people who embrace religion and God see positive outcomes in virtually every area of life: divorce is lower with a higher level of marital satisfaction and happiness, poverty rates are lowered, morality increases, suicide, drug abuse, out-of-wedlock births all drop, crime is lowered, people have lower rates of depression, higher self-esteem, children are more mentally fit, successful recovery from addictions like alcoholism increase, and general physical health is better.[3] On the other hand, part of the trouble in Western society is a rejection of God and the hope God offers which in turn fosters a rise in fear and despondency among our youth. Whether it is about climate change, the right image, bullying, drugs, or general despondency, it may help explain why teen suicide is on the rise. Indeed, in the past decade alone, the CDC says that teen (15–19 years of age) suicide has increased 76 percent.[4] God knew what he was doing when he instituted proper worship of the Creator of the universe and humanity.

What Western scientific/rationalistic thinking fails to consider, or at least what they seek to reject, is the fact that God will not be marginalized. The Bible is replete with examples of God bringing judgment upon the nations because of their sin (Isa 13–23; Jer 46–51; Ezek 25–32; Amos 1–2; Zeph 2).[5] In Genesis alone, we find God passing judgment upon the world for sin in chapters 6–9, and then upon the cities of the plain in Genesis 19 for sexual sin. In our modern "coexist" climate, many may think that the God of the Bible does not have dominion over them because they worship some other god. They would be wrong of course. I am reminded of the words of the prophet Ezekiel when the nation of Israel decided that they would be like the nations, a desire that was against the will of God. God's response was unequivocal: "'As I live, declares the Lord Yahweh, with a strong hand and outstretched arm, and with wrath poured out I will be King over you!'" (Ezek 20:33; my translation).

We can think that we will eliminate God from our lives, and God may allow us to go on for a period of time living in this delusion, but it will not last. Sooner or later the chaos that we create will implode on us

---

3. Watkins, *New Absolutes*, 233. See also the conclusions of Patterson and Kim, *The Day America Told the Truth*, 61.

4. Power of Positivity, "CDC."

5. See also Grudem, *Politics*, 85–86.

and God will once again have to be reckoned with. There is a reason God placed the Tree of the Knowledge of Good and Evil in the middle of the Garden of Eden. Adam and Eve were forced to decide each day whether they would follow and obey the law of God. They had to choose, and so do we. Each day we are faced with a decision on who will be the god of our lives: self or God in heaven?[6] What is evident from history is that God has a way of getting people's attention. God does not live on the edges of society; God is central to all we do. Jesus also picked up on the centrality of God when he warned his disciples that "If anyone comes to Me, and does not hate his own father and mother and wife and children and brothers and sisters, yes, and even his own life, he cannot be My disciple" (Luke 14:26; NASB). Right now, as I write this paragraph, I am holed up in my office as the world faces a global pandemic of Covid-19. Many are asking or wondering if this is not perhaps God trying to get our attention. We certainly need to repent of our sin. And it is not a coincidence that the well-known verse in 2 Chronicles 7:14 ("and My people who are called by My name humble themselves and pray, and seek My face and turn from their wicked ways, then I will hear from heaven, will forgive their sin, and will heal their land." NASB) is prefaced by verse 13 which lists famine, locust plagues, and pestilences as sent by God to get his people's attention and as the impetus for God's people to call out for his mercy. Now while some may push back against this type of application of OT texts, which are geared to a covenanted people,[7] the truth is the principle of God's mercy being extended to a repentant nation—any nation—is clearly stated in Jeremiah 18:5–10.[8] Therefore, the same God who sends these types of warnings is the same God who can be petitioned to remove them! It sounds contradictory but that is how God has consistently worked in the Bible. Again, it is a message that is clear: humanity cannot live without God because God will be central to all we do whether we agree to it or not.

Now that does not mean that we cannot reject God; many do just that. But in time we will know that God is still in control. This brings us full circle to the question at hand. If God is central to all we do, and if God is sovereign, then does he have a final say as to what is acceptable about our behavior, ethics, and place he plays in our lives? The answer of

---

6. Americans have been moving in this direction since the 1990s and before. See Patterson and Kim, *The Day America Told the Truth*, 25–27.

7. E.g., Longman, *Bible and the Ballot*, 27.

8. See also, Gaines, "2 Chronicles 7:14."

course is a resounding, Yes! It is for this reason that the West's attempts to remove God from our sexual ethics and morality will not stand but will ultimately fail. God will see to that, as he has done with societies throughout history. Marriage, family, sexuality, environment, species distinctions as established in the Genesis mandates of Genesis 1 and 2 may be flouted for a period, but God will have the final say.

This also raises another issue, namely, the reading of God's Word. Evangelicals claim to be people of the Book, so to speak, but fail to read or study it regularly. I am reminded of my life's verse from Hosea 4:6a "my people perish for lack of knowledge." I am also amazed at the biblical illiteracy among young people from many of the dominant evangelical denominations. I see them regularly in my classes. Many simply do not know what the Bible says on the key cultural and moral issues. I do not blame them per se, I blame pastors, parents, and Christian educators who have chosen to entertain children as opposed to teaching them. And when it comes to instruction in the OT it is not acceptable to simply bypass this portion of the Bible with the statement "Well, that was for the Jewish people and doesn't apply to Christians." This is simply to miss the clear instruction of Paul that *all* Scripture is inspired and good for teaching and correction unto all righteousness (2 Tim 3:16). Peter points out the Holy Spirit's inspiration of the Hebrew Bible as well (2 Peter 1:21). Back on November 8, 2011 then president of the American Bible Society, Lamar Vest, appeared on Fox News and gave an update on the biblical literacy project that he was promoting. In the interview with Lauren Green, Vest noted that only 20 percent of Americans read the Bible regularly.[9] Much to my surprise is the fact that Vest also notes that about 54 percent of Americans suggested that the Bible needed a greater platform in society, but this is not happening. How is society supposed to change if Americans, and specifically evangelicals, are not reading the Bible? The reason we are facing a moral and ethical crisis in Western culture is the failure of professing believers to engage and understand God's instruction to his people. The church has become impotent because of this lack of knowledge. How can we expect the next generation to change culture or buck the cultural trends for that matter, if all they have is a "Veggie Tales" knowledge of the Bible?

While certainly anecdotal, I have been keeping records for my freshmen OT classes for a decade now regarding their basic biblical

---

9. See also Vest, "Most Americans."

knowledge upon entering my class. I give all my students what I have termed a "pre-semester exercise" which usually consists of fifteen basic biblical questions from the OT. These are big-picture questions. What I have found is that most students get on average about three to six correct answers out of fifteen. The good news is that I do see some improvement after they have taken my class, but it is not to the level I would like to see. If this is the case for a Christian university that thankfully requires religion and Bible classes, what does this say for the majority of students, evangelicals mind you, who go to state schools and other universities that never teach Bible, theology, and biblical ethics classes? What this again tells me is that we evangelicals have a huge responsibility as pastors, educators, parents and grandparents to teach our kids the entirety of the Bible and its moral injunctions, because the church is not doing it in a few minutes once or twice a week.

America's Drift from God: Was America Ever a Christian Nation?

From its earliest settlement, America's founding fathers had a strong belief in the role of natural law as endowed by the Creator.[10] This is made evident in the opening lines of the Declaration of Independence. Historians have traced this quasi-Christian history from the landing of the Mayflower to modern day.[11] Indeed, the fear of God and morality is central to America's social fabric.[12] One clear example comes from John Adams; the second president of the United States stated, "We have no government armed with power capable of contending with human passions unbridled by morality and religion. Avarice, ambition, revenge, or gallantry, would break the strongest cords of our Constitution as a whale goes through a net. Our Constitution was made only for a moral and religious people. It is wholly inadequate to the government of any other."[13] Put differently, Adams assumed that the populace would govern

---

10. Carson, *Christ and Culture Revisited*, 134. See also Meacham, *American Gospel*; and Holmes, *Founding Fathers*. These as noted by Carson 134n33.

11. E.g., Fea, *Believe Me*, 75–113. Fea vacillates on the issue even though he spends almost a third of his book laying out the Christian and God-centered founding of the nation.

12. See also, Wallis, *God's Politics*, 59.

13. Adams, "Letter to Officers," 229 as cited by Watkins, *New Absolutes*, 62. Fea (*Believe Me*, 69–70) uses these types of sayings from the founding fathers to bludgeon

themselves to a degree through self-control, realizing that their actions would be judged by God.[14] To be sure, as with Adams's concerns, D.A. Carson is correct to note that the American experiment, and democracy in general, runs the constant risk of imploding because it affords freedom to people to live as they see fit: for good and for evil.[15] Despite this early faith in a Higher Power to direct the affairs of American culture, there has been an ever-increasing push to downplay our godly heritage and to marginalize Judeo-Christian principles, which put God at the center of moral and ethical demands. This more recent trend has caused a very rapid downward spiral in American culture.[16]

The rapidly changing face of American culture is perhaps best exemplified in the rise of oppressive litigation and governmental restrictions of our religious freedoms. The oft-cited Constitutional grounds for the silencing of believers in the public square is the First Amendment to the US Constitution which states: "Congress shall make no law respecting an establishment of religion, or prohibiting the free exercise thereof." Yet, instead of being able to exercise a freedom of religion, organizations like the ACLU and others of their ilk have pushed the belief, which has been adopted by most governmental institutions, especially the courts, that this is freedom *from* religion. Jim Wallis is correct to call out these groups as "secular fundamentalists" who misunderstand the central role that religious language, God, and morality has played in the history of America.[17] Indeed, if one challenges the moral issues of abortion, homosexuality, or transgenderism then Christians, as Carson notes, "are inevitably charged with smuggling Christianity into the public arena."[18] On the other hand, if Christians rally against homelessness, the plight of the poor, issues of public welfare, and the dangers of consumerism, "then

---

conservative evangelicals as being inconsistent when viewed along with other statements from the founding fathers on the need for an upright character of the nation's leaders (*The Federalist Papers* 57 and 68 written by James Madison and Alexander Hamilton respectively), that is, Fea is speaking of Donald Trump's indiscretions. The reality is that many evangelicals recognize the problems with Trump's temperament and indiscretions but find the downward trajectory of the nation more important than the man who will occupy the Oval Office for a maximum of eight years. The enacted laws and appointment of judges by a president has a lifetime effect.

14. Strand, "The Founders."
15. Carson, *Christ and Culture Revisited*, 128.
16. So, too, Brown, *Jezebel's War*, 35–37.
17. Wallis, *God's Politics*, 65–71.
18. Carson, *Christ and Culture Revisited*, 127.

they are widely (if sometimes condescendingly) thought to have prophetic voices."[19] One set of moral issues is acceptable to address, the other is off limits. Why? Because sexual and moral ethics strike at the heart of the individual and their personal accountability before their Creator.

As succinctly noted by John Eastman, professor of law at Chapman University, separation of church and state never appears in the Constitution: it is actually a phrase that appears in a letter written by Thomas Jefferson to the Danbury Baptist Church Association of Connecticut in 1802 which reaffirmed that the government should not infringe upon an individual's freedom of religion.[20] In other words, it was a "wall" to protect the individual from the government, not the government from the individual. In fact, it was understood that God should be on "both sides of the wall."[21]

The cultural changes began to pick up steam in 1947 when the Supreme Court adopted Jefferson's 1802 wording—from the Danbury Baptist letter, not the Constitution—in their *Everson v. Board of Education* ruling. Even though the ruling was in the favor of Catholic private schools using tax dollars for busing, the separation of church and state language was nonetheless now on the proverbial radar screen for future rulings. This came to fruition in 1962 when the Supreme Court struck a blow to religious liberty in their ruling of *Engel v. Vitale* which removed from schools even the most benign of generic prayers to God. Whether accurate or not, since then it has become common fare to connect America's moral collapse to this decision. For example, from the 1960s onward America has seen the rise of premarital sex, an explosion of pregnancy and births outside of wedlock, the exponential increase in violent crimes in schools, and a dramatic drop in academic performance. Of course, some will argue that correlation is not causation, but there can be little doubt that the rejection of God at every level of Western society has only fueled the degradation of culture.

Instead, every other secular humanistic ideology and pagan practice is generally allowed a hearing without question while the mention of Jesus, God, or prayer evokes terror in the hearts of those in control of these governmental institutions as they run for cover in fear of the litigation shockwaves. It is fine to promote the religion of secular humanism,

---

19. Carson, *Christ and Culture Revisited*, 127.
20. Eastman, "Separation."
21. Strand, "The Founders."

God as Sovereign Creator

but the mention of God is a bridge too far. This is where America and many Western democracies (e.g., Canada) find themselves since we have yielded the ground of the public square to those with a godless and leftist ideology who insist that their way of understanding the First Amendment is the only way. Of course, removing religious instruction, specifically Christian instruction and principles, from the public square, court houses, schools, and houses of Congress, has paved the way for a depraved secularism that is devoid of ethical decency and morality, concepts that have held America together since its founding.[22] Indeed, we have arrived at the moment when the words of Isaiah 5:20 ring true: "Woe unto them that call evil good, and good evil; that put darkness for light, and light for darkness; that put bitter for sweet, and sweet for bitter!" (KJV). Of course, as noted in my previous chapter, another tendency of current postmodern thought is the rejection of absolute truth, especially as mandated by a Higher Authority.[23]

One wonders how long it will be before God will judge our immoral extremes exemplified by our increased secularism. In the last half of the twentieth century and the beginning two decades of the twenty-first, we have seen a steady spiritual and moral decline in Western culture because we have placed our own debased morality above God's clearly defined moral commands.[24] Unfortunately, today, any remotely Christian themes, concepts, or practices by believers in or near government-controlled institutions are regularly challenged in the courts or outright forbidden by governmental and educational administrators.[25]

For some time now, Americans have been moving away from faith in God, at least as being divinely sovereign over their morality. Even though they may believe in the existence of God, they do not submit to God's commands as detailed in the Bible. For example, many Millennials feel they do not need religion or religious organizations to teach their children morality. As a matter of fact, many feel they are a hindrance. This is to fundamentally miss how we gained our morality in the first place. It is based upon the existence of a Creator. Clearly Americans have

---

22. Watkins, *New Absolutes*, 64.
23. Kelly and Dew, *Understanding Postmodernism*, 220.
24. Watkins, *New Absolutes*, 248.
25. See the numerous examples cited by Watkins, *New Absolutes*, 49–55, 248.

become their own moral compass as they decide what is right and wrong for themselves as opposed to relying on the church or the Bible.[26]

Recently I ran across an article which analyzed a Barna study on how Americans view Satan and God. The findings of the study were startling. While slightly more than half of those surveyed still believe in an all-powerful and good Creator, only thirty years ago this number was closer to three quarters of the population.[27] What is more, practically every denomination saw declines in orthodox thinking on this subject with Pentecostal and Charismatic churches having the greatest shift with a 27 percent decline.[28] As a Pentecostal, I find this deeply troubling, although not surprising, seeing how many churches have opted for children's programs and adult services more akin to entertainment than solid biblical instruction. Based upon the Barna findings, scholars concluded that basic beliefs, which were once held by most people, are now being rejected, with the most troubling assertion being the belief that Jesus himself was a sinner in need of salvation—a position held by 40 percent of American adults.[29] With such unorthodox beliefs pervading America, not to mention the fact "that more people believe in the existence of Satan than the God of Abraham,"[30] it does not take much evaluative thought to realize why we as a country are in deep moral and ethical decline, not to mention spiritual danger.

Another problem is that leaders in America are becoming more and more vocal with their hostility towards God and their rejection of his sovereignty. On Monday, April 13, 2020, during the Covid-19 quarantine, the Democrat governor of New York, Andrew Cuomo, haughtily declared that the state had dropped the infection rate "because we brought the numbers down. God did not do that, fate did not do that, destiny did not do that. A lot of pain and suffering did that. That's how it works. It's math. And if you don't continue to do that, you're going to see that number go back up. And that will be a tragedy if that number goes back up."[31] Such arrogance reminds me of the words of Nebuchadnezzar in Daniel 4:30: "Is this not Babylon the great, which I myself have built as a royal

---

26. This paragraph reflects the insights of Patterson and Kim, *The Day America Told the Truth*, 199–206.

27. Mouser, "Barna."

28. Mouser, "Barna."

29. Mouser, "Barna."

30. As cited by Mouser, "Barna."

31. Brown, "Governor Cuomo"; and Prestigiacomo, "Cuomo."

residence by the might of my power and for the glory of my majesty?" (NASB). Of course, we all know what happened to Nebuchadnezzar immediately following this proudful declaration: he became like an animal for a period of time and lost his sanity until God restored him.

The Effects of Secular Education vis-à-vis America's Rejection of God

It goes without saying that young evangelicals in the West have been influenced, by culture and media of all types, to reject God. For those who have raised, and are raising, their children in a Christian setting, this may be mitigated to a degree. Nevertheless, by the time they head off to university, many times the seeds of dissent are already planted within them by the culture at large. Once at university, there are two ways the further erosion of faith in an all-powerful and sovereign Creator can potentially continue. One is through religion classes, which you would think would do just the opposite, and the second is through general education classes in Science and the Humanities.

To begin, depending on how they are taught, religion classes, which often include Bible, theology, ethics, and comparative religions, can have either a profoundly positive or negative effect on young people coming out of evangelical churches and homes where hard questions have been glossed over, or only shallow answers have been given. While I do not have the space to delve into the many ways this can happen in every discipline, nor would I claim to be an expert in them all, I do know that one of the easier and subtler ways young people are influenced negatively is how the Bible is taught. If, for example, much of the opening chapters of Genesis are presented as mythology, and scientific evolution is correct, then answering to a God who is no different than all the other ancient gods, especially concerning moral and ethical standards, is easily rejected. Now of course there are certainly people who can handle challenges to their interpretive approaches to the Bible, but if the student is not shown how to handle properly the opening chapters of Genesis, then it is certainly understandable why young people begin to question their faith in God. This is particularly poignant when dealing with ethics and the Old Testament, especially when addressing troubling texts like those found in Deuteronomy and Joshua, which deal with God's judgment on foreign nations. Many times, this ethical issue is handled as either being unhistorical, or presented as a picture of a tyrannical God. To be sure, Richard Dawkins and the New Atheists love to throw these texts into the faces of young impressionable Christians to get them to reject the God of the Bible. Sadly, many do just that.[32]

A second major issue is the continued and ever-present naturalistic perspective of human origins propagated by Darwin and fueled by those in both the hard sciences (e.g., biology, astronomy, physics, chemistry, geology) and the soft sciences (psychology, sociology, anthropology, etc.). This is the case for most universities worldwide, even Christian institutions. Now I am in no way trying to belittle science, nor am I attempting to explain away or trivialize the debates about how God created all things. But behind Darwin's thinking was a godless philosophy of naturalism that made no room for God.[33] Who needs a God when the natural world can be explained by natural selection and evolution, and religious belief can be chalked up to humanity's tendency to believe in superstition?[34] Thus, by removing God from the picture, naturalists also remove the image of God in humans. I would like to look at the treatment of the unborn as a case study of how a rejection of God as creator can lead to horrific outcomes.

Following the lead of Darwin, abortion advocates teach that unborn children are nothing more than another clump of "parasitical" cells to be discarded at will. Indeed, this is often the very language used by pro-choice advocates when they are confronted with the horror of their actions. Since the *Roe v. Wade* decision in 1973, educational institutions have pushed this belief harder and harder despite the growing scientific and medical ability to visualize a child in the womb. It should be of no surprise why pro-choice advocates are pushing so hard against the use of ultrasounds to show a woman her baby before an abortion. The technology is so advanced now that pro-choice advocates know once a woman sees her child, who is not a clump of parasitical cells as they suggest, as an actual living and moving infant in utero, many choose life. When humanity begins to make moral and ethical judgments on their own, apart from God, objectivity is lost. Harvey Cox notes this well when he states, "Secular man's values have been deconsecrated, shorn of any claim to ultimate or final significance . . . they are no longer the expression of

---

32. I would point my readers to Copan, *Is God a Moral Monster?* (2011) and Copan and Flannagan, *Did God Really Command Genocide?* (2014).

33. See also Carson, *Christ & Culture Revisited*, 116.

34. Watkins, *New Absolutes*, 75.

the divine will. They have become what certain people at a particular time and place hold to be good. They have ceased to be values and have become valuations . . . ."[35] And when one's own thinking becomes the final arbiter of right and wrong it is not hard to understand how society begins to devolve. Part of this devolution is the rise of atheism, which is the ultimate rejection of a sovereign God.

Atheism and the Rejection of God

To remove God from the human experience invites a re-evaluation of what constitutes moral good and evil. Back in the 1930s, social anthropologist Joseph Daniel Unwin noted that part of the cultural decline of societies is the rejection of sexual ethics and mores coupled with a rejection of God.[36] Despite what appears to be short-term gains when sexual mores are rejected, Unwin's research showed that putting restraints on sexual promiscuity before and during marriage brought about the most long-term good and societal flourishing.[37] But to suggest such an ideal today is often viewed as outdated, and in some cases, "evil" for not allowing people to be their true selves. Yet, what is "evil" is the move away from a Judeo-Christian ideal.

Many in the West, and America in particular, have rejected God's laws and have set themselves up as the moral standard by which to live. This has caused confusion and chaos for the individual and for society as a whole.[38] Even evangelicals are walking away from their belief in God and their Christian faith.[39] Recent studies have shown that atheism is on the rise among younger people such as Gen Z (13 percent as opposed to 6 percent among adults).[40] Much of this change is due to a rejection of Christianity because of the problem of evil in the world, and the rejection of the church's general stance on social issues related to immigration and sexual ethics.[41] Another issue, which is related to the influence of science

---

35. Cox, *Secular City*, 31 as cited by Waltke, "Reflections," 4.
36. Durston, "Sexual Morality."
37. As pointed out by Durston, "Sexual Morality."
38. Patterson and Kim, *The Day America Told the Truth*, 31–34.
39. Joshua Harris of the "I've Kissed Dating Goodbye" fame and other Christian artists have turned their back on faith and God. See Parke, "Christian Singer."
40. Barna, "Atheism Doubles."
41. Barna, "Atheism Doubles."

noted above, is young people's desire for proof that God exists.[42] Jesus' words to Thomas immediately come to mind: "Blessed *are* they who did not see, and *yet* believed" (John 20:29b; NASB). Part of the natural outcome of this shift is a rise in relativism when it comes to sexual ethics and morality. If God's Word is not the final arbiter, then once again "self" must be the measure of right and wrong. This fits naturally within the educational system where secular philosophical thinking dominates.

As Kelly and Dew have pointed out, philosophical thinking, post Enlightenment (e.g., Hegel, Nietzsche, Marx, Freud), tended to redefine the notion of "self" by eliminating the concept of the eternal soul as classically defined within Christianity. Without a soul to define the self, one is merely a conglomeration of thoughts and impulses. Not surprisingly, in this historical and academic setting, Friedrich Nietzsche (1844–1900) pushed the idea that the natural outworking of the Enlightenment is that God must be set aside; that God is dead and atheism in all its facets, should be embraced.[43] It did not take long for this philosophical elitism by someone as influential as Nietzsche to cause those in Western culture to embrace this stance. Even if believers do not admit it, we are in many ways "Christian atheists" by our actions: we live as though there is no God in many cases. Nietzsche's philosophical position affected Western anthropology and our perspective of "self" more than anything else: "If there is no God, or anything like God, then there is nothing left to define us and each person is left to determine who and what they will be for themselves."[44]

On the heels of such thinking naturally arose the concept that human life has no meaning, at least eternally. If God is dead, then humans being "made in the image of God" becomes a meaningless concept.[45] Not surprisingly, postmodern thought is heavily influenced by this philosophical conclusion and therefore notes that the human nature/self/personhood is merely a social construct and does not exist outside of cultural influences and pressures.[46] Of course, this flies in the face of Genesis 1:26–27 and God's declaration that all people are made in the image of God, and, as I will stress in later chapters, are made distinctly male and female.

---

42. Barna, "Atheism Doubles."
43. Kelly and Dew, *Understanding Postmodernism*, 125.
44. Kelly and Dew, *Understanding Postmodernism*, 125.
45. Kelly and Dew, *Understanding Postmodernism*, 132.
46. Kelly and Dew, *Understanding Postmodernism*, 137.

Despite the dim view of life proposed by neo-atheists there are those who suggest that Western society must and will return to its Judeo-Christian roots. Jewish-American sociologist, Philip Rieff (1922–2006) is one of these. Rieff concludes that the atheistic desire and push to undermine the social order will fail.[47] This is where I can appreciate modern thinkers like Jordan Peterson. Peterson has become world-renowned because of his engagement with culture through his online videos and his most recent bestseller *12 Rules for Life* (2018). While not a professing Christian to my knowledge,[48] he makes it very clear to his audience that he lives as though God exists.[49] Peterson's perspective is important if we hope to bring Western culture back from the brink. Put differently, as a culture we must live as though God exists even if there may be some among us questioning that reality. Indeed, belief in God is a good first step. This will hopefully help us further realize that God is the sovereign Judge and has the right to demand of his creation moral and ethical standards. This will in turn set the stage for possible conversions which will bring about a changed heart. Perhaps this is the reason the Great Awakenings were effective in early America. While Deism and Christianity may have dominated throughout our early history, at least the belief in God was at the heart of the country's moral and ethical trajectory despite the heinous stain of slavery. That was then: today there are other ways the West has rejected God and his moral foundations, and that is in the rise of occult practices and false religions.

The Age of Harry Potter

Witchcraft, the occult, paganism, satanism, Wicca, wizardry, New Age philosophy, astrology, fixation on the paranormal, you name it, all reject the true God as sovereign. Make no mistake, God will triumph but in the short term, the rejection of God through various satanic and pagan philosophies has greatly influenced Western cultures. I titled this section "The Age of Harry Potter" for a reason: the influence of the occult, be it ever so "innocent" and benign in our entertainment and reading is anything but. It has prepared an entire generation to question and reject outright the God of the Bible, and by extension, God's laws.

---

47. As noted by Ashford, "Jordan Peterson," 11.
48. On this see the discussion of Ashford, "Jordan Peterson," 23–26.
49. So, too, Ashford, "Jordan Peterson," 12–13.

Some may already be rolling their eyes and saying that this type of children's entertainment is all in good fun and that I am blowing things out of proportion. For those who think this way I suggest they do a quick Google search on the rise of witchcraft in America. It is staggering how many are now getting involved in every facet of occultic behavior. Many do it halfheartedly to be sure; but dabbling with it at any level is no joke. Where this becomes important to our overall discussion is the direct connection between a rejection of God and God's mandates, and the radical and troubling movements and changes in Western culture. These include: the rise of radical feminism, sexual immorality, the rejection of marriage and gender roles, the embracing of a culture of death through abortion, the belittling of humans and the elevation of animal welfare, the worship of mother earth, and the general chaos in our sexual ethics. This is the work of the Enemy and it should come as no surprise that as increased attacks on the Genesis mandates began in the 1960s, witchcraft also began to rise especially among radical feminism. Brown has traced these connections at length so I will not rehash them here.[50] Suffice it to say, that the renewed focus on all things anti-God in Western culture should not surprise us.

The Enemy knew what he was doing by lulling an entire generation with the so-called innocence of the Harry Potter franchise. As of 2018, the Harry Potter series had sold 500 million books.[51] Do you think that this will not influence anyone? Millennials in particular, those who cut their teeth on Harry Potter and the Twilight series, the latter of which glorified vampirism and "darkness" in general, are leaving the church for witchcraft and astrology.[52] Indeed, Western culture in general has rejected not only God, but the role the church has played throughout the past 2000 years of history. The sad part about this reality, is that we as parents and grandparents have played a key role in this rejection of church and by extension, God, through our own lukewarmness and by turning a blind eye to what was influencing our kids and grandkids through movies and print.

---

50. I owe much of the general content of this section to Brown's chapter on the rise of witchcraft in the West (*Jezebel's War*, 119–32).

51. Brown, *Jezebel's War*, 121.

52. See Brown, *Jezebel's War*, 130.

Conclusion: A Rejection of Church

I will conclude this chapter by pointing out the role that we as parents and grandparents play in teaching our children about the value of God and church. It is easy to lay all the blame for America's rejection of God and his divine mandates at the feet of education, but the truth is, older generations have taught their children that God and his teachings in the Bible are not important through their own rejection of church. Americans simply do not attend church in the numbers they once did especially in the mid-twentieth century. The most recent two generations (Millennials and Gen Z) have followed their parents' lead and are leaving churches and not coming back.[53] This is fueling the anti-God and anti-Genesis-mandate push in Western culture.

In one recent study researchers found that much of the reason for the shift away from belief in God and religion in general, especially among Millennials, is due in part to their parents' ambivalent attitude about religious affiliation. "According to the AEI [American Enterprise Institute] survey, 17 percent of millennials said that they were not raised in any particular religion compared with only five percent of Baby Boomers. And fewer than one in three (32 percent) millennials say they attended weekly religious services with their family when they were young, compared with about half (49 percent) of Baby Boomers."[54] What this tells us is that those of us in older generations have dropped the ball in how we raised our kids. This naturally leads to our children and grandchildren making life decisions that will affect not only them, but also their children and so on. One way this begins is in their choice of spouses. If they have been shown that God and faith are not important, then they will naturally choose a spouse with those same values. Again, it is telling when the same study showed that almost 75 percent of Millennials, who have no religious affiliation, chose a "nonreligious partner or spouse."

The same study noted above pointed out that in bygone eras in America, even those who did not attend church regularly as a youth tended to return to church when they began to have children. They saw the need to make sure their kids were raised with some fear and knowledge of God, a concept that harks back to the words of John Adams noted above. Yet, this is not the pattern for younger Americans. When life changes happen for them, such as beginning a family, they still do not make the move to

---

53. Dimock, "Defining Generations."
54. Cox and Thomson-DeVeaux, "Millennials."

return to church or faith. This is going to have devastating effects on the future of Western culture when it comes to putting God at the center of their lives and political decisions. In this regard, the same study sounded the warning of the dangers to children's moral and ethical development when religious affiliation is removed. The natural progression is that now less than half of those in the Millennial generation assert that one does not need "to believe in God to be moral," a noticeable shift from the Baby Boomer generation who understood the value of religious instruction for children's upbringing.[55] The study concluded that some in the younger generation are rejecting religion because of its association with the Republican Party, nevertheless, children raised in godly Republican homes generally do return to their faith roots. On the other hand, those children who identify as Democrats generally do not return to their faith.[56]

Parents therefore cannot look at Western culture and blame only education, or politics, or the church. We must take responsibility for our lack of consistency in modeling a faith in a sovereign God who demands ethical and moral living. We also need to model the importance of church for aiding in the teaching of our children. If we do not stop the slide, can we be surprised when Western culture continues to hurtle towards the abyss? As such, the importance of marriage, as established by God for the flourishing of society is a good place to start our analysis of Western culture's rejection of the Genesis mandates. Indeed, the lack of strong biblical marriages is at the heart of many of society's ills and moral collapse.

---

55. Cox and Thomson-DeVeaux, "Millennials."
56. Cox and Thomson-DeVeaux, "Millennials."

Chapter 4

The Marriage Mandate Part 1
Biblical Marriage and Sexuality

GOD'S MANDATE OF MARRIAGE appears in Genesis 2:24 and is intimated in God's earlier command in 1:27–28 for male and female to be fruitful and multiply and fill the earth. When God created sex, his plan was for sexual activity to be fulfilled in the confines of marriage. When churches (at least the conservative ones) speak of the definition of "biblical marriage," Genesis 1 and 2 is what they have in mind. What has been evident over the past half century or so in Western culture is that the institution of marriage, and even its definition, has been under attack. It is not surprising that the Enemy attacked this mandate first. The marriage unit was already in trouble when Adam and Eve sinned in the garden in Genesis 3 and God declared that there would be trouble in the marriage relationship because of the tension between the man and the woman due to the fall (Gen 3:16b).

As we will see, from a Christian perspective, scholars, evangelical and mainline alike, are lining up to offer their latest biblical insights into the contemporary marriage discussion. New interpretations for marriage based upon what is often called the "fluidity" or "contradictory" nature of the biblical presentation of marriage are being proposed even though these approaches are seriously flawed. For example, scholars fail to note the difference between prescriptive and descriptive language in the biblical accounts. As I will demonstrate below, most of these scholars' "contradictory" examples of marriage fall into the latter category. While the biblical presentation of marriage is indeed multifaceted (e.g., polygamy, the use of concubines, surrogates, war brides, and levirate marriage), the diversity of exemplars are not the model established by God himself. Indeed, the principles for God-ordained marriage established at creation are reinforced by Jesus and the authors of the New Testament (Matt 19:1–9; Eph 5; Col 3).

Western cultures have been all too willing to aid in the deconstruction of this fundamental mandate through a variety of anti-biblical actions. In this chapter, I will examine a number of these issues related to the undoing or rejection of this mandate. These include the problems associated with the sexual revolution, the troubling rise of divorce rates, and the rejection of marriage through cohabitation. I will handle the redefining of marriage in the next chapter. While the Enemy has used the postmodern philosophical tenet of the rejection of moral absolutes as a starting point to undo every Genesis mandate that is vital for human flourishing and societal health, the Bible is clear on what God has mandated for humanity when it comes to the purpose of sex. Sex and all its blessings are to be utilized in the context of the covenant of marriage. This is clearly demonstrated in the biblical model.

Sex and Marriage: A Biblical Perspective

Scholars have noted the centrality of marriage to God's greater plan for humanity, which is highlighted by the fact that the Bible begins and ends with heterosexual marriage, one literal and the other metaphorical. In Genesis 2, Adam and Eve are the literal model whereas Revelation 21–22 presents the metaphorical relationship between Jesus and his bride.[1] The physical and emotional complimentarity of heterosexual marriage, highlighted by Adam's comment that Eve is bone of his bone and flesh of his flesh (cf. 2 Sam 19:12–13), reflects the Triune God and the complimentarity found within this image.[2] As we will see in our next chapter, same-sex marriage can never do this. Marriage was so fundamental to the building of the family unit that God mandated newly wedded men to be free from military service for a year so that he and his wife could enjoy each other (Deut 24:5),[3] and no doubt to make sure a child was conceived before the possible untimely death of a man in war. On the other hand, acts

---

1. O'Reilly, "What Makes Sex Beautiful?" 197–212.
2. See O'Reilly, "What Makes Sex Beautiful?" 197–212 esp. 203.
3. Sider, *Completely Pro-Life*, 113.

of adultery and premarital sex are outside of, or remove the individual from, the covenant found within the marriage union. Adultery breaks the marriage vows thus displaying a similar lack of trust in the God-human relationship, and premarital sex makes us vulnerable without a covenant.[4] At the same time, marriage is more than a companionship connection or a mere kinship bond as is often argued by gay-affirming scholars;[5] it is an intellectual, emotional, spiritual, and physical union of bodies which, as we will see in a later chapter, was meant to produce children. Indeed, male and female bodies are made for one another.[6] All other forms of sexual union undermine the sanctity of the male-female union established by God for human procreation. Homosexual unions in particular are a direct affront to the sanctity of heterosexual unions as is any form of incest, which the Bible also condemns (Lev 18:3–18; 20:11–20; Deut 22:30//23:1 in Hebrew; 1 Cor 5:1–8).

Because marriage serves as an encapsulating image of the Bible as I noted in the first paragraph of this section, clearly God views marriage as an important part of the human and spiritual experience. And some have gone so far as to argue that the marriage union in Genesis 2:24 is the foundation for sexual ethics.[7] In defining marriage from a biblical perspective, then, we can say that marriage is the God-sanctioned union between a man and a woman. This is made clear when God gave Eve to Adam (Gen 2:22) and followed it up with the ensuing marriage union between the man and the woman in 2:24–25. Because this mandate appears in the opening eleven chapters of Genesis, it has universal significance (cf. Lev 18:3, 27–30; Mark 6:17–18) and is not legislation for Israel alone. In other words, this portion of Genesis established the pattern to be followed by all people of all times.[8]

Jesus also sanctioned marriage by his presence at the wedding at Cana in John chapter 2, a commonly quoted passage at weddings even today. Moreover, when defending the sanctity of marriage, Jesus quotes both Genesis 1 and 2 as the model to follow (Matt 19:3–6): marriage was supposed to be between a man and a woman who were brought together by God for life. I find it telling of modern scholarly hubris when scholars

---

4. O'Reilly, "What Makes Sex Beautiful?" 197–212.
5. See for example this position by Brownson, *Bible, Gender, Sexuality* (2013).
6. Wilson, *Mere Sexuality*, 80–81.
7. Levering, "Thomas Aquinas," 165–80.
8. Grudem, *Politics*, 118, 214–16, 233.

have the audacity to suggest that Jesus misunderstood these texts or was "selective" in his choice of texts.⁹ Others suggest there is no mandate for marriage present in Genesis 1 and 2 or that Jesus downplayed the institution of marriage.¹⁰ Clearly, the texts Jesus cites are about male and female coupling and marriage, even if scholars cannot grasp this reality. The sanctity of marriage is also brought to the fore in Paul's teaching on proper sexual ethics, divorce, and marriage in 1 Corinthians 7.¹¹ He tells a believing spouse not to leave an unbelieving spouse showing the permanency God intended for marriage.

It is also telling that God established the institution of marriage before any other institution, be that for nations, government, religion, or whatever. God's reason? Marriage was to be the foundation of society. Without this sacred institution, societies will collapse. Marriage and morality in sexual ethics are built into all cultures by God himself. Indeed, as noted in my previous chapter, in social anthropologist Joseph Daniel Unwin's classic work, *Sex and Culture* he examined 86 tribes and civilizations covering roughly 5000 years of history and showed that they all began to collapse after three generations because of a rejection of monogamous marriage and pre-nuptial chastity.¹² In fact, once pre-nuptial chastity and monogamy were rejected or modified, the rejection of deity quickly followed as did the collapse of culture.¹³ Conversely, a consistent preservation of absolute monogamy and pre-nuptial chastity allowed for the flourishing/productivity of culture and its expansion (e.g., the arts, sciences, craftmanship, environmental control).¹⁴ Unwin goes on to note that "No society can display productive social energy unless a new generation inherits a social system under which sexual opportunity is reduced to a minimum. If such a system be preserved, a richer and yet richer tradition will be created, refined by human entropy."¹⁵ Interestingly, Un-

---

9. E.g., Coogan, *God & Sex*, 94.

10. Knust, *Unprotected Texts*, 56, 64–69.

11. Contra Knust (*Unprotected Texts*, 93–94, 100), who erroneously argues that Paul is just concerned about putting "body parts" where they should not be. On the contrary, this is about the spiritual union involved with sexual acts and the sanctity of marriage and the marriage unit. The marriage covenant is used to show God's relationship with Israel as it is with Christ and the church.

12. See also comments by Grudem, *Politics*, 216–17, 370.

13. Unwin, *Sex and Culture*, 368–69, cf. 424.

14. Unwin, *Sex and Culture*, 411–12, 428, 431.

15. Unwin, *Sex and Culture*, 414.

win concludes that the most productive societies are those where both the male and the female have equality and where sexuality is confined to monogamous marriage,[16] the picture of Adam and Eve before the fall.

Marriage was God's way of channeling sexual activity into a productive and God-ordered ideal. On this point, Jewish commentator Dennis Prager notes well that Judaism's forcing of sexual activity to the confines of marriage allowed for the growth of western culture and society.[17] When commenting on Genesis 2:18 Prager notes, "Now, presumably, in order to solve the problem of man's aloneness, God could have made another man or even a community of men. But instead, God solved man's aloneness by creating one other person, a woman—not a man, not a few women, not a community of men and women. Man's solitude was not a function of his not being with other people; it was a function of his being without a woman."[18] Therefore, despite what postmodern thinkers suggest, God's mandate for marriage is meant to be very narrowly defined despite humanity's attempts to redefine it as they see fit. One of the ways some attempt to get around this clearly defined mandate is to look at other models for marriage also found in the Bible.

Alternate Biblical Marriage Arrangements

Today it has become common fare to point to the numerous other marital arrangements in the Bible as a basis for undermining God's mandate of monogamous heterosexual marriage.[19] It is true that within the book of Genesis alone we find polygamy practiced by Lamech, Abraham, the Pharaoh (intimated), Esau, and Jacob. We also see levirate marriage in 38:8, and the possibility of war brides in the Shechem fiasco in 34:29. What is clear, however, is that whenever these types of arrangements are made by humans, trouble is not far behind. One need only look to the troubled married lives of Abraham and Jacob to get an appreciation for this reality. These types of marriages, even though regulated in the law code (Exod 21:10; Deut 21:10–17), were always to be understood as descriptive (e.g., Judg 8:30; 1 Sam 1:1–2; 2 Sam 5:13; 12:8; 2 Chron

---

16. Unwin, *Sex and Culture*, 432.
17. Prager, "Why Judaism."
18. Prager, "Why Judaism."
19. E.g., see Knust, *Unprotected Texts*, 47–48; DeFranza, "Common Ground," 69–101, and DeFranza, *Sex Difference*, see esp. 178, 203–6, 262–72, 287.

11:21; 13:21), and not prescriptive. By this I mean that the Bible is merely recording and telling what happened or what humans *thought* acceptable as opposed to what God had mandated. God's mandate of monogamous marriage challenges the negative realities of polygamous marriages. For example, polygamous marriages do not allow the husband to be completely devoted to one woman and robs the woman of the closeness with which marriage was supposed to function.[20]

The clearest rebuke of laws that regulated alternate marriage forms comes from Jesus himself when he goes back to Genesis 2:24 to demonstrate the plan of God for marriage (Matt 19:8). What is more, whenever God speaks of marriage or whenever it is used as a metaphor the picture is always monogamous heterosexual marriage. The prophets use this imagery consistently to demonstrate God's relationship with his people (e.g., Hosea 1–3; Jer 2–3; Ezek 16 and 23) as does the NT (Eph 5; Rev 21). If monogamous heterosexual marriage is God's mandate for all people, what does that mean for those who reject marriage and practice fornication, deviant sex, or adultery? And can sexual activity happen outside of the covenant of marriage and still be blessed by God?

Sex is for Marriage Alone

As noted above, gender and sex were created by God in Genesis 1. Their creation is immediately followed by the account of Adam being alone, a fact that God says is not good (Gen 2:18). This was God's first and only negative comment about creation. It is no coincidence that the covenant of marriage follows immediately after God brings Eve to Adam in the garden. The natural order is for man and woman to come together and enter a life-long monogamous relationship. The marriage relationship is specifically designed for the fulfilment of sexual pleasure between the man and the woman. This is the mandate of God for the use of sex. We can assume that Adam and Eve were first attracted to each other for pleasure not procreation, even though this was a natural and expected outcome.

Sexuality is not wrong, and intercourse is good (contra Augustine).[21] Sex was created for the marriage bed and for the enjoyment of the man and the woman not as a means of entertainment and pleasure for those who reject marriage. Conversely, in the biblical law, adultery is

---

20. Wilson, *Mere Sexuality*, 82–84.
21. Balswick and Balswick, *Authentic Human Sexuality*, 69.

consistently spoken against with legislation demanding the death penalty for such a violation of the God-established union (Exod 20:14; Lev 20:10; Deut 5:18; cf. Matt 19:18; Rom 2:22; 13:9; James 2:11). The mandate and presentation in Genesis 1 and 2 are clear as to what God's plan for sexuality is for all people: we are all created sexual beings, but marriage is where our sexual drives are to be fulfilled. Indeed, the physical intimacy of marriage is what makes friendships different than marriage.[22]

Unfortunately, some scholars have taken other biblical presentations of coupling and suggested that the Bible is contradictory on how sex is to be used. For example, some argue that premarital sex is sanctioned in the Song of Solomon, a carefree return to Eden of sorts.[23] However, this is simply not true. The picture painted in the Song of Solomon is indeed reflective of Eden—a man and a woman enjoying sexual passion accompanied by garden imagery. It is the idyllic scene pre-fall where the man and woman function as equals (Song 2:16; 6:3; 7:11).[24] From this vantage point, the book depicts how a young couple are to come together in the confines of monogamous marriage and how sexual activity is to be used in this context alone.[25] This is the reason the author of the book reminds his readers at key junctures not to awaken love before its time (Song 2:7; 3:5; 8:4), that is, do not have sexual contact before marriage.

Another common misconception is that Ruth and Boaz had premarital sexual relations on the threshing room floor in Ruth 3.[26] Again, this is to impose a modern sexual ethic of "free sex" onto an ancient text and context. The truth is, when read through the lens of a consistent biblical sexual ethic whereby sex is for marriage, both Ruth and Boaz remain chaste. Boaz not only goes out of his way to protect Ruth's reputation, but he is also fully aware that there is someone closer to her relationally who could redeem her and Naomi's land (Ruth 3:11–14). Had they had sexual relations on the threshing floor Ruth could have gotten pregnant and both would have been disgraced. Therefore, these types of modern readings reflect more of the sexual ethic of the scholar as opposed to that of the Bible.

22. Wilson, *Mere Sexuality*, 82.

23. So, Coogan, *God & Sex*, 17–18. See also Knust, *Unprotected Texts*, 5, 24–29, 46.

24. Carr, *Erotic Word*, 132–34.

25. For an excellent commentary on the Song of Solomon that develops this perspective, see Garrett, *Proverbs, Ecclesiastes, Song of Songs*, 347–432. And contra Carr (*Erotic Word*, 116) who says there is no consummation in the Song of Solomon.

26. Knust, *Unprotected Texts*, 36.

Another troubling point is how some modern evangelical scholars and counselors teach about premarital sex apart from what the Bible teaches. For example, when giving advice on the use of premarital sex, some do not hold to a biblical model per se, but rather try to rationalize premarital sexual involvement.[27] While many have tried to justify varying levels of promiscuity as somewhat natural, especially from a post-sexual-revolution perspective, the Scripture is clear on fornication before marriage.[28] Every precaution must be taken to avoid sexual involvement before marriage. Now that is not to say that people will not fall, we all know this can happen. Rather, we should not cede the ground to a postmodern relativism where sexual activity before marriage is a given and therefore just needs to be guided by principles.

Once again, the goodness of God's plan for human coupling cannot be overstated, especially considering the sexual depravity of the surrounding cultures of Israel's day and age. God chose to reveal to the Jewish people his ideal in this regard and to set the standard for all peoples. To be sure, the Torah and the rabbinic Talmudic instruction were countercultural and held Israel to moral and ethical ideals, which combatted all forms of sexual perversion especially bestiality and homosexuality. [29]

Marriage Stabilizes Societies

Besides serving as a God-honoring institution within which sexual fidelity is to be practiced, marriage also brings stability to societies. Wayne Grudem lists several positive features which marriage brings to society: economic wellbeing for the family, "educational and economic benefits for children, the transmission of moral and cultural values to the next generation, and a stable social unit for interactions within society."[30]

Societal confusion vis-à-vis sexual promiscuity and a rejection of marriage was not always the American way. On the contrary, marriage played a key role in America's history and social fabric. In the early years of America, sex outside of marriage was not only frowned upon, it was

---

27. See the troubling comments of Balswick and Balswick, *Authentic Human Sexuality*, 155; and Allender and Longman, *God Loves Sex*, 119–20.

28. So, too, Grabowski, *Sex and Virtue*, 117–18.

29. See comments by Prager, "Why Judaism."

30. Grudem, *Politics*, 221.

illegal, as was abandonment of one's family or spouse.[31] Adultery, for example, was punishable by public shaming, fines, floggings, and in some cases, the death penalty.[32] While I may personally reject some of these more severe penalties, the shame of such actions did in fact dampen promiscuity. Yet, many sociologists and psychologists are attempting to remove any level of shame from people who practice sexual deviancy by claiming that shame is bad. But the truth is the emotion of shame has its value and place. After the fall, Adam and Eve felt shame and rightly so (cf. Gen 2:25; 3:7). Shame can keep people from doing that which is against God's commands.[33]

America's history boasted a strong belief in marriage and its benefits. French aristocrat and diplomat, Alexis de Toqueville "commented in the early 19th century on the deep commitment to marital union in the American republic. 'There is,' he wrote, 'certainly no country in the world where the tie of marriage is more respected than in America, or where conjugal happiness is more highly or worthily appreciated.'"[34] Yet, based upon today's rejection of this Genesis mandate, one would never know that God's plan for sex and human flourishing was for monogamous heterosexual marriage. Postmodern thinking about sex is contrary to this important mandate.

Sex and Western Culture

It goes without saying that Western culture has obliterated the mandate of marriage and sex. Postmodern perspectives on the institution of marriage have helped to undermine this foundational mandate due to what are often perceived as archaic requirements for marriage. These include, but are not limited to, sex is to be reserved for the marriage bed, the overrating of fidelity within marriage, and the rejection of traditional gender roles. And, as we will see in the next chapter, many within the same-sex community simply reject these principles as only applicable to "heterosexual" marriage, and not conducive for homosexual marriage. Despite the growing rejection of fidelity in marriage, sex is a powerful force to be

---

31. Shinkoskey, "Without Law," 5–6 as noted by Watkins, *New Absolutes*, 120.
32. Shinkoskey, "Without Law," 6.
33. See Patterson and Kim, *The Day America Told the Truth*, 56–59.
34. Shinkoskey, "Without Law," 5.

used in the confines of marriage so that when, and if, children do come from the union, they will have a stable environment in which to grow.

Today in America and Western cultures sex outside of marriage is the norm. Virginity is mocked and those who adhere to it are labelled prudes, uptight, unnatural, or whatever pejorative scoffers choose. In fact, as of the early 1990s studies showed that fourteen percent of children lose their virginity by the age of thirteen.[35] Sex is no longer something to be reserved for the confines of the marriage bed. Surveys have also shown that well over thirty percent of Americans are involved in extra-marital affairs.[36] It is a pastime and entertainment for Americans in ever-increasing numbers since the wild and radical days of the 1960s. All forms of media (print, movies, internet, sports, etc.) promote sex before marriage as the normal way to live. This position makes sense in light of today's highly effective means of "birth control." With abortion on demand and contraceptives available to younger and younger children, the consequences of sexual "mistakes" are easily remedied. As part of the new healthcare push, the common mantra of "women's health" has become code for both abortion on demand and free birth control, paid for by the American taxpayer no matter what your moral leanings may be.

Some studies have shown that over half of self-identifying Christians have no problem having premarital sex or cohabiting with someone after only six months of dating.[37] Evangelicals fare no better with a 2019 Pew Research poll showing that 46 percent now feel premarital sex is fine if you are in a committed relationship.[38] This type of promiscuity at all levels has led to a rise in juvenile sexual crimes with more than one quarter of all sexual offenses against children being perpetrated by children themselves.[39] It is not enough that sex and sexual experimentation have become the most popular form of relationship "play," every type of sexual fantasy is now becoming more and more mainstream in America with virtually no shame attached to the most degrading acts.[40] For example, America's obsession with the 2011 book and 2015 movie by the same

---

35. Patterson and Kim, *The Day America Told the Truth*, 100, 103.

36. Watkins, *New Absolutes*, 116; and Patterson and Kim, *The Day America Told the Truth*, 94.

37. Wilson, *Mere Sexuality*, 126.

38. Mouser, "Pew Research."

39. Brown, *Jezebel's War*, 52.

40. Watkins, *New Absolutes*, 116–18. See the nonchalant way Benshoff and Griffin (*Queer Images*, 6) list the most perverse types of sexual media as normal.

name, *Fifty Shades of Grey*, made S&M mainstream and the fantasy of many. One pornographic website lists no less than 26 categories of sexual "entertainment" some of which are simply too vile to mention.[41] Christians are not exempt from this trend. Numerous sources have pointed out the staggering statistics on the use of pornography by Christians.[42] This has had devastating effects on marriages with some reporting that pornography is a leading cause of 60 percent of divorces.[43]

As I have noted already, when sex is separated from marriage and its purpose of bringing joy and pleasure to the marriage unit as well as for procreation, then it becomes nothing more than a commodity.[44] Sexual promiscuity is rampant and is leading to devastating consequences. The Office of Adolescent Health notes that "Adolescents ages 15–24 account for nearly half of the 20 million new cases of STDs each year. Today, two in five sexually active teen girls have had an STD that can cause infertility and even death. Also, though rates of HIV are very low among adolescents, males make up more than 80 percent of HIV diagnoses among 13- to 19-year olds."[45] Some health professionals note that this rise in sexual promiscuity can be attributed in part to the increase in "hook-up" apps available on electronic devices which make sexual liaisons more accessible and seemingly "permissible."

These changes stemmed from the rise of contraception and the sexual revolution of the 1960s which advocated for "free love."[46] The mandate of marriage became one of the first casualties of the sexual revolution as women found new freedom outside of the home, and culture began to downplay the shame associated with sex outside of marriage. As I have noted earlier, shame plays an important role in keeping people "in line," but today shame is no longer seen as a limiting emotion; it is something to be shunned and rejected as bad. This paves the way for sexual deviancy of all types. For example, the infamous Ashley Madison website, which promotes adultery, boasts that from its inception until 2017, they signed up 52.7 million users.[47] Despite this disturbing trend, when a survey of

41. As noted by Benshoff and Griffin, *Queer Images*, 6.
42. Brown, *Jezebel's War*, 46–49, 54–60; and Isom, *Conversations*, 61–68.
43. Brown, *Jezebel's War*, 49.
44. So, too, Wilson, *Mere Sexuality*, 98.
45. Office of Adolescent Health, "Adolescent Development" as noted by Brown, *Jezebel's War*, 50.
46. Gushee, *Getting Marriage Right*, 27–28.
47. As noted by Brown, *Jezebel's War*, 51.

Americans was conducted asking them what they were most ashamed about, adultery ranked first.[48] Scholars and counselors can say whatever they want, but God's plan for humanity cannot be thwarted without consequences. God will not allow people to practice sexual promiscuity and deviancy with emotional impunity.

Marriage is also being rejected because of the investment of time and effort which is required to maintain a strong and healthy relationship. Of course, marriage was never meant to be an agreement or an arrangement of convenience; it is hard work.[49] Ask anyone who has tried it. But it is a good and beneficial type of "work," one that yields benefits in bringing stability to our lives, our children's lives, and to society as a whole. This was God's plan in the first place. Unfortunately, this is not where Western society finds itself today.

As noted in the previous chapter, the main reason for the instability of the institution of marriage in Western culture is the rejection of God and the demands he has placed upon us as outlined by the Bible, most readily seen in the opening chapters of Genesis. If these opening chapters are viewed as mythology, which is commonly taught in university religion classes in both mainline and now many evangelical seminaries, then why should we adhere to a man-made myth or set of rules? Therefore, the Genesis mandate of self-sacrificial love and union exemplified in the bond between God and Israel, and Christ and the church has been replaced with a different mandate—lust and self-fulfillment—the biblical model offers security whereas this new model offers only insecurity and chaos.[50] Confusion and chaos are the desire of the Enemy, and Western societies are imbibing at the well of this One's relativistic, rationalistic, and anti-God tripe. Part of that "tripe" is the assertion that marriage is not a permanent institution, it can be dissolved through divorce.

Divorce

One cannot address the downward spiral of Western culture's sexual ethics and morality without laying appropriate blame at the feet of systemic divorce and remarriage within culture and the church itself. From a biblical perspective it is obvious that some marriages did in fact end in

---

48. Patterson and Kim, *The Day America Told the Truth*, 57.
49. See also Watkins, *New Absolutes*, 96–97.
50. Watkins, *New Absolutes*, 98.

divorce. Abraham appears to have divorced Hagar (Gen 21:12–14) and I have argued elsewhere that Moses may have divorced Zipporah because of her rejection of the Abrahamic covenant which required circumcision (Exod 4:24–26; Num 12:1).[51] Moses also allowed for divorce because of the hardness of Israel's heart (Deut 24:1–3; cf. Mishnah *Gittin* 9:10). In the New Testament some believe that Jesus made no allowance for remarriage after a divorce (Mark 10:1–12). Others note that Matthew's inclusion of the exception clause for fornication (Matt 5:32) along with Paul's instruction in 1 Corinthians 7:12–15 dealing with an unbelieving spouse departing, are examples of going beyond Jesus' teaching (or rejecting it[52]) and allowing for remarriage. This of course is debated.

From an evangelical perspective, we have failed to model the biblical standard of marriage for the world around us and the next generation of Christian young people. As such, we are complicit in the devaluation of marriage. As some evangelicals have pointed out (e.g., Michael Brown), it may be time for the church to reconsider what it classifies as a "biblically" approved divorce and what is not. As pastors, educators, parents, and grandparents instructing the next generation, our own modelling of the godly ideal is vital to sound biblical instruction on this foundational mandate.

While divorce rates have fluctuated throughout the history of America, it was not until the period after World War II that increased divorce rates began to take a detrimental toll on the wider culture.[53] The divorce rate spiked between 1970 and 1980 after no-fault divorce was first passed in California in 1970. Since the 1980s the divorce rate has dropped 32 percent,[54] but this is not a true indicator that marriages are staying together. As we will see in the next section, the outright rejection of the mandate of marriage and the rise in cohabitation explains much of this change. Researchers have noted that "Since sociologists have found that cohabiting before marriage increases the risk of divorce later, they speculate that those who cohabit would be the type to break up more easily if they had gotten married. Thus, one likely reason divorce is declining is simply that those folks are not getting married to begin with."[55]

---

51. Peterson, "Scriptural Precedent," 43–62.
52. Collins, *Biblical Values*, 98–101.
53. Shinkoskey, "Without Law," 5.
54. Feldhahn and Whitehead, *Good News*, 26.
55. Feldhahn and Whitehead, *Good News*, 27.

Even more telling of the changing ethical tide in America is the rising acceptance of divorce as morally acceptable, which according to a recent Gallup poll (2017), shows that 73 percent of Americans now think it is morally acceptable while 51 percent of the "very religious" feel it is so.[56] This flouting of God's marriage mandate and the purpose of sex for marriage is only aiding in the downward spiral of culture. Marriage is also being negatively affected by the West's rejection of the traditional roles of husband and wife as outlined in the Bible and experienced throughout history in most cultures. Studies now show that egalitarian-focused marriages are the most tenuous and tend to dissolve at higher rates than traditional marriage unions.[57]

Even though we have not been the best witnesses to the sacredness of marriage, there is some good news for the church when it comes to divorce rates. For years we have been told that surveys showed that the divorce rate in the church and the wider culture was the same, hovering at or near 50 percent. The problem was that the surveys were based upon the question of those who held *beliefs* in Christian ideology not those who were actual believers.[58] As such, the data became skewed especially in a country like America where the majority of people *identify* as "Christian." Those who attend church regularly have a 25–50 percent lower divorce rate than the broader culture.[59] When it comes to evangelicals, a Barna poll from 2008 showed that the divorce rate for those who attended church regularly was 25 percent, and for Catholics was even lower at 22 percent.[60]

While the divorce rates in the church are not as bad as most realize, it still is troubling. And the wider culture is increasingly showing the signs of a rejection of God's plan for permanent marriages and stable families. Within Western culture it is now assumed that people will cohabit before marriage, a practice that does nothing to improve marriage.[61]

---

56. Dugan, "Divorce Rate."
57. Watkins, *New Absolutes*, 97.
58. Feldhahn and Whitehead, *Good News*, 68.
59. Feldhahn and Whitehead, *Good News*, 66. See also pages 71–73 and 154–55.
60. Feldhahn and Whitehead, *Good News*, 70–71.
61. Wilson, *Mere Sexuality*, 86.

Cohabitation

More and more people are cohabiting today with many doing it out of convenience or fear of marriage failure. Originally, cohabitation tended to occur among the "lower classes" or "disadvantaged youth," but in the past forty years it has become popular among the middle classes as well.[62] For example, among working women and high school graduate men, three quarters of their first unions in the late 2000s involved cohabitation, up from 58 percent twenty years earlier.[63] As a result, more than four in ten children are born out of wedlock,[64] with some putting the numbers as high as 50 percent.[65] And evangelicals are not helping the problem. Based on national surveys, between 2014 and 2018, self-identifying evangelicals who cohabited rose from 3.9 to 6.7 percent, a 72 percent increase.[66] Overall, support for cohabitation in the wider populace increased just 11 percent in this same period.[67]

What this shows is that society, and many evangelicals, no longer value marriage as an institution. From a long-term perspective the rate of change is even more troubling. For example, from 1960 to 2006 the rate of cohabitation increased twelvefold.[68] While percentages tend to be more benign, the actual numbers are staggering at their exponential increases.[69] In 1970, 523,000 couples cohabited, ten years later the number had tripled to 1.6 million, and by the early 1990s it was at 3 million.[70] In just one year from 2009 to 2010 the number jumped 13 percent from 6.7 to 7.5 million.[71]

During the 1970s scholars suggested that cohabitation would strengthen future marriages because of the gained experience sexually and relationally and the chance to winnow out mates that were not compatible

---

62. Balswick and Balswick, *Authentic Human Sexuality*, 164.
63. Feldhahn and Whitehead, *Good News*, 26–27.
64. Feldhahn and Whitehead, *Good News*, 6.
65. Brown, *Jezebel's War*, 50.
66. Regnerus, "Marriage," 37.
67. Regnerus, "Marriage," 37.
68. Balswick and Balswick, *Authentic Human Sexuality*, 163.
69. See Michael, et al, *Sex in America*, 40, 96–100; and Patterson and Kim, *The Day America Told the Truth*, 87–90.
70. Watkins, *New Absolutes*, 94–95, see also 115–16.
71. Kreider, "Cohabiting Couples," 1.

for marriage.[72] The truth is 70 percent of cohabiting relationships end within a little over a year and do not lead to marriage, and those who cohabit before marriage have a 50 percent higher divorce rate than those who do not.[73] The cohabiting experiment has failed miserably especially in the areas of marital interaction, marital disagreements, marital instability, and higher rates of divorce.[74] Put simply, cohabitation is deleterious to the family structure, especially for children who lack stability in a living arrangement that has a high divorce rate and other destabilizing factors such as sexual and physical abuse, assault and even murder.[75]

Conclusion

Marriage is no longer a covenant to be honored, it is merely an institution to be experimented with and cast aside like an old coat when it no longer "fits" or is "out of style." The Enemy has been effective with diminishing its importance since the rise of the sexual revolution and the rejection of moral standards that once were the bedrock of society. Divorce, cohabitation, and pre-marital sex have undermined God's good mandate for lifelong marriages. Again, Western postmodern culture can insist that their ways are better than God's plan, but God's reality not only sheds light on the fallacy of such thinking it also shatters false perceptions. This is no less true of Western culture's desire to redefine what marriage actually is. With marriage belittled and marginalized, what is the big issue with redefining it? It is to this topic that we now turn.

---

72. Balswick and Balswick, *Authentic Human Sexuality*, 170.

73. Balswick and Balswick, *Authentic Human Sexuality*, 163, 169.

74. Balswick and Balswick, *Authentic Human Sexuality*, 170; and Gushee, *Getting Marriage Right*, 30–32.

75. Balswick and Balswick, *Authentic Human Sexuality*, 174–75, 179; and Gushee, *Getting Marriage Right*, 31.

Chapter 5

The Marriage Mandate Part 2
Marriage Redefined

IF YOU ARE LIKE me, Christmas is the best time of the year. Sadly, even this sacred and holy celebration is now under assault by the postmodern sexual revolution. The 2019 and 2020 Christmas seasons marked seismic shifts in how Western culture celebrated this blessed and hallowed time of the year. Hallmark Channel's 2019 Christmas movie season introduced traditional families in America to the "new normal" when it comes to the cultural definition of "marriage" in America. As we watched our Christmas specials, the advertisements for an online wedding planning company revealed Hallmark's greater plan to "educate" traditional America on diversity. One of the advertisements depicted two lesbians kissing at the altar during their "marriage" ceremony. The backlash from conservative America was immediate and rightly so.[1] Hallmark responded by quickly removing the ads only to reverse their position within hours because of pressure from GLAAD and others to reinstate the ads, which they did.[2] On December 12, 2020, Hallmark moved beyond just advertising gay marriage when they featured a male homosexual couple in a feature movie titled *The Christmas Setup*. The 2019 season was the test run. By 2020 Hallmark made it clear what their agenda was. We can assume this is just the beginning. Based upon the response of many Christians in 2019 (One Million Moms in particular)

1. Gaynor, "Hallmark."
2. Associated Press, "Backlash."

I am sure many were, and are, asking how did we get here? As noted in the previous chapter, the rejection of the sanctity of marriage has had many unintended consequences. If marriage is not based upon a hard and fast moral precedent that is defined as being between one man and one woman for life, then maybe it is not as "untouchable" as the church and culture have implied for millennia.

What is shocking is the speed with which Western culture, and America in particular, made the shift in what defined marriage. The entire process of redefining marriage took only a little over forty years. This spanned the period from the APA's removal of homosexuality from its list of disorders in 1973 until the SCOTUS decision in 2015 to legalize same-sex marriage. One could narrow it even further by beginning with the *Defense of Marriage Act* passed in 1996, which would make the transition just under twenty years. Or we could really get technical and point out that when President Obama came to office in 2008, he held a traditional definition of marriage (at least in public to maintain the conservative African American vote[3]) but by 2012 he had changed his official position.[4] Three years later same-sex marriage became the law of the land. By 2020, the normalizing of same-sex marriage was all but complete when Democrat presidential contender, Pete Buttigieg, proudly declared his marriage to another man. In a nationally televised interview Buttigieg, a self-professing "Christian" gay man, declared his pride in his marriage to his "husband."[5] He continued in the interview by stating that those who challenge his position are homophobic. Of course, this is meant to shut down any further debate or discussion on the matter.

Based upon the forty-year block of time noted above for this change in marriage, it is important to keep in mind that there were other things happening during that time in the church and culture at large to aid in the seismic shift. During that same period, the culture and the church normalized a variety of other types of marriage arrangements. Even though there have always been blended families in the church and the wider culture, the general acceptance of them within both settings changed during the period in question. Not counting common-law or cohabitation arrangements, these new "acceptable" marriage arrangements included blended families of all stripes but generally fell into three

---

3. Brown, *Jezebel's War*, 102–3.
4. Stein, "Gay Marriage."
5. Wallace, "Pete Buttigieg."

categories: a divorcee with or without children and a person in their first marriage; two divorcees with or without children entering a second (or more) marriage; and divorcees with children prior to remarriage and now with children from the new marriage. Now to be sure, the biblical legitimacy of these types of marriages is up for debate, and has been debated, by evangelicals at length.[6] Yet, at the end of the day, all of these blended types of marriage coupling still fall within the broader category of heterosexual unions, and to a certain degree, are defensible biblically.

With this brief overview in mind, in this chapter I will trace how the culture, the church, and scholars have come to accept same-sex marriage as "biblically" mandated and acceptable and how that change is certain to have a deleterious effect on Western culture. The undermining of God's good mandate of marriage as the foundation of culture and as beneficial for human flourishing was just one more step towards the total undoing of the Genesis mandates and the usurping of God's plan for creation. While many may scoff at such an assertion, the simple fact that Western culture has placed its morality and sexual ethic above God's proves that we are one step closer to divine judgment.

America's Road to the Legalization of Same-Sex Marriage (*Obergefell v. Hodges*)

Throughout US history the role of government to establish the parameters for what constitutes a legal union has been vital for maintaining the stability of society. It is a good thing when government mandates that children or those from close family relations should not marry, or that polygamous unions are not in the best interest of society. Nevertheless, long before Western culture was faced with the issue of same-sex marriage, SCOTUS was faced with a similar redefinition of marriage when Utah applied for state status seven times between 1845 and 1895. At issue was the problem of the Mormon practice of polygamy. In the Supreme Court case *Murphy v. Ramsey* (March 23, 1885) the Court ruled "For certainly no legislation can be supposed more wholesome and necessary in the founding of a free, self-governing commonwealth, fit to take rank as one of the coordinate states of the Union, than that which seeks to establish it on the basis of the idea of the family, as consisting in and springing from the union for life of one man and one woman in the holy

---

6. See my discussion and numerous sources in "Scriptural Precedent," 44.

estate of matrimony; the sure foundation of all that is stable and noble in our civilization; the best guarantee of that reverent morality which is the source of all beneficent progress in social and political improvement."[7] As noted clearly in this SCOTUS decision and in the previous chapter, marriage in America and throughout Western cultures, as a general rule, was understood as being between one man and one woman as mandated in Genesis 2.

From the late nineteenth century until the mid-twentieth century, marriage, as traditionally defined, remained intact with only minor pushback from the periphery. However, since the mid-1950s, marriage as an institution did not just slip, it began to freefall. While some of this was due to the rising divorce rates and the repercussions of the sexual revolution as noted in our previous chapter, another reason for the changing tide on marriage and what it meant in general can be laid at the feet of second-wave feminism. Much of this rise in the socially motivated and, in some cases, militant voice of women stemmed from their time in the work force during the Second World War and immediately afterwards when they took over traditional male jobs and roles.

By the late 1960s radical feminist groups advocated for the dissolution of marriage due to its supposed enslavement of women.[8] Lesbian authors often downplayed marriage as unimportant in their pursuit of "love" in the arms of other women.[9] Scholars have rendered scathing evaluations of the feminists of the 1960s for several reasons: for elevating females to the point of almost god-like status; for being hostile towards "anything male"; for devaluing the unborn through abortion; for rejecting marriage and the family; for distorting the religious heritage of America; and for promoting immorality and irrational assertions about life and reality.[10] While some may recoil at this summary of second-wave feminism, it has hit at the heart of much of what is behind modern feminism, especially when it comes to appreciating God's greater plan for the family and procreation for the purpose of establishing a stable society. Indeed, a number of leading second-wave radical feminists see "man-hating" as honorable, insist on the destruction of the nuclear family and the "abolition of marriage" because

---

7. See *Murphy v. Ramsey*, 114 U.S. 45 (1885) at http://supreme.justia.com/us/114/15/case.html. As noted by Grudem, *Politics*, 223.

8. Morgan ed., *Sisterhood is Powerful*, 536–37. See also comments by Sider, *Completely Pro-Life*, 118–19.

9. Rule, *Lesbian Images*, 1–11 esp. 5.

10. So, Watkins, *New Absolutes*, 153–54.

it is built upon "rape," and seek the elimination of, or a vast reduction in, men.[11] What is more, Brown notes that they are parroting the philosophy of the Marxist, Leon Trotsky, who said, "To alter the position of women *at the root*, is possible only if all the conditions of social, family, and domestic existence are altered" (italics original).[12]

Where this becomes important for the current discussion on marriage redefinition is that same-sex marriage advocates had a ready ally in the feminist movement because they both saw themselves as "oppressed" by the traditional values of Western culture, and the longstanding view of marriage. This would play a key role in many of the cultural, legal, and political changes regarding the definition of marriage and the family towards the end of the twentieth century and in the first two decades of the twenty-first century.

Another way feminism aided marriage redefinition is their desire to divorce sex from pregnancy and having children.[13] Once contraceptives and abortion became widely accepted (and legal), it solved the problem of the unwanted byproduct of a "free" sexual lifestyle, namely, children, and paved the way for a redefinition of family. If two people could come together and form a unit simply for the purpose of sexual pleasure without the fear of having children, then the die was cast for other non-childbearing unions. It should not be surprising that the liberation and so-called emancipation of women was quickly followed by the LGBT movement in the 70s and onward. These other pairings could just as readily meet the criteria of "family" and add to the patchwork quilt of society.

The winds of change regarding marriage and same-sex rights began to blow ever stronger in the last decade of the twentieth century forcing politicians to take a stand on the definition of marriage. The 1996 *Defense of Marriage Act* signed into law by Bill Clinton was supposed to set firm parameters for what constituted marriage—the union of one man and one woman. Little did we all realize then just how quickly these winds were going to turn into an all-out hurricane. The winds began shifting in 2003 with Massachusetts legalizing same-sex unions. Although as late as the first decade of the 2000s state courts decided along the same lines as the 1885 SCOTUS decision noted above,[14] in the second decade of the

11. These all come from a list of numerous feminist quotations found in Brown, *Jezebel's War*, 83–84.

12. As cited by Brown, *Jezebel's War*, 85.

13. Watkins, *New Absolutes*, 101–4.

14. See the numerous decisions of state courts in Indiana, Arizona, New Jersey,

twenty-first century, no longer was the one-man and one-woman model for marriage the accepted norm in wider culture. Rather, chaos became the order of the day during the first two decades of the twenty-first century as a number of state supreme courts (e.g., Massachusetts, Connecticut, California, Iowa[15]) ruled same-sex marriage as "constitutional" paving the way for SCOTUS to rule favorably for the redefinition of marriage. The first step was full recognition of same-sex couples as a legitimate pairing which opened the door for adoption rights in 2013. Then, in June of 2015 in *Obergefell v. Hodges*, SCOTUS ruled that same-sex marriage was in fact constitutional thus codifying into law the erroneous belief that same-sex marriage is a valid expression of the marriage union. What is so troubling about this decision is that in this one ruling it nullified state amendments—thirty as of 2008—that had amended their constitutions to clarify that marriage was defined as being between one woman and one man.[16]

Christians may wonder how all this cultural change took place so quickly. Put simply, the judicial branch usurped the prerogative of the legislative branch and began "making law" by "finding" precedents in the Constitution and its Amendments for such things as abortion, gay marriage, and special protected class status for sexual orientation.[17] As I noted earlier, and will reemphasize in a later chapter, this is why Christians, especially evangelicals, need to take note of who they are voting into office. The legislative and executive branches of the US government are all too willing to cede this power to nine unelected justices on the Supreme Court simply because they know that the majority of people in the US would not go along with such an undermining of our moral principles. What politicians cannot pass through the legislative process can simply be enacted into binding law on all people of the US simply by tipping the court in the favor of the current desired moral trajectory even if most Americans disagree with it.

In more recent years, the elite class (politicians, educators, Hollywood actors and actresses, etc.) has consistently moved to the left of center even though the average American is more centrist. In order to enact their ethical and moral ideals, they have needed the courts to enact

---

and New York noted by Grudem, *Politics*, 228.

15. See the more detailed presentation of court rulings in the first decade of the twenty-first century in Grudem, *Politics*, 228–31.

16. Grudem, *Politics*, 231 see also 140–44.

17. Grudem, *Politics*, 134–54.

their agendas, agendas that would never pass legislatively. It is no surprise that the 2016 election caused such a vitriolic reaction from the Left. With Donald Trump's election, he was given the right to appoint Supreme Court justices. It was bad enough when he nominated Neil Gorsuch to replace Justice Antonin Scalia, but when he nominated Brett Kavanaugh to replace Justice Anthony Kennedy to SCOTUS the Left went apoplectic realizing the threat to their "sacred cows" like *Roe v. Wade* and gay marriage. The unexpected death of Ruth Bader Ginsburg just prior to the 2020 election did not foment as great a pushback due to the fact that the Democrats assumed they would win the election and then "pack" the court, which they are currently attempting to do. It is a sad day in America when the highest courts of Western democracies hold the reins of power when it comes to the moral direction of our countries, but this is exactly what has taken place.

Believers need to get involved and be informed about what is at stake when we elect presidents and governors.[18] The time for voting party line simply because "that is what I have always done" is long since passed. And those who suggest that Christians have a "liberty of conscience" to vote for either party because both parties promote "biblical" ideals is simply not true.[19] In order to bring our country back from the moral brink it is going to take a concerted effort from all those professing Christ as savior both within our churches and in the culture at large. Unfortunately, it seems unlikely that professing believers will act in the best interests of our children and our grandchildren. We have become too polarized and myopic to see the true Enemy behind the proverbial curtain. And just to clarify, this is not a call to nostalgia and the good old days. Nor is it intended to enact some form of fundamentalist "triumphalism" as some would suggest.[20] On the contrary, it is a call for a return to the basics; to the foundational principles incumbent upon all societies of all times. It is a call to return to cultural sanity as defined by the Genesis mandates.

Is Same-sex Marriage on Par with Heterosexual Marriage?

One of the dominant propaganda points of same-sex marriage proponents is that same-sex marriage is no different than heterosexual marriage. In

---

18. So, too, Grudem, *Politics*, 153–54.
19. Note this troubling stance by Timothy Keller in Jackson's article, "Tim Keller."
20. So, Carson, *Christ & Culture*, 210.

fact, in some cases, the LGBTQ victory has emboldened some radical elements of their movement to suggest that this ungodly coupling is superior to heterosexual marriage.[21] News outlets now regularly report about the "nuptials" of same-sex athletes and celebrities as though this was the way society always viewed marriage.[22] But is same-sex marriage on par with heterosexual marriage? We certainly do not have the data yet because of the recent status of the "new normal," but based upon what we know of homosexual activity in general we can be pretty certain that the acceptance of same-sex marriage is not as "good" as we were told. Even if gay couples offer a more stable "family" environment for children than an abusive or dysfunctional heterosexual couple, this does not mean that it is right. It may "work," but we should not redefine marriage because the heterosexual ideal has not been met by certain families.[23] The presence of a mother and a father is God's ideal and will always be the better choice for society.

As noted above, the benefits of heterosexual marriage for all involved and the broader society has been shown time and again by statistical studies. In this vein, scholars have noted that children benefit with higher educational achievement; a better economic standard; better physical and emotional health; are more likely to uphold stronger moral standards and less likely to commit crimes and engage in risky behavior like substance abuse; they are less likely to experience abuse, both physical and sexual; and they are also more likely themselves to establish strong families benefiting future generations.[24] The benefits for the husband and wife are no less important especially when it comes to giving stability to each other and society as a whole.

Conversely, despite what the culture and media present, the serious issues created by the legalizing of same-sex marriage and the normalizing of these unions has not been fully appreciated or reported to society. The truth is that multiple factors push against same-sex unions as "beneficial" and "normative" when one considers the medical issues generated by same-sex coupling. In this regard, psychiatrist, Jeffery Satinover has noted several concerns. A few of these include, "A significantly decreased likelihood of establishing or preserving a successful marriage;

---

21. See Berg, "Extinction."
22. E.g., Gaydos, "Ali Krieger and Ashlyn Harris."
23. Dallas, *Gay Gospel*, 57.
24. Grudem, *Politics*, 224–25.

A twenty-five to thirty-year decrease in life expectancy; Chronic, potentially fatal, liver disease—infectious hepatitis, which increases the risk of liver cancer; Inevitably fatal immune disease including associated cancers; Frequently fatal rectal cancer; Multiple bowel and other infectious diseases; [and] A much higher than usual incidence of suicide."[25] This does not even take into consideration the dominant sexual promiscuity of same-sex coupling, especially among men, even within so-called "monogamous coupling."[26] Indeed, the main problem with gay marriage is the double standard. Is monogamy expected of them in the same way it is expected of heterosexual couples? One study of 156 male same-sex couples showed that only seven couples claimed to be monogamous; however, by their fifth year of union, none remained so.[27] And British social commentator Douglas Murray notes that at least one leading gay couple in Britain does everything in their power to hide the fact that they are in an open marriage because of the damage it would cause to the gay-marriage movement.[28] These types of stories are just the tip of the proverbial iceberg. By adopting an unorthodox definition of marriage, society is put at a disadvantage in that the next generation will see these unions as normal which will inevitably lead to an increase in other forms of non-biblical coupling.

Implications of Accepting Same-sex Marriage

As noted above, the general cultural perspective of the past decade is that same-sex marriage is no different than heterosexual marriage. Another false premise is that this egregious flouting of God's mandate of marriage will have no unintended or unforeseen consequences. Those who believe this false premise are sadly mistaken. For decades leading up to the legalization of same-sex marriage, conservatives were mocked when they brought up the slippery slope argument that asserted that once the Pandora's Box was opened on the redefinition of marriage, any number of coupling combinations would be next (e.g., multiple males with one

---

25. Satinover, *Homosexuality*, 51.

26. For the staggering statistics see Grudem, *Politics*, 226–27; and Gagnon, *Homosexual Practice*, 395–432. See also Patterson and Kim, *The Day America Told the Truth*, 97.

27. Satinover, *Homosexuality*, 55.

28. Murray, *Madness of Crowds*, 40.

female, or vice versa, or people married to something other than a person). Even before the legalization of same-sex marriage Western culture was being prepared, through television shows (e.g., *Big Love* and *Polyamory: Married & Dating*) and news reports, showcasing polyamorous relationships.[29] These are coming at us so rapidly now it is virtually impossible to keep up with them.

One of the newest trends is the concept of "throuples" which includes the sexual coupling of three people.[30] For example, on February 12, 2020, *People.com* reported that after seventeen seasons of success, HGTV House Hunters broke new ground by featuring its first throuple on an episode titled "Three's Not a Crowd in Colorado Springs."[31] Brian and Lori, who are legally married with two children, met Geli at a bar, fell in "love" and went through a "commitment ceremony" binding the three together in this polyamorous relationship.[32] The article ended by citing a number of approving fans who watched this episode calling it "progressive" and "educational." Similarly, in a news report, a couple told their story of how they met and had a "spiritual marriage" before the female of the pair fell in love with another woman. Currently they are documenting their polyamorous relationship on YouTube. The male in the relationship declared, "It's finally time to just be who we are, to accept the gift that God has given us, which is the ability to love infinitely in all directions."[33] The warping of God's mandate of marriage soon will know no bounds as deviancy and perversion dictate what is acceptable sexual behavior.

Michael Brown was right to point out that this is the trajectory we have been heading on all along once marriage was redefined by the Supreme Court.[34] As just noted, despite the warnings from conservatives, we were vilified by detractors who said we were using the slippery slope argument. But now here we are being faced with another ethical fence being torn down in the name of equality and progress. Brown goes on to point out that if marriage is not between a man and a woman, then what is so sacred about the number two? Cannot three men or women marry

---

29. See the numerous citations in Hammer, "Remember."
30. See Puhak, "'Throuple.'"
31. Chung, "HGTV."
32. Chung, "HGTV."
33. Bartiromo, "Sexually Fluid."
34. Brown, "Slippery Slope."

or four? Who's to say that you can't marry yourself?[35] Polyamory is sure to be next. In this regard, the ground was already being made ready by a 2009 Newsweek issue, which featured a piece by Jessica Bennett titled "Polyamory: The Next Sexual Revolution," and began by stating, "Only You. And You. And You. Polyamory—relationships with mutually consenting partners—has a coming-out party."[36] These issues are changing so fast that just this week in July 2020, Sommerville, Massachusetts, passed legislation giving polyamorous relationships the same rights as other marriage arrangements. Councilor Lance Davis said, "I don't feel it is the place of government to define a family."[37] Indeed, it is not their place to make these definitions, the Bible has already done this, but politicians are trampling all over it just the same. If we recall, Massachusetts was the first to legalize same-sex unions in 2003. More perversion is not just coming; it is now here! Brown also points out that self-marriage known as sologamy is becoming more and more popular with websites[38] promoting the practice which several states apparently now recognize in some form.

The Complicity of Christian Scholars and the Church

The redefinition of marriage could not have taken place as smoothly and as rapidly as it did if the church had not also been prepared to accept the new normal. During the forty-year period noted above, mainline seminaries were preparing a new generation of pastors to think differently about same-sex relationships, especially when several high-profile mainline and conservative church leaders either came out as homosexual or were already living openly homosexual lifestyles during this time period. When this educational drive was coupled with a continued push within the broader culture to accept homosexuality as normal, which was influencing those in the pew, a perfect storm emerged in which the church was ready to affirm this new form of marriage and to reject or reimagine the biblical mandate of heterosexual marriage. Now to be sure, fierce battles raged, and continue to rage, within many denominations because of the traditionalists who simply would not stand idly by and allow their denominations to be hijacked by cultural shifts, especially ones

---

35. Brown, "Slippery Slope."
36. Brown, "Slippery Slope."
37. Sorace, "Ordinance."
38. See Lazar, "Sologamy."

that were so completely beyond the teaching of Scripture. Non-affirming proponents knew all too well that the Bible clearly rejects all forms of same-sex coupling as noted in multiple texts like Leviticus 18:22, 20:13, Romans 1:26–28, 1 Corinthians 6:9, and 1 Timothy 1:10, but rejected or reinterpreted them. These texts were pejoratively labeled the "clobber passages" by affirming scholars and systematically reinterpreted and/or dismissed as being not applicable to modern loving same-sex relationships. I will give a more detailed analysis of these texts in a later chapter.

Those who refused to go along with the redefinition of marriage tended to split from their denominations and form conservative counterparts to the original. One such example was the splitting of the American Episcopal church in 2008. The conservative branch ended up forming ACNA (The Anglican Church of North America). Others decided to stay within their denominations and attempt to reform them from within. The Anglican Church in Canada is one example. Many, although not all, of the churches of this denomination have chosen to stay together. Early on, the thinking of the traditionalists was that they would continue to dialogue on this issue and allow the "wheat" (non-affirming members) to grow among the "tares" (affirming members) in the hopes of allowing God to sort it out. Unfortunately, this was a copout because those holding an affirming view simply were biding their time until a new generation of affirming clergy and lay people replaced the older non-affirming members. Within a few short years denominations that were once split on the issue had enough votes to change the overall position of the denomination.

It is no surprise that a recent survey revealed the shift within mainline churches as well as the seeds of dissent that are now growing in more conservative denominations related to same-sex marriage. *LifeWay Research* shows that 47 percent of pastors of mainline churches now support same-sex marriage while 8 percent of evangelicals do.[39] The survey breaks down the denominations as follows: "Presbyterian or Reformed (49%), Methodist (47%), Lutheran (35%), and Christian/Church of Christ pastors (20%) are more likely to see nothing wrong with same-sex marriage than Baptist (3%) or Pentecostal pastors (1%)."[40] The reason for the divergence has a lot to do with how each denomination views the authority of Scripture and the role of the church within the broader

---

39. As cited by Brown, "Shocking Difference."
40. As cited by Brown, "Shocking Difference."

culture. It is no secret that many mainline churches are being pastored by men and women who allow culture and experience to influence their interpretation of Scripture and to trump scriptural authority. For example, some ordained leaders reinterpret the Text to justify redefining marriage as two women and a baby by pointing to Ruth and Naomi, or as two men by referencing David and Jonathan.[41] This is not only poor biblical interpretation, it is reading one's modern bias onto an ancient text. Not surprisingly, the higher the degree one receives within the pastorate (doctorate—27 percent, masters—32 percent, bachelors—9 percent) the more likely the pastor/educator is to be in support of same-sex marriage.[42] This is not based upon some enlightenment achieved as they advance through school, it is instead reflective of indoctrination from educators who hold to these positions at seminaries and graduate schools.[43]

If the church no longer holds a clear understanding of marriage, how are we to expect the broader culture to endorse the Genesis mandate of marriage? The answer is clear. They will not. Adding to this confusion and the redefining of traditional marriage in the last few years were several evangelical and mainline scholars who were writing popular and scholarly-level works supporting the new normal. One of the ways they did this was to downplay the clear teaching on marriage in Genesis 2 by muddying the waters with questionable and erroneous interpretations that are supposed to allow for God's approval of same-sex marriage. This group of scholars is growing rapidly and is being given a voice by many of the leading Christian publishers. Because I have handled a lot of this discussion elsewhere, I will give only a broad overview of the main biblical arguments.[44]

The Reinterpretation of the Genesis Mandate of Marriage

Because I will handle the so-called "clobber passages," which I noted above, in a later chapter, here I will focus on the opening chapters of Genesis and the arguments that are often used to support same-sex marriage.

---

41. See Knust, *Unprotected Texts*, 37, 39. Even mainline scholars who are honest about these texts refute such poor exegesis. See Coogan, *God & Sex*, 118–21.

42. Brown, "Shocking Difference."

43. Brown, "Shocking Difference."

44. See Peterson, *Sin of Sodom* (2016); Peterson, "The Sin of Sodom Revisited" (2016); Peterson, "Same-sex Marriage" (2017); and Peterson, "Ezekiel 16:49–50" (2018).

One might wonder how scholars can get around the clearly articulated mandate of monogamous heterosexual marriage as presented in Genesis 2. There are three predominant arguments affirming scholars use to support same-sex marriage from the first two chapters of Genesis and one argument from Genesis 3. Most affirming scholars use a combination of these arguments when defending their position. I will handle these arguments in what I feel is a descending order of persuasiveness. I will save my rebuttal to the end of this brief overview.

The first main argument relies heavily on historical critical source theory which says that Moses did not write Genesis and that the opening two chapters present two very different understandings of creation and marriage. Chapter 1 is often presented as being written by the putative Priestly author who saw human coupling for the purpose of procreation (Gen 1:27–28). On the other hand, chapter 2 is said to have been written by the so-called Yahwist to show that marriage is for the purpose of remedying loneliness (Gen 2:18). In this latter case, procreation is not the focus. Because of these two presentations, affirming scholars argue that chapter 1 promotes heterosexual marriage where procreation is a natural outcome and chapter 2 opens the door for any other marriage combination which can combat loneliness but not necessarily lead to procreation.[45] Of course, they argue that this must be confined to "acceptable" coupling such as elderly couples, people who are barren, and yes, same-sex couples.

The second argument is like the first in that affirming scholars argue that chapter 2 is for the purpose of creating kinship bonds between two people. Evangelical New Testament scholar James Brownson has offered one of the most sustained arguments for this view.[46] He argues that the oft-cited passage—read at most weddings today—dealing with the one-flesh union in Genesis 2:24 presents the coupling of individuals for the purpose of kinship bonds. Again, affirming scholars insist that there is nothing in chapter 2 that points to procreation as the natural outworking of marriage.

The third argument suggests that these opening chapters do not present a complete picture of creation. For example, we do not see the

---

45. See for example the arguments of Brownson, *Bible, Gender, Sexuality*, 32–34, 86–97; McNeill, *Sex as God Intended*, 23–26; and Johnson, *A Time to Embrace*, 120, 123. Johnson (p.123) calls Gen 2:18 "the most important verse in all of Scripture for the gay marriage debate."

46. Brownson, *Bible, Gender, Sexuality* (2013).

intermediate life forms such as amphibians, which can live on dry land and in the water. Rather we only see the creation of distinct land, air, and water creatures. Similarly, we only see the distinction of male and female genders and not the intermediate form of intersex. Because of this "incomplete" picture of creation, we can assume that the presentation of marriage in chapters 1 and 2 is also not complete. As such, same-sex marriage fits nicely into this "intermediate" state as do intersex people who fit neither the male nor female categories.[47]

A fourth argument suggests that we must live in light of the fall and that since the fall in Genesis 3 all sexuality is broken. Because we accept blended families that result from divorce, an issue related to the fall as well, accepting same-sex relationships should be no different than accepting other "broken" forms of marital relationships.

Before beginning my response, I want to point out two things. First, I will not address the debate about the differences between Genesis 1 and 2 vis-à-vis the creation pattern. This is beyond the scope of my current discussion. Instead, I will focus on the marriage issue alone. Second, affirming scholars who understand the clear teaching of the Bible and are honest with their readers have made it clear that the Bible in no way supports same-sex acts in any form, loving, committed, or otherwise.[48] Instead they choose to follow their *experience* and move beyond the Bible and accept same-sex marriage and lifestyles. I appreciate their honesty even though their conclusions are nonetheless dangerous. These points being noted, I will now offer a rebuttal to the above four arguments.

First, the argument that Genesis chapters 1 and 2 offer completely different creation accounts by two different authors is highly theoretical and unprovable. I have argued elsewhere, as have others,[49] that chapter 1 seems to be presenting the creation of the universe and earth whereas chapter 2 seems to be zeroing in on Genesis 1:26–28 and expanding on how God created the first two people and their home, namely, the Garden of Eden. If this is true, which seems to be the case, arguments based upon a bifurcation of the two creation accounts can be rejected before they begin.

---

47. Evangelical Megan DeFranza has written in support of this view. See DeFranza, *Sex Difference*, see esp. 178, 203–6, 262–72, 287 and DeFranza, "Common Ground," 69–101.

48. Loader, "Homosexuality," 17–48; and Johnson, "Homosexuality."

49. See Peterson, *Genesis as Torah*, 32; and Sailhamer, *The Pentateuch as Narrative*, 98–100.

Second, even if one accepts two different sources for the creation accounts that does not mean that they both do not present procreation as the expected outcome of marriage. The kinship-bonds argument is true only insofar as it correctly notes the strong familial bonds created by marriage.[50] The reference to the "one-flesh" union includes this bond but does not negate procreation. On the contrary, two people becoming one-flesh implies children because two people literally become "one-flesh" in their creative activity which mirrors the creative work of God.[51] Therefore, the "one-flesh" union is exemplified in the combining of two people to make a third—a child.[52] Interestingly, the 1662 *Book of Common Prayer* (BCP) actually notes that the first purpose of marriage was to procreate.[53] The second and third reasons for marriage include the fulfillment of sexual desires and the building of society. Not surprisingly, the changes to the Episcopal US BCP in 1979 moved procreation to the last spot and removed any hint of marriage as a remedy for falling into sexual sin. Of course, this is fitting with the direction the Episcopal Church in the US has moved over the past forty years or so.

Third, the assertion that chapter 2 deals with loneliness that can be remedied with same-sex coupling as readily as heterosexual coupling is to miss the heart of what God is presenting in chapter 2. Adam had plenty of company in Eden, but he did not have a partner suitable for himself (Gen 2:18, 20). The animals could not procreate with him or communicate at the level required for human thriving. God set up this scenario to show Adam and the rest of humanity that we need each other, and more specifically, that marriage is part of the good plan of God. The key word in this discussion related to God's making a helper for Adam is the term *kenegdo* in Hebrew which is often translated as "suitable" in most English translations of 2:18 and 20. In the Hebrew Bible, it only appears in these two verses and is a combination of three Hebrew words meaning "like, in front of/opposite, him." Not to be crass, but when male and female persons are standing in front of each other, biologically they "fit" and are the "opposite" of each other. God thus created a companion that was

---

50. Balswick and Balswick, *Authentic Human Sexuality*, 89. See also, Pruss, *One Body*, 132–37, 168–71, 244.

51. So, too, Carr, *The Erotic Word*, 24; and Song, *Covenant and Calling*, 13.

52. Contra Longman, *Bible and the Ballot*, 221–22.

53. So, too, Pruss, *One Body*, 247.

both Adam's equal and opposite from a psychological and a physiological perspective. Same-sex coupling simply will not fit into this model.[54]

Fourth, the assertion that the creation accounts do not present a complete picture of creation is to push the creation account too far and misses the technical language of the Hebrew text. To begin, the creation account was never meant to be exhaustive in its presentation by listing every animal that God created. Instead, the author used terms that had broader appeal and included all creatures whether amphibian or not. The terms for "creeping things" (*remesh*) in Genesis includes all kinds of animals no matter what their land or water status (1:21, 24, 25, 26, 28, 30). What is more, the issue of intersexuality does not fit into the creation account because it is a result of the fall.[55] While I am in no way belittling the human value or worth of those who are faced with this condition, it is nonetheless, a result of the fallenness of humanity that we have birth defects and issues of physiological gender confusion.[56]

Fifth, the argument that the fall allows for a further redefinition of marriage cannot be sustained. As noted in my previous chapter, polygamy, war brides, levirate marriage and the like are the results of human fallenness and are not God's plan for humanity.[57] This is not the model that the Bible presents for us to follow.[58] As evangelical scholar Wesley Hill notes, "God intends in Jesus Christ the reconstitution of marriage, not its redefinition."[59] We simply cannot continue to pervert marriage because of our fallenness. This also holds true for our support of legislation that attempts to recognize these types of unions.[60] I do not believe this is God-honoring for believers.

Finally, while Genesis 2 may be used to support the marriage of elderly people and those who are barren, that does not mean that we can include same-sex marriage because these couples are "barren" as well. Whether elderly or barren couples can have children or not does not diminish the fact that heterosexual marriage is the only coupling model

---

54. For a fuller discussion, see Peterson, *Sin of Sodom*, 51–52.
55. See my discussion in Curley and Peterson, "Eve's Curse Revisited," 1–16.
56. See more in Peterson, "Same-sex Marriage," 692–94.
57. So, too, Longman, *Bible and the Ballot*, 47–48.
58. Contra, Coogan, *God & Sex*, 79.
59. Hill, "Gay Christians," 31–43 at 42. Here Hill critiques the work of Song, *Covenant and Calling*, x, 18.
60. Wallis, *God's Politics*, 11. Here Wallis argues for supporting "gay civil rights and legal protection for same-sex couples."

ever offered by the Bible that is God-honoring.[61] The truth is there are numerous barren and older women in Genesis and the rest of the Bible who are granted children because of God's miraculous intervention (e.g., Sarah, Rebekah, Rachel, Tamar, Hannah, Samson's mother, Ruth, Elizabeth, etc.). And even though Genesis 2 does not explicitly mention procreation, this does not mean it was not a central concept in Genesis. Genesis is replete with genealogies and the command to be fruitful and multiply and fill the earth.

Conclusion

The rapid changes in Western culture regarding marriage have left many believers reeling and scratching their heads about how we got here and how we can get out of this mess. There is no easy solution now that the Pandora's Box has been opened. This is now both a spiritual and political battle. At the same time, it is important to realize that sex outside of marriage is always wrong as is any form of same-sex sexual activity in any setting. Nevertheless, there is a differentiation between sinful sexual activity outside of marriage by a man and a woman and that practiced by same-sex couples. Sex between a man and a woman who are not married can still result in marriage. The Hebrew Law required that a man who had illicit sex with a virgin, who was not betrothed, was to marry the woman if her father (and no doubt the girl) agreed to it (Exod 22:16–17). On the other hand, same-sex activity in any form or setting is never accepted in the Bible, nor can it lead to a God-honoring marriage.

For those living in Western cultures today, we now find ourselves in a sad situation. The biological bonding of the two sexes for creating children has now been hijacked for another unifying feature of marriage: love. The world, and many Christians as well, now ask the question: If two people love each other and can form a loving union to combat loneliness then why should we prohibit them from being happy?[62] To answer that question people must appreciate God's next mandate, the mandate of family as the foundation for society. As I will show in my next chapter, the nuclear family serves this very function. God intended the family to consist of a man and a woman because of the benefits that each gender brings to the marriage and in raising children. Statistics show that single

---

61. So, too, Levering, "Thomas Aquinas," 179.
62. See discussion by Dallas, *Gay Gospel*, 55–56.

parent homes, especially where no father is present, increases the risk to children, especially males, who are often the ones who become violent offenders, sexually active earlier, and struggle with suicide.[63] God's mandate for marriage had purposes beyond procreation and combatting loneliness. It was to be the foundation of society and a stable place for children—God's precious gift to parents—to be raised in security.

---

63. Dallas, *Gay Gospel*, 56–57.

Chapter 6

The Mandate of Family and Procreation Part 1

Family

I COME FROM A family of eight children. I grew up in a small town of about one thousand people with most of my extended family living within a few miles of my parents' home. In fact, my home was located on the front portion of my uncle and aunt's farm. I knew the "chaos" of living life in such a setting. You could not step out of line without someone knowing and quickly rendering the correct discipline. For me this was not restrictive, it was formative and liberating. When hard times came, and they did, I knew that my family would always be there for me. Growing up in this setting gave me a strong tie and responsibility to my family. I am now a father of five children all under the age of ten. I know the "chaos" of living in this setting as well, and I often wonder how my parents did it with eight children. But it is a good kind of chaos. My goal is to raise my children with the same sense of family responsibility and importance with which I grew up. Although I live far from my siblings, I make it a point to take my children "home" so they can remain connected to their extended family. The reason I relate these facts is to stress the blessing of family and the role that family plays in bringing stability not only to the immediate family unit, but also to society as a whole. I cannot imagine what my life would have been like had I not had the strong support of my family. Sadly, what is happening in Western culture in this regard is nothing short of transformational. What happens when children no longer have a sense of duty and responsibility to a family unit because it is non-existent? What happens when they do not have a connection to their extended family or perhaps do not even know who their extended family is? And what happens when the family unit is undermined or belittled at every turn by the wider culture? What are the repercussions for society? I can tell you that chaos is not far behind. God's plan for the family unit to be the bedrock of society was no mistake. It was to bring stability to societies.

Up to this point we have looked at the mandate of marriage as being one of the first of God's mandates to be attacked by the Enemy and undermined by Western culture. However, one cannot separate the idea of marriage from the family unit, a fact I have touched on at various junctures up to this point. The thing that is important to keep in mind is that family, namely, procreation and the creation of the family unit, are the plan of God for building societies and his greater plan for all creation. I am certainly not the first to note that God designed the family structure as a place where children could be raised and disciplined in a godly manner thus limiting broader societal chaos. When the family unit breaks down (e.g., fatherless and/or broken homes), many times the chaos of undisciplined and improperly instructed children bleeds over into society forcing society to become the "parent," duties for which it was never intended or designed.

When one looks at Western culture today, it is impossible not to recognize the chaos that is prevalent at all levels of society especially among our youth: mass murders, school shootings, disrespect for all levels of authority, psychological issues such as anxiety, suicide, depression, drug abuse, bullying and the list goes on. Why is there chaos everywhere we look? As noted in the previous two chapters and as will be expanded upon below, Western culture has consistently undermined marriage, and by extension, it has undermined the basis upon which God intended to create thriving societies. You cannot redefine and reject biblical sexual ethics and the family structure with impunity. It will affect the wider culture. Indeed, if we flout God's plan for stable societies and humanity in general, we are certainly going to reap the consequences. Undermining the family unit, especially the place of fathers, opens the door for sexual chaos among the family and paves the way for various pathologies, one of which, as we will see in a later chapter, is the rise in homosexual activity that destabilizes future generations.[1] Unfortunately, currently we are

---

1. Satinover, *Homosexuality*, 214.

reaping a whirlwind due to sixty years of undermining God's mandate of family building. Once again, this mandate is made evident in the opening book of the Bible.

The Family in Genesis

God's mandate to be fruitful and multiply is one of the most repeated phrases in the opening chapters of Genesis, both pre- and post-fall (1:22, 28; 8:17; 9:1, 7). For the ancients of every culture, having children was vital. Without them, one ceased to live on after death (2 Sam 21:1–14).[2] Already, we can see a disconnect between ancient concepts about the importance of family and today's Western culture. Today, some either forego raising a family or reject the notion outright in an attempt to "save the planet." There is certainly nothing wrong with responsible family planning, but such extreme positions make it clear that the planet has taken precedence over the mandate of family, a point I will examine in more depth in a later chapter.

This being noted, even a cursory reading of Genesis reveals that all the patriarchs and the matriarchs sought to have children in order to fulfill God's greater purpose of establishing families for solid societies and for continuing godly influence and God's blessing to future generations. Abraham and Sarah's family line is indeed important in this regard because it is through them that God established the line which would bring forth the Messiah, who would bless all the nations of the world (Gen 12:2). However, along with being aged (e.g., both Abraham and Sarah), barrenness plagued many of the matriarchs (Eve—4:1; Sarah—11:30; Rebekah—25:21; Rachel and Leah—29:31) making the family-building mandate impossible without God's intervention.[3] Along with these miraculous interventions, Genesis is punctuated with genealogical lists (4:17–22; 5:1–32; 10:1–32; 11:10–32, etc.) showing the natural progression of societal growth and the importance and beauty of families in God's greater plan to bless his creation and bring about stable societies.

The backbone of the Genesis narrative comes immediately after the devastation of the flood when God promises Abraham in Genesis 12:2 to make him into a nation. The ancestral narratives focus on the unfolding

---

2. See a further discussion in Peterson, "Gibeonite Revenge," 201–22. See also Knust, *Unprotected Texts*, 189.

3. See Curley and Peterson, "Eve's Curse Revisited," 1–16.

of that promise and the human drive to fulfill that plan. It also reveals God's plan to bless the world. While reading these narratives, however, the reader quickly realizes God's promise of blessing is something that extended into the distant future as well. It is a promise that does not come to fruition until four hundred years later (Gen 15:13; Exod 1). The lesson from Genesis in this regard is clear. Family building is not just a mandate which affects a married couple in the here and now. It is intended to extend into the future and be a part of the continued growth and blessing to the wider creation. This is the full impact of the family unit as designed by God, especially for those who place God at the center of their family. To be sure, the Bible makes it clear that those who fear God and keep his law will bring blessings to their family for a thousand generations (Exod 20:6).

The Role of the Family

As just highlighted, the family is the most fundamental unit of society. It is within the family unit that instruction is given and parents teach values to their children. These values include, spiritual instruction, sexual ethics and morality, discipline and self-control, respect for authority and country, knowledge of how to deal with anger and conflict responsibly, appreciation for how to work with others, proper discipline administered lovingly when children are wrong or rebellious, and the list goes on.[4] When these are handed over to public schools and government institutions, the family unit fractures and "group think" can occur. Indeed, the autonomous family unit is a buffer to the overreach of government through indoctrination.[5] When examining this brief list, to which many things could be added, is it any wonder we are facing the group think of today's culture? Parents have abdicated many of these responsibilities to daycares, public schools, afterschool programs, and public universities. And in rejecting church, God, and godly ethics and morality, parents have allowed their children to be indoctrinated into a religion of secular humanism. Change will only come when we change our methods in this regard.

---

4. Sider, *Completely Pro-Life*, 126–29.
5. Sider, *Completely Pro-Life*, 127, 144–46.

The Centrality of the Family Unit in History

The autonomous family unit is vital to Western culture, a reality attested to by history. To be sure, the biblical instruction on the value of the nuclear family did not fall on deaf ears for most early Americans, especially its founders. The founding fathers knew their history well,[6] and understood that Judeo-Christian ideals, especially the importance of the family unit established by the covenant of marriage, were what transformed and stabilized Rome, Europe, and Western culture as a whole.[7] The excesses and instability of pagan Roman culture with its limitless iterations of "family" and sexual entanglements is evident in Paul's letters to the Romans and the Corinthians, and in many ways mirrors the excesses of Western cultures today.[8] Similarly, prior to its Christianization, the influence of Christian values in Europe helped end the practice of rich men having multiple wives, a practice which led to the degradation of society and the rise of many poor single men who turned to a life of crime.[9]

This was a similar scene just prior to the flood when society devolved because rich rulers (i.e., the sons of God/godly sons) were marrying at will (Gen 6:1–4) and leaving many of the lower class of men without women to marry.[10] Genesis 6 tells of the chaos at that time, a situation that led to the constant violence of humanity (6:5). Here in the opening chapters of Genesis, the breakdown of society at its basic level, namely, the family unit, led to the destruction of all things. There surely is a lesson to be had here. Western culture cannot expect to continue to redefine and undermine the family unit and society with impunity. God simply will not allow it. This was never the plan of God for humanity. And it certainly was not how the American experiment was founded.

Families were central to colonial life with divorce a rare event. Large families allowed family businesses to excel as well as provided for the protection of parents and grandparents as they aged: children were not a detriment, they were a blessing to both the family and wider society.[11] With the shift from an agrarian-based market to an industrial-based

---

6. Ellis, *Breakdown*, 90–94.

7. Watkins, *New Absolutes*, 104.

8. Watkins, *New Absolutes*, 104–7.

9. Watkins, *New Absolutes*, 108.

10. See my discussion in Peterson, *Sin of Sodom*, 25 and Peterson, *Genesis as Torah*, 64–65.

11. Watkins, *New Absolutes*, 110.

economy, Western cultures have removed the need for large families. Despite this shift, that does not mean that children are not still vital to cultural success. The positive and practical aspect of rearing children to help care for the elderly, which is a biblically supported concept, is still important even though it has been transformed in Western cultures today through the implementation of a social safety net. Yet, even in cultures that have programs like social security, children are still needed to help fund and continue these important support systems.[12] There is a reason why America is facing a troubling future in this regard: our birthrate of 1.93 children per family (as of 2019) is now unable to sustain these programs. The more recent trend away from family-centered ideals to individualism, namely, an adult-centered focus versus a child-centered focus in marriage, has caused the birthrate to decline even more.[13]

The Centrality of Family for Culture

Considering the above discussion, the family unit is a blessing from God and is built upon a healthy interaction between the husband and wife and their children. A strong family unit is vital to the functioning of society. It is its foundation. God's plan was for both parents to be a part of the rearing of children. Indeed, children have a right to be raised by one's father and mother.[14] Now while there are certainly extenuating circumstances that prohibit this ideal in some cases (death of a parent, abuse), in reality many in Western culture are often too quick to give up this responsibility for selfish reasons. These reasons are often related to our own selfish sexual desires outside of the marriage covenant, which in turn fractures the sanctity of the family. Sex apart from the family unit creates discord and disorder and as such must be controlled with God's help (Gal 5:19–20; Col 3.5). Chastity is key. But chastity is more than refraining from sex before marriage, which may produce "unwanted" children who are aborted or deprived of a father, it also means fidelity within marriage so that sexual promiscuity does not sever the marriage bond.[15]

From a biblical perspective, the centrality of the family unit held Israelite society together even when things became difficult (e.g., slavery

---

12. See the stats in Grudem, *Politics*, 245–47.
13. Gushee, *Getting Marriage Right*, 28.
14. Levering, "Thomas Aquinas," 166.
15. Levering, "Thomas Aquinas," 167–69.

in Egypt and exile in Babylon). Part of the "glue" that held the nation together was the importance of Sabbath and the intentional focus on God and family time one day out of the week (Exod 20:9–11; Deut 5:13–15). To this day, Jewish culture promotes family as the center of society with modern Shabbat celebrations reflecting this ideal. In this regard, the divorce rate in modern Israel is one of the lowest of Western democracies, although this is changing as they become more secularized.[16] In biblical times there was also a strong connection between family units, the extended family, and the broader "culture" of Israel. Their faith in God and the covenant at Sinai gave Israel commonality. Now certainly they were not always in agreement nor did they always practice a pure religion/faith in God, nevertheless, there was a common spiritual identity within the broader culture.

For many generations this was no less true of Western, and particularly American culture. The common threads were a belief in God, the value of family, church, love of country, and traditional values. Today, that is no longer the case. The idea of the traditional family no longer holds the place it once did. This is also the case for church attendance, which fosters biblical values. Biblical instruction and church attendance are important for a stable and sexually ethical culture. A recent Pew Research poll concluded that 84 percent of children raised in homes where both parents attend church generally stayed in church.[17] This statistic shows that we as parents are key to teaching our children the value of church and God. With the decrease in church attendance is there any wonder why we are seeing a devaluing of biblical ethics as outlined in the Genesis mandates? Is there any wonder why we are seeing a fracturing of our culture? The "glue" that once held us together, namely, church, the Bible, and family values, is no longer present.

The rapidly changing culture in the West is causing traditionalists to be pitted against non-traditionalists, capitalists against socialists, the religious against the non-religious, and the list goes on.[18] As pointed out in my previous chapter, how can two people agree on what is good within society when we cannot agree on what constitutes a family? Personal choices related to family, church, God, and the Bible, thus have more

---

16. See Toi Staff, "Jewish Divorces."

17. Religion and Public Life, "One-in-Five."

18. The issue of race and reversed racism on college campuses is not just troubling, it is downright scary considering what awaits the future of America. See Murray, *Madness of Crowds*, 128–37.

The Mandate of Family and Procreation Part 1

far-reaching consequences than one's own home. It bleeds into society. It shapes and defines what society is. We are deeply divided because the traditional values, which most Americans held for generations, have been cast aside in the name of progress and individuality. Values are now relative and are not founded upon cultural tradition but rather upon what each person says is important—a dominant postmodern tenet.

Attacks on the Family and Society in Western Culture

The decline of the family unit within Western culture is not just happening due to pressures from within the family related to abuse, infidelity, addiction, rejection of God and church values, and marital break ups. Culture in general has been hostile towards traditional families for some time now. We saw this in our last chapter when dealing with the redefinition of marriage and what comprises a family. Here I would like to examine several factors that are exerting ever-increasing pressure on the family unit, which many often do not stop to consider.

Government Intrusion into the Family

One of the more subtle ways Western culture is diminishing the value and importance of the family unit is through legislation and tax policy.[19] In post-revolutionary America, family planning became so important that laws were enacted against contraception,[20] abortion, and even the dissemination of literature instructing on how to stop or limit pregnancy.[21] In other words, early in America's history, the governing bodies had a vested interest in keeping the nation strong through legislating against those things that would hinder or diminish the family unit. Conversely, the easing of divorce laws over the past eighty years or more has wreaked havoc on the family unit. During and after World War II, marriages that were entered into hastily before men went to war suffered from an increase of infidelity and divorce; the result was governmental ambivalence

---

19. Shinkoskey ("Without Law," 4) also points to oppressive tax legislation from the past that favored singles over families. See also, Sider, *Completely Pro-Life*, 117.

20. For a more detailed treatment of the controversies related to contraception, see Pruss, *One Body*, 263–327.

21. Shinkoskey, "Without Law," 6.

when enforcing marriage and infidelity laws.[22] As noted in my previous chapter, California's no-fault divorce first passed in 1970 opened the floodgates for the collapse of the family unit. One also cannot overlook the unintended side effects of Lyndon B. Johnson's social experiment known as the Great Society (1964–1965), which has devastated African American families.

The courts have also continued to undermine the family unit through legislative decisions that remove decision-making rights from parents relating to their minor children.[23] In many cases, the courts promote turbulent conditions in the family unit when they allow minor children free reign over their own lives. For example, as early as the 1980s, the court ruled in some states that minors as young as twelve could get an abortion without their parents' consent.[24] This is still happening today. Massachusetts is set to pass a bill allowing minors to get abortions without parental consent: a minor needs parental permission to get the flu shot but not an abortion.[25] Allowing children to make adult decisions too early as well as allowing them to reject parental supervision has been devastating to Western culture as children make life-altering decisions on their own. And studies have shown that poor decision-making increases astronomically in single-parent homes, which in turn affects the wider culture.

The breakdown of the family unit is happening at all levels but is particularly devastating for youths. In one fifty-year snapshot of American history (1933–1983) juvenile arrests increased 8,000 percent.[26] No longer do schools deal with the minor issues of delinquency and profanity; today they are dealing with armed assault, rape, drugs, murder and all forms of mayhem.[27] This disturbing trend seems to be associated with one of the more recent trends, historically speaking, which rejects the disciplining of children using corporal punishment. Much of the reason for this is the rejection of the fact that humans have a fallen nature that needs to be guided and corrected. I am not speaking of abuse here, but rather I am dealing

---

22. Shinkoskey, "Without Law," 6.

23. See Sider, *Completely Pro-Life*, 64–65, 140–43.

24. This is based upon a 1981 Oklahoma Supreme Court decision. See Shinkoskey, "Without Law," 7.

25. Mouser, "ROE."

26. Shinkoskey, "Without Law," 7.

27. Shinkoskey, "Without Law," 7.

The Mandate of Family and Procreation Part 1

with the reality that children require direction. And when that direction is implemented, sometimes physical coercion is required.[28]

Other legislation such as *Roe v. Wade* pitted men against women and even husband against wife, as a woman's right to choose was placed in the woman's hands which allowed her to override what her husband may want.[29] And as noted in my previous chapter, the redefining of marriage in 2015 has had the direct effect of the cultural redefinition of families. This will be detrimental to society in the long-term because of its flouting of God's law. Now, same-sex couples are hailed as being able to have their own families either through adoption or through surrogacy. The problem is, in the latter case, rarely is the opposite sex "parent" involved in births connected to same-sex parents. Put differently, rich same-sex couples like Elton John and his partner, David Furnish, simply pay someone to have a child with one of the men's DNA.[30] Lesbian couples are less hindered in this process especially with the availability of sperm banks, an act which has ethical and moral implications of its own.[31] Legislation allowing adoption for same-sex couples as well as marriage is not aiding in the stability of American culture despite the cry of the crowd.

One also must take into consideration the rise in single-parent families because the shame of having children out of wedlock has diminished and has added fuel to the fire. In the wake of the sexual revolution, single young women who have children and want to stay at home can now be supported by another means other than a husband: government is the new "husband" of the unwed mother. I will return to this below.

Educational and Personal Goals

Western culture has placed more and more emphasis on individualism and the importance of higher education. With the introduction of student loans and grants from the government, larger numbers of people are now eligible and able to attend colleges and universities with the result that marriage is pushed off until later in life. As such, educational and career goals exacerbate the rising age for first-time marriages, which reduces a woman's childbearing years dramatically. And, as touched on above when

---

28. See Grudem, *Politics*, 256–60.
29. Gushee, *Getting Marriage Right*, 28.
30. Murray, *Madness of Crowds*, 41–42.
31. See Brown, *Jezebel's War*, 87–88.

dealing with declining birthrates, the self-centered focus of young people is making marriage and family planning a secondary focus as opposed to a primary focus. Many now view marriage as the "capstone" of a young adult life, not the foundation.[32] Young people who used to marry in their early 20s are now waiting until their late 20s and early 30s because they do not want to be tied down or committed to one person nor do they want to give up their freedom to do all they want in life as a young person. At the heart of much of this self-centeredness is the fact that young people do not want the sacrifice that comes with marriage and raising a family.[33] Again, in a culture where sex before marriage is the norm (see Chapter 4), marriage and family no longer play an important role. This is particularly true of men who can now find sexual fulfillment without a marriage commitment. This has in turn had devastating effects on the family dynamic.

The Marginalization of Fathers in the Family Unit

It is self-evident that a "family" of sorts can be created without a father being present. As noted immediately above, sex before marriage may sound liberating but the side effect is often the birthing of children without a committed father being present in the home. As such, America's out-of-wedlock birthrate has skyrocketed across all demographics. Instead of recoiling at this change, culture has embraced the new norm making it appear as though fatherless homes are perfectly fine and normal. Who needs a father anyway when moms can do it alone, after all, they are the smart ones in the home, right?

For the past three decades, Western culture has been programmed, through media of all types (TV shows, commercials, music), to believe that fathers are not only second-rate parents to mothers, but more tragically, that they are incidental to the family unit. Commentators have noted the troubling trend that has moved from fathers as central to the family in shows like *Leave it To Beaver*, *My Three Sons*, *Ozzie and Harriet*, and *Father Knows Best* to the more negative portrayals of fathers as doofuses in shows like *The Simpsons* and *Everybody Loves Raymond*.[34] With such a low view of fathers, and with an ever-increasing trend for fathers

---

32. Regnerus, "Marriage," 38.
33. Regnerus, "Marriage," 38–39.
34. See Brown, *Jezebel's War*, 88–91.

to shirk their responsibilities as active parents in their children's lives, it should be no surprise that someone or *something* stepped into the gap to replace them, namely, the government.

As noted earlier, the government's assuming of the role once held by husbands and fathers in the family structure is not a positive thing. God knew what he was doing when he established the husband-wife pairing for the prospering of the family unit. Since the sexual revolution and the rise of radical feminism, men have been viewed with ever-increasing suspicion and vitriol as the reason for many of Western culture's ills. The extremes of the #MeToo movement highlighted this antagonism against men all too well.[35] This belittling of the father's value to the family unit and children is clearly on display in divorce laws. When divorce began to increase in the last half of the twentieth century, fathers rarely gained custody of children in divorce proceedings—the exact inversion of what had been the case in earlier centuries. And, as noted above, men have been removed from decisions related to abortion.

In a recent TEDx talk, divorce lawyer Marilyn York gives startling statistics on the effects of children growing up without fathers.[36] The statistics are clear: fathers play a vital role in the wellbeing and stability of children. Suicide, incarceration, runaways, and stunted psychological development are just a few of the problems associated with children growing up in fatherless homes. For example, according to the CDC 90 percent of all runaways come from fatherless homes, as do 71 percent of high school dropouts, and 63 percent of youth suicides.[37] Conversely, York notes that children whose fathers are present and active in their lives "have better cognitive and motor skills; elevated physical and mental health, become better problem solvers, and are more confident, curious, and empathetic." Not surprisingly, the main contributors to fatherlessness are divorce and out of wedlock births. York goes on to point out that "every thirteen seconds someone in America gets divorced. That equates to almost 2.5 million divorces a year . . . currently more than 40 percent or 1.5 million babies are born out of wedlock each year in the US." York notes that from 1960 to 2016 children growing up in a home with just their mothers nearly tripled from 8 percent to 23 percent. Other studies have shown that promiscuity among female children, adolescent

---

35. See my more detailed discussion in Peterson, "Sexual Exploitation," 693–703.
36. York, "Fatherhood."
37. See also, Shinkoskey, "Without Law," 5.

pregnancy, and abortion increases when fathers are not in the home.[38] One can only imagine what the long-term negative effects will be on children in same-sex families. While society for decades perpetuated the myth that fathers were not important to a child's life, the statistics clearly state otherwise. Indeed, studies are now showing that the presence of weak or "emasculated" fathers or the total absence of a father increases the likelihood of sons identifying as gay because of the failure to "fully gender-identify."[39]

Adding to this rejection of the family, and by extension the belittling of the role of men, was the tendency of many second-wave feminists to spurn motherhood in favor of careers. Some feminist academics of the 1980s boldly propounded that the traditional American family (mother, father, and kids) represented "a dysfunctional family unit" and that dildos could easily take the place of men.[40] Ironically, some feminists have since noted the tradeoff may not have been worth it.[41] The most recent wave of feminism, what is sometimes called the "fourth wave" has attempted to downplay the importance of men in a more troubling manner. It is not enough for them to push for equality in all areas of life, now they insist that "Everything that is good is female. Everything that is bad is male."[42] In the age of social media, this new wave uses hashtag lines such as "Men are trash" and "Kill all men," which apparently are not supposed to be taken literally but rather as representative of the vitriol women feel towards the "patriarchy" of western society.[43] I am sure many first-wave feminists would be rolling over in their graves if they knew where their push for equality has landed.

Family and Social Marxism

Another means of attack on the family has been in the social and political changes among the children of people from Generation X (1965–1983). These children are known as the Millennials. Millennials, especially, have

---

38. Schwarzwalder and Tax, "Fatherlessness," as noted by Brown, *Jezebel's War*, 106.

39. See the numerous sources in Brown, *Jezebel's War*, 106–7.

40. D'Souza (*Illiberal Education*, 202) here citing Dana-Michele Brown of the University of Washington at Seattle. See also D'Souza, p.213.

41. Murray, *Madness of Crowds*, 243–44.

42. Murray, *Madness of Crowds*, 97.

43. Murray, *Madness of Crowds*, 98–105.

endorsed socialist policies. Much of this has been due to the indoctrination of students from preschool until they leave university (see Chapter 2). An August 2018 Gallup poll showed that 51 percent of 18–29 year-olds had a favorable view of socialism with 57 percent of Democrats now having a positive view of it, a first for the Democrat party.[44] Communistic and socialistic tendencies are creeping into every aspect of education, which in turn has serious consequences for the family, especially the authority of the parents versus the authority of the government.

Recently, my wife related to me a clear example of what is often viewed as a "benign" form of socialistic ideology. She told me of a situation in a local public-school district where some of the teachers required their students at the beginning of the school year to put all their pencils into a pile and then allowed any student to pick whatever one they wanted. Those whose parents had purchased expensive pencils for their children did not necessarily get them, someone else did. The teachers were trying to make the classroom a level playing field, but in doing so had modeled a communist tenet to these young children: what you own does not belong to you, it belongs to the collective. And what those from well-off families have, can be taken from them and given to those who do not have as much. Now while I am all for Christ-like behavior and helping those less fortunate, what this type of educational policy is teaching is not that. These types of forced policies indoctrinate children to adopt socialistic policies and communistic thinking without them even realizing it. Later in life this will lead to an easier acceptance of even more radical anti-God and anti-family tendencies which are becoming all too common in the West.

What younger Americans do not realize, usually because they have not studied Marxism, is that socialist tenets proposed by Karl Marx and his friend Friedrich Engels pushed for the dissolution of the family as the basis of society and argued for its replacement by the state/government. In their Communist Manifesto they wrote that they envisioned a world where "the single family ceases to be the economic unit of society. Private housekeeping is transformed into a social industry. The care and education of the children becomes a public affair."[45] This is exactly what is going on in the West as more and more emphasis is being placed on the government's role in raising children in daycares and in the public

---

44. Ellis, *Breakdown*, 113.
45. As cited by Roys, "Socialism."

school system including tuition-free state universities. The government with its godless policies is indoctrinating children from the cradle to the end of college. And the acceptance of the BLM agenda is already reflecting similar issues with one school district in Buffalo, New York, teaching elementary school children to question the value of the nuclear family.[46] This is straight up Marxist ideology masquerading as a legitimate racial justice and social movement.

What is troubling is that many Christians are erroneously equating socialism to being "Christ-like" when it is anything but. The Bible is replete with evidence of the ownership of private property, personal responsibility, a rejection of covetousness, and the central role of family as the basis of society. The story of Naboth's vineyard is one such case (1 Kings 21). Ironically, Jesus explicitly taught about greed and rejected forcible seizure of someone else's property (Luke 12:13–15). Our political shifts are just one more piece of evidence that Western culture is rotting from within. Education, or should I say the lack thereof, is leading younger generations down a godless path. Because of the rejection of biblical principles and the refusal to study history, young people are quick to adopt political ideologies that are radical and clearly anti-scriptural. As I was writing this chapter, I took a break to listen to a radio broadcast. During the show, the commentator noted how young people from conservative homes are being indoctrinated by radical Marxist professors who thrive on driving a wedge between their students and their parents. As an example of one among many such cases, a young lady had turned against her father simply because he did not endorse her radical political agenda as she had learned in university. It brought division to the family.

So, what are we to do to thwart these attacks against the family unit? Recently, I had a concerned grandmother come to me after one of my talks and ask me this very question. My response was twofold. First, we need a spiritual awakening, which will draw people back to the truths of God's Word. Second, we need to take responsibility for educating our children, both in history and in the Bible, even if this means the sacrifice of one parent's job so that children can be homeschooled. Now to be sure, this latter part of my response may be viewed as radical by some, but we are talking about the greatest gift God has given us: our children! (Ps 127:3). Not surprisingly, even homeschooling is being challenged as educators are now insisting that all children should go to public schools

---

46. Halon, "Nuclear Family."

(see more in Chapter 10).⁴⁷ Of course, this would allow secular educators to indoctrinate every child. This is no less true of the educational system's usurpation of how children are educated about important life decisions, especially related to sex and family building. Looking back on that brief discussion I had with the concerned grandmother, I would add that we must be mindful of where we send our children to school and university. The Enemy is using the educational system to corrupt our children at every turn (see Chapter 2).

Education's Attack on the Family Unit

During the recent increase of homeschooling due to the Covid-19 outbreak, some parents in Seattle, Washington, found out firsthand what their children were being taught in the public-school system. One couple intercepted the text messages from the local school's sex-ed teacher to their 12-year-old daughter. In the text, the teacher gave instructions on how to have safe sex during the coronavirus outbreak. This was for pre-teens! The absolute corrupting nature of many aspects of the education system in America is causing the moral corruption and destruction of the innocence of our children.

By now, I would hope that you, the reader, would have come to realize that the all-out attack on the family is not just through divorce, cohabitation, and the rejection of marriage in general. We also see a rising trend in the education system to corrupt children at a younger and younger age. The children that the Enemy does not kill through abortion, he focuses on "killing" spiritually by destroying their innocence. In this regard, in recent years there has been an increase in the attack on the family from a variety of outside sources not the least of which is the putative "sex education" classes offered in public schools and on university campuses. The issue with many of these programs is the questionable "educational" nature of the material especially when it comes to the graphic sexual content and the sexually and morally twisted practices hailed as normal. These classes are not just oral presentations. Many are accompanied with full color photos and videos depicting the most base and vile sex acts between homosexual couples, bi-sexuals, and heterosexuals.⁴⁸ This is all

---

47. Snibbe, "Homeschooling." For the original article, see Bartholet, "Homeschooling."

48. For a more detailed discussion on the explicit nature of the material, see

done in the name of diversity and variety. School concerts, pageants, special lectures, and invited guests promote sexual deviance as normal, fun, and exciting. Some of the proponents of these programs encourage keeping parents in the dark about the content because of their graphic nature and because, they argue, the presentations would be misunderstood out of context. Are we supposed to believe that context is going to help us understand the need for such perversity being taught, not to university-level students mind you, but to students in middle school and younger?

Not surprisingly, Planned Parenthood is a ringleader in sex education material boasting on its website that they reach an estimated 1.5 million people with their programs, 64 percent of whom, are in middle school and high school.[49] I find it telling that the founder of Planned Parenthood, Margaret Sanger (1883–1966), was not just known for her racial eugenics positions, but also for her unapologetic push for birth control, which meshed well with her documented sexual promiscuity.[50]

I am sure most people are not against age-appropriate responsible sex education for their children; however, this is not what is being pedaled in many public schools today. It is obvious that organizations like Planned Parenthood have the goal of normalizing sexual activity and deviancy at a younger and younger age. Topics like BDSM, oral and anal sex, masturbation, "protected" sex, homosexuality, and the like are common curriculum content. Many of these topics are accompanied by cartoon-like books with full imagery on display. I can personally attest to the fact that I went through sex-ed when I was in junior high and high school, but it looked nothing like what is being taught to our kids today. And then people wonder why many of us homeschool our children.

It should come as no surprise that when it comes to sexual activity among adolescents, America ranks among the top nations in the world in adolescent birthrates.[51] Of course, along with these increased pregnancies comes an increase in abortion. About one out of five abortions is performed on adolescent mothers.[52] And, as Watkins noted more than twenty years ago, this is all happening in a country that is supposed to be

---

Watkins, *New Absolutes*, 142–45.

49. For a more detailed and graphic discussion on the role of sex education and Planned Parenthood's involvement, see Fox, "Exposed."

50. Watkins, *New Absolutes*, 82–83.

51. Watkins, *New Absolutes*, 121.

52. Watkins, *New Absolutes*, 121.

on the cutting-edge with its sex education programs.[53] This is all a ruse to rob our children of their innocence. The Enemy is working overtime with those at the head of the sex education programs and curriculum to corrupt and instill ungodly values concerning sex, especially sex before marriage.[54]

Sex-ed has become much more than simple education about one's body, it is about corrupting and stimulating young people to become sexually active at younger ages. And, as I just noted, every kind of sexual perversion is now seen as good and formative for young people to explore.[55] This works well for organizations like Planned Parenthood, whose founder Margaret Sanger famously stated that "The most merciful thing a large family can do for one of its infant members is to kill it."[56] Planned Parenthood is on the receiving end of government assistance for "women's health" concerns and the profitable destruction of unwanted babies. When faced with the abysmal failure of government-sponsored sex-ed programs, those promoting them double down and blame those who cling to a higher moral compass: Christians are the problem because we are not teaching our kids how to use condoms and other forms of contraception properly and we are naive to think that our children are not having sex.[57]

The connection this has to the family unit discussion falls into two categories. First, family as defined and designed by God is now passé. In our postmodern context, education like that noted above, seeks to demean conservative biblical morality[58] and pervert and undermine the family structure by getting children sexually active much earlier. When sex-related services are needed for things like STDs and unwanted pregnancy, guess who is ready and waiting to assist? You got it, government-funded Planned Parenthood. In situations all too common today, sex is not reserved for marriage and for family building, it is now passed off as nothing more than something to enjoy whenever a person is "ready." Marriage and

---

53. Watkins, *New Absolutes*, 121–22.

54. This is not an over exaggeration. See the disturbing citations noted by Watkins, *New Absolutes*, 122.

55. See also Patterson and Kim, *The Day America Told the Truth*, 104.

56. Sanger, *Women*, 67 as cited by Watkins, *New Absolutes*, 81.

57. See the disturbing account of President Clinton's Surgeon General, Joycelyn Elders's radical policies on sex education in Arkansas and then expanded to American schools. As noted by Watkins, *New Absolutes*, 123–30.

58. See the pejorative comments against conservatives by Benshoff and Griffin, *Queer Images*, 2–3.

family do not come into the discussion generally. The second, and just as insidious, plan is evident in one of the promotional descriptions of the goal of Planned Parenthood. They seek to redefine family by normalizing homosexuality in order to help control population growth.[59]

Again, I cannot stress this enough. At the heart of the issue is the role of parents in educating their children and protecting them from harmful "educational" content. When morality and sexual ethics have been corrupted by a Western postmodern mindset, where everything is relative and everyone's sexuality and sexual expressions are okay, then the biblical design for family and sexuality quickly falls by the wayside. Is it any wonder why sexual deviancy, promiscuity, and a decreased interest in marriage dominate the worldviews of younger and younger people in Western culture?

The Impersonal Nature of Social Media

Social media has also made us more detached from one another and aided in the fracturing of society with impersonal interactions often punctuated with vitriolic attacks and name-calling. I can speak personally on this as I have watched family connections become strained and fractured because of the impersonal nature of social media and online posting of the most divisive and hurtful comments. What used to be confined to the four walls of the family home and worked out in as loving a manner as possible is now being aired before the world and viewed by millions. In these situations, embarrassment and shame lead to family tension.

A Loss of Patriotism

In my short lifetime, I have watched as patriotism and a connection to one's past have been eroded and now reviled. Part of establishing strong families and by extension, strong communities and societies is the sharing in common traditions like the way Israel shared together during feast days. Unfortunately, today community gatherings and national holidays are just another chance to spew hatred for our "racist" institutions. We no longer find wholesome community-and-family-building clubs, groups, and community organizations as important as they once were.[60] Western

---

59. Fox, "Exposed."
60. Balswick and Balswick, *Authentic Human Sexuality*, 315.

society is divided and walking different paths without common goals or even common historical values. We need look no further than the basic American tradition of reciting the pledge of allegiance or honoring the flag. Whole segments of society see the American experience as a failure and in need of radical transformation. Indeed, at the heart of these once-loved societal ideals is the Judeo-Christian belief in God, family, and country, which are now being marginalized as an unimportant, or worse, an unwelcomed return to the "racist and unjust" period of our past. We are now divided and pitted against each other more than ever before. How is a society to survive if there are no common guiding rules, values, moral principles, or accepted history? The truth is it cannot. It will dissolve.

Is Western Culture Headed for Collapse?

Scholars have long noted the importance of the nuclear family to societal stability. Any time the centrality and importance of the nuclear family are diminished or marginalized throughout history, societal decay follows in its wake. Some of the warning signs of this trajectory include: easy divorce, reduced family size, a belittling of the marriage agreement and what it stands for, a rejection or demonizing of past historic heroes and figures in favor of a modern elitism, a rise in cohabitation, a rejection of traditional family values and roles, an embracing of anti-family values, a minimization of the deplorability of adultery, a rise in the disrespect of parents and authority by children, and an acceptance of all forms of sexual perversion.[61] But all of these troubling trends start with the nuclear family and how we view and treat God's mandate of family and societal building. Joe Dallas appears to be correct when he notes that the threat to the nuclear family is not homosexuality per se, it is the nuclear family itself.[62] This threat has arisen through the promotion of abuse, incest, divorce, adultery, violence and the like.

But these are symptoms, not the cause. Returning to my discussion in Chapter 3, the cause is better understood as a rejection of God and God's laws and the elevation of the self and self-interest.[63] To be sure, self-serving individualism that shirks the responsibility and self-sacrifice

---

61. See also Watkins, *New Absolutes*, 236–37.
62. Dallas, *Gay Gospel*, 54.
63. Watkins, *New Absolutes*, 237–38.

to have a family coupled with sexual laxness is at the heart of the demise of society. As I have been stressing throughout this chapter, God instituted the family as the basis of society for a reason. When we choose to reject that order, chaos ensues. This is reinforced by studies that show that when people reject God, society, built upon the family unit, begins to deteriorate.[64]

God establishes rules for sexuality because it is needed for human thriving. Returning to my discussion from Chapter 4, Joseph Daniel Unwin's 1930's examination of 86 tribes and civilizations revealed some troubling trends that are common to all societal collapses. Unwin discovered that when sexual continence is enforced within society, and more specifically in the family unit, the culture advances; whereas, conversely, an "extension of sexual opportunity" brings about a decline of the culture.[65] Unwin's extensive study showed that when cultures jettison sexual ethics and morality in the family unit, the cultures collapsed by the third generation. One of the more interesting discoveries Unwin made is encapsulated in his comment,

> it is often supposed that female emancipation is an invention of the modern white man. Sometimes we imagine that we have arrived at a conception of the status of women in society which is far superior to that of any other age; we feel an inordinate pride because we regard ourselves as the only civilized society which has understood that the sexes must have social, legal, and political equality. Nothing could be farther from the truth. A female emancipating movement is a cultural phenomenon of unfailing regularity; it appears to be the necessary outcome of absolute monogamy. The subsequent loss of social energy after the emancipation of women, which is sometimes emphasized, has been due not to the emancipation but to the extension of sexual opportunity which has always accompanied it. In human records there is no instance of female emancipation which has not been accompanied by an extension of sexual opportunity.[66]

Keeping in mind that Unwin wrote his book in the 1930s, one could not have prophesied a more accurate picture of the results of the sexual revolution, which began in 1960's America. We may be thinking that we are on a trajectory towards a positive outcome for our Western culture,

---

64. Watkins, *New Absolutes*, 238.
65. Unwin, *Sex and Culture*, 326, see also 365.
66. Unwin, *Sex and Culture*, 344.

but the reality is just the opposite. There are simply no exceptions to the rule. All societies that diminish sexual continence both before marriage and within marriage (through divorce and open marriages) end up imploding or being conquered by another culture that has higher sexual values.[67] While Unwin focused on sexual issues, what he really discovered is what happens when the family unit is marginalized in society. In this regard, Unwin goes on,

> The history of these societies consists of a series of monotonous repetitions; [. . .] after a period of intense compulsory continence, the human organism seizes the earliest opportunity to satisfy its innate desires in a direct or perverted manner. Sometimes a man has been heard to declare that he wishes both to enjoy the advantages of high culture and to abolish compulsory continence. [. . . But] these desires are incompatible, even contradictory. The reformer may be likened to the foolish boy who desires both to keep his cake and to consume it. Any human society is free to choose either to display great energy or to enjoy sexual freedom; the evidence is that it cannot do both for more than one generation.[68]

Thus, while the first generation to enact sexual freedom may not suffer immediately, Unwin's research showed that the next two generations certainly do. When the data is analyzed through a modern grid, commentator Kirk Durston, to whom I owe a debt of gratitude for bringing Unwin's research to my attention through his online blog, notes that if Unwin's generation equals 33 years, then "Looking at our own sexual revolution, the 'having your cake and eating it too' phase would have lasted into the early 2000's."[69] I would revise Durston's assertion and point out that the first generation really would have ended in roughly 1993 if we start in 1960. The second generation would thus run from 1994 to 2027, the generation of which we are quickly coming to the end. That means that unless something changes soon, cultural and societal collapse in America will take place during the 2028–2061 generation. The disorder in our education system, the turmoil in our sexual ethics and family structures, and the pandemonium in our political and media institutions

---

67. See also a similar conclusion by Satinover, *Homosexuality*, 17–18.
68. Unwin, *Sex and Culture*, 412.
69. Durston, "Sexual Morality."

does not leave me optimistic that we will survive even this long unless we turn our hearts to God and beg for mercy (2 Chron 7:14).[70]

Conclusion

Throughout this chapter I have laid out an argument that God's mandate of family is vital for building strong societies. When the family unit breaks down, societal chaos ensues. I also showed that what is often at the heart of the collapse of the family unit is a carefree approach to sex and sexual fidelity in marriage. America has been on this dangerous trajectory for more than six decades now. We may think that we are the exception to the rule, but the reality is that history proves just the opposite: judgment is coming. Returning to my central thesis of this chapter, Durston rightly notes that at the heart of our social upheaval (mass shootings, mental health concerns, depression, suicide, and "extreme identity groups") is the rejection of the family unit and the extended family connections (e.g., aunts and uncles and cousins, etc.) and the stability that that unit offers to young people and children.[71] By the third generation the effects of society's acceptance or rejection of sexual restrictions from the previous two generations is felt to their full extent.[72] As just noted, but it bears repeating, most of this is related to a "modified monogamy" (divorce and open marriages) and the removal of pre-nuptial sexual restrictions.

From a modern perspective, one could make the application that if the church holds to a solid sexual ethic, it will have a positive effect on society at large and perhaps stave off judgment. However, if it adopts the sexual ethic of the larger culture, which it seems to be doing at a record pace, it will aid in bringing about the rapid decline of Western culture.

Some may scoff and pass this off as fear mongering once again. Even if Unwin is not "prophetic" or is wrong to suggest that sexual promiscuity caused past societal collapse (the correlation vs. causation argument), what we can be assured of is that failure to protect the natural outcome of sexual promiscuity, namely, children, will certainly bring God's judgment. Based upon the words of the prophetic voice of the Bible, any time a society refuses to protect the most vulnerable in society God is sure to judge that nation (read Amos and Micah). Who is the most vulnerable

---

70. See also, Brown, *Jezebel's War*, 43.
71. Durston, "Sexual Morality."
72. Unwin, *Sex and Culture*, 429.

in our society today? It is not the "widow, the orphan, and the alien" of the biblical period (e.g., Deut 10:18; 14:29; Isa 1:17; 16:11, 14; Jer 7:6; 22:3; Zech 7:10; Mal 3:5), even though we must care for them, in Western culture it is the plight of the unborn. It is to this disturbing and heartbreaking topic that I now turn.

Chapter 7

The Mandate of Family and Procreation Part 2

Procreation—Abortion and Culture

A country that shrugs off the evidence of what abortion really is and chants all the louder about 'freedom' and 'equality' can never claim to achieve either. *Roe v. Wade* is the litmus test to end all litmus tests. That's because abortion is the moral 'issue' to end all issues. It is uniquely defining of a culture and an individual. People who support the act of butchering the most defenseless and innocent of all human beings, blithely calling it 'choice' can hardly plant their flag on a civilized hill. A nation that considers killing its own children to be the *pièce de résistance* of its fight for empowerment and justice is suffering a suicidal delusion.[1]

THIS COMMENT BY JENNIFER Hartline captures the essence and the logical summation of the abortion atrocity. It is a heinous practice that should cause all people, especially Christians, to recoil. And it is a practice for which America will certainly be punished (cf. Ps 106:34–40). Some have said that the death of 600,000 men during the US Civil War was

---

1. Hartline, "Kavanaugh."

punishment for the blight of slavery. If this is true, what will our punishment be for killing over 62 million babies?

In the previous chapter I examined the importance of the family unit for the building of a stable society. While this is important, one cannot speak of "family" without appreciating and acknowledging the role that procreation plays in making possible a family and an enduring legacy. As an illustration of this point, recently, I was teaching a class on Ecclesiastes and needed to demonstrate how quickly generations come and go. To help my students visualize the cycles of these generations, I arranged a PowerPoint slide showing seven generations of the Peterson men over the past two hundred years beginning in the early nineteenth century and extending up to today. As I reviewed it, I realized the power of procreation and the value of passing on one's legacy to the next generation. God's mandate of procreation in Genesis 1:28, and intimated in 2:24, was intended to do just that. Despite this obvious reality, the mandate of procreation, a natural outworking of the marriage mandate, has been under attack with even more ferocity than the marriage mandate itself. While there are a number of issues related to the mandate of procreation that could be discussed (e.g., adoption, contraception, invitro fertilization, infertility, etc.) here I will focus on what has been the most disturbing rejection of the mandate of procreation. It is not our current trend of simply refusing to have children, it is what is often the militant desire to destroy children when they are in the safety of the womb through the blight of abortion. I want to note, however, that this assessment is not directed necessarily at women who find themselves in a variety of troubling situations which often leads to abortion;[2] rather, I am focusing on the act of abortion itself and the militant push to keep it enshrined in law.

Due to the breadth of this topic, it is impossible to handle comfortably in one chapter. As such, I will handle the discussion in two parts. In this chapter, dealing with the mandate of procreation, I will focus on the cultural issues that led to the legalization of abortion, and how culture continues to promote this heinous act. I will reserve the scriptural arguments against abortion and how Christians handle this topic for my next chapter.

---

2. So, too, the perspective of Brown, *Jezebel's War*, 62.

A Brief History of Abortion in America

Historically, America has taken a strong stance against abortion. As already noted in my previous chapter, in post-Revolutionary America it was illegal to even possess literature that propagated abortion and birth control.[3] What is more, in 1821, Connecticut enacted a law that prescribed life imprisonment for any doctor who performed an abortion.[4] While there certainly were "back-room" abortions that took place throughout the history of America, for all intents and purposes, abortion was marginalized and frowned upon by most people in society. This was no doubt due to the Judeo-Christian influence on the general populace. This was the case until the turn of the twentieth century when global upheaval and the rise of rationalism began to shake the once-entrenched understanding of godly principles and the value of human life. If Darwin is correct in that we are all nothing but evolved creatures, which do not answer to a Higher Power, then what is the harm in managing one's own reproduction? And if world wars can kill millions at will, where is the value of life?

These and a variety of other factors led to the secularization of America post-World War II, which in turn began a shift in the way politicians, the courts, and America in general, viewed reproductive rights and procreation. This can be seen in several court rulings that began the process of eroding the sanctity of life and family building. This erosion began when the courts enacted anti-contraceptive legislation (e.g., *Griswold v. Connecticut* in 1965 and *Eisenstadt v. Baird* in 1972). Within this same period, abortion advocates were laying the groundwork for the pro-abortion law of *Roe v. Wade* in 1973. In the interim, doctors joined the fight to be allowed to save women's lives by performing abortions when medically necessary. They argued that in cases of fetal abnormalities, incest, and rape, women should have access to abortion services. More liberal-leaning states like New York allowed most abortions prior to the 1973 ruling and a few other states allowed it for specific cases of rape, incest, and the health of the mother. Still others had outlawed it completely. In this changing season of "reproductive health," American culture was heading into a period of social, political, moral, and ethical turmoil that it had never experienced before. The sexual revolution of the

---

3. Shinkoskey, "Without Law," 6.
4. Shinkoskey, "Without Law," 6.

1960s would push America in a direction that no one could have ever dreamed of twenty years earlier.

The turbulent period of the 1960s provided the perfect setting for the *Roe v. Wade* ruling of 1973. The sexual revolution and the introduction of oral contraceptives known as "the pill" in 1960, set the stage for female "liberation" and the rejection of marriage (see Chapter 4). The problem with this new freedom was what to do when unmarried women found themselves with an unwanted pregnancy. The rise of second-wave feminism (see more below) sought to address these types of concerns by lobbying for access to legal abortions anywhere in the United States. Indeed, feminists have long been on the forefront of the attack against the unborn child by advocating for a woman's "right" to dispose of an unwanted baby, or as some have labeled it, an "uninvited being growing in her womb."[5] In the chaotic era of the Vietnam War, student protests, free love, exotic drugs, and Woodstock, politicians felt the growing pressure to "get with the times" and pass comprehensive legislation on the abortion issue. The problem, however, was that most Americans opposed such a barbaric law.[6] Nevertheless, where politicians lacked public backing and moral integrity on the issue, the unelected judges on the Supreme Court had no such restraints. With the right members of SCOTUS in place, the *Roe v. Wade* decision of 1973 became the law of the land sweeping away any individual state's anti-abortion legislation.

Not surprisingly this SCOTUS ruling coincided with the proliferation of feminist writings on the liberated woman.[7] Among these, many spoke callously about the plight of the unborn vis-à-vis abortion. For example, in 1973, Mary Ann Warren "memorably argued that fetuses were no more morally significant than fish, and abortion no more morally serious than cutting hair."[8] With this type of rhetoric one can easily understand why the Christian Right was aghast at what had transpired in America. Over the next three decades or more, the fight only intensified as many Christians fought to overturn the *Roe v. Wade* ruling, with those supporting abortion intent on keeping it codified in law. The problem is that since the "culture wars" of the 1970s and 1980s, many "Christians" have now come to support abortion laws. The troubling part of this is that

---

5. Kamitsuka, *Abortion*, 177.

6. According to Blake ("Abortion," 548), in the last few years of the 1960s, 80 percent of the white population of America disapproved of elective abortion.

7. See the collected essays by Morgan ed., *Sisterhood is Power* (1970).

8. Warren, "Abortion," 43–61, as noted by Reader, "Abortion," 134.

49 percent of white self-identified evangelicals also support the legalization of abortion[9] and 52 percent of Protestant African Americans want abortion legal in almost all cases.[10] Again, much of this change in opinion can be traced to the influence of biased higher education and media indoctrination. The church is quickly reflecting the values of secular culture. We will never change the abortion issue if this trend continues. Indeed, the current state of affairs is not promising.

The Current State of Affairs

No topic garners as much immediate vitriol than the issue of curbing or ending abortion rights. There could not be a starker contrast of opinions than that between the pro-life and the pro-choice sides of the abortion debate. A good example of this can be seen in a comparison between the interviews conducted with participants of both the pro-choice Woman's March and the pro-life March for Life in January 2020 in Washington, DC.[11] A quick online search of videos from both marches shows the stark differences. On the one hand, the March for Life had a somber and often God-fearing tone. Conversely, the Women's March was punctuated by vitriolic and obscene rhetoric[12] and the most extreme arguments and positions for abortion and, in some cases, infanticide. Women were recorded cheering and bragging about their abortions. While some may argue that this is an extreme, the truth is I have yet to find a pro-choice march video without troubling and obscene rhetoric. Many Christians rightly note that the "spirit" behind abortion advocacy is demonic. This makes perfect sense when one considers the obvious desire of the Enemy to undermine God's good mandates for creation.

From the political perspective, during that rally, Democrat New York Senator, Chuck Schumer, made threats against two of the newest judges on the Supreme Court (at that time) warning them that they would be in serious trouble if they attempted to undo *Roe v. Wade*.[13] While he

---

9. See the changes noted in the Pew Research article by Fingerhut, "Roe v. Wade," and the charts from the 1980s presented by Kellstedt, "Abortion," 211–13.

10. Pew Research Center, "Black Protestant Tradition."

11. E.g., TFP Student Action, "Marches."

12. This type of rhetoric is also favorably noted by "Christian" feminists such as Peters, *Trust Women*, 191.

13. Brown, "Conservative Justices."

later recanted, it is clear what is in the heart of the average pro-choice individual. This vitriol against pro-life justices and individuals is reaching a fever pitch and will only increase now that Amy Coney Barrett has joined SCOTUS.[14] The vitriolic language of lawmakers and pro-choice radicals is only a foretaste of what is sure to follow if *Roe v. Wade* is ever overturned in America. The troubling language is not just an issue in America though.

Western culture's flippant and callous disregard for the ugly reality of abortion was on full display during a recent teachers' strike in Ontario, Canada. A protestor for the teachers' union, who was protesting the government's cutbacks, held up a placard that showed a picture of one of the government legislators with the caption, "A problem an abortion could have solved."[15] Not only does this show the depravity of a culture it shows the obvious numbing and callousness of how many, in the West, view abortion. But this should not be surprising considering the frequency with which it is practiced.

In America, one in five pregnancies end in abortion (some put it at one in four[16]), and of those, depending on the survey, 40–50 percent of the women claim to be Christian.[17] While this statistic may be troubling, I am not too convinced on the self-identifying language of the survey participants. Just because you identify as "Christian" does not make it so. For example, one 24-year-old unmarried woman named "Ashley," who self-identifies as evangelical, states, "Jesus and I are tight. And I don't think he is mad at all about me having an abortion."[18] To have such a cavalier perspective about the killing of an infant is troubling to say the least. We have lost what the holiness of God is and what God requires of those who claim to be his followers. Just the same, even if the number of abortions is lower for "Christians," the statistic is nonetheless disturbing and telling of where we are as a church and as a country. The fact that 20–25 percent of all pregnancies end in abortion prove that the old quip "safe, legal,

14. So, too, Hartline, "Kavanaugh."
15. Ontario Proud, *Facebook*.
16. Gushee, *Getting Marriage Right*, 29.
17. Kamitsuka, *Abortion*, 3; and Green, "New Survey."
18. This citation is from a 2008 Harvard Divinity School dissertation by Linda Ellison titled "Abortion and the Politics of God: Patient Narratives and Public Rhetoric in the American Abortion Debate," page 66 as cited in Kamitsuka, *Abortion*, 129n31. This dissertation analyzes 700 self-professing "conservative Christians" who have had abortions. Eighty percent of them never told anyone about the abortion (Ellison, p.64).

and rare," which was used by President Bill Clinton to promote abortion legislation, was a ruse from the start. Since 1973, Americans have aborted over 62 million babies, with Planned Parenthood accounting for almost nine million of those since 1970.[19] For many, although certainly not all, abortion is no longer something to be troubled about or frowned upon. Now women's abortions are championed and bragged about with proponents seeking no restrictions at any time. Of course, when the Enemy introduces sin into the world, he is never happy to leave it at the bare minimum: Satan wants chaos and sin to be championed as the norm. At the forefront of the march to preserve abortion as the law of the land are the second, third, and now, fourth-wave feminists.

Feminists and Abortion

During the first wave of feminism in the late nineteenth century, many of its primary leaders viewed abortion as horrific, murder, infanticide, and a blight on society.[20] Conversely, many feminists over the past six decades have been the primary voices advocating for abortion in the heated debate about pro-life and pro-choice decisions. No matter how one views the debate, it is evident that there is a push to demonize those who are pro-life as being anti-woman. The feminist mantra of "reproductive justice" (coined by twelve African American pro-choice women[21]), even espoused by some self-professing "Christians," undergirds the push for legalized abortion up to the point of birth.[22] Many pro-choice advocates not only want all laws and restrictions on abortion repealed, they want full access to free contraceptives, and they insist that the taxpayer (by repealing the Hyde Amendment) or health insurance should foot the bill.[23]

While I will address more of the logical disconnects of feminist support of abortion below—apart from my general revulsion with the whole premise of abortion—there are two troubling things I find about the feminist call for reproductive justice and their rejection of putative male

---

19. See the startling statistics related to abortion in real time at http://www.numberofabortions.com. As of 2020, the US alone is approaching 62 million aborted children since 1973, whereas the global count since 1980 is over 1.5 billion.

20. See comments by Brown, *Jezebel's War*, 68–69.

21. Peters, *Trust Women*, 189.

22. E.g., Peters, *Trust Women* (2018).

23. Peters, *Trust Women*, 194, 197.

The Mandate of Family and Procreation Part 2

"patriarchy" and "domination." First, I find it quite ironic that "justice" is denied to the unborn child, while feminists scream for justice for the one who is pregnant. The child is the innocent one and should receive the justice of their right to life. On the other hand, and generally speaking, the woman, except for rape (both inside and outside of marriage), is the one who knowingly makes a choice to have sexual relations with the possibility of a resulting pregnancy.[24] Failed birth control is not a viable defense for killing a baby in the womb. There was a reason why God mandated the covenant of marriage as the framework for sexual fulfillment. Second, the ones who were the most supportive of abortion in the 1960s were not women, it was college-educated men.[25] They knew that abortion would give them a freer rein in their pursuit and exploitation of women without the dangers of being forced to support an unplanned family. Proverbially speaking, women played right into men's hands. While I have cited Leon Kass elsewhere,[26] his point bears repeating. When addressing this very issue of female emancipation, Kass notes that "not surprisingly, the result was emancipated male predation and exploitation, as men were permitted easy conquest of women without responsibility and lasting intimacy."[27]

Since the rise of second-wave feminism, many of their arguments have been refined due to scientific and medical advancements. For example, when they argued for abortion prior to "viability" back in the 1960s and 70s, this meant they could abort their babies into the late second or early third trimester. However, since then medical procedures now can save premature babies born as early as twenty-two or twenty-three weeks of gestation. The more astute among them realized that arguing for abortion based upon viability could quickly come back to haunt them if medical procedures were to develop whereby a child could survive outside of the womb in the second or even first trimester. This may sound like science fiction, but we have no idea how medical procedures will advance over the next century. Feminists have anticipated this possibility as well.

Considering these matters, arguments based upon more philosophical premises have begun to take over the abortion debate among feminists. For example, arguments like a woman's right not to extend "hospitality" to the "embryonic guest" in her womb is one of the more

---

24. So, too, Sider, *Completely Pro-Life*, 42–44.
25. Blake, "Abortion," 548.
26. Peterson, "Genesis Mandates," 129.
27. Kass, "Dinah," 38.

recent troubling arguments.[28] Based upon this line of thinking, it is fine to turn down "hospitality" to the unborn child if it does not suit the woman. In these cases, a woman's self-determination overrules the life of her child in utero. I find this a strange way of looking at a pregnancy especially considering the requirement, whether Christian or not, to extend hospitality to the needy. For the "woke" crowd, social justice is a central tenet of their thinking. This apparently does not apply to the unborn. But then nothing surprises me when society decides to reject such a basic mandate given by God.

Another disturbing feminist argument for abortion is that a woman, once pregnant, has the right, as a mother, to decide whether to end her mothering responsibilities "early" by killing her child in utero. Adoption is not an option for those holding this perspective because it would still mean that the woman would be a "mother" to a child "somewhere in the world." The only viable option to remove any mothering responsibilities would be to kill her child before birth.[29] Instead of rearranging her own life entirely by carrying the child to term, raising the child, and being a mother to it, she can choose simply to cut the whole process short.[30] I will return to this in a moment.

Finally, as noted above, the argument for "reproductive justice" is often touted as a "moral good" when it comes to making the "courageous" choice to abort a child in the face of objections from "bullies and hate-mongers who seek to shame" a woman for killing her child.[31] The language of "reproductive justice," however, is nothing more than an effort to remove the focus from what abortion truly is—the death of a child—in favor of focusing on every other possible facet related to a woman's life when considering whether to birth a child. Among other issues, this can include a mother's mental state, socio-economic status, family support, concerns with domestic violence, and poverty.[32] While all of these are important, these concerns do not diminish the reality that a child's life is being terminated. These issues are as old as time and unlike in an earlier era, most Western societies have excellent social-safety nets,

---

28. E.g., Gray, "Original Habitation," 79, 85.
29. Reader, "Abortion," 143–44.
30. See more in Kamitsuka, *Abortion*, 127–38.
31. Peters, *Trust Women*, 206.
32. So, Peters, *Trust Women*, esp. 190, 206.

not to mention the option of adoption.[33] Another way proponents of this view marginalize the value of the unborn child is to state that getting pregnant is not a blessing of God, it is mere biology. If bearing children is such a blessing, then why does God allow women to be infertile? A God who would allow this is capricious and unloving. From this conclusion, it allows them to focus on a woman's "sexuality" and sexual enjoyment as being God's primary blessing as opposed to getting pregnant.[34] Apart from the clear biblical teaching against such assertions (e.g., getting pregnant *was* a blessing from God; cf. Gen 4:1; 29:31; 30:22), the problems of infertility or other reproductive issues do not mean God is not just or good.[35] It simply shows that we live in a post-fall world.[36] Moreover, such positions seem to advocate for the use of sex outside the confines of marriage. Simply put, this argument only muddies the water to disguise what is truly at stake.

Though I could go on, these types of arguments smack of the naturalistic and God-rejecting education system and culture, which has exploded over the past century and a half. At the heart of many of these arguments is the assertion that the mother is the "creator" of life and therefore has the moral position to choose to allow a child to live or die: in this case, the mother takes on the role of God.[37] Not surprisingly, those who hold this position recognize that infanticide is a natural outworking of this perspective.[38]

When it comes to the honest and ugly truth of what abortion is, professor emeritus, Margaret D. Kamitsuka of Oberlin College, states plainly, "abortion must be starkly defined morally as a decision to kill a living being in utero—a momentous decision that only the gestating mother has the authority to make."[39] Surprisingly, Kamitsuka turns around in the next paragraph and repudiates anyone who would challenge such a decision made by a mother. Yet, by her own definition, abortion is taking

---

33. See the discussion of Gardner, *Abortion*, 155–66.
34. Peters, *Trust Women*, 202–3.
35. Peters, *Trust Women*, 202.
36. See discussion by Curley and Peterson, "Eve's Curse Revisited," 1–16.
37. So, Reader, "Abortion," 144. While they would no doubt shy away from the language of being "God," this is in essence what they have become in determining the life and death status of their child.
38. Reader, "Abortion," 145–48.
39. Kamitsuka, *Abortion*, 131. I will engage with Kamitsuka's biblical arguments in my next chapter.

a life. For Kamitsuka, the real issue is the question of when personhood begins and how one views the sacredness of embryonic life. On the latter, she acknowledges that life is to be valued at any stage in the pregnancy; however, she rejects personhood language for the unborn child, and thus accepts abortion at any point "whether early or late in the pregnancy."[40] Personhood appears to start with live birth for Kamitsuka.[41]

On the face of it, this stance is simply abhorrent to most logical and morally attuned persons. While Kamitsuka may argue for a mother's, as opposed to the state's right to end a life in the womb,[42] the reality is Kamitsuka's stance embraces a rejection of God's sovereignty over life and her too one-sided reliance on the fallenness of humanity. For her, Christian mothers who abort are sinners like anyone else and should not be villainized. While I would agree with this last assertion, this does not give a person a pass to murder an unborn child any more than it gives a mother the right to murder her child a day after birth. The state is put in place and mandated by God, whether those in power realize it or not, to protect the innocent and thwart lawlessness and anarchy (Rom 13:1–3; 1 Peter 2:13–15; cf. Gen 9:6). Thus, a mother does not have the right to end life, only God does, or the state in capital offences.

The push of radical abortion practices is evidence of the complete fallenness of humanity and our depraved nature as God's mandates and gift of life are pushed to the side in the name of expedience. When mothers (or fathers) can make a state-sponsored decision to end their baby's life out of expediency, or for any other reason, then we have crossed a moral threshold from which it is hard to return. I find it hard to read feminist pro-choice arguments, which callously discuss when it is okay to kill an unborn baby, or as some put it, a "potential child."[43] To me, these writers reduce the discussion of life and death for these innocent children to pure semantics on when, or if, an unborn child is a person. In an attempt to whitewash the barbaric reality of abortion, they argue using philosophical and moral elitism and doublespeak which seems more like hairsplitting and smacks of similar reasoning and sanitized and sterile language used by the likes of the notorious Josef Mengele of the Third Reich. Interestingly, Mengele also studied racial ideology during

---

40. Kamitsuka, *Abortion*, 138, cf. 141, 211–12.
41. Kamitsuka, *Abortion*, 151–53.
42. Kamitsuka, *Abortion*, 153.
43. Peters, *Trust Women*, 199.

his philosophy degree similar to the founder of Planned Parenthood, Margaret Sanger.

Disturbing trends connecting race and abortion are not fictitious. In New York city, for example, more African American babies are aborted than are born! And overall, almost forty percent of all African American babies are aborted; this is nothing less than a direct attack on the African American community by the Enemy.[44]

Gender selection is also directly tied to abortion practices. In this regard, the sad irony is that feminists refuse to acknowledge that the legalization of abortion has been an attack on females. In many countries such as India and China, female babies are aborted at a much higher rate than males thus perpetuating feminists' so-called problem of "male dominance." As such, male dominance, at least numerically, is literal because of a loss of female babies to abortion. Take for example China's one-child policy. After a generation of the policy being the law of the land, the Chinese government had to reverse its decision because of the plummeting birthrate of female children. And in just one city in India, Bombay, a review of eight thousand abortions showed all but one were females.[45] This type of gender selection is not just happening in distant cultural settings, it is also happening in America.[46] Put differently, the putative "war on women" in many cases is being waged by women themselves!

This putative war on women is also perpetuated by feminists' rejection of adoption as a viable option to killing an unborn child. As a "sisterhood of women" (feminists' terminology) one would expect them to come to the aid of infertile women through adoption, but this is not the case. From a feminist perspective, if a woman is a lesbian then adoption is a good thing, but if you are a heterosexual woman, especially a married one, desiring to adopt a newborn, you are unimportant to their cause.[47] Such radical positions against the unborn help to explain why same-sex marriage is praised by so many in the feminist camp. No children can come from such unions unless specific unnatural steps are taken, or adoption is an option.[48] Again, I am not speaking of the unfortunate circumstances of a young woman who finds herself pregnant for the first

---

44. So, Brown, *Jezebel's War*, 108–9.
45. Watkins, *New Absolutes*, 165.
46. Sider, *Completely Pro-Life*, 42; and Watkins, *New Absolutes*, 165.
47. Watkins, *New Absolutes*, 165.
48. Watkins, *New Absolutes*, 169.

time and is scared to death of what her parents and family will think or do. I am speaking of the growing number of militant feminist voices who revel in their abortions and their support for this industry of death. What is really at the heart of their abortion drive is a rejection of God's mandate to procreate and be mothers themselves. This rejection of God's mandate is troubling at so many levels not the least of which is Western culture's rejection of the inherent value of an unborn child and the clear evidence that these precious children are indeed persons with a soul.

In this regard, it is not surprising that feminists, especially those who declare themselves to be "Christians," never take note of books like *Heaven is for Real*, which directly address the issue of the plight of a child who dies in the womb. This could be due to their ignorance of the existence of these types of books or simply due to a rejection of the premise.[49] This specific book details four-year-old Colton Burpo's experience of going to heaven while at the point of death in an emergency room. While in heaven, Colton met his sister. Through the intense prayers of his father, Colton survived his emergency room ordeal. In one chapter, Colton's father relates an account of his son's revelation to his mother that he had two sisters.[50] In reality, Colton's mom had only one *living* daughter, Cassie. Colton went on to tell his mother how one of her daughters had "died in her tummy." While his mom had never known the sex of her miscarried child, her son Colton described her to his mother. He also told her how his sister had met him in heaven and would not stop hugging him. When he asked his sister her name, she told him that her mom and dad had not named her, which was true. Colton's mom had also never told their young son about the earlier loss of their baby. If a few more pro-abortion writers would read *Heaven is for Real* perhaps they would view abortion differently.

Now while some may see this as anecdotal, completely unprovable, and fanciful, the truth is that Jesus—speaking the words of Abraham—warned that even if someone should return from the dead, people would not believe (Luke 16:31). Here a child testified to the reality that

---

49. Kamitsuka (*Abortion*, 219, 223n104) seems to reject the premise that aborted children go to heaven. I was also somewhat surprised to find a similar ambivalence to the plight of miscarried or aborted children by evangelical OT scholar Tremper Longman III. In a recent book, he asks the question of whether we will be reunited with a miscarried child in heaven, but then does not answer it. He seems to be presenting a rhetorical question with an assumed "no" response (*Bible and the Ballot*, 148).

50. See Burpo and Vincent, *Heaven is For Real*, 93–97.

miscarried children are in heaven. If this is the case, can we honestly say that unborn children are not persons? This should be the death knell to the abortion debate especially for believers, but I guess you would have to believe in the supernatural. The cold hard truth is that abortion is the killing of an innocent child in the womb. For those who have experienced an abortion, and are honest, they would tell you it is not as harmless as we have been led to believe by abortion advocates.

The Psychological Toll of Abortion

Despite the sentiments of the insensitive "Shout-Your-Abortion" movement, the dirty ugly secret about those who abort their children is that many times it does not bring peace or normalcy to their lives. I can personally attest to the fact that a friend of mine who had an abortion struggled with the decision for the rest of her life. Often women who abort feel guilt and shame to the point, in some cases, of wanting to kill themselves, while others turn to advocacy for abortion through feminist groups in an effort to try and make abortion "right" so that they will not feel so much guilt.[51] It is telling that 50–70 percent of relationships end after an abortion.[52] The self-loathing and guilt is understandable.[53] What woman in their right mind would not ponder the life they have taken? Now to be sure, there certainly are some, who fall into the category, as the Bible says, of having their conscience seared by a hot iron (1 Tim 4:2).[54] For example, one Reddit user on the "Child Free" forum bragged about the abortion of her twin babies this way:

> I am on my way to Planned Parenthood to purge the two parasites that somehow implanted into my uterus despite me being on the pill. I can't [explicative] wait to stop being nauseous and throwing up and being unable to keep water down. I can't wait to be rid of this hyperemesis gravidarum that destroyed my Christmas and ruined my [New Year's Eve] and is ruining my life. I can't [explicative] wait to be done with the anxiety of knowing these things are in my uterus and knowing that I will not have to birth dribbling horror goblins, will not have

---

51. Watkins, *New Absolutes*, 157–60; Patterson and Kim, *The Day America Told the Truth*, 33; and Sider, *Completely Pro-Life*, 40–41, 50.

52. Watkins, *New Absolutes*, 160.

53. See the numerous such testimonies in Brown, *Jezebel's War*, 72–73.

54. See also Brown, *Jezebel's War*, 62–63, 69–72.

disgusting leaking [breasts], will not go home from the hospital in a nappy and with a stitched [sic] up vagina, I will not have post-partum depression or be left disfigured with stretch-marks. My relationship with my [significant other] will not be ruined. I am dedicating this double fetus purge to the anti-choice movement because no matter how hard you try, you will not force us to be your handmaids. HAPPY 2020![55]

Such rhetoric is the reason why pro-life advocates shudder at the callousness of the pro-choice movement. Another disturbing trend is the call for aborting boy babies, which is hailed by radical feminists.[56] It is not a stretch to recognize the long-term psychological suffering that such approaches to procreation will have on young boys as they are reared in such a hostile environment. As I have noted before, the #MeToo movement has all the markings of suppressing anything masculine that the radicals may deem unworthy of their standards. Again, this is a rejection of how God created male and female, a point to which I will return in a later chapter.

God has given women the innate desire to protect their children. The above discussion does not even take into consideration the psychological toll that abortion can have on minor children in the family. Many young children, who learn of their mother's decision to abort a baby, can question if their mother loves *them*.[57] Because of the moral bankruptcy of Western culture and the rejection of the Genesis mandates, specifically those dealing with sexual abstinence, the sacredness of the marriage bed, and the natural outcome of building families, we are witnessing traumatic side effects from abortion. God knew what he was doing when he established marriage as the place for sexual fulfillment and enjoyment. And even married women who abort are not exempt from the trauma that can follow such a radical decision. We all must face the fact that dismembering and "evacuating" a child from the womb is a gruesome occurrence that should never be normalized in civilized societies as it is today. Yet, the gruesomeness and abhorrent nature of abortion is not just what happens in the procedure itself it is also what happens in its aftermath.

---

55. As cited by Shiver, "Reddit."
56. Pavlich, "Baby Boys."
57. Gardner, *Abortion*, 159.

The Gruesome Reality of Abortion

For anyone following the news over the past few years, the abortion debate became front and center when undercover videos of Planned Parenthood workers and administrators emerged in which they detailed the harvesting and sale of the body parts of aborted babies.[58] The medical use of tissue and organs from aborted babies is not just disturbing, it is downright barbaric to most civilized individuals. What is often suppressed in the abortion discussion is the fact that from the earliest days of the abortion industry, heinous acts were undertaken on living aborted fetuses and unborn babies that were handicapped all in the name of science.[59] And the complete disrespect for life perpetrated by the abortion industry was on full display when thousands of aborted babies were found stored in a deceased Illinois abortion doctor's home.[60] This type of grotesque treatment of the unborn exemplifies the heinous nature of the abortion industry.

Other heinous acts associated with this ungodly practice is the vile procedure of partial-birth abortion (scientifically called D&X and D&E). This involves partially delivering a baby feet-first. While the baby's head is still in the birth canal, the abortionist drives a sharp instrument into the baby's skull and sucks out their brain. If this is not the height of barbarism I do not know what is. Pro-choice advocates scoff at pro-life proponents when this practice is brought up insisting that this is only used to "save the life of the mother" or to terminate the life of a "severely deformed child." Let me be clear, they are spewing the abortion industry's propaganda. The reality is just the opposite. When I was reading the testimonies from nurses who have been involved in this process, it literally made me weep having just witnessed the birth of my own daughter one day earlier. Testimonies from doctors and nurses who have worked in these death mills acknowledge that most of these types of abortions are performed on perfectly healthy children or in some cases, on children with nothing more than a cleft palate or a child with down syndrome.[61] And today as I write this chapter Planned Parenthood is being

---

58. Brown, "Planned Parenthood."

59. See Sider, *Completely Pro-Life*, 38–40, 66.

60. Betz, "Fetuses."

61. Watkins, *New Absolutes*, 84–85. See also Brown, *Jezebel's War*, 66–67; and Rovner, "'Partial-Birth Abortion.'"

investigated for harvesting tissue and organs from living aborted babies.[62] Something needs to be done. Allowing the radical Left to trample the precious lives of the unborn is something that every believer should be ready and willing to stop. But again, this takes the political will to act. It also requires making sure we elect God-fearing politicians who will not bend to the pressure of the abortion industry. Returning to the undercover videos of Planned Parenthood workers, these people were not brought to justice for their actions, instead, the abortion industry brough the full weight of the pro-choice government and judicial system against the whistleblowers (see for example Kamala Harris's involvement in the above case[63]). The ones exposing the atrocities of Planned Parenthood were the focus of reviling hate, not the ones who truly deserved to be reviled and imprisoned. Again, this shows the ungodly "marriage" of the abortion industry with political operatives.

Abortion and Politics

As noted above, the state of the abortion discussion is so volatile in America that sitting senators are now threatening Supreme Court justices that if they do not toe the line then there will be repercussions (what those repercussions are was not made clear).[64] And Planned Parenthood president, Cecile Richards, insists that Democrats must be pro-choice and that the party should not support pro-life candidates even though polls show that approximately one quarter of Democrats are pro-life.[65] The reality is that the position of Richards is not a one off, it is actually becoming the dominant position of the Democratic party, a party that has moved far away from the standards of even twenty or thirty years ago.

The push for reigning in abortion and its barbaric practices has been ongoing in the political arena. While the US Congress tried to outlaw the barbaric practice of partial birth abortion, President Bill Clinton vetoed the legislation in November 1995.[66] In 2003, under President George W. Bush, the practice was outlawed and subsequently upheld in a Supreme Court challenge in the 2007 case, *Gonzales v. Carhart*. When

62. Dorman, "Testimony."
63. St. John, "Harris."
64. Re, "Rebuke."
65. Ertelt, "Cecile Richards."
66. Watkins, *New Absolutes*, 84.

The Mandate of Family and Procreation Part 2

the 2018 midterm elections flipped a number of state legislatures to the Democrats, several of these Democrat-run states, with their newly acquired majorities in state houses and senates, rushed through extreme abortion bills that allowed for abortion up to the point of delivery. When this type of bill was passed in New York in early 2019 (and yes, I have read it), the politicians cheered and lit up the One World Trade Center in pink.[67] In one well-known case related to proposed legislation on late-term abortion, the governor of Virginia, a doctor himself, casually talked about what to do with a child who survived an abortion. He plainly stated that the mother and the child would be "kept comfortable" until a decision could be made about the future/life of the child. What he was proposing is nothing short of infanticide. While some came to the governor's defense, the reality of what was being proposed became crystal clear during the debate period in the Virginia Congress. When asked point blank what the proposed legislation allowed, the Democrat congress woman, Kathy Tran, who proposed the HB 2491 bill, admitted that a child could in fact be killed at any point even when the mother was dilating.[68] In this case, because of a lack of Republican support, the bill was tabled. These laws are so vile, one should be appalled. What this also shows is the close connection of the abortion issue and political parties.

Even so-called news outlets are on the side of abortion advocates doing everything in their power to destigmatize abortion and the barbarism that accompanies it, especially when a baby survives an abortion. The proposed federal law known as the Born-Alive Abortion Survivors Protection Act has been mocked and downplayed in an effort to stop the bill. Radical pro-choice senators and the left-leaning media attempt to paint the bill as restricting a woman's right to choose, when in reality it is a bill to stop infanticide after a botched abortion.[69] As with the scholarly debate about when a baby becomes a person, the liberal media[70] has joined in the madness and are suggesting that a fetus that survives an abortion is not a baby like a newborn baby. Again, this is doublespeak and a dumbing down of our senses about what abortion actually is. Note especially the use of the acronym POC for "Product of Conception" for post-abortion babies often used in tissue harvesting.

---

67. See also comments by Brown, *Jezebel's War*, 66.
68. North, "Controversy."
69. Schow, "CNN."
70. See Grudem, *Politics*, 555–71.

This desensitizing of America and the use of euphemistic terminology is the same as the abortion lobby's rejection of state-sponsored heartbeat bills. Opponents state that a baby's heartbeat in the womb is nothing more than "embryonic pulsing" or "fetal pole cardiac activity."[71] We have reached a sad day in America when a baby born alive is left to die of exposure due to lack of medical care simply because the mother and doctor say it is okay. I have a warning for America in this case: God will judge us! God cares about how we treat our children and the most vulnerable in our societies. In chapter 16 of his book, Ezekiel, a prophet of the exile, rejected the practice of allowing children to die from exposure by presenting God as saving and caring for an exposed female infant, a metaphor for Israel. Exodus also relates God's harsh treatment of the Egyptians and Pharaoh who were forcing Israelite mothers to kill their male children by throwing them in the Nile (Exod 1:22). God in turn killed the Egyptians' firstborn children (Exodus 12). Based upon biblical precedent, killing children will not go unpunished. Where is the church's voice on this issue?

Although I will address this in more detail in my last chapter, the reality is that there is a political divide between left-leaning evangelicals and conservatives on this issue. While many evangelicals tend to vote Republican due to issues of abortion and sexual ethics, liberal evangelicals tend to lean Democrat. They may identify as "pro-life" and they may be sympathetic to the concerns of pro-life advocates, but they choose to focus their "pro-life" concerns elsewhere, namely, on social issues (e.g., poverty, race issues, and war).[72] I will be addressing the scriptural problems with this position in my next chapter. This divide is exacerbated by the fact that many Christians simply find the acceptance and/or the turning of a blind eye to the atrocity of abortion, beyond what can be accepted by a believing Christian. Both sides may think that they are reflecting the values of Jesus, and personally they may be doing so, but the reality is that neither party is doing what needs to be done to stop the abortion madness. If 49 percent of white evangelicals and 52 percent of Christian African Americans now support abortion legislation, as I noted above, then the church has become part of the problem. As we will see in the next chapter, the question of "What would Jesus do?" is important in this case. He would follow the Bible and do everything in his power to stop the senseless slaughter of the

---

71. Schow, "CNN."
72. Gushee, *Still Christian*, 55–56.

innocent. This should be the driving factor behind one's politics and faith not some nebulous mantra of "I support life from the womb to the tomb." Indeed, since I started editing this chapter two days ago, close to 5,000 babies were aborted in America alone. I know of no other social concern upheld by left-leaning evangelicals that has this staggering death rate. This is why conservative Christians are up in arms.

Conclusion

On the issue of abortion and the rejection of God's mandate to procreate, I readily agree with John MacArthur when he states plainly that America's heinous crime of murdering the most "defenseless and harmless of people created in God's image will not escape His eventual punishment."[73] Instead of repentance for such heinous sins, Western culture and its social activists have remade society in their image,[74] and in doing so, have brought America and society in general to the brink of absolute chaos. The very foundations of God's plan for society are reviled and rejected while profane machinations of humanity are viewed as blessed and good. Some are now trying to justify abortion as pleasing to God and not a sin of which they need to repent.[75] This is a dangerous position to take. We live in a time that Isaiah the prophet foresaw when he declared, "Woe unto those who call evil good and good evil and replace darkness for light and light for darkness" (Isa 5:20a; my translation). Also, Paul gave a clear warning about this type of thinking when he said, "See to it that no one takes you captive through philosophy and empty deception, according to the tradition of men, according to the elementary principles of the world, rather than according to Christ" (Col 2:8; NASB).

It is one thing to hold a pro-choice position for yourself, but when you try to teach others through publications, sermons, and classroom settings that murder is fine, then the words of James certainly ring true:

73. MacArthur, *Why Government Can't Save You*, 50.

74. Watkins, *New Absolutes*, 170.

75. Kamitsuka, *Abortion*, 207–13. Kamitsuka (pp.202–7) attempts to justify the killing of unwanted children based upon a few Medieval women's accounts of seeking to serve God by abandoning their own children, even newborns. Many of these mystics supposedly had "visions" from Jesus and angels telling them it was fine to do so. I cannot begin to stress the theological and biblical problems with such a conclusion. God does not contradict his Word. Due to this fact, I would challenge from whence these putative "visions" came.

"Not many of you should become teachers, my fellow believers, because you know that we who teach will be judged more strictly" (James 3:1; NIV). Even though many have convinced themselves that abortion is not murder,[76] when the Bible says you shall not murder (Exod 20:13)—especially the innocent and righteous (Exod 23:7a)—we had best take note of God's prohibitions for God does not acquit the guilty (Exod 23:7b). As many have noted, you can say you do not believe in gravity but that does not change the fact that it exists. And you can say something is not sin or murder, but that does not mean that you are right. Simply saying it does not make it so. I cannot help but recall the words of Jesus to his followers when they tried to stop children from coming near Jesus. Jesus said, "allow the children to come unto me and do not stop them for such is the Kingdom of heaven" (Matt 19:14; my paraphrase). Furthermore, he gave a stern warning to those who would offend children or hurt them. Jesus said it would be better for that person to put a millstone around their neck and be drowned in the sea (Matt 18:6). He continues, "Woe to the world because of *its* stumbling blocks! For it is inevitable that stumbling blocks come; but woe to that man through whom the stumbling block comes!" (Matt 18:7; NASB). This is a stark reminder that God views children in a special way. The Bible is clear on this fact. The Bible also supports an anti-abortion stance. It is to this topic that I now turn.

---

76. Kamitsuka, *Abortion*, 210–11.

Chapter 8

The Mandate of Family and Procreation Part 3

Procreation—Abortion and the Bible

> On every point, my research tells me, pro-life claims are biblically weak, conceptually misleading, theologically mistaken, and even dangerous.[1]

THIS COMMENT BY MARGARET D. Kamitsuka appears in one of the more recent books dealing with abortion from a "Christian" perspective. As a biblical scholar, I am immediately drawn to the conclusion that *someone* is obviously wrong. Either I, and many other biblical scholars, have missed the mark, or Kamitsuka is the one doing the "misleading." What I have found is that the term "dangerous" should not be used for some so-called misinterpretation of Scripture, but rather should be applied to the plight of the unborn child: they are the ones dying!

In the last chapter I looked at the cultural and political influences on the issue of abortion. In this chapter, I will examine what the biblical arguments are when dealing with abortion. Is Kamitsuka correct to say that the arguments are "biblically weak"? I must preface this discussion by noting that entire books have been written on this one issue, and I certainly cannot do justice to this topic in a few short pages. From the

---

1. Kamitsuka, *Abortion*, 1.

beginning of the debate in the mid-twentieth century moving forward, abortion has been addressed at almost every level, by biblical scholars and theologians alike.[2] Nevertheless, in light of the ongoing discussion on the Genesis mandates, it is clear that many scholars have made the truthfulness of God's mandates appear as though they are not applicable to, or in sync with, today's "evolved" and enlightened culture. From the outset of the Bible it is obvious where God's heart lies when it comes to the mandate of procreation: God is for it and to suggest that God is okay with abortion is to miss the overall tenor of Scripture.

That said, in this chapter I will examine two key concepts. First, I will examine the biblical passages that are often brought to bear on the abortion discussion. I will allow you, the reader, to decide if they are as "biblically weak" as Kamitsuka suggests. Second, I will look at how many Christians, especially those within evangelicalism, have seemingly justified their silence on this important issue. In the discussion that follows I will interact with two of the more recent works that have in some way addressed this topic, one from a mainline perspective (Margaret D. Kamitsuka, *Abortion and the Christian Tradition*, 2019) and one from an evangelical worldview (Tremper Longman III, *The Bible and the Ballot*, 2020).

Abortion and Scripture

To begin, I have limited my discussion only to texts dealing with preborn children. If I were to include all the texts related to child sacrifice it would be overwhelming. Suffice it to say that if God was vehemently opposed to the killing of one's newborn children during the worship of false gods, like that practiced in the worship of the pagan deity Moloch (Lev 18:21; 20:2–5; 2 Kgs 23:10; Jer 32:35), then you can be assured that God is not in favor of killing them in the womb.[3] In the discussion that follows I will address specific texts at some points while grouping others together that have similar themes related to the topic in question. This is not meant to be a comprehensive listing but rather an overview focusing on some of the more important texts, which in some way deals with the abortion discussion.

---

2. See Barth, *Church Dogmatics*, III.4, 415; Gardner, *Abortion* (1972); and Waltke, "Reflections," 3–13. I strongly disagree with Gardner's suggestion that it is okay for Christians to get abortions (p.273).

3. See the heart-rending discussion by Brown, *Jezebel's War*, 62–64.

The Mandate of Family and Procreation Part 3

Genesis 1:27

Up to this point we have been examining the clearly defined mandates of God as presented in the opening two chapters of Genesis. It should come as no surprise that one of the most heated modern discussions about abortion comes from these opening chapters, namely, God's comment that humanity is made in the image of God, what is often referred to as the *imago dei*. Pro-choice proponents argue that the opening two chapters of Genesis cannot be used for the abortion discussion because of the scholarly confusion on what constitutes the image of God in people, especially an unborn child.[4] It is no secret that pro-choice advocates have long argued for the ability to define the unborn child's "humanness" however they see fit.[5] These types of arguments are not based upon solid exegesis but rather flimsy assertions and misconceptions of what the image of God actually entails.

For centuries Christians have debated what the image of God means, with some simply stating humans are valuable because God says so, that is, it is part of "God's rights" to make such a declaration.[6] This would mean that humans have value because God extends those rights to his creation. One can hear the echoes of this concept in the opening lines of the Declaration of Independence: "We hold these truths to be self-evident, that all men are created equal, that they are endowed by their Creator with certain unalienable Rights, that among these are Life, Liberty and the pursuit of Happiness." The simple fact that God declares that humans have value and "rights" is indeed true, but this does not get to the heart of what it means to be made in the image of God. There is something more tangible, and basic, implied in the text of Scripture and applies to all human life whether one believes in God or not.

A straightforward reading of Genesis, especially 1:27 and 9:6, seems to imply that the image of God is the eternal nature of humans versus the finite nature of all other creatures. I will return to this in a minute. Now obviously there are many things that play into the functional aspects of the image of God in humans (e.g., our creative abilities through procreation;

---

4. Kamitsuka, *Abortion*, 52–59.

5. See the troubling statements by professor of biology, Hardin, "Abortion," as noted by Waltke, "Reflections," 5–6.

6. Gushee, *The Sacredness of Human Life*, 39–54 at 46, 52. See also Sider, *Completely Pro-Life*, 48–49; and Waltke, "Reflections," 3–13.

our mandate to have dominion;[7] our innate understanding of morality [cf. Rom 1]; and our relational capabilities[8]) but this does not answer the most challenging question according to pro-choice advocates. How can an unborn child fulfill or meet any of these requirements when they are nothing more than a "blob" of cells (using pro-choice language) in the earliest stages of gestation? *If* these concepts are used to define the image of God, then their arguments may have merit. However, even a basic application of some of these proposed definitions creates problems for pro-choice advocates at the most basic level. For example, if part of the meaning of bearing the image of God has to do with our creative ability, that is, our ability to procreate, then pro-choice advocates not only reject this aspect of the image of God for themselves, they remove this possibility from the unborn by ending their lives. In fact, the potential to enact any of these suggested definitions of the image of God would be removed from the unborn child by the selfish actions of the mother. While some may protest such a simplistic understanding of the image of God, there is a more legitimate rebuttal of the pro-choice position when dealing with the image-of-God question.

As noted in the previous paragraph, all these arguments fall short because they fail to consider that all humans have eternal souls. Based upon the consistent presentation of Scripture regarding human responsibility before God and concern for our *eternal* souls (Eccl 3:11; Matt 10:28; 1 Thess 5:23), I conclude that our *eternality* is what it means to be made in the image of God. Thus, because of the eternality of all human life, no matter at what juncture of development, to end that life is an afront to God.[9] This is in keeping with God's requirement of the death penalty for anyone who takes the life of a person because they are made in the image of God (Gen 9:6). The arguments of when a person gains a soul is something that cannot be known with certainty, but based upon our discussion concerning the presence of miscarried children in heaven (see previous chapter), it is best to err on the side of caution and reject abortion on its face. And few Christians would disagree that once a baby is viable (23–24 weeks) they certainly would be considered persons with a soul. Yet even with viability at this early stage of gestation, many

---

7. So, Song, *Covenant and Calling*, 16–17.
8. So, Balswick and Balswick, *Authentic Human Sexuality*, 76–78.
9. See also Waltke, "Reflections," 7–10; and Sider, *Completely Pro-Life*, 49.

The Mandate of Family and Procreation Part 3

pro-choice advocates still push for the "right" to kill unborn *viable* babies.[10] As we will see, the value of preborn children is only strengthened as one examines more of the biblical texts.

Genesis 1:28; 2:24; 9:1, 7 and Genealogies

I have already stressed the importance of these texts throughout so I will only summarize my findings up to this point. The fact that God's mandate included the command to procreate flies in the face of a pro-choice position from the start. It pushes the bounds of credulity to suggest that God would be okay with killing a baby in the womb simply because it was "unplanned" or a "mistake." What is more, God's plan for procreation is implicit in the numerous genealogies listed throughout Genesis and beyond.[11]

Genesis 25:23 et al

One of the dominant textual arguments used in support of the value of the preborn is God's and other authors' references to babies in their mother's womb. Many of these texts prophesy of these children's calling or purpose in life (Gen 25:23//Rom 9; Isa 49:1; Jer 1:5; Pss 71:6; 119:73; 139:13, 16; Luke 1:41; Gal 1:15; cf. Isa 44:24; Job 10:11; etc.). In Genesis, the classic example is God's prophetic word to Rebekah concerning the futures of her twin boys, Jacob and Esau. Kamitsuka tries to downplay these numerous passages by arguing that just because some preborn children may be called and predestined to be leaders does not mean that all children are.[12] She also downplays the poetic genre form of some of the passages while overemphasizing the theological implications of the pre-existence of souls prior to conception. In the latter case, she argues that the part of the passage from Jeremiah 1:5 which states "Before I formed you in the womb I knew you, And before you were born I consecrated you..." (NASB) implies the pre-existence of souls and therefore is theologically problematic.

I cannot begin to unpack the numerous problems with these lines of argumentation, but I will point out the major logical fallacies with these positions. First, Kamitsuka is not convincing to suggest that just

---

10. Kamitsuka, *Abortion*, 154.
11. Peterson, "Genesis Mandates," 128.
12. Kamitsuka, *Abortion*, 63–69.

because most people are not called to some prophetic or special ministry that they can be eliminated in the womb. This is pure nonsense. For one thing, one could just as easily argue that we are all "called" to spread the Gospel (Matt 28:19; Mark 16:15) even though many may refuse to do so (John 3:16; Matt 7:13–14). Second, Kamitsuka quickly jumps over the text dealing with John the Baptist's and Jesus' unborn status which clearly undermines her position. While John the Baptist was still in the womb, he was aware of the presence of the Son of God, who was in Mary's womb (Luke 1:41) and was filled with the Holy Spirit in utero (Luke 1:15). This certainly sounds like God cares about and can act upon the unborn. Third, just because a text is poetic does not mean it is not true or real. Metaphors and poetic language still carry meaning and in each case it is clear that the unborn have value.[13] If the genre form is the criteria for reality or legitimacy, most of the prophetic books, which contain poetic content, would be eliminated. Fourth, even though there may only be a few passages dealing with God's interaction with the unborn, this does not mean that we should not take them seriously. Frequency is not a criterion for legitimating any theory, especially one so vital to the life and death of the unborn. As the inspired text, even if the Bible states/prescribes something only once it still makes it binding, especially if it is directed to all people or is in a universal context. Fifth, Kamitsuka's suggestion that when pro-life scholars cite Jeremiah 1:5 they are implying that they believe in the pre-existence of souls as advocated by Origen is no more than a strawman argument. No one of sound theological thinking would adhere to this heresy. She neither allows for the poetic license of Jeremiah, nor the language of foreknowledge in God's greater plans, neither of which require a belief in the pre-existence of souls.[14] What cannot be denied is the clear, and acknowledged, medical reality that life does in fact begin at conception.[15] Finally, despite her claims otherwise, it is up to Kamitsuka to prove her point that God is okay with aborting children in the womb, a point at which she certainly fails. Simply to point out supposed weaknesses in scholarly *interpretations* of the Text does not

---

13. So, too, Longman, *Bible and the Ballot*, 146–47.

14. This heresy stems back to the church father, Origen (185–253 CE). Put simply, he proposed that there was a "berry bucket" of souls from which God chooses as children are born. This is unbiblical and theologically problematic. At its heart, it takes away from the creative process in procreation and it smacks of reincarnation.

15. Sider, *Completely Pro-Life*, 48.

in turn open the door for the killing of innocent unborn children at any stage in their development.

Exodus 21:22–25

This text has been discussed *ad nauseum* with no solid conclusion or consensus.[16] It deals with a situation where a pregnant woman is hit during a fight between two other people and gives premature birth as a result. It falls within the Covenant Code or legal portion of Exodus. As law, it fits the genre of other ancient Near Eastern law codes. Even though most law codes had no provisions for or against abortion, one legal code does stand out as unique. The Middle Assyrian Laws (MAL A §§50–53 ca.1400 BCE) mandated the death penalty for voluntary abortion.[17] Already one can assume that if a pagan empire valued unborn life, the God of Israel and all humanity would have valued the unborn no less.

That said, here in Exodus 21, there is uncertainty about whether the injury to the woman is accidental or purposeful. Because the killing of a mother or her child in this case elicited the death penalty, some argue that it appears that the striking of the woman was not accidental because killing someone accidentally was considered manslaughter and was not punishable by death (Exod 21:13; Num 35:9–15, 22–29).[18] If it was an accident, and the child was premature or miscarried, then the punishment was a fine to be paid to the father (Exod 21:22). Again, this does not mean the author devalued the life of the unborn. As just noted, accidental killing did not require the death penalty. On the other hand, if it was an accident and God required the death penalty—if either the mother or the child died—then this points to an even greater value placed upon the lives of both the mother and the child—a precedent in Jewish law. Any of these conclusions push against the devaluation of an unborn child.

---

16. See Hoffmeier, "Abortion," 57–61. Hoffmeier engages several scholars who have argued at length for the value of the unborn child. This debate started with furor in the late 1960s on the eve of the *Roe v. Wade* decision. See also Kline, "Lex Talionis," 193–201; Congdon, "Exodus 21:22–25," 132–47; Loewenstamm, "Exodus 21:22–25," 352–60; Kaiser, *Toward Old Testament Ethics*, 168–72; and Longman, *Bible and the Ballot*, 139–42.

17. See Driver and Miles, *Assyrian Laws*, 116–17; and Peterson, "Genesis Mandates," 131–32.

18. Grudem, *Politics*, 159–60.

These concerns being noted, the main issue in the text is how to translate the word used to describe the unborn child's premature birth (*yatsa'*). The English translations are divided with some calling it a "miscarriage" (implying the child is born dead; cf. NASB, TNK, RSV) with other translations saying that the baby was born early and alive (NIV, NLT, NKJV, see also the LXX). Literally, the word *yatsa'* means to "come out." In the context, it clearly is addressing the child being born and if any ensuing harm followed (i.e., the death of the child or mother) then the perpetrator was to die. If the author wanted to say this was a "miscarriage" there are other Hebrew words for that (*nephel*="to fall" connoting the idea of a deceased child "falling" from the womb on its own through a spontaneous miscarriage; and *shakal*, which means to be bereaved of a living child; cf. Gen 31:38; Exod 23:26; Job 3:16; 21:10; Ps 58:8//9 in Hebrew; Eccl 6:3; Hos 9:14). What is more, those who suggest that this is just a miscarriage and not an actual baby need to keep in mind that the language here is of a "child" (*ben*) not the regular word used for "miscarriage" as elsewhere.[19] Therefore, it seems that the author wanted to point out that this was not a regular birth, nor was it a miscarriage, but rather it was a forced birth, hence the use of the term *yatsa'*. I am confident that this passage,[20] along with a number of others, does in fact help paint a fuller picture of the value of life in the womb despite the ambiguity and vacillation on the topic by later rabbis and Jewish interpreters such as Josephus and Philo.[21] While some may see it as ambiguous, which I do not, this does not give license to individuals to adopt a "Christian" pro-choice agenda.

Numbers 5:11–31

This strange passage is sometimes cited in favor of "God-sanctioned" abortion.[22] It describes a ritual ordeal whereby a husband suspects his wife of unfaithfulness. In this case, the woman is brought to the tabernacle and forced to drink a concoction of dust from the floor of the tabernacle mixed with water. This part is clear; what follows is debated.

---

19. Grudem, *Politics*, 160.
20. Contra Gardner, *Abortion*, 119.
21. Longman, *Bible and the Ballot*, 142.
22. See comments by Brown, "Killing the Unborn."

Does God bring about an abortion, as some suggest,[23] or does something else happen to the woman? The interpretive issue is what it means for the woman's "thigh to waste away" and her "abdomen to swell" (Num 5:21, 22). While it is true that "thigh" can mean one's genitalia or "loins" (Gen 46:26; Exod 1:5; Judg 8:30), it does not always mean this. Most of the times when genitalia are in view the phrase is rendered "under my thigh" (Gen 24:2, 9; 47:29). Therefore, there seems to be something other than an abortion taking place.

In light of these concerns, I would argue that the woman may have been smitten with a severe case of hemorrhoids or something gastro-intestinal, because her "thigh" is literally "falling" not "wasting" as rendered by many translations.[24] Something related to the bowels or urination would make sense if the woman is *drinking* the potion. This is bolstered by the fact that in the Song of Solomon, "thigh" is used to speak of the woman's shapely thighs/posterior (Song 7:2). Second, there are ANE curses brought about by the gods which speak of one passing bloody discharges either by the bowels or urination.[25] These curses sound very similar to the curse that is happening in this text. Third, there is no indication in the text that the woman is pregnant. In fact, after the ordeal, if the woman is innocent, she can conceive children implying that she was never pregnant. Fourth, *God* is the one who brings about the ordeal, not a person. So, even if one were to believe that a God-induced spontaneous abortion happened, this would never give a doctor or anyone else the right to abort a woman's baby. Therefore, due to the ambiguity and the alternate interpretations, this text should never be used to condone abortion.

Ecclesiastes 6:3–5

While somewhat tangential, Tremper Longman also notes Ecclesiastes' use of the image of the miscarried child in 6:3–5 for instructing on the value of life.[26] Qoheleth—the author of Ecclesiastes—notes that someone who does not appreciate God's good gifts is worse off than a miscarried child. To begin, this example is a non-starter in the abortion discussion

---

23. Longman, *Bible and the Ballot*, 142–43.

24. If this is a miscarriage or an abortion one would expect a similar term as was used in Ecclesiastes 6:3 (*naphel/nephel*), which comes from the same root as used here.

25. King ed., *Boundary-Stones*, 62; and Crawford, *Blessing and Curse*, 180.

26. Longman, *Bible and the Ballot*, 144–46.

because a miscarried child is not the same as a *living* unborn child. In this case, Qoheleth speaks only of the former, not the latter (cf. Eccl 11:5). Second, Longman's conclusion that this actually reflects the way people of Qoheleth's period viewed the unborn, namely, that "it does not have the same status as a child after birth"[27] is reading too much into Qoheleth's ethical worldview. This is an apples and oranges comparison. If anything, Qoheleth uses the image of the miscarried child for the purpose of showing the complete waste of a person's life when they do not enjoy God's good gifts: unlike the value of a *living* unborn child, the miscarriage is already *dead* in the womb, and the person who refuses to enjoy life is "dead" outside of it! The miscarried child will not have to experience oppression and turmoil in life, nor will the child be held accountable for their actions, unlike the person who is living and refuses to acknowledge God.[28] For these reasons, this text should not be used for the abortion discussion.

Amos 1:13

This prophetic text in Amos deals with the gruesome practice of the Ammonites cutting open pregnant women from the neighboring region of Gilead during battle in order to kill their unborn children, and no doubt the women themselves. This prevented the conquered people from expanding in their own land. That is, this was a direct attack against procreation by means of a most barbaric form of abortion. Amos, a prophet of social justice, delivered the word of God to the Ammonites for this atrocity declaring that God would burn their cities and send them into exile (Amos 1:14–15). Put plainly, God would execute many (the death penalty) and deport others (they would lose their right to their land). To me, this is one of the clearest demonstrations of God's disgust and hatred for violent acts against the defenseless—the unborn and women—and attacks against the procreation mandate. How can we possibly think that God is not taking note of the similar butchering of defenseless children for the sake of personal expedience, while blatantly attacking the mandate of procreation? If anything, this should serve as a warning that God's judgment is coming if we do not change our ways. We must remember that it was King Manasseh's shedding of innocent blood that sealed the

---

27. Longman, *Bible and the Ballot*, 146.
28. See Peterson, *Qoheleth's Hope*, 94.

fate of Judah in the days leading up to the exile (2 Kgs 21:16; 24:4; cf. Jer 19:4; 22:3, 17 etc.).

Luke 1:41–44

While I touched on the content of this text above, it is important to note that when the biblical authors speak of living children in the womb, they consistently call them babies and not fetuses or some other sanitized word which would make aborting them more acceptable. For example, when Elizabeth heard the salutations of Mary, her "baby" (*brephos* in Greek) leapt in her womb. *Brephos* is the same term used for Jesus after he was born (Luke 18:15; 2 Tim 3:15).[29] I already noted this same phenomenon in the Exodus 21 passage above where the term *ben* ("child"/"son") is used for a baby in the womb.

Summary and Some Final Notes

While I will be dealing with the ethical dimension of the prophets vis-à-vis God's care for the defenseless in more detail below, what this brief textual survey has shown is that there is no way to conclude from the numerous biblical texts, which speak of the preborn, that God or the Bible is in any way supportive of abortion rights. If anything, the Bible is univocal on the value of the unborn. Those who go to the biblical Text in search of support for this heinous act will find nothing to support their actions. Their work mirrors the special pleading employed by those who try to use the Bible to affirm homosexuality and same-sex marriage. Finally, the question of whether abortion is equivalent to murder will be answered by people differently depending on their ethical worldview. The fact that death was the penalty in Exodus 21 (and implied in Amos 1:13) tells me that God took seriously the value of *all* life.

Before leaving this topic, it is important to point out a troubling trend within evangelical scholarship when it comes to abortion and the Christian response, namely, that access to some level of abortion is good. Longman falls into this category.[30] Personally, I think that Longman's equivocating on the issue of abortion and his failure to take a strong

---

29. Grudem, *Politics*, 158.

30. So does Gardner (*Abortion*, 273) even though he wrote just prior to *Roe v. Wade*.

stand on the importance of changing the laws of the land about abortion is problematic.[31] He ends his discussion on abortion by saying "there may be wisdom in making abortion rare and safe."[32] To me, this sounds eerily similar to the mantra of Planned Parenthood and the Clinton-era quip of abortion being "safe, legal, and rare." Of course, it is anything but rare today. The Enemy loves death. What is more, Longman's logic is flawed. He says that trying to outlaw abortion would just cause people to do it illegally or unsafely while the rich would just go to another country.[33] If this is the logic we are going to employ when making laws then should we do away with laws against illegal drugs? After all, people still get them illegally, and rich people can go and get them in other countries. This is simply ludicrous. Why would Christians not want abortion to be illegal? It is immoral on its face. Even if some people choose to break the law, that does not mean keeping such a horrendous law in place is "wise" as Longman concludes.

My solution is for Longman to follow his own interpretive principles about the "redemptive-ethical trajectory"[34] of Scripture, something with which I readily agree. While Longman is certainly correct to note the lack of explicit teaching on abortion in the Bible, and while he is also correct to note the biblical teaching on the value of life—both born and unborn—he drops the ball by not seeing how science has aided us in appreciating the complexity and wonder of human life in the womb. Simply put, the ancient writers did not have the wherewithal to understand what was going on in the womb (see Eccl 11:5) and as such did not use language that a pro-life advocate would use today. However, due to medical advancements, we know much more about when life begins, how babies are formed, and the ability of the unborn child to feel pain. With sonograms and ultrasounds so advanced, there is no excuse for the butchering of children in the womb. We know more now and therefore we are more culpable than were the ancients. "To whom much is given, much is required" (Luke 12:48). It is telling when pro-choice advocates at the highest levels push against legislation requiring ultrasounds before a woman gets an abortion.[35] Of what are they so afraid? The fact that

---

31. Longman, *Bible and the Ballot*, 151–53.
32. Longman, *Bible and the Ballot*, 153.
33. Longman, *Bible and the Ballot*, 152.
34. Longman, *Bible and the Ballot*, 44–45.
35. Grudem, *Politics*, 164–65.

women will see for themselves who they are about to kill: their baby? We have also seen how the abortion industry is devastating the African American community and female babies. As such, Christians should employ Longman's redemptive-ethical trajectory and withstand abortion at every turn and advocate for pro-life candidates and pro-life legislation. Anything less than this is not "wise," to use Longman's language. This brings us to the second part of this chapter, namely, Christian arguments for abortion.

Christian Arguments for Abortion

I have often said that if close to two thirds of Americans identify as "Christian" then we could outlaw abortion in one election cycle.[36] This, I know, is wishful thinking because there is both ambiguity and a wide interpretation of what the label "Christian" actually means.[37] There are four basic camps of Christians when it comes to abortion. The first says it is always wrong. The second group has no problems with abortion: it is a woman's right to choose. The third camp thinks it should be rare, but it is okay in certain situations especially if it is agreed to by both parents after prayer.[38] And the fourth camp are those ambivalent towards the practice. This last group exemplifies many Christians today, evangelicals included, who try to sidestep the blight of abortion by using weak and easily refuted arguments, which in many cases, reveals their lack of will to effect real change. People's silence or refusal to do anything is tantamount to approval.

The Imposed Morality Argument

To begin, some make the argument that the reason that they support maintaining abortion legislation is because they do not want to impose their morals upon someone else.[39] This smacks of insincerity and sidesteps the real issue and begs the question: Whose morals should we

---

36. So, too, Brown, *Jezebel's War*, 76–77.

37. See also Brown, *Jezebel's War*, 37.

38. So, Gardner, *Abortion*, 273–74, 276. Published in 1972, Gardner's book represents his era where he thinks bi-racial (what he calls, "Half-Caste") children are best aborted because of the social stigma both the child and the mother would feel (p.192).

39. See discussion by Grudem, *Politics*, 168–69.

follow then? The world's? The Enemy's?[40] We have moral instruction in the Bible about murder, incest, stealing, and the like, and have no problem imposing those morals on people. At the heart of these types of arguments is the reality that these Christians have no problem imposing their morality on culture if culture agrees with them. If culture rejects their biblical position, then is it no longer appropriate to continue pushing for what is right? This was the same poor reasoning that allowed slavery and racial injustice to go on for so long. It took courageous men and women standing up and saying, "Enough!" Despite what culture thinks is right or wrong we need to push back when we see injustice, especially at the gruesome level of abortion. No society should allow the killing of innocent children at any stage.[41] The truth is that the morality that Christians should be following is that of God.

The Ambiguity Argument

Another argument is that due to the lack of clarity of biblical teaching on abortion, one's views on abortion should not be a "litmus test for biblical values."[42] As I noted above, while the Bible may not have explicit language about abortion, no doubt due to its rarity, that does not mean that any normal thinking Christian cannot see the evil in this act. The Bible does not speak about killing Jews in gas chambers either, but Christians recognized that this was heinous and wrong. When a professing Christian supports or turns a blind eye to something as barbaric as abortion then it should indeed serve as a "litmus test" of their "biblical values" (Matt 7:16; Eph 5:3–20).

The "It-is-just-another-sin-and-God-will-forgive-me" Argument

This argument basically makes abortion on par with every other sin, which is covered by the finished work of Christ. There is no question that all unconfessed sin can condemn someone to hell, but the gravity of abortion, which is taking a life, should not be trivialized in this manner. God can indeed forgive those who abort their babies, but passing abortion off as just another sin is to miss the gravity of certain sins. The

---

40. So, too, Grudem, *Politics*, 70.
41. Sider, *Completely Pro-Life*, 53–57.
42. So, Collins, *Biblical Values*, 58.

truth is some sins have greater penalties (Matt 10:14–15; 11:23–24; Luke 10:11–12; John 19:11) and have long-lasting repercussions for a nation and a person. A nation that sheds innocent blood will not go unpunished (I will return to this in a minute), and a woman who aborts her baby often suffers long-term psychological torment such as guilt and remorse. What is more, Paul's words ring true here as well: "What shall we say then? Are we to continue in sin that grace might increase?" (Rom 6:1; NASB). Finally, to suggest that if one has "peace" with God about aborting a baby then it is the right decision to make,[43] is to grossly overestimate the ability of the heart and intellect to guide one's decisions. The heart is deceitfully wicked and is deeply marred by sin (Jer 17:9). The Bible must be our guide, not one's *feelings* of "peace."

The "Pro-Life" and Social Justice Fallacies

Since the next two arguments/fallacies are often used in tandem, I will therefore handle them together because many of my responses to both arguments follow the same logic. It is important to note that many of those promoting these positions tend to be left-leaning Christians who have chosen to support one political party in particular and have also embraced much of the social agenda in Western culture, which I have been addressing throughout this book. While this list is certainly not exhaustive, and while everyone may not endorse all of these positions, usually those in this camp also push for the acceptance of same-sex marriage rights, so-called transgender rights, the acceptance of illegal immigration or open border policies, and the endorsement of problematic "equity" and "social justice" movements (racial, gender, sexual, and environmental).

The "Pro-Life" Fallacy

While I have touched on this concept in earlier chapters, the central tenet of this argument is encapsulated in the slogan "we need to be pro-life 'from the womb to the tomb.'"[44] Variations of this position are captured in statements like Christians need to have "a consistent ethic of life,"

---

43. Gardner, *Abortion*, 273.
44. Yeh, "Orthopraxis," 105. See also Claiborne, "Evangelicalism," 162–63.

which includes issues of capital punishment, war, care for the poor, immigration justice, the environment and so on.[45]

The "Social Justice" Fallacy

A second fallacy closely connected to the "pro-life" fallacy is encapsulated in the mantra of "justice"/"social justice" often touted by the evangelical left and mainstream churches. Justice for all people, not just the unborn, they say, is what God seeks and *they* are the ones doing it while the rest of the conservative evangelical churches are dropping the ball.[46]

Response

While both these arguments sound wonderfully "Christian," they are in many ways copouts when addressing what is truly problematic. When this group of Christians support the election of people who are supposedly "pro-life" for all and "pro-social justice"—without dealing directly with the blight of abortion—they somehow feel justified that they are helping the poor, widows, orphans, and foreigners according to Jesus' words (Matt 25:31–46). They also insist they are following the ethics of the prophets like Amos and Micah (e.g., Micah 6:8). While I am in no way trying to minimize the ethical and moral issues related to many of these social concerns, the premise often misses the heart of the "Gospel," as they would call it, and the central ethical focus of the prophets. Space will not allow me to go into too much detail, but I will highlight some of the major problems with this line of thinking.

First, perhaps the most misguided aspect of these types of arguments when it comes to the abortion debate is the complete misunderstanding of what the prophets' ethical intention was when they spoke of taking care of the widow, the orphan, and the foreigner. In an ancient context, especially a patriarchal framework,[47] these three groups of people had no one to protect them within society; they had no legal rights as a rule; they were the most vulnerable within virtually every culture. As such, God spoke through the prophets and warned Israel that they needed to defend

---

45. See "Pro-Life Evangelicals for Biden"; and Wallis, *God's Politics*, xviii, xxiii–xxiv, 8, 300–301. See a critique of this position by Grudem, *Politics*, 176–77.

46. See this type of position propounded by Harper, "Evangelicalism," 19–30.

47. See more in Richter, *Stewards of Eden*, 68–78.

The Mandate of Family and Procreation Part 3

these defenseless people. God even enshrined their protection in the Law (Lev 19:10; 23:22; Deut 10:18; 14:29; 24:14, 17, 19–21). God judged Israel and other nations on how they treated the defenseless (Amos 1–2; Micah 6). What is more, Jeremiah the prophet added to this list the need to stop the shedding of innocent blood (Jer 7:6; 22:3; cf. Ps 106:34–40), something rarely if ever mentioned in the modern discussion. "Innocent blood," of course, covers a wide range of killing, but especially the unborn (see Amos 1:13 above).

Now while I am not saying that believers should not support or offer aid to these same three groups today, the reality is that widows, orphans, and foreigners have rights and protections under the Constitution and laws of America and other western democracies. No one can kill members of any of these groups with impunity. However, if the prophets were speaking to America today, they would call out the church on their complacency regarding the unprotected in our culture, namely, the unborn. I am reminded of an interview with then-presidential-candidate, Hillary Clinton, and Chuck Todd on *Meet the Press*. When asked directly about whether the law protects the unborn, Clinton said that an unborn child had no protections under US law.[48] Indeed, the unborn are the only ones in our country who have no protection under the law. They represent the "innocent blood" being shed noted above. Although some may retort that illegal immigrants have no protection under the law, this is a false dichotomy. Illegal immigrants *choose* to come to this country illegally and as such do not have the same rights as citizens. Often this illegality is what leads to exploitation for them and their children whom they may have brought with them. Moreover, even when they are caught, they are not executed for being in an unprotected group. On the other hand, the unborn are at the mercy of the mother and society. When society turns a blind eye to their plight, God is sure to judge that society.

Second, these types of arguments fail to differentiate between the role of the believer in helping the poor and disenfranchised and the role of the state. Every believer is required to fight for the oppressed, but the state has other responsibilities beyond this, which *may* conflict with the church or beliefs of some Christians (e.g., border protection and restrictions, fighting wars, the use of nuclear weapons, capital punishment). Christians who try to make the state do the job of the church are misguided. It appears that some move in this direction so they will not have

---

48. Schwartz, "Chuck Todd."

to respond or get involved personally in the giving of their time and resources. They would prefer to let the government do it. Nevertheless, aiding the poor, widows, and new immigrants is something anyone can do. As just noted, legislation is already in place that protects these classes of people. On the other hand, the church cannot change the law on abortion and morality related to sexual ethics. These issues are politically driven and must be changed by both whom we elect, and by grassroots efforts that lobby the government and politicians to hear our voices and undo or reject these unbiblical laws.[49]

This brings me to my third point. The Bible consistently presents a position of law and order as being from God (Gen 1; Exod 20–23; Deut 5–26; 1 Cor 12, etc.). Policies that promote chaos in a society (e.g., immigration chaos), or are unbiblical (abortion, sexual and gender confusion), are not godly and should be rejected by the church. The Enemy is the author of confusion not God (1 Cor 14:33).

Fourth, the legislating of problematic moral issues related to sexual ethics is something every Christian should be appalled by. Christians must push against and denounce these unbiblical laws. Nevertheless, the truth is that the blight of abortion is the most pressing issue within Western culture when it comes to moral atrocities. Over 62 million deaths and counting has not gotten the Christian Left's attention. Think about that number for a moment. We have killed close to the population of Canada twice since 1973 with no mass public outcry. If anything, the Left in general is only getting worse in their anti-God and anti-biblical policies. Those who say they are "pro-life" but focus only on those they can see at the border or those that they see on a news report are part of the problem. While these are the visibly "oppressed" people according to some, in the back rooms of abortion clinics, millions of babies are being butchered. Most conservative evangelicals would agree heartily that the wellbeing of children should be the main issue, but conservatives focus first on the children without a true voice: the unborn. Instead of acting on behalf of these truly voiceless children, in some instances, the religious Left is praising the abortionists. In one such example, the National Abortion Federation appointed a lesbian Episcopal priest (Katherine Hancock Ragsdale) as the new CEO and president.[50] Ragsdale, who is married to another lesbian priest, went on to praise abortionists as "heroes" and

---

49. So, too, Sider, *Completely Pro-Life*, 57.
50. Prestigiacomo, "Lesbian Priest."

"modern-day saints." Pro-life advocates have rightly called out these people as "false prophets."[51]

Fifth, the call for "social justice" obviously only extends to those who are outside of the womb for many of these proponents. If they truly wanted justice, they would stop electing politicians who are hostile or ambivalent to the plight of the unborn. Their actions speak much louder than their words. In this regard, just before the 2020 election, I was stunned to see a website established by so-called "pro-life evangelicals" in support of Joe Biden. The website touted the signatures of evangelicals with credentials at all levels of publishing and academia. Along with this group, the website included a list of over three thousand other self-professing evangelicals who had signed their names. This type of biblical and spiritual blindness is breathtaking and seems to reflect more of a hatred for Donald Trump than a knowledge of what the Bible has to say about the shedding of innocent blood.[52] It is mindboggling and spiritually troubling to consider how so-called evangelicals could elect a man who represents a party that seeks to kill babies at all levels of gestation and now even outside of the womb! And this does not even take into account the vice president Kamala Harris, who was the most liberal senator in the US senate. This type of willing rejection of God's laws will not go unpunished by God and I fear for those who would willingly allow such delusion to encapsulate them. Instead they want to focus on racial issues, poverty, healthcare, climate change and the like. As just noted, most Christians desire to stop wars, feed the hungry, help the sick, see prison reform, and so on, but this is not what is most pressing on western democracies. On the contrary, we do not see millions of people in western democracies dying because of these things. What we do see, is the death of millions upon millions of children in every western democracy. At 41 million deaths, abortion was the number one cause of death worldwide in 2018,[53] and in 2020 the number was 42.6 million.[54] This is why I think Jesus gave some of the harshest statements about judgment on those who offend the least of these (i.e., the children). He mandated the death penalty (Matt 18:6; Mark 9:42), something that is sure to go against many left-leaning thinkers' sense of justice. It seems to me that the reason these self-identified

---

51. Prestigiacomo, "Lesbian Priest."
52. See the excellent response to this by Brown, "Pro-Life Evangelicals."
53. Brown, *Jezebel's War*, 77.
54. Ford, "Abortion."

"elites" tend to support left-leaning policies (or at least politicians) is that they do not want to be associated with the "Religious Right," a phrase that is almost always used pejoratively in their writings. They refuse to acknowledge that their time in the ivory towers of education being indoctrinated by left-leaning professors has affected the way they view the Bible and cultural agendas.

Sixth, it is a false dichotomy to assert that Christians must be known for what they are *for* as opposed to what they are *against*.[55] Most evangelicals should rightly recoil at this statement. One can be both *for* the rights of the oppressed and be *against* cultural degradation and corruption. It does not have to be an either-or proposition. What this usually reveals is the Left's desire not to be seen as adversarial. Ironically, those in this camp are quick to note that they are following the positions of Jesus and the prophets; yet, even a quick reading of the life of Jesus and the prophets would show that they were not only adversarial, they called out ungodliness and anti-God policies, both politically and culturally, on a regular basis and were hated for it.

Seventh, the hypocrisy of left-leaning Christians is evident in their judgmental attitude against anyone within evangelicalism who does not see their brand of "justice" as legitimate. How can someone call for justice for the oppressed in one breath and turn around and deny justice to millions of unborn babies? And the current move to divide the country based upon "racial justice" while the plight of the unborn is ignored, especially African American babies, is inexcusable. Ironically, the way some left-leaning evangelicals speak pejoratively of white people and conservative believers is itself nothing less than racist and unchristian.

Eighth, the oft-cited argument that Christians are focused on one issue and should instead be focused on *all* the "justice" issues is only to muddy the waters with faulty logic. Just because abortion is the major issue for conservative evangelicals does not mean that they do not care about the other issues. We just realize that this is the most pressing issue of our day. The truth is, historically when people advocate for everything, nothing gets accomplished. Focusing on one key issue at a time was how slavery, the oppression of women, and racial injustice were tackled and defeated, the church and biblical teaching being instrumental in effecting change in each case.

---

55. So, Yeh, "Orthopraxis," 117. See a similar statement by Claiborne, "Evangelicalism," 154.

Ninth, some Christians insist that abortion is needed, especially for cases of incest, rape, and saving the mother's life in certain circumstances. In Jewish tradition in the Mishnah, rabbis suggested that a woman who was unable to deliver a child should be saved by cutting up the baby to save the more valuable life of the mother (*m. Ohalot* 7:6). Of course, most know that Rachel died giving birth to Benjamin (Gen 35:18). Even though difficulties, and even death, still occur during pregnancy and birth in the developed world, even America, the medical advances have severely curtailed these deaths.[56] Abortions related to saving the mother's life in truly life-threatening situations account for only 0.118 percent of all abortions.[57] One does not need an open-ended abortion policy to handle these rare cases. Such arguments are akin to the red herring fallacy. These situations were already protected under the law prior to *Roe v. Wade*.[58] Finally, on a personal level, I do not feel abortion is ever the solution for the brutality of rape and incest. Answering one form of brutality with another does not seem like a good solution.[59]

Finally, when left-of-center Christians use the sanitized phrase "reproductive justice" in their writings and rhetoric instead of the more negative phrase "pro-choice," conservative evangelicals recognize that this is code for abortion rights. As long as culture continues to destroy unborn children, conservative Christians will fight to stop this practice through "justice" for the unborn first and foremost. We will continue to wage political and spiritual warfare until these laws are changed.

Conclusion

As can be seen by the overview above, Scripture in no way supports a position for abortion. Every text which we looked at actually promoted life in the womb as opposed to downplaying it. The mandate of procreation finds ample support throughout the Bible. I also pointed out that Christians should reject arguments that belittle the travesty of abortion through calls for nebulous and ineffective "pro-life" policies from the "womb to the tomb" or under the banner of "social justice." No matter

---

56. The rate is roughly 28 deaths for every 100,000 births with half of these being preventable. See Agrawal, "Maternal Mortality," 821–26.
57. Grudem, *Politics*, 163.
58. See Gardner, *Abortion*, 151–54.
59. So, too, Sider, *Completely Pro-Life*, 50–51.

what some self-professing Christians may say, we *should* try to change laws that allow abortion. As I will handle in my closing chapter, it is important for believers to get involved with electing pro-life presidents and politicians, especially senators, who confirm SCOTUS judges, in the hopes that someday the heinous *Roe v. Wade* law can be overturned.[60] As parents, pastors, and educators, we need to instruct our children about the sanctity of life and the heinous nature of abortion. Public schools and universities are not doing this. We must also work and pray that Western culture can once again respect life in the womb and value children as clearly stated in God's mandate for procreation. I am hopeful, although not too optimistic, that this can happen. I temper my enthusiasm because it is hard to remain optimistic based upon Western culture's further undoing of the Genesis mandates through gender confusion. This is the topic of my next three chapters.

---

60. Grudem, *Politics*, 175–76.

Chapter 9

The Mandate of Gender Distinctions Part 1

A Biblical Introduction

The elimination of gender distinctions, in terms of biological gender identity assigned at birth, is something that will lead to massive confusion at the very heart of what it means to be human.[1]

THIS COMMENT BY AL Mohler in 2014 captures the chaos that the Enemy has foisted upon Western culture in recent years. It is something most of us could have never imagined even a few short years ago. For the most part, the gender distinctions of male and female are God's way of bringing order to creation. Without gender distinctions for humanity, creation was not good according to God in Genesis 2:18. Adam found himself alone without a suitable partner with whom to share his life. Gender distinctions are as Mohler notes, what it "means to be human." Most people know this firsthand if you have ever had children.

As I have noted before, I am the father of five children. In fact, just a few days ago my wife and I welcomed our fifth child, Cassie, into the world amidst the Covid-19 crisis. What has made every one of our children's births so unique and exciting is not knowing what the gender of our child was until they were born. It was like receiving a Christmas gift

---

1. As cited by Brown, *Jezebel's War*, 112.

and surprise each time. In every case, we had names picked out and ready for whatever gender the child may have been. In all five births the doctors said, "It's a boy!" or "It's a girl!" Not once did they say to us, "Well, we are not sure what gender your child is, I think you should let them decide when they are a little older." Now do not get me wrong, I am not trying to belittle the trauma of children born intersex. On the contrary, I am trying to make a point about the gender madness and confusion that is being pedaled in Western cultures today. The clearest mandate given to humanity by God, one that no one can deny, barring some hormonal, genetic, or physiological abnormality, is the obvious distinction of gender differentiation. Unlike the mandates of marriage, procreation, and family building, in which some may choose or not be able to participate, gender is something set by God for all people.

Only fifteen years ago few would have challenged these concepts, but this is not the situation in our current state of cultural confusion. Gender distinctions have not just been blurred; they are being obliterated by the radicals of Western culture. Before moving forward, a couple of examples will suffice. First, more liberal states (e.g., New York, California, Oregon, Washington, New Jersey) are passing legislation that allows parents to choose a neutral/undesignated gender for newborns on their birth certificates.[2] Others have opted to identify their babies as "theybies" in an effort not to "confuse" the child with a gender with which they may not identify later.[3] Such craziness is nothing less than child abuse, a point noted by others as well.[4] Adults are supposed to be setting an example, but instead they are aligning with the new "wokeness" of Western culture and in turn creating a world of chaos for their kids. One can only imagine the confusion for these children as they go through the first few formative years of their lives.

In this vein, and as a second example, Planned Parenthood is getting into the fray peddling their own form of gender confusion by offering "guidelines for parents" on sex and gender, which includes instructing children as young as four that their genitals do not determine their gender.[5] They insist that their stance is all in the effort to stop "gender stereotypes." But anyone who is even half alert will recognize this has more

---

2. Prager, "LGBTQ Organizations."
3. See Compton, "'Boy or Girl?'"; and Muhammad, "Theyby Babies."
4. Prager, "LGBTQ Organizations."
5. Tucker Carlson Tonight, "Planned Parenthood."

to do with shoring up support and empathy for the LGBTQ community. According to Planned Parenthood, even talking to your preschool daughter about growing up and liking boys and marrying one (or vice versa), can cause confusion for them if they do not know their sexual orientation yet.[6] In their guidelines they note how easily influenced children are and how we need to be careful about how we talk to them about gender and sex. Yet Planned Parenthood is doing just that. They are doing everything in their power to influence younger and younger children with confusing discussions about gender fluidity, gender non-conforming identities, transsexuality, you name it. According to Planned Parenthood, children should be allowed to choose for themselves without the pressure from parents which can be something as "dangerous" as putting a girl in a pink bedroom or putting a boy in a blue bedroom. (I do not know what Planned Parenthood would say to those of us who grew up in large families and had to share a room, whatever color it was, or what they would say to people who do not even have a bedroom to call their own—only in the West would we be so elitist.) In other words, culture is pushing parents to perpetuate the gender and sex confusion of children by allowing children to decide what they *feel* about gender and sexuality without parents trying to influence them along traditional paths. And guess who is there with children's programming, "educational" books, and sex-ed programs filling the void left by silent parents? You guessed it, Planned Parenthood and the LGBTQ-linked agenda.

When I read these articles and putative guidelines it sickens me as a father. This is the world in which our children are growing up. I cannot help but hear the harsh warning of Jesus ringing in my ears concerning those who would "offend the least of these" (Matt 18:6). America is in a mess, and we need Jesus now more than ever when raising a family in such confusing times. When culture rejects something as basic as gender distinctions, how much is left before God judges? As the church we need to wake up. This is coming at us and our children from all angles. We need to be informed.

In light of these concerns, in this chapter, I will examine the biblical mandate of gender distinctions as found in Genesis 1:27 and 2:22–23. I will also point out the continued slippery slope of allowing this type of gender confusion madness to continue. What is the "natural" progression of humanity's sin if sexual deviance is allowed to proliferate? We are

---

6. Planned Parenthood, "Preschooler."

seeing it in a rise of homosexuality, transgenderism, pedophilia and yes, even bestiality. Because of the depth of these discussions, I will handle these topics over the next three chapters.

The Biblical Mandate of Gender Distinctions

While defining "authentic human sexuality" Judith and Jack Balswick point out six biblical principles to follow: "1) Human sexuality is established in the differentiation between male and female and in the unity established between them. 2) Sexuality is a good gift, meant to draw persons to deeper levels of knowing self, others and God. 3) Humans are born with an innate capacity for sexual pleasure, and human sexuality can best develop within an emotionally caring, trustworthy family environment. 4) Sexuality and spirituality are intricately connected. 5) After the Fall, sexuality became distorted and in need of redemption. 6) Christ offers restoration and renews our potential for authentic sexuality."[7] As can be seen by this multi-point list, there are many moving parts to our sexuality as mandated by God. And the fall has not made living with our sinful sexual desires and confusion any easier. It is easy to understand how people within our confused culture, especially those without the power of Jesus' blood applied to their lives, can be led astray. Nevertheless, despite the fall, as spiritual beings we are responsible to God for how we use what he has given to us for our flourishing. The opening two chapters of Genesis make this clear.

Genesis 1:27

In the opening chapters of Genesis, the author notes the distinction of male and female for humans and animals six times (Gen 1:27; 5:2; 6:19; 7:3, 9, 16). In the binary distinctions of chapter 1 (i.e., heaven and earth, upper and lower waters, sea and dry land, light and darkness, and male and female), however, it is only humans that are explicitly labeled with binary gender. The reason is self-evident moving forward. God's plan for humans is unique and included the coupling of male and female for life within the confines of marriage. While it is implicit in the text that the animals were created male and female (1:22; 6:19; 7:3, 9, 16), the purpose of binary gender as being a mandate for human propagation carries

---

7. Balswick and Balswick, *Authentic Human Sexuality*, 60.

greater theological weight because humans were made in the image of God. Humans are the pinnacle of creation, not an afterthought or chance of evolution.[8] Based upon the creation mandate, gender differences are established by God and are not fluid or on a spectrum for us to adjust at will. God established them in Genesis 1 and does so in a context of creating what is "good."[9] This is further supported by the positive instruction on the coupling of Adam and Eve in Genesis 2.

Genesis 2:22–23

The second chapter of Genesis, often called the second creation account, focuses on the creation of Adam and Eve and the Garden of Eden. In the account, God fashions Adam out of the dust of the ground but he has no counterpart suitable for him. As a result, God causes Adam to fall into a deep sleep and God takes one of his ribs and fashions (literally "builds") a woman for him (2:21). A common scholarly argument championed by feminist Phyllis Trible was that Adam was actually androgynous, being equally male and female, and God simply divided Adam into two parts.[10] This, she argues, is the reason that the man and the woman cleave to one another and seek to once again become "one flesh" (Gen 2:24). Even if this is correct, which contextually I doubt, this in no way diminishes the importance of gender distinctions today *post* creation. As I noted in a previous chapter, Genesis 2 seems to be an expansion of what was highlighted in 1:26–28. Therefore, the context points to a male human alone in need of an opposite, yet corresponding counterpart. When Adam sees God's creation of the woman, there is an immediate connection and he calls the woman bone of his bone and flesh of his flesh (2:23). Following on the heels of this proclamation, marriage is instituted in 2:24 which brings the man and woman together for the purpose of intimacy and procreation.

These two accounts make it clear that God establishes binary gender as a part of his good creation. Gender distinctions naturally come before any discussion about marriage, procreation and family. Nevertheless, God's creation of binary gender was fundamental to humanity's perpetuation. What is also important about gender distinctions is the role the male and female play in the family and within society. As noted in Chapter 6,

---

8. So, too, Branch, *Affirming God's Image*, 40–41.
9. Wilson, *Mere Sexuality*, 35–36.
10. Trible, "Eve and Adam," 74–81.

when addressing the important role that fathers play in the family dynamic, God intended both male and female distinctions to play a vital role in raising a family and in the family structure. On this point, Denny Burk comments, "Adam's role as leader, protector, and provider is inextricably linked to his biological sex. What does this mean? It means that God has so made the world that there is a normative, holy connection between biological sex and gender identity."[11] Similarly, others have noted that the physical strength of the man vis-à-vis the woman is purposeful to show the imbalance, yet shared power, of Christ and the Church.[12]

Despite the common practice in scholarly circles to argue that the creation accounts of Genesis 1 and 2 are not complete pictures of all that God created, and as such transgendered people, homosexuals, and intersex all fall within the spectrum of the two genders, male and female,[13] I have demonstrated earlier that this is a poor understanding of the creation narrative. As a reminder, while I can readily agree that the creation narratives are cursory, to argue that transgenderism, homosexuality, and intersexuality are all part of God's good creation is simply a bridge too far. It is important to keep in mind that while all people are equally loved by God, these aberrations are a result of the fall and/or personal sin, not a part of God's good creation. What is more, as detailed in earlier chapters, these arguments miss the general nature of the language used to describe God's creative process for the species. There is simply no biblical evidence supporting these postmodern perspectives. In fact, a couple of texts push against sexual confusion, especially transgenderism.

Deuteronomy 22:5 and 23:1

Deuteronomy 22:5 is one text that stands out as unique in the transgender discussion. At first glance, the text seems to prohibit men and women from crossdressing, that is, wearing the clothes associated with the opposite gender. However, J. Alan Branch is indeed correct to note that this extends beyond just clothing; the verse also prohibits people from appropriating even the "articles" (22:5a) of the opposite gender.[14] Put differently, God is prohibiting people from wearing clothes, jewelry,

11. Burk, "Transgender Test," 95.
12. See Hiestand, "Theodicy," 101–18.
13. Collins, *Biblical Values*, 62. See also DeFranza, *Sex Difference* (2015).
14. Branch, *Affirming God's Image*, 43–46.

makeup, and so on, that would cause them to present themselves as the opposite gender from what God had created them, thus confusing God's good creation of gender distinctions. This is certainly more than mere cross-dressing; this would include all forms of gender dysphoria. This law reinforced God's earlier laws and instruction related to gender distinctions in Genesis 1 and 2.[15]

In the second passage (Deut 23:1//v.2 in Hebrew), the law prohibits someone from entering the assembly of God who has been emasculated (i.e., their testicles are crushed or removed causing sterilization) or has had his sexual organ removed. While this could be the result of a variety of unfortunate events such as a war injury or an accident while working, it does not preclude someone who removed their penis for the purpose of cultic activity in a pagan context (cf. 23:17//v.18 in Hebrew), as was common in the ancient Near East with the worship of pagan deities, especially Ishtar.[16]

Already there will be those who reject these texts as not applicable for a modern audience. Like many of the other Jewish laws, scholars argue that they are no longer applicable. It is here that I agree with Longman and Gane when they argue for an application of the principles behind laws that may no longer directly apply today. However, in the case of these two texts there is a clear one-to-one connection, something obvious to any reader. People who confuse their birth gender, or surgically alter their physical body are in violation of God's commands. In other words, transgender people who choose to live as the opposite gender are certainly guilty of breaking the first prohibition, and the use of hormone therapy, which leads to sterilization, or invasive surgery, which removes or alters one's sexual organs, applies in the second case. It is also important to keep in mind that Jesus' teaching that there are those who make themselves eunuchs for the sake of the kingdom (Matt 19:12) no doubt refers to a choice to be celibate, not literal surgery of any kind.

Again, Branch is correct to note that the tendency of transsexuals is to practice homosexuality as well.[17] As I will demonstrate in a later chapter, this is against the teachings of Scripture. Furthermore, transsexuals separate the body from the soul, namely, their mind tells them they are the opposite sex trapped inside the wrong body. With such a perspective,

---

15. See Harland, "Menswear and Womenswear," 73–76.
16. Branch, *Affirming God's Image*, 45–46.
17. Branch, *Affirming God's Image*, 48–49.

they fail to recognize the full repercussions of the fall and the clear teaching of Scripture that we are created body and soul and that we are *one* being made in the image of God.[18]

The New Testament and Gender

In the NT, Jesus is the only one to make a direct reference to the creation of binary gender as noted in Genesis 1 (Matt 19:4; Mark 10:6). That said, binary gender categories are a given in the NT with only passing references to those who are eunuchs (Matt 19:12; Acts 8). Paul does make note of the removal of the concepts of Jew and Greek, bond and free, male and female when it comes to salvation (Gal 3:28), but this in no way suggests, as some have tried to argue, that gender does not matter to God, or that people can identify with whatever gender they want.[19] This flies in the face of Paul's teaching on the use of gendered sexual activity in Romans 1:25–28 (cf. 1 Cor 6:9; 1 Tim 1:10; see next chapter).

From a NT eschatological perspective, some have insisted that biological sex as a gender distinction is not just for the here and now but will also be important in the resurrection.[20] On this point, Matthew Mason comments, "the resurrection of the body shows that gender reassignment is a rebellion against the moral order God has written on our bodies in creation in their sexual form as male or female."[21] While some may reject this concept, it is obvious that sex and gender are important for humanity. This is supported by the fact that Jesus still appeared as a man after his resurrection.

Before moving on to my next topic I want to make one more point. A common assertion today is that we should not deny our sexual expressions (i.e., through intercourse) because that is what makes us human. This is a fallacy. Jesus did not need sexual "fulfillment" to be human. He was chaste. And the common trend to insist on the identification of people by their sexual preference is troubling and flies in the face of biblical teaching. It is telling of the state of humanity today when sexuality

---

18. Branch, *Affirming God's Image*, 49–53.

19. E.g., Song, *Covenant and Calling*, 49–50. See also the numerous erroneous assertions made by Saylor and O'Hanlon, "Homosexuality." See also a refutation by Slattery, *Rethinking Sexuality*, 181.

20. Wilson, *Mere Sexuality*, 48.

21. Mason, "Gender Dysphoria," 144. See also Jones, "Embodied," 26–27.

and gender are said to be fluid and therefore subject to our whims.[22] Ironically, we live in a time when people have rejected the science behind sex and gender distinctions and have instead opted for feelings over reality. People insist with matter-of-fact certainty that there is no difference between men and women, or boys and girls, and that gender is all a social construct with no scientific evidence to prove their point.[23] Now while gender *roles* certainly can be socially constructed,[24] the differences between male and female are evident to those living in the real world—especially outside the university bubble[25]—and have ever raised children. As a father of five young children, I have noticed that the differences between my boys and girls extend beyond what they do. It is also how they think and react to different circumstances, how they react emotionally, and how they show empathy. Males and females are different because God made them that way. This brings me to my next point, are intersex people made this way by God?

Intersex and Gender Discussions

A recent development in how the church should view gender distinctions is the focus on the issue of intersexed persons.[26] Intersex is the rare medical condition (1 in 2000 children) related to genetic, hormonal, and/or physiological issues which occur in utero which cause the sex of a child in some way to be ambiguous.[27] While this condition can affect a person for life, most of these issues are treatable by hormone therapy, surgery, or both. As noted above, Jesus notes this condition when he says that some are born "eunuchs" (Matt 19:12). In an effort to affirm trans individuals, the intersex and eunuch discussion is often used as a precedent.

This is problematic for several reasons. First, intersex issues are biological in nature, not psychological as is usually the case with LGBTQ identities.[28] Put differently, transsexualism is usually identified as

---

22. Wilson, *Mere Sexuality*, 49–51 esp. 51n15.
23. Ellis, *Breakdown*, 123–26.
24. See discussion by Benshoff and Griffin, *Queer Images*, 7.
25. So, too, Ellis, *Breakdown*, 18.
26. See the work of DeFranza, *Sex Difference* (2015).
27. See further discussion by Balswick and Balswick, *Authentic Human Sexuality*, 33–38.
28. Murray, *Madness of Crowds*, 188–90 at 188.

a "software" issue versus a "hardware" issue. Second, trans persons, for the most part, rely completely on "testimony," that is, how someone perceives themselves as opposed to the reality of a scientifically/medically determined gender confusion of those born intersexed.[29] Third, there is nothing sinful about a person who is born intersex. They are still made in the image of God but have been affected by the fall in the same way any child who is born with some physical impairment or issue is affected by the fall. Isaiah the prophet actually commends eunuchs' faithfulness and their place within God's eschatological plan (Isa 56:4–5). Practicing LGBTQ individuals, however, go against God's good creation. In the case of trans people, it is common for them to mar their perfectly functioning bodies in an effort to match their physical bodies with their perceived sex. Conversely, when intersex people have surgery generally it is to fix some physical defect. Fourth, for those who are "made eunuchs by men" it seems that this was usually against their will for the purpose of working in a harem. Even then, they still identified as men as opposed to claiming gender dysphoria issues.[30] As such, these types of gender confusion must be given over to God. Again, it is natural to ask how we got to this point. It did not happen overnight.

The Path to the Rejection of Gender Distinctions

The war on gender did not start in the past few years. This has been going on for some time. In fact, feminists led the charge back in the 1960s and 70s when one feminist group better known as "Feminists—A Political Organization to Annihilate Sex Roles" made it clear that their agenda was to remove gender distinctions.[31] As I have noted in an earlier chapter, feminists' rejection of traditional roles paved the way for the LGBTQ movement. If gender roles are constructed by society, why not the very idea of sexuality?

Scholars have long noted that some aspects of gender distinctions are determined by culture.[32] Historically, sexuality and the norms for sexual expression have changed drastically from the Puritan, to the Victorian,

---

29. Branch, *Affirming God's Image*, 42–43; and Murray, *Madness of Crowds*, 195–99.
30. Branch, *Affirming God's Image*, 47–48.
31. Brown, *Jezebel's War*, 105.
32. Balswick and Balswick, *Authentic Human Sexuality*, 15–20.

to the roaring 20s and beyond.[33] At the same time, secular sociologists suggest culture should define what is "normal" and acceptable sexually.[34] This is a problem; the Word of God must do this. Culture changes but God's Word does not. To be sure, part of the postmodern attack on the creation mandates related to sexuality is the incessant attack from the Left, and particularly the social sciences, that the designations of male and female are oppressive and limiting. So how do they get around such an obvious distinction of sex differentiation readily apparent in almost 99 percent of the population? They simply muddy the waters by divorcing biological sex from psychological or "feeling-based" gender.[35] It did not take the social scientists long to suggest that if gender is a "social construct," which is supposedly the result of patriarchy and hierarchical power structures (e.g., White Privilege), then sex is something which can be modified to match one's "true" gender identity.[36] Science no longer matters, and biology is unimportant in this "brave" new world.[37]

While the removal of gender distinctions may have been proposed in an effort to free one's self of past restrictions, it is just one more step down the road of rebellion against God's design. Indeed, every such step leads us closer to Paul's admonition in Romans 1, which declares that people exchanged the truth for a lie. When creation itself reveals God's good plan, and people rebel against this clear revelation, disaster is sure to follow. As I have been noting throughout, the absolutes of the Genesis mandates related to morality cannot be sidestepped with impunity. There will be consequences.

Western civilization consistently rejects these absolutes but deep down most know when something is not right, especially when it comes to sexual perversion and moral laxness. Yet we still see a concerted effort to reject and rebel against God in this regard. I am reminded of Ezekiel's words to the house of Israel. They were a rebellious people who rejected their past and the realities of what God had done for them. They had had the presence of God in their midst, yet they rejected the truth for idols.

---

33. Balswick and Balswick, *Authentic Human Sexuality*, 20–27.

34. See discussion by Balswick and Balswick, *Authentic Human Sexuality*, 25–27.

35. Branch, *Affirming God's Image*, 22–23. The division was pioneered by Harry Benjamin and later, by professor of psychiatry at UCLA, Robert Stoller (1924–1991), in his 1968 book *Sex and Gender: On the Development of Masculinity and Femininity*. As noted by Branch, *Affirming God's Image*, 11–14.

36. See Butler, *Gender Trouble* (2007).

37. See also comments by Peterson, *12 Rules for Life*, 311.

As such, judgment came upon them in 586 BCE at the hand of the Babylonians. This certainly sounds like Paul's message, and the reality quickly approaching the church, the evangelical world included.

Ironically, for the radicals who push for gender fluidity, their designation of sexuality as an *orientation* is anything but fluid. For these zealots, sexuality is fixed and immovable.[38] To suggest otherwise is tantamount to Inquisitional heresy. Heaven forbid that a pastor, counselor, or even a regular layperson suggest that someone can change their sexual orientation. Rosaria Butterfield learned this the hard way at Wheaton College on January 31, 2014. Butterfield, a converted (in every way) "leftist lesbian professor," who is now married with adopted children, was protested by self-proclaiming evangelicals when she delivered a message in Wheaton College Edman Chapel. Her sin? She declared the radical power of God to change people's sexual desires and orientation.[39] When "evangelical" students have been indoctrinated to the point that they cannot rejoice in the power of Christ to change lives and radically transform even a Rosaria Butterfield, then the church must take note.[40] At the heart of the Gospel is the power of God to change even one's sexual orientation. For the Left, especially the LGBTQ community, such assertions are to be crushed because they fly in the face of *their* dogma.

Regarding the ongoing gender-confusion discussion, Brown notes that "the moment gay activists attempted to redefine marriage, they also rendered gender meaningless within marriage, since for them marriage was no longer the union of a man and a woman but the union of any two people, irrespective of gender. And once you render gender meaningless within marriage, you render it meaningless in society as a whole."[41] At the heart of postmodernity's push for the right to obliterate gender distinctions is the "I" word. It is for self-fulfillment and self-satisfaction. It is to place self on the throne and remove God.[42] It is, as Jeremy Treat says, "Eden all over again,"[43] but not in a good way, it is the rebellion that brought about the fall. In this worldview, "each individual is the great I AM" where science no longer dictates the facts about someone's gender,

---

38. Murray, *Madness of Crowds*, 58.
39. Tracy, "Wheaton."
40. See also comments by Brown, *Evangelicals at the Crossroads*, 118.
41. Brown, *Jezebel's War*, 111.
42. See also Ashford, "Christian Politics," 450.
43. Treat, "Sexuality," 48.

the individual does![44] It is interesting that the subjective nature of self-determination, when it comes to gender, is being hailed as reality and what is right and good.

Barring a great awakening and a spiritual renewal, there is no end to the rebellion and chaos in sight in the near future. Indeed, the chaos is present at almost every level of our lives. Our social media accounts even reflect the chaos. For example, the gender selection of Facebook allows for fifty different choices plus a fill-in-the-blank option.[45] The Enemy loves chaos and Western culture is reveling in it when it comes to gender confusion. Something so basic is now a hodgepodge of elided pronouns and gender identities. And as I write this book gender madness is being enshrined in law by the highest court in the country. On June 16, 2020 SCOTUS legislated special protections of homosexuals and transgendered persons based upon Title VII and the Civil Rights Act of 1964, which included protections for race, religion, color, sex, or national origin. Despite what five SCOTUS justices believe, "sex" in the 1960s certainly did not mean orientation and the baggage it carries today. The chaos continues.

Of course, the mental health professionals have been all too willing to support the chaos of the elimination of gender distinctions through attacks on what it calls "toxic masculinity." But it is not just the toxic masculinity that is the issue, even "traditional masculinity" is an issue to be cautioned against. In this regard, Murray relates how the American Psychological Association wrote to its members noting that an "Awareness of privilege and the harmful impacts of beliefs and behaviours that maintain patriarchal power have been shown to reduce sexist attitudes in men and have been linked to participation in social justice activities."[46] So according to the APA, masculinity is therefore not a gift from God, it is harmful to society in general. Is it any wonder why our young boys are facing confusion as to how they are to act? Every aspect of their very being is challenged on a daily basis while they are told that they are the villain for simply being male.

We have also been rewarding the gender chaos within the educational system. Being from a sexual minority of the LGBTQ community

---

44. Treat, "Sexuality," 48.
45. Brown, *Jezebel's War*, 112; and Wilson, *Mere Sexuality*, 64.
46. As cited by Murray, *Madness of Crowds*, 63.

gives a person a leg up in admissions and hiring at elite universities.[47] In every area of life, the obliteration of gender distinctions is no longer something to be rejected, it is a prized commodity and literally opens doors to opportunity. But what other "opportunities" has the obliteration of the mandate of gender distinctions afforded our depraved society? It is to this that I turn and end this chapter.

The Dangerous Progression

There can be no question that this section will create angst for some people while others will say I have moved beyond the pale and have ventured into the area of fearmongering again. Before you, my reader, make such an evaluation, however, let me remind you that back in my Preface to this book I pointed out that books written only a decade ago issuing strong warnings about the continued downward spiral in our sexual ethics and morality are now outdated because Western culture has not only reached the points of those previous warnings, it has blown past them. While I could have chosen to address these issues in any of the following chapters, I have chosen to address them here because of their connection to the downward progression of societies when the mandates of Genesis are rejected. To be sure, if marriage and family are meaningless, and if procreation is not important to marriage and sexual relationships, and if something as obvious as gender distinctions is no longer important, then why not allow for other sexual deviancies as part of the patchwork quilt of Western sexuality? Not surprisingly, two other sexual perversions are on the horizon with one now in the process of being "normalized." These sexual deviancies are pedophilia and bestiality.

Pedophilia

Simply defined, pedophilia is the seeking of sexual gratification through sexual encounters with children.[48] While historically the definition of who constitutes a "child" has been somewhat fluid, in Western cultures today this tends to be someone younger than eighteen or even sixteen years of age. With the recent news blitz regarding the sexual deviance of the late Jeffrey Epstein and his elite band of cohorts, the issue of

---

47. D'Souza, *Illiberal Education*, 5.
48. For a more detailed definition, see Grabowski, *Sex and Virtue*, 120–21.

pedophilia has been front and center even if some insist that "Soliciting sex from minors is not the same as pedophilia" (so, Lady Collin Campbell: Good Morning Britain).[49]

Former homosexual, and now ordained Christian counsellor, Joe Dallas, correctly notes the similarities between psychiatrists' and doctors' arguments for the normalization of homosexuality in the 1960s and 70s and those being used to normalize pedophilia today.[50] While many homosexual men and women would rightly cringe at the thoughts of normalized pedophilia, the truth is their push for the removal of boundaries is paving the way for the next step in the downward spiral of Western culture. Fences that were put in place not only by God, but also by society and the state, are being torn down in the name of sexual justice. It will not be long before those who reject such a move will be labeled haters and pedophobes (if there is such a word).

Today pedophilia is being promoted with ever increasing intensity as once again science comes to the aid of another form of sexual deviance labeling it an "orientation." The magazine *Paidika*, which ran for twelve years (1987–1995), was devoted to advocating for the rights of pedophiles while being bolstered by "expert" sexologists, psychologists, historians, and lawyers. In fact, the editors openly acknowledged their pedophilia and their desire to educate the general public about their sexual "identity" while fighting back against the "repression of sexuality" they feel in Western culture.[51] Sound familiar?

While this publication is defunct, its assertions certainly are not. In an article from August 2019, culture and news magazine, *Vice*, pushed for the destigmatizing of pedophilia.[52] This article is based upon the work of Berlin's Project Dunkelfeld. The article states, "Another objective of Project Dunkelfeld is to destigmatize pedophilia. Dr. Klaus Beier, who created the program, argues pedophilia is a sexual orientation and not a crime if the person has not acted on it. 'Nobody chooses this,' he said. 'And as long as he would not [sic] act out, it would be very, very inhuman to judge such a person. And I would always vote to integrate him in society.'"[53] Of course, the first step is acceptance, the next is allow-

49. Grant, "Lady Collin."
50. Dallas, *Gay Gospel*, 50–53; and Watkins, *New Absolutes*, 147–48.
51. Statement of Purpose at http://www.drjudithreisman.com/archives/Paidika_Statement_of_Purpose_OCR.pdf.
52. See Vice News, "Pedophiles."
53. Vice News, "Pedophiles."

ing "consenting" children to partake in the deviancy with these troubled adults. In this regard, gay-friendly groups are attempting to lower the age of consent in America (e.g., NAMBLA—North American Man-Boy Love Association), and some politicians are lobbying for variations of this concept.[54] Again, while I am not trying to draw a direct connection between pedophilia and homosexuality, the statistics do show that the rates of pedophiles who are gay (males predominantly) is 11 to 1 versus 36 to 1 among heterosexual men.[55] The reality is, this is yet another slippery slope down which the West is heading.

On this topic commentator Lauren Chen is correct to note that this "type of thinking is exactly how slippery slopes happen, [. . .] And I am fully convinced at this point that pedophilia will be the next slippery slope our society tumbles down. In fact, as we've seen, it's already started. Like it or not, we are living in a world where nearly every single slippery slope that people tried to warn us about [. . .] has come to fruition."[56] If Christians do not wake up and begin to act, we will be living in a society that we could never have imagined, but then again, it may be what we deserve because of our complacency and unwillingness to get involved and call our lawmakers to account.[57] What was once reviled and marginalized within society is now being viewed as an orientation similar to homosexuality. Even though many may not view this as mainstream, the rapidity with which homosexuality and transgenderism has swept over the church and Western society does not leave me optimistic. Recently, I read where one Presbyterian pastor in California allowed a self-identified pedophile to work with children unsupervised. This included overnight excursions with children, which were encouraged by the pastor. When it was finally revealed—by the pastor's own transgendered child, no less—that this was happening the pastor's defense was that "pedophilia was like homosexuality."[58] The slippery slope argument is true once again.

If the assertion that pedophilia is an unalterable orientation, how long will it be before we accept such lifestyles in our Western society? We may not be there yet, but that seems to be changing. Although since removed from the TEDx talks, in May of 2018, at the University of

---

54. Brown, "California."
55. Satinover, *Homosexuality*, 65.
56. Chen, "VICE."
57. See a similar conclusion by Watkins, *New Absolutes*, 148.
58. Briggs, "Ortberg."

Würtzberg in Germany, German medical student, Mirjam Heine, argued for the acceptance of pedophilia as an orientation following the natural conclusions of the LGBTQ trajectory.[59] These feelings, she argues, are not their choice; they were born with them. While Heine insisted that acting upon those feelings was wrong, she concluded that having them was "natural" to pedophiles. Therefore, we should not stigmatize them or marginalize them. The fences are being probed for weaknesses once again and right there to aid in the probing is the media through film.

In this vein, in February 2020, the film festival in Germany known as Berlinale 2020 featured a film by an Austrian filmmaker named Sandra Wollner called "The Trouble with Being Born." In the movie, a father has a sexual relationship with an android meant to take the place of his lost ten-year-old daughter. This not only highlighted pedophilia, it also included the glorification of incest. Clearly this is an attempt to mainstream one of the remaining frontiers of sexual taboos.[60] While some hailed the film as a "gem," at least one honest film critic called it for what it truly is: "Let's not pretend that this isn't about mainstreaming the last sexual perversion—other than bestiality—that isn't socially acceptable. [. . .] Of course, if you live like an atheist and have a worldview that this world is all there is and that human beings aren't any more than a conglomeration of cells accidentally swirled together, to both begin and end without meaning in the world, then why wouldn't you build a kiddie sex robot, thus softening your resistance to going and getting a real kid? Hello, pagan morality."[61]

Netflix is also getting in on the action. This year they released a new movie called *Cuties* which features the sexualization of eleven-year-old girls in dance routines in which they dress seductively, "twerk," and behave in an inappropriate and a sensual manner.[62] The natural reaction of many people was revulsion and disgust, especially in light of the objectifying of children sexually, which is sure to draw the attention of pedophiles. Netflix administrators held their ground and defended the movie. They insisted that the movie was highlighting the problem of objectifying children. I find this response disingenuous and troubling. So, you make a movie that objectifies children in order to protest and combat

---

59. The talk is available through McLean, "TEDx Speaker." See also, Watkins, *New Absolutes*, 147–48.
60. Activist Mommy, "Child Robot."
61. As cited by Activist Mommy, "Child Robot."
62. Dumas, "Netflix."

objectifying children? You cannot make this stuff up. We are living in a twisted world.

From a legislative perspective, California just passed a law (SB 145; note also bill AB 1145[63]) lessening the penalty for those engaging in sex with minors if there is a ten year or less age gap between the individuals.[64] The argument of the bill's author, state Senator Scott Wiener (Democrat from San Francisco), is that previous legislation unduly targeted LGBTQ people because of the illegality of anal and oral sex (the dominant forms of same-sex sexual activity) as opposed to vaginal intercourse.[65] That would mean that a 24-year-old person could have sexual encounters (e.g., anal and oral sex) with "consenting" minors as young as 14 without necessarily being charged with any serious crime such as being a sex offender for pedophilia. It is obvious that this new legislation will allow gay men especially, to target younger males and groom them for the gay lifestyle without fear of prosecution. Gay-affirming groups in California praised these new laws.[66]

Sexual deviance and the undermining of God's mandates go hand-in-hand and are only going to increase as society becomes immune to the horrors and depravity of such acts. We certainly have moved in that direction about other sexual deviancies in the past. And, as just noted in the above critic's quotation, bestiality is the other "taboo" of sexual deviance that is now coming into view. Even though many think bestiality is beyond reasonable decency even to discuss, the Enemy has no problem unleashing this sexual perversion upon an unwitting public.

Bestiality

When I began planning the direction of this book, I included in my proposal a brief discussion on the issue of bestiality as one of the many perversions of sexuality present in Western culture. When one of the editors for a leading evangelical publisher, to whom I was pitching this book idea, read the proposal, he suggested that I remove any reference to bestiality due to the outlandish nature of the deviancy. I said I would consider

---

63. This bill lessens the requirements for reporting statutory rape.
64. Lamm, "California Bill."
65. Presently, judges can use discretion when vaginal intercourse occurs as to whether it is consensual and therefore not meriting sex-offender status or registry.
66. Brown, "Legislators."

his request. The very next time I turned on the news I was greeted by a headline noting the practice of bestiality by a man. The amazing thing is that instead of a sense of shame at the act, the man actually threatened his neighbors if they did not allow him to have access to their animals.[67]

To be sure, I am not saying that bestiality is coming to a community near you any time in the immediate future, but I am not too convinced that it is not too far off before we turn a blind eye to it, even though it may never be mainstream. We are doing this already with cases of pedophilia as I noted above. And for the last several decades, all forms of same-sex acts and relationships are now viewed as normal. Now again, I am not trying to say that those struggling with same-sex attraction are on par with pedophiles or those who engage in bestiality. What I am trying to point out is the trajectory of sexual and moral decline prevalent in Western cultures. There is a reason why God established his mandates in Genesis and then enacted laws against the practice of breaking those mandates in the Torah (e.g., Lev 18 and 20). Incest, homosexuality, transgenderism, and bestiality are all prohibited within the Torah.

As I was reading about the state of college campuses vis-à-vis sexual depravity I read one disturbing quotation from a gay activist who joked, "What's wrong with a little bestiality?"[68] In keeping with many people's concerns with gay activism, some in this camp are obviously okay with the further degradation of Western culture in this regard. In my country of birth, Canada, recently a man who was brought up on charges of bestiality, which included sexual acts between animals and his children, was not charged because of a loophole in the law. The judge could not convict the man because the law dealt only with sexual penetration of an animal. Canada had to pass a new bill (C-84) in June of 2019 in order to fix this loophole. Finally, one detailed study of the sex habits of Americans found that one of the sexual fantasies they had was bestiality, with seven percent of men and three percent of women following through with the act.[69] These numbers are staggering when placed within the context of a country the size of America. As a society, we have moved far beyond human decency and are quickly heading for the abyss unless God intervenes, and we pray for God's mercy and forgiveness.

---

67. Fox News, "New Jersey Man."
68. D'Souza, *Illiberal Education*, 12.
69. Patterson and Kim, *The Day America Told the Truth*, 77, 81.

Conclusion

I would like to conclude this chapter by noting a pertinent comment from Todd Wilson. He says, "Despite the consistent messaging of our culture, you are not who you desire sexually. Instead you are who God has created you to be in his image and likeness, whether male or female."[70] The Enemy has certainly created confusion beyond description as we face the ongoing chaos of our society. To a degree, today's rejection of gender distinctions is a return to a form of dualism or better yet, Gnosticism.[71] What the body is, is unimportant. What the "spirit" or intellect tells the person is more tangible and "real" than actual bodily realities. Thus, we have a disconnect between reality and spirit. But then again, the heart is deceitfully wicked. We also need to recognize the effects of the fall on our bodies and on the way we perceive ourselves. Our bodies and minds are marred by the fall and sin. Thus, our perceptions of right and wrong, of sexuality and gender, of what God wants from us, and our perceptions of "how God made us" are also warped by sin. This includes any possible genetic abnormalities, that may cause one to be inclined in a certain direction sexually. Despite the results of the fall on our genetics, we are still accountable before God in the same way an alcoholic or a drug addict, who is genetically predisposed to these sins, is accountable.[72] A person still has a choice of whether or not to act upon those tendencies.

Our bodies as male and female will not be done away with, they will be redeemed. At the same time, holiness cannot be reduced to being male or female, it is committing ourselves, soul and body, to God and living in accordance with God's Word. For those who minister to people who are sexually confused, my heart goes out to you. This is an important calling, and many are offering help for those ministering in this area.[73] Nevertheless, as ministers, educators, parents, and grandparents we must never accept sexual deviance in any form as normal for us or our children. Nor should we say it is sanctioned by God's Word. To do so is to be unfaithful to our calling. Not surprisingly, Western culture and the church specifically have been doing this very thing when it comes to same-sex activity, the topic of my next two chapters.

---

70. Wilson, *Mere Sexuality*, 75.
71. So, too, Branch, *Affirming God's Image*, 108.
72. Branch, *Affirming God's Image*, 64–67.
73. See Mouw, "Continuing the Task," 59–70.

Chapter 10

The Mandate of Gender Distinctions Part 2

Homosexuality and Culture

> By and large, it is society, not the individual, that chooses whether homosexuality will be widely practiced. A society's values, much more than individual tendencies, determine the extent of homosexuality in that society. Thus, we can have great sympathy for the exclusively homosexual individual while strongly opposing social acceptance of homosexuality. In this way we retain both our hearts and our values.[1]

THESE COMMENTS BY JEWISH commentator, Dennis Prager, capture well the tension between cultural acceptance of homosexuality and pastoral care for those who struggle with same-sex attractions. Despite how or which of the Genesis mandates people reject, as believers and the church, it is our job to minister to them and bring healing through the power of Jesus Christ. Yet, as believers we are still part of culture and should seek what is best for our country. But what happens when a culture embraces same-sex activity and coupling as normal? This is the scenario we face in western democracies. What is telling is that most of these nations, America in particular, declare themselves to be Christian. America has rejected the authority of God's Word and God's mandate of gender

---

1. Prager, "Why Judaism."

distinctions. Put differently, the law of God has come into conflict with the law of the land. Those holding to an orthodox belief in the sinfulness of same-sex acts find themselves at odds with the wider culture in a similar way Daniel and his three friends found themselves at odds with the laws of Babylon. This is no less true of Jesus and the early church who found themselves at odds with Rome. While we may not have come to the point of life and death, the conflict is inevitable if you declare yourself to be a follower of God.

As I have queried in other chapters, how has Western culture arrived at our current situation? While the acceptance of homosexuality as "normal" did not happen overnight, it did happen with more rapidity than previous attacks on the Genesis mandates (e.g., marriage, family, and abortion). Within forty years, culture went from almost a complete rejection of same-sex activity to almost a full acceptance. As I will demonstrate in this and the following chapter, the Enemy effected this shift on two fronts: one cultural and one ecclesial. In light of this two-prong approach, in this chapter I will examine how the shift within culture transpired, and in my next chapter I will look at the biblical and church positions on same-sex activity.

Before beginning this discussion though, I want to make three comments. First, as introduced in the last chapter, same-sex activity is at its heart a rejection of the mandate of gender distinctions and God's plan for humans to find companionship within heterosexual pairing. Second, because I have touched on some of the cultural and biblical issues concerning same-sex activity when dealing with marriage redefinition, there is inevitably bound to be some overlap. I will attempt to limit this as much as possible. Third, I want my reader to know that I am coming at this subject as someone who has read extensively on this topic and published in this area. I also have had personal interaction with those who struggle with same-sex attraction both within my family and among my close friends. At the same time, while I recognize that the results of the fall have affected our sexuality, I know that God is greater than our sin and can bring about transformation despite the fact that we are being told that sexual orientation is immutable. I will begin this chapter by giving a brief history of how same-sex activity became mainstream in America.

Homosexuality in America: A Brief History

The deviance of same-sex activity is as old as time. Most cultures tolerated homosexual activity but marginalized it as outside of the mainstream of what was deemed normal. One need only look at Paul's words in Romans 1 to recognize that nature teaches humanity that homosexual activity is not the normal mode of sexual expression. In this vein, for over 400 years of English and American history, legislators such as Sir William Blackstone in England and American patriots James Otis and Alexander Hamilton, noted the power of natural law (i.e., God's law) to supersede human law, especially when it came to homosexuality and bestiality.[2] That was the general attitude towards same-sex activity throughout most of American history until the rise of social-scientific studies in the first half of the twentieth century.

The Influence of Alfred Kinsey

The proverbial beginning of the end of biblical sexual morality in America (and Western culture) came with the work of Alfred Charles Kinsey (1894–1956). In this vein, Watkins says "What Malthus did for population control, Darwin for evolution, and Sanger for birth control, Kinsey did for sex—and the fallout has been every bit as devastating."[3] Kinsey, a follower of Darwinian evolution found that Judeo-Christian morals were a hinderance to the truly freeing nature of deviant sex, namely, homosexuality, pedophilia, bestiality, and bi-sexuality.[4] While others have detailed Kinsey's "scientific studies" on human sexuality, Kinsey's "studies" are so perverse in nature that I refuse to note them here. In fact, some of his "scientific" studies are not just perverse, they are criminal, especially when it comes to Kinsey's "observations" related to child sexuality.[5] Put simply, Kinsey was a deeply flawed individual when it came to his sexual proclivities and deviances.

Despite his major moral flaws, it was from his studies in human sexuality from the 1940s that the oft-touted statistic that four percent of the population is homosexual arose, a statistic that is based upon faulty

---

2. Watkins, *New Absolutes*, 132–33.
3. Watkins, *New Absolutes*, 131.
4. Watkins, *New Absolutes*, 134–36.
5. Watkins, *New Absolutes*, 138–39.

data and has been called into question in various studies.[6] Many studies have shown that number to be as low as one to two percent.[7] What is most troubling is the way Kinsey gathered his data, which primarily derived from active homosexuals, prison inmates, prostitutes, pimps, rapists, and so on. Today, any honest scientist would quickly note that all of these groups by their very nature do not represent the American mainstream.[8] Put differently, Kinsey's study would be the modern equivalent of asking a room full of Playboy Playmates how they felt about posing nude and then taking their responses and applying them to the wider society. Kinsey's subjects almost all fell within the fringe of society during his day, and in some cases, even for our time. As a case in point, to assume that homosexual activity is commonplace in the prison system is an understatement. Of course, many of these subjects are going to have had homosexual encounters. Yet, despite Kinsey's methodological flaws, his studies on human sexuality have become mainstream in America,[9]—no doubt due to his favorable view of deviant sex—and regularly receive government funding through the Kinsey Institute at Indiana University. Not surprisingly, Hugh Hefner of Playboy fame was a big fan of Kinsey and used his lead when he established his hedonistic lifestyle and business model, which undermined the Genesis mandates and human sexual mores in general.[10]

America Post-Kinsey

In the wake of Kinsey's work, the following two decades saw a push for acceptance of same-sex practices within Western culture, and the church in particular.[11] As a predominantly "Christian" culture, in order to change public opinion on homosexuality, the Enemy knew he had to change the way the church viewed same-sex activity. One of the earliest affirming statements from a religious scholar was the book titled *Homosexuality*

---

6. See the listing in Watkins, *New Absolutes*, 136–39.
7. Dallas, *Gay Gospel*, 127–30.
8. Watkins, *New Absolutes*, 137–38.
9. Note the approving way Benshoff and Griffin (*Queer Images*, 5) cite Kinsey.
10. Watkins, *New Absolutes*, 141.
11. See Dallas (*Gay Gospel*, 64–79) for a brief overview of the history of the gay "Christian" movement. Much of the next three sections are a summary of Dallas's excellent overview. See also Benshoff and Griffin, *Queer Images*, 3–9.

and the Western Christian Tradition written in 1955 by Derrick S. Bailey, a British Anglican theologian. Bailey started what today is often termed the reimagination of Scripture vis-à-vis the homosexual question. Less than a decade later in 1963, the first religious group to affirm homosexual activity came from the Quakers in a pamphlet titled "The Literary Committee of the Friends Home Service in England." Joe Dallas notes that in this pamphlet, "It allowed for premarital sex, approved of adultery in some cases, and viewed homosexuality as acceptable."[12] Beginning with this slow trickle in England, Western culture was beginning to reimagine the place of same-sex activity.

Throughout the 1960s the gay movement steadily gained steam as the gay sub-culture began to organize and demand recognition as being "normal." The gay movement reached its "flash point" and "point of no return" with the now famous Stonewall Riots in New York's Greenwich Village in 1969. In the immediate aftermath of this event, the gay movement organized and declared war on anyone who stood in their way for full acceptance. It is important to remember that early on during the gay rights movement like Stonewall, gay proponents did not advocate for gay marriage.[13] Nevertheless, it did not take them long to realize that in order for them to be viewed as "normal," marriage rights were a must. By the end of the decade homosexual activism in America reached a fever-pitch. From a religious perspective, in 1968, former Pentecostal pastor Troy Perry organized the first gay denomination, the *Universal Fellowship of Metropolitan Community Churches* (UFMCC).

Dallas notes that there were three prongs to the gay agenda: come out; form alliances; and confrontation.[14] The slogan "gay power" emerged, and advocates insisted that homosexuality was no longer to be viewed as a behavior to be fixed or shunned, but rather was an "identity" which was immutable like one's race or gender.[15] This had an immediate ripple effect for the gay Christian movement. If it is true that homosexuality is immutable and part of one's being, that is, homosexuals were created by God this way, then how could this be a sin? The die was cast for the forward momentum of the movement to tackle the "abuse"

---

12. Dallas, *Gay Gospel*, 65.
13. Murray, *Madness of Crowds*, 5.
14. Dallas, *Gay Gospel*, 71–76.
15. Dallas, *Gay Gospel*, 70–71.

heaped upon the gay community by the church's so-called "misuse" and "misinterpretation" of Scripture.

America Post-Stonewall

After the cultural earthquake of Stonewall, a growing number of voices advocating for the full acceptance of homosexuality began an all-out push to change public perception of homosexuality. The gay movement made alliances with Hollywood, mainline churches, media personalities, and politicians.[16] A major breakthrough for the gay movement came in 1973 when the APA (American Psychiatric Association) removed homosexuality from its list of disorders in their *Diagnostic and Statistical Manual* (DSM) and renamed it "sexual orientation disturbance."[17] This paved the way for the full acceptance of homosexuality as "normal" sexual behavior (the World Health Organization followed in 1992). Over the years since this change in the DSM, the APA has moved away from Judeo-Christian language, which affirmed heterosexuality as the "norm" against which everything else is measured, to language reflective of the changing culture or the "spirit of the age" thus removing the categories of deviant sexuality that the Bible calls sin.[18]

From an academic perspective, following the lead of Christian authors like Bailey in the late 1950s, others began to publish works to change specifically Christian perspectives on the topic. One of the most influential and earliest volumes on the topic was the 1978 publication of *Is the Homosexual My Neighbor?* coauthored by Letha Scanzoni and Virginia Ramey Mollenkott. After approximately twenty years of marriage, Mollenkott (b. 1932) divorced her husband and went on to become a vocal advocate for LGBTQ issues, and later married her lesbian partner.[19] For anyone already suspect of the motives behind the "re-education" of American culture and the church vis-à-vis homosexuality, books written by those who had a "vested interest" in the legalization and acceptance of homosexuality is problematic on its face. It is no wonder why several of the so-called "groundbreaking" books of this period were written by self-identifying homosexuals. The secular media promoted these works

---

16. Dallas, *Gay Gospel*, 73–75.
17. See Branch, *Affirming God's Image*, 29.
18. Branch, *Affirming God's Image*, 30.
19. Virginia Ramey Mollenkott at https://www.virginiamollenkott.com/.

to bring about their goals of transforming American culture. Since the 1970s, Christian bookstores and publishing houses have been churning out literature on both sides of the debate. Sadly, many well-known and well-meaning evangelicals have joined the affirming bandwagon and written books and articles reinterpreting every biblical passage on homosexuality (see more in the next chapter).

With changing opinions within the church, medical fields, and general public, in the 1970s, and under the banner of "civil rights," the gay movement took their fight to the government with the purpose of striking down anti-sodomy laws, changing the military's position on gays, radically changing how schools taught on homosexuality, and attacking and marginalizing churches, or any other organization that had previously, or currently, deemed them as "sick" or "disturbed."[20] Evangelicals were now confronted with how they were going to react to this new push.

Evangelicals and the Gay Agenda

At first, most evangelicals thought that the growing gay movement would not be an issue that would require immediate response, and to a degree, they were right. Nevertheless, by the late 1970s, state and local legislators took up gay rights issues and ballot initiatives that soon forced believers to take a stand. Jerry Falwell Sr.'s organizing of the Moral Majority in 1979 helped bring to the fore the growing concern about the war against traditional values, which had prevailed in the United States since its inception.[21] The 1980s and 1990s marked the turning point for the moral soul of America as the gay movement became increasingly active in promoting their agenda while effectively marginalizing the Christian Right. Although it would be another decade or more before evangelicals also found themselves in the quagmire of the same-sex debate, the handwriting was on the wall: it was just a matter of time.

In 1981 openly gay Yale historian, John Boswell, released his book *Christianity, Social Tolerance, and Homosexuality*, which became the ammunition many gay Christian advocates and affirming scholars had been looking for in order to undermine biblical authority and its teaching against homosexuality. Boswell showed how homosexuality was not a major issue within the church until the Medieval period and

---

20. Dallas, *Gay Gospel*, 75.
21. Dallas, *Gay Gospel*, 78–79.

later. He also reinterpreted all the key passages on homosexuality in the Bible "proving" how they supposedly did not teach that homosexuality was wrong.[22] Similar to the concerns raised about Mollenkott's biased agenda, one can easily see why conservative evangelicals tended to ignore Boswell's work.[23] On the other hand, Dallas correctly notes that most liberal mainline churches accepted Boswell's thesis with little trouble due to their general lack of serious scriptural engagement on the issue. Conservatives, however, who took seriously the authority of Scripture and the study of the original languages, were not so easily convinced even though numerous scholars were beginning to parrot Boswell's conclusions.

But the gay movement was not to be discouraged. They took advantage of the AIDS crisis in the 1980s putting the blame on the church for teaching hate and shame about homosexuality, which in turn caused gays to be so self-loathing that they engaged in unsafe sexual practices.[24] Into this mix, two gay men from Harvard, Marshall Kirk and Hunter Madsen, added their perspective of how to change the anti-homosexual sentiment throughout America, especially in conservative churches. They wrote a book in 1989 titled *After the Ball* in which they laid out a detailed roadmap using eight propaganda strategies as to how homosexuality would become legitimized in America.[25] The key was to go on the offensive and stigmatize and marginalize any person who disagreed with their agenda using pejoratives of every kind. They also set forward how the gay agenda would take over media coverage on the topic.[26] At the heart of the offensive was the push to stop all opposition to the gay movement.[27] Many during this time insisted on presenting homosexuals as the same as heterosexuals. They did this by keeping the general public in the dark as to what actually took place sexually between homosexuals, especially gay men: full disclosure would have immediately turned off the wider populace.[28] The strategy worked well especially when coupled with the assault on educational content, media propaganda, and the

---

22. Dallas, *Gay Gospel*, 84–88.
23. Dallas, *Gay Gospel*, 86–87.
24. Dallas, *Gay Gospel*, 92–93.
25. Kirk and Madsen, *After the Ball* (1989).
26. See for example, Benshoff and Griffin, *Queer Images* (2006). Media in the West, and especially in America, leans left and therefore promotes left-leaning agendas, many of which are anti-biblical. See Grudem, *Politics*, 555–71.
27. Dallas, *Gay Gospel*, 94.
28. Satinover, *Homosexuality*, 52.

The Mandate of Gender Distinctions Part 2

rapidly changing church culture. For example, former evangelical professor Mel White established the gay activist organization Soulforce (seeking to "Sabotage Christian Supremacy" according to their website), which spawned the Freedom/Equality Rides of the late 1990s and early 2000s, both of which sought to change the policies and positions of evangelicals towards homosexuality.[29] The Equality Ride actually made it to my school in 2006 prior to my employment in 2011 and was greeted with Christian love and caring, something they did not expect.

The gay movement also had a ready-made contingent of celebrities that would help sway the hearts and minds of America, especially younger generations. Ellen DeGeneres, Rosie O'Donnell, Boy George, George Michael, Elton John along with numerous others gave credence to the gay movement broadly.[30] Along with celebrities, movies, and pop music, television series and specials aired gay-themed content non-stop throughout the 1990s and 2000s. *Will and Grace, The Modern Family, Queer as Folk, Queer Eye, Shameless, The L Word, Brokeback Mountain* (2005), and the like bombarded the airwaves with the goal of making gay "normal." America, and by extension the church, was becoming desensitized to the stigma once placed upon the gay lifestyle. To a certain degree, Christians are just as much to blame for consuming this programming. An entire generation of Millennials and Gen Z have cut their teeth on these types of shows. This indoctrination has continued into the second decade of the twenty-first century. As noted in an earlier chapter, the family-friendly Hallmark channel decided to air gay-themed commercials and movies during the 2019 and 2020 Christmas seasons. And recently a Brazil-based comedy group released a Christmas movie depicting Jesus as a gay man.[31]

This brief historical overview highlights the process of how America came to accept same-sex activity as normal. The intensity of the fight was felt most readily in the 1970s through the 1990s. From the early 2000s and onward, it was a foregone conclusion as to what direction Western culture was moving, especially in the US. While the church continued to push back against the seismic changes through political and theological opposition, America's rejection of the Genesis mandate of gender distinctions was all-but-complete by the turn of the millennium. Gallup

---

29. Dallas, *Gay Gospel*, 95–96.
30. Dallas, *Gay Gospel*, 94.
31. McCarthy, "Netflix."

polls showed that in 1987 only 32 percent agreed that same-sex activity between consenting adults should be legal with 57 percent disapproving. During the 1990s, people began to vacillate with percentages almost equally split in the mid-forties. By 2003, however, the gulf between the two sides began to widen and by 2020, 72 percent approved and only 24 percent disapproved.[32] As we will see in the next section, the changes in favorability towards same-sex activity during the first decade of the millennium correspond not only with changes in cultural perspective but also with the legal process. What could not be mandated legislatively due to opposition by traditionalists, was enacted through the judiciary.

Legislative Changes

As just noted, the activism and propaganda campaign of the LGBTQ community since the 1970s has caused most people in the West today to look favorably upon same-sex lifestyles. What is more, the legal process of the past sixty years has enshrined many rights and precedents into law for LGBTQ groups. Clearly this has fundamentally changed the moral and ethical landscape of America, even though most Americans would argue that these changes are good and needed. The first step in legalizing same-sex activity was the need to remove anti-sodomy laws. Illinois was the first to do this in 1962 followed by a similar, although much later, SCOTUS decision in 2003 (*Lawrence vs. Texas*). This ruling reversed the earlier 1986 *Bowers v. Hardwick* decision. During the late 1980s and the early 1990s some cities (e.g., San Francisco and D.C.) began allowing for domestic partnerships with some states (Hawaii) inching closer to legalizing same-sex marriage.[33] While the *Defense of Marriage Act* (DOMA) in 1996 was meant to alleviate the fears of mainstream America from the growing threat to traditional marriage by limiting "federal marriage benefits" (e.g., joint tax filing, immigration sponsoring of a spouse, the extension of social security benefits to a spouse),[34] the handwriting was on the wall for the demise of traditional marriage. For example, that same year, Hawaii legalized same-sex marriage, but it was quickly voted down by the people in a constitutional amendment in 1998.[35] By 1999 Califor-

---

32. Gallup, "Gay and Lesbian Rights."
33. History.com Editors, "Gay Marriage."
34. History.com Editors, "Gay Marriage."
35. History.com Editors, "Gay Marriage."

nia became the first state to legalize domestic partnerships for same-sex couples, followed in 2000, with Vermont becoming the first state to legalize same-sex unions.[36] In 2003, Massachusetts was the first to pass legislation legalizing same-sex marriage, which set the stage for rapid changes within American culture related to the issue. Although some states passed constitutional amendments in the early 2000s banning same-sex marriage (e.g., Oregon, Texas, and Kansas), the legal challenges to traditional marriage laws only increased in the first five years of the new millennium with several states following Vermont's lead to legalize same-sex unions (e.g., Connecticut, Iowa, and New Hampshire).[37] The raucous legal period of the first decade of the 2000s gave way to the changing moral fabric of America in the second decade when, for the first time, several states legalized same-sex marriage through *voter-approved* state constitutional amendments (Maine, Maryland, and Washington).[38] In several key legal cases from 2010 to 2015, DOMA was challenged and ruled to violate the "equal protection clause" of the Constitution, with the Obama administration refusing to defend it.[39] The death knell for traditional marriage sounded in the landmark 2015 *Obergefell v. Hodges* SCOTUS decision, which legalized same-sex marriage nation-wide. This decision helped cement the "acceptable" status of the same-sex "family."

But the LGBTQ agenda was not done with their push for "equality" and "normative" status. How could they be viewed as normal when there were "homophobes" in America still advocating for what has become known as "reparative therapy." Indeed, many Christian counselors and therapists hold that same-sex orientation is not immutable but can be changed with the help of God and prayer. What started as an internal push to ban reparative therapy among the mental health community in the early 1990s,[40] has now found solid footing in the age of acceptance and tolerance. LGBTQ proponents, many of whom now hold political office, are going after the "hateful," "bigoted," and "unscientific" practitioners of reparative therapy. As a result, conversion therapy is now outlawed for minors in Virginia with other states soon to follow suit. California Democrat Ted Lieu along with 144 Democrat cosponsors, introduced

---

36. History.com Editors, "Gay Marriage."
37. History.com Editors, "Gay Marriage."
38. History.com Editors, "Gay Marriage."
39. History.com Editors, "Gay Marriage."
40. Satinover, *Homosexuality*, 35–37.

Bill HR3570 (the *Therapeutic Fraud Prevention Act*) on June 27, 2019 to the House in Congress while Senate Bill 2008 was introduced by Democrat Senator Patty Murray, which is the senate version. This bill seeks to outlaw conversion therapy by anyone who charges for their services, that is, professional counselors, psychologists, and psychiatrists.[41] Put simply, practicing therapists can no longer help those struggling with same-sex attraction to change or convert to a heterosexual lifestyle.[42] Again, the LGBTQ community feels that these types of legislative "protections" are not enough. Now legislation, which seeks to give LGBTQ people special protections (Bill HR5 *The Equality Act*),[43] has not only been introduced, but SCOTUS has established a precedent in the June 2020, *Bostock v. Clayton County, Georgia* ruling that extended protection to LGBTQ workers from being fired for their orientation. While this has been hailed as a great victory, the full implications of the law are yet to be felt. Many Christians feel that this has opened the door for Christian organizations and institutions to be sued if they fire or refuse to hire a practicing LGBTQ individual. Thus, the clash continues between the church and a culture, which has embraced same-sex activism.

The Clash of Culture and Conservative Christianity

The militant and intolerant attacks of many in the radical wing of the LGBTQ community is not just happening at the judicial level, it is becoming more visible in their open rejection of anything and anyone that may threaten their status. Now to be sure, not all LGBTQ people are univocal in this regard. In fact, even within the LGBTQ community there is division. For example, Murray points out the distinct difference between those who identify as "gay" and those who prefer the label "queer." He notes that gays want to be accepted as "normal" like everyone else and live out their lives like straight people. Queers, on the other hand, want to be distinct and different from society. They want to tear down the old norms in favor of *their* reality with ubiquitous public displays of

---

41. See https://www.govtrack.us/congress/bills/116/hr3570 and Congress.Gov, "S.2008."

42. Associated Press, "Conversion Therapy."

43. Congress.Gov, "S.2008."

lewdness, debauchery, and all-around indecency in their "Pride" parades throughout Western democracies.[44]

Despite the divide within the LGBTQ community, there seems to be unanimity when it comes to their disgust, hatred, and disdain for conservative Christians, especially conservative evangelicals. They seek, and in some cases succeed, in silencing the voice of evangelicals who preach the Bible. Recently, the Liverpool, England, Labour LGBT Network petitioned and forced the cancelation of Franklin Graham's evangelistic service labeling him a "homophobic hate preacher."[45] Since then, the number of venues rejecting Graham's ministry to the UK has grown to seven.[46] Graham has enlisted legal counsel with the tour being postponed until a legal remedy can be found.[47] I am not hopeful of a positive resolution when even evangelicals in the United Kingdom are resisting his ministry by writing to news outlets expressing their opposition.[48] I guess these evangelicals forgot Paul's admonition for believers to keep their disputes in-house (1 Cor 6:1–6). It is not that hard to grasp what this type of opposition means for the preaching of the Gospel in such a hostile environment where politically correct evangelicals side with the LGBTQ mob. Billy Graham would have a much harder time ministering today. Just this week I read that over 12,000 "Christians" are now seeking the removal of Franklin Graham from leadership of *Samaritan's Purse* simply because they do not agree with his political stance and his position on social justice issues like homosexuality.[49] As I will develop in Chapter 14, much of this hostility is nothing more than petty partisan politics and a fundamental difference related to biblical morality. Conservative Christians are being marginalized because of their rejection of "social justice" concerns of left-leaning "Christians," who often push for the normalizing of LGBTQ lifestyles in the church.

A similar attack happened in June of 2019 in Toronto, Canada, when a street evangelist was arrested for preaching God's love in the gay section of Toronto. He was accosted by a mob of gay and pro-gay people

---

44. Murray, *Madness of Crowds*, 36–37.
45. Parke, "Franklin Graham."
46. Mouser, "Franklin Graham."
47. See the news release at https://grahamtouruk.billygraham.org/status-of-the-tour/.
48. Sherwood, "Franklin Graham."
49. Jackson, "Petition."

and verbally and physically assaulted; yet he was the one arrested, while the LGBTQ people played the victim.[50]

This is fitting. The most effective way the gay lobby has brought about its proposed changes to Western culture is through the stance of victimhood. Now to be sure, many times homosexuals throughout history have been treated unfairly, and in worse case scenarios have been brutalized and even killed, a reality that is unacceptable. However, homosexuals in Western societies have gone from what may have been a legitimate concern for safety, to advocating for the outright rejection of any person or group, especially conservative Christians—evangelicals in particular—who in any way disagree with their position and agenda.[51] Even to disagree with the lifestyle while expressing genuine love and concern for the person is not enough to quell their attack against those who hold to traditional beliefs on sexuality and marriage.

Conservative evangelicals are labeled or branded homophobes and haters for no other reason than that they disagree with the LGBTQ agenda and lifestyle because of their Christian convictions founded upon God's Word. Indeed, many have written on this topic showing how Christians are consistently faced with attacks from LGBTQ groups.[52] The LGBTQ movement knows full well that it is easy to get the general and nominal-Christian populace on the side of the "oppressed," especially in a postmodern context. Who would not want to be on the side of the underdog? Yet, the reality is that even though Christians are viewed as the oppressor, we are quickly becoming the underdog even though the media presents it as just the opposite. Conservative evangelicals are being marginalized for what they believe, how they vote, and for the people with whom they associate. Interestingly, politicians and governors of entire states are declaring implicit and explicit war on those with traditional beliefs.

Recently the governor of New York said that those holding pro-life and conservative beliefs (that is code for Christian values), do not belong in New York because they do not represent NY values![53] Imagine if a governor of a more conservative state said homosexuals and pro-choice people are not welcome in an entire state; the media would go into a frenzy! Of course, what are we to expect when most news outlets have a

50. Hoffman, "Pastor Arrested."

51. See also Dallas, *Gay Gospel*, 135–36.

52. E.g., Osten and Sears, *The Homosexual Agenda* (2003); Floyd, *The Gay Agenda* (2004); Sheldon, *The Agenda* (2005).

53. Chasmar, "Gov. Cuomo."

progressive, left-leaning bent and agenda?[54] Once again, this is all part of the marginalization of believers and the rejection of the divine mandates of God on sexuality and gender distinctions.

Similarly, former Democrat presidential candidate Elizabeth Warren declared that gender non-conforming people were the backbone of American democracy.[55] Really? A small fringe group are the "backbone" of American democracy? What does that mean for the majority who have worked to make America into the nation it is today, a nation built upon Judeo-Christian ideals? This type of evidence proves that many politicians are now more concerned about pandering to minority groups within society, some of which have a goal of dismantling past norms and ideologies, than listening to the majority, many of whom declare themselves to be Christian. Christians are brushed aside as unimportant to the discussion about where society is heading. The majority must be silenced in order to elevate past oppressed groups because, they erroneously argue, an "oppressed" group cannot themselves exhibit prejudice and oppress others. Clearly our politicians are disconnected from reality.

While slightly tangential to our discussion, it still is important to note that one of the clearest examples of the disconnect between the LGBTQ community (and the Left in general) and reality is their close alliance with those of Islamic faith. Former Islamic people have sounded the warning about this trend.[56] This "unholy" alliance is troubling to say the least. The radical Left is nothing more than a pawn or the "useful idiots" in the hands of the Islamic agenda. Islam rejects many of the tenets of the Left, not the least of which is homosexuality and liberalism in general. Yet, these two camps have joined together to tear down the tenets of Western society which are built upon Judeo-Christian values. The truth is Islamists adhere to the old saying "the enemy of my enemy is my friend" until it no longer suits them. In this case, both the Left and Islam have Christianity as an "enemy." Thus, the groups on the Left, including the LGBTQ community are "useful idiots" for Islam's greater purposes: the takeover of Western culture and the annihilation of Judeo-Christian values. Their most useful means of doing this, barring war or military

---

54. See Grudem's discussion with full stats on the media's left-leaning bias in *Politics*, 555–71.

55. Freiburger, "Warren."

56. See Mohammed, *Unveiled* (2019). See also Mohammed's interview on The Rubin Report, "Ex Muslim." Note also, Ayaan Hirsi Ali's numerous books on the topic and her appearances on YouTube.

tactics, is through *hijrah*, which is the immigration of Muslims to non-Muslim regions and then using birthrates to take control of a region. According to Pew Research, by 2060 Islam is projected to increase by 70 percent compared to Christianity's 34 percent. In the ten years from 2007–2017 Muslims increased by one million in America alone.[57]

What is at stake for the believer? President of Southern Baptist Theological Seminary, Al Mohler, says it well when faced with a quickly changing culture that is embracing every aspect of the sexual revolution, especially the gay agenda. He states, "This is the reality we now face, and the onslaught is coming fast. Major LGBT organizations are now pressing their demands and gaining traction. A host of politicians are ready to support any legislation that will make them appear, by their calculation, on 'the right side of history,' not to mention on the winning side of the ballot box. An entire universe of regulative bodies ranging from the National Collegiate Athletic Association (NCAA) and the American Bar Association to accrediting agencies and local school boards is poised to drop the hammer on any individual or institution that stands in the path of the sexual revolution."[58] Mohler continues the warning by noting that while some may think that they can appease both worlds, there is in fact no middle ground or being neutral on this issue: the movement in Western culture will not allow it, they will find you and force you to make a decision. Either the church accepts and celebrates the LGBTQ agenda, or we will face political, institutional, and economic demise, and perhaps someday soon, even lose our freedom. Conservative Christians, many of whom are evangelical, are the last hold outs on this issue and the LBGTQ community knows it.[59] But not to worry, they have a plan to remedy that. They are focusing on our children.

The Indoctrination of Our Children

In 1958, after an unsuccessful summit, gay activist Allen Ginsberg shouted proudly and defiantly: "We'll get you through your children!"[60] He was indeed "prophetic." Western culture has done a 180 degree turn on the issue of homosexuality, and the main way this has been achieved

---

57. Lipka, "Muslims and Islam." See also Fea, *Believe Me*, 54.
58. Mohler, "David Gushee."
59. Mohler, "David Gushee."
60. Ginsberg, "Project," as cited by Brown, "Pixar."

is through the indoctrination of our children. Throughout this book I have been laying out the grim statistics of the changing morality within culture and the church, even evangelical churches. Based upon what I see in the classroom on a yearly basis, Ginsberg was correct. As parents and grandparents, we need to be aware of this heinous plan to steal the innocence of our children through both subtle and overt indoctrination.

In previous chapters, I have already noted the public-school system's sex-ed and gay-themed curriculum. For example, one school district in Maryland is developing an entire curriculum that not only affirms, but celebrates LGBTQ lifestyles and people.[61] And according to *USA Today*, New Jersey's Garden State Equality organization has now approved a pilot program for public schools involving three schools to begin with which will incorporate LGBTQ topics into school curriculums.[62] The major problem is there is no "opt out" option for parents. The obvious purpose of LGBTQ advocates to push their preferences upon the majority is problematic on its face. This does not even take into account the fact that sexuality and sexual preferences are now a central focus of the curriculum. Despite LGBTQ contentions that they are only teaching about contributions of their community and not about sex per se, it is obvious that these two cannot be separated so easily in the minds of students. Indeed, younger and younger students will be faced with, and indoctrinated by, sexual issues and ideology as opposed to history, science, math, and so on. While we may feel that we are insulating our children through private Christian schools or homeschooling, this is also being challenged by some. Harvard Law professor, Elizabeth Bartholet, who is the director of the Child Advocacy Program at Harvard Law School recently wrote an extensive article warning of the dangers of homeschooling, especially for children from conservative evangelical settings, who are being "indoctrinated" by parents and not being exposed to the "alternative values" of society.[63] Astute readers know exactly what those "alternative values" are. For now, there is some protection through alternative schooling but for how long, one cannot be certain. Despite our best efforts to shield our children from a corrupt educational system, there is another way the LGBTQ agenda plans to get their message to our children, through their entertainment.

61. Peetz, "LGBTQ Class."

62. Adely, "LGBTQ History."

63. Snibbe, "Homeschooling." For the original article, see Bartholet, "Homeschooling."

Indoctrination through Entertainment

Although there are numerous examples I could cite of indoctrination from children's entertainment, I will point out a few of the more overt cases. First, in May of 2020, Disney released an animated film titled *Onward*, which features an openly LGBTQ character voiced by Lena Waithe.[64] The character is a purple cyclops who is a police officer. While a child would never catch the irony, for those of us who are attuned to the brazen indoctrination, I find Disney's use of a gay cyclops fitting for the myopic perspective of the LGBTQ community and Western culture's willingness to accept their propaganda without pushback. Second, Disney's Pixar is now streaming a nine-minute video for children called *Out* depicting a gay man moving in with his boyfriend and having to reveal his homosexuality to his parents.[65] There is certainly no hiding the agenda in this short film. What was formerly more inuendo or focused on minor roles now is front and center. The short film, which was animated by two gay men, was praised by GLAAD and was strategically released on Harvey Milk Day.[66] Steven Clay Hunter, one of the two animators, commented, "We're moving towards more visibility. It doesn't mean we're taking over. We're just trying to tell our stories like everyone else . . . And we're not going anywhere. We're here to stay."[67] Third, PBS has been called out for their agenda-driven children's programing. Programs like Sesame Street, Arthur, and Clifford the Big Red Dog have integrated lesbian couples, LGBT "star" crossdressers, gender confusion themes, and homosexual marriage just to name a few.[68] The LGBTQ agenda is no longer masked or implicit, they are now at the stage of overt attacks on our children's innocence. This is happening across all areas of children's programming with increasing frequency.

The mainstreaming of the LGBTQ agenda is all but complete. Now children speak about their sexuality as though it is just another childhood issue which they must navigate, something unheard of only a few decades ago. Recently the *New York Post* reported that during a 2020 presidential rally in Aurora, Colorado, a nine-year-old boy asked openly homosexual Democrat presidential candidate Pete Buttigieg if he would

---

64. Day, "'Onward.'"
65. Coyle, "Pixar."
66. Coyle, "Pixar."
67. Coyle, "Pixar."
68. Activist Mommy, "Reboot."

help him come out as gay. Buttigieg brought the boy and his mother up on stage and praised him for his bravery.[69] Later the boy told a local news outlet that he was "inspired by Pete."[70] Many may feel this is no big deal, but the truth is it is a symptom of the moral sickness of our society when an audience of four thousand applaud such an action. Sexual sin will not be curbed by praising "alternative" lifestyles, nor will it be lessened if we continue to elevate people living these lifestyles as people to emulate. It will only lead more and more children astray as seen in this case. So how should we respond? We need to combat the propaganda of the LGBTQ agenda with facts that challenge or disprove their lies.

Exposing the Lies and Misinformation of the LGBTQ Agenda

It is important to remember that the downward spiral of Western culture is not the fault of any one group. It is the rejection of God's mandates by our collective society. And while I am in no way trying to diminish the sincere emotional and sexual attractions of homosexuals to those of the same sex, I do want to point out that those who choose to flout the teaching of God's Word will not flourish, whether that be heterosexuals practicing sexual sin, or people engaging in same-sex activity. Any time we try to deviate from God's ideal, trouble follows. For any attuned believer it is self-evident that there are agendas that are being driven by demonic spirits set on destroying any goodness that may be found in Western culture, especially as it relates to God's laws. That said, there are several problems with the LGBTQ agenda and what they have been foisting upon wider society. Although I certainly cannot cover them all, I do want to point out a few of the key problems with the assertions that the LGBTQ lifestyles are "normal" and in no way harmful to themselves, children, and society.

For decades now, well-meaning researchers, and some professing Christians, have attempted to persuade the church that homosexual lifestyles are acceptable and that those involved in the gay community lead ordinary lives and have ordinary relationships just like the average heterosexual couple.[71] While I am sure that there are those homosexuals

---

69. Brown, "Mayor Pete."
70. Jacobs, "Pete Buttigieg."
71. E.g., Scanzoni and Mollenkott, *Is the Homosexual My Neighbor?* 88–109.

who may fall into this category, the truth is that the homosexual lifestyle tends to lead in a direction that is anything but normal. In fact, several scholars have documented the promiscuity that is perpetuated by self-identified "Christian" homosexuals.[72]

In this regard, the facts are self-evident. Even though it is now two decades old, Robert Gagnon, in his book *The Bible and Homosexual Practice* (2001), has compiled an impressive array of scientific studies showing just the opposite of what many have tried to convince the church of for so many years. When people indulge in sexual deviancy of any kind, it will begin to affect other areas of their lives. For example, Michael Brown documents this well in his book *A Queer Thing Happened to America* (2011). In one chapter, Brown points out the perverse presentations being passed off as scholarship at the annual meetings of one of the world's leading biblical studies organizations. These presentations were not being presented by "non-believers" off the street. These were being presented by professors and church leaders who align with the gay movement.

The Truth about Changes Made by the APA

Although the LGBTQ community likes to tout the APA's decision to remove homosexuality from their list of disorders, this was not done due to some scientific breakthrough about the harmlessness of homosexuality, whether psychological or physical. On the contrary, the APA changed their manual only after much pressure, lobbying, bullying, disruption of meetings, dissembling, and infiltration of the APA by the gay agenda; it was purely political.[73] In fact, the APA committee's decision to change their position on homosexuality was approved because only one third of the membership cast their mail-in ballot dealing with the approval of the change.[74] Because there was no science behind the change, many psychiatrists withstood the decision. Four years after the vote, a survey showed that 69 percent of psychiatrists still disapproved of the decision.[75]

72. I would direct my reader to the works of Joe Dallas, Robert Gagnon, and Michael Brown just to name a few.

73. Satinover, *Homosexuality*, 18–19, 31–35.

74. Satinover, *Homosexuality*, 35.

75. Satinover, *Homosexuality*, 35. See also the discussion by Brown, *A Queer Thing*, 458–69; Dallas, *Gay Gospel*, 127–30; Watkins, *New Absolutes*, 218; and Reilly, *Making Gay Okay*, 117–42. Reilly (p.127) concludes that "there is no credible science to substantiate this assertion."

Nevertheless, the change to the DSM remained due to both internal and external pressure. Two years after the APA made their change, the much larger (by three times) American Psychological Association followed suit.[76] At this point it is important to keep in mind that even if the APA says that homosexuality is normal, that does not make it so. As former homosexual Joe Dallas notes, we should never take our moral "cues from the mental-health profession. What is deemed mentally sound by man may not be morally viable to God."[77] Since 1973, each updated DSM has reflected current cultural trends more than sound science when it comes to gender and sexuality issues.[78] The assertion that sexual orientation is immutable is simply not true.

Sexual Orientation is not Immutable

Many scientific studies are now being hailed as evidence that people are born with an LGBTQ identity and therefore it is immutable. The truth is none of these studies have been conclusive and many have been proven inadequate to explain sexual orientation and transgenderism.[79] As I noted in my conclusion in the previous chapter, even if there is some biological or genetic predisposition or connection to one's orientation, this does not mean that people are free to act upon these proclivities if it is against the Bible any more than someone who is genetically predisposed to being an alcoholic or drug addict can righteously partake in these acts.[80] This is nothing more than "biological determinism" and smacks of a naturalistic and evolutionary worldview.[81]

What is true is the fact that many people have been transformed by the power of God often coupled with therapy despite the politicization of the reparative therapy debate.[82] A quick online search of testimonies of those who have been delivered by the power of God from same-sex lifestyles reveals that the LGBTQ groups' assertion about the

---

76. Satinover, *Homosexuality*, 35.
77. Dallas, *Gay Gospel*, 127.
78. Branch, *Affirming God's Image*, 31.
79. Branch, *Affirming God's Image*, 55–80. See also Gagnon, *The Bible and Homosexuality* (2001).
80. Branch, *Affirming God's Image*, 64–67.
81. Branch, *Affirming God's Image*, 79.
82. See Satinover, *Homosexuality*, 168–70.

immutability of sexual orientation is simply not true. I have already noted God's transformational work in the lives of Rosaria Butterfield and Joe Dallas. Dallas goes so far as to say that the "immutable" argument is a myth.[83] Other examples of transformed lives abound. For example, two survivors of the Pulse Night Club shooting in 2016 have since become Christians and been delivered from the gay lifestyle. They, along with hundreds of other transformed and former gay men and women, joined in a recent march in Orlando, Florida, declaring the transformative power of Jesus.[84] They also lobbied the government to scrap anti-reparative therapy legislation. They are living proof of the power of God proving that sexual orientation is not immutable.[85] This is no less the case for many others who have come to the realization that Jesus is the answer to the sinful desires of homosexuality.[86]

One's sexuality can be redeemed and healed. Dean Bailey, a former gay man who has been restored noted in an interview that, "People often wonder why would the gay activists be trying to outlaw professional means of therapy and counseling for the pursuit of freedom from unwanted homosexual behaviors, if they truly embrace the 'tolerance' that they preach? What is it that they are actually so afraid of? I will tell you that what they fear the most is the breakdown and destruction of the inward lies that form the foundation of their own 'gay' identity, and everything that the 'gay rights' movement has been built upon. That is why gay activists will always insist that this form of dysfunctional sexual behavior is 'who' they are. It is the only way for them to remain secure in the falsehood."[87]

Now, is a sexual orientation difficult to change? Absolutely, especially when someone has "wired" their brains to think and react a certain way due to sexual activity.[88] It should be no surprise that Paul in his letter to the Romans noted the power of sin to alter the mind and thus declared that it is the power of God that renews the mind (Rom 12:2). The power of God to change people is still real even if some do not experience a change in sexual temptations immediately, or ever. Like all sin, sometimes

---

83. Dallas, *Gay Gospel*, 119–24.
84. Casanova, "Orlando."
85. CBN News, "Former LGBTQers Testify."
86. See Bailey, *Beyond the Shades of Gray* (2011).
87. Baklinski, "Ex-Gay Man."
88. Branch, *Affirming God's Image*, 76–77.

people have to cope daily with temptation with God's help. Despite these concerns, many have indeed changed with God's help, and their changed lives make it clear that for those living in the gay lifestyle, they are lying to themselves when they say this is "normal." Even if certain character traits are "inborn" that does not mean we should embrace them. And we certainly should not celebrate a lifestyle that can kill you spiritually and, in some cases, physically. This brings me to the putative "science" behind the LGBTQ position and the medical concerns of alternate sexual lifestyles.

LGBTQ's Flawed "Science"

The trend within society and churches to trust the "science" that affirms homosexuality as "normal" because of its association with innate, immutable, traits is troubling to say the least. I can in no way begin to address the numerous studies conducted over the years that have rendered conflicting results. I will leave that to those who are experts in their field.[89] What is clear, as with the issues with transgenderism, is that genetic and behavioral research in this area is notoriously problematic and inconclusive. For society, and worse still, the church, to rely on these studies as a basis to change biblical morality is rife with spiritual and societal repercussions. We should never acquiesce in this regard. The Bible, and therefore God, has the final say on morality and sexual ethics. Nevertheless, I would like to point out a couple of the more popular-level arguments that are made by affirming people.

First, some well-meaning affirming scholars and researchers assert that same-sex behaviors of animals, the most famous of which are Roy and Silo, two male chinstrap penguins at New York's Central Park Zoo, help prove the fact that same-sex attraction and sex can be "natural" for those who identify as homosexual.[90] This line of argumentation is troubling on a number of fronts. First, while I would not deny that animals can exhibit such characteristics, this is not at all the norm. In fact, relatively speaking, it is extremely rare. Second, most of these studies are based upon evolutionary biology which is naturalistic in its bent and rejects the existence of God. Third, and most applicable to our discussion, is the

---

89. Although somewhat dated, I would point my reader to scholars like Jeffrey Satinover, *Homosexuality and the Politics of Truth* (1996).

90. See Moskowitz, "Same Sex Couples"; Pappas, "Behavior"; and Scanzoni and Mollenkott, *Is the Homosexual My Neighbor?* 65.

fact that we should not in any way apply the sexual actions of animals to humans. If this were the case, why not practice polygamy because of the regular traits of dominant males in different species to mate with multiple females? Put simply, human sexual ethics and morality must never fall to the level of the beasts. This is another reason why I can see how Western cultures have begun blurring the lines between species distinctions: human and animal (see Chapter 13).

Another troubling trend in the LGBTQ community is the belief that there is absolutely no difference between same-sex and heterosexual families. In some cases, they propound that gay lifestyles are even better than heterosexuality. Indeed, any inclination of same-sex attraction at any age is assumed to mean that this is one's rightful orientation in life even though they may later become heterosexual: to reject the same-sex attractions or experimentation of one's youth is tantamount to living a lie.[91] In other words, homosexual tendencies are good, heterosexuality is bad. As I will show in the next section, LGBTQ groups' oft-noted "scientific studies" are more akin to propaganda when they hail the advantages and benefits of gay coupling for long-lasting marriages and for children in these marriages: children are supposedly "healthier and happier."[92]

The Medical Facts about the LGBTQ Lifestyle

As noted in my chapter on same-sex marriage, there are several increased health risks for those engaging in same-sex activity. Gay sex is rife with STDs, and the CDC reports that STDs

> have been rising among gay and bisexual men, with increases in syphilis being seen across the country. In 2014, gay, bisexual, and other men who have sex with men accounted for 83% of primary and secondary syphilis cases [. . .] in the United States. Gay, bisexual, and other men who have sex with men often get other STDs, including chlamydia and gonorrhea infections. HPV (Human papillomavirus), the most common STD in the United States, is also a concern for gay, bisexual, and other men who have sex with men. Some types of HPV can cause genital and anal warts and some can lead to the development of anal and oral cancers. Gay, bisexual, and other men who have sex with men are 17 times more likely to get anal cancer than

---

91. Murray, *Madness of Crowds*, 24.
92. For these studies see Murray, *Madness of Crowds*, 42–43.

The Mandate of Gender Distinctions Part 2

heterosexual men. Men who are HIV-positive are even more likely than those who do not have HIV to get anal cancer.[93]

Beyond these specific terrible diseases, the list of infections and diseases associated with the dangers of anal sex is staggering.[94] Simply put, first, there is no such thing as "safe" anal sex for anybody, heterosexual or homosexual, and the statistics show that homosexual men are the ones who do this the most—13 times more frequently than heterosexuals and with 12 times the number of partners.[95] Studies have shown anal sex is homosexual men's favorite sexual activity by far, especially when it is unprotected sex.[96] Second, HIV and AIDS is not going away: advances in medicine are merely able to manage and treat it better than in the past. Sadly, the highest rates of increase of HIV and AIDS is in the young African American community.[97] As a point of clarification, even though sexually transmitted diseases and cancers are rarer among lesbians because of their less risky sexual behavior and reduced promiscuity,[98] that does not mean that it is any less problematic from a spiritual and psychological perspective.

The staggering statistics are no less the case with the issues of mental health among same-sex couples. According to a 2016 report from *LifeSite News*, "The National Health Interview Survey (NHIS) has found that gays, lesbians and bisexuals have significantly greater health problems than heterosexuals."[99] The report went on to note that the *Journal of the American Medical Association* "revealed that of 69,000 adult participants, homosexuals 'were more likely to report impaired physical and mental health, heavy alcohol consumption, and heavy cigarette use.'"[100] In fact, the report goes on to cite numerous examples of how homosexual men and women rate significantly higher in incidences of mental and physical distress. For example, psychological distress among homosexuals is much higher than heterosexuals (females: 28 percent vs. 22 percent;

---

93. CDC, "Diseases." See also Jin et al, "Anal Cancer," 2322–27; and Roark, "Anal Dysplasia," 433–43.
94. For a listing, see Satinover, *Homosexuality*, 66–68.
95. Satinover, *Homosexuality*, 22–23, 55.
96. Satinover, *Homosexuality*, 58–60.
97. Brown, *Jezebel's War*, 108.
98. Satinover, *Homosexuality*, 52.
99. Hodges, "Homosexuals."
100. Hodges, "Homosexuals."

males: 26 percent vs. 17 percent). Of course, this is often attributed to the cultural stresses like stigmatization and discrimination. However, since the 1990s, homosexuals and their lifestyles have been praised and celebrated in most Western democracies with little to no pushback from mainline cultural groups. And the mental impairment and struggles are not just experienced by those in same-sex relationships, it affects those around them, especially family members.

In this regard, the report notes that "The journal *Depression Research and Treatment* (DRT) analyzed data from the National Longitudinal Study of Adolescent Health that showed that the percentage of adult children of same-sex partners reporting ongoing depression was nearly triple that of adult children of heterosexual parents (51 percent vs. 22 percent)."[101] What is more, the erroneous assertion that the children of same-sex couples fair just as well if not better than heterosexual couples does not hold up under close scrutiny. The data shows the opposite. Obesity, physical, emotional, and sexual abuse are more prevalent, often as much as 50 percent higher.[102]

Sociologist Dr. Mark Regnerus from the University of Texas at Austin made the candid conclusion that the gay activist community is not only being untruthful with their assertions that children of same-sex coupling fair the same or "no different" than those of heterosexual coupling, they are "torturing" the data and/or refusing to allow anyone to scrutinize it.[103] What this demonstrates is that the increase in obesity, abuse, mental distress, and depression, among a variety of other issues, among children and young adults of same-sex couples has been overlooked for far too long in the name of political correctness. The Bible is clear that marriage coupling between a man and a woman is God's plan for society. When humanity decides otherwise, then the fallout will affect far more than just those involved: innocent people suffer as well.

Conclusion

Former homosexual and former member of the gay-affirming Metropolitan Community Church, Joe Dallas, noted in his revised 2007 edition of *The Gay Gospel* that "America may one day receive, from her own

---

101. Hodges, "Homosexuals."
102. Hodges, "Homosexuals."
103. As cited in Hodges, "Homosexuals."

churches, a definition of normality that includes (and approves of) gay marriage, pro-gay education (beginning with primary grades) on the normality of homosexuality, and the general portrayal of same-sex unions as healthy and legitimate . . . [once this happens] both church and society will begin to reap the spiritual and cultural consequences."[104] In less than two decades since the publication of his book, American churches and culture have blown past these predictions by Dallas and are now heading straight for cultural chaos as has never been seen before in the West. Dallas rightly notes that at the heart of this type of movement is the rejection of the authority of God's Word.[105] Once that is undermined, what is left? The church and society are set on a path of moral chaos because God's revealed will through his Word has been minimized and disregarded and will certainly be disregarded when the next sin that people want to accept as "normal" comes along. The repercussions of allowing sin to enter the church is the further slippage in other areas.

The rapid rise of the LGBTQ movement in America and Western cultures and its takeover of many aspects of our lives is staggering. It is affecting practically every area of our lives and in many cases is unforgiving. Just the other day I read about a man who was sentenced to more than fifteen years in prison for burning an LGBTQ flag.[106] Now while I am not trying to defend hate speech and acts, and while there may be much more to the story than meets the eye, it does, nonetheless, seem a little excessive if more heinous crimes get much shorter sentences. It is clear there is an example being set. Do not cross us! The gay agenda is loud and proud and makes no bones about it. When a recent poll showed that the gay population in the United Kingdom had reached one million, the UK's Pink news praised the announcement but insisted that the number was not high enough.[107] They want more of the deviance. This harks back to my earlier discussion on the LGBTQ's desire to indoctrinate children. They are doing their job well. One study shows that only two thirds of Gen Z identify as "exclusively heterosexual."[108]

In light of the rise of the LGBTQ agenda and its effect on Western culture, what should our response be? It is obvious that Western cultures

---

104. Dallas, *Gay Gospel*, 42.
105. Dallas, *Gay Gospel*, 42–43.
106. Betz, "Iowa Man."
107. Murray, *Madness of Crowds*, 28.
108. Murray, *Madness of Crowds*, 23.

have been engulfed by the ungodly sexual ethics of postmodernity and that they have rejected the Genesis mandate of gender distinctions. Those holding to the truthfulness of God's Word must be prepared to face the challenges of a post-Christian society. Along with fervent prayer and solid Bible teaching, the attacks can be thwarted in our lives and the lives of our children because God is greater than the Enemy. Unfortunately, some evangelical scholars are not pointing out the dangers and scriptural problems with same-sex activity. For example, social scientists, Jack and Judith Balswick, conclude their study on homosexuality with the troubling statement that "We acknowledge that some gay Christians may commit themselves to a lifelong, monogamous homosexual union, believing that this is God's best for them. They believe that this reflects an authentic sexuality that is congruent for them and their view of Scripture. Even though we hold to a model of a heterosexual, lifelong, monogamous union, our compassion brings us to support all Christians who pursue God's direction for their lives. A suffering Jesus knows the way and longs to meet those who seek him."[109] While I can agree with the last part of this statement, the truth remains that Jesus does not want people to stay in their sin. He wants them to follow his Word. The Balswicks' response is problematic on its face. They are conceding that homosexual monogamous marriage is okay because some who are from a same-sex persuasion feel that the Scriptures support such a stance. As we will see in the next chapter, this conclusion is patently false and misleading and offers a false hope instead of warning of the dangers of unconfessed sin.

---

109. Balswick and Balswick, *Authentic Human Sexuality*, 136.

Chapter 11

The Mandate of Gender Distinctions Part 3

Homosexuality, the Church, and the Bible

HAVING COVERED THE ISSUES of the LBGTQ agenda and culture in my last chapter, it is now time to look at how the church has fared when dealing with this issue especially considering biblical teachings on the subject. As the bride of Jesus Christ, it is important that we reflect his purity and holiness as well as listen to God's Word. Unfortunately, this has not been the case when addressing the Genesis mandates and biblical teaching on sexual ethics and morality. There has been growing division within the wider church, specific denominations, and the evangelical scholarly world concerning the LGBTQ issue. What is the reason for this division if the Bible and church tradition is univocal on the topic of same-sex activity? And are evangelicals correct in "holding the line" in this regard? These are important questions which need to be answered. Some may think that we are too caught up in the culture wars and are not showing the "love" of Jesus if we reject *practicing* same-sex individuals from entering into full fellowship in our churches. This is simply not true. We are fighting for the soul of our nation and our churches while defending the authority of God's Word.

Back in 2015, one affirming author, who formerly identified as evangelical, suggested that the reason evangelicals are so adamantly against homosexuality being normalized and accepted in the church is because they see it as the "final frontier, the last line of defense."[1] Again, this is a false premise. The reason evangelical non-affirming scholars and the larger church reject same-sex practices is because it is against what the Bible teaches. What is more, we also recognize that it is not the "final frontier." On the contrary, accepting deviance in one area will only lead to more depravity as witnessed in the past five years with the rise of the culture war related to the fluidity of gender, which I will address in more detail in my next chapter. Despite what they think, affirming scholars are not remedying injustice or correcting "improper" biblical interpretation, they are throwing the doors wide open for even more perversion and anti-biblical lifestyles. I can hear the words of Jesus in this regard, "wide is the gate that leads to destruction" (Matt 7:13). These well-meaning authors are not a part of the solution, they have become a part of the problem. And, as I have been noting throughout and will handle in greater detail in my final two chapters, one cannot simply pass issues of morality to the state and allow the church to move along on its merry way.[2] As I have noted before, the author of Proverbs certainly recognized the dangers of such a position when he states, "Righteousness exalts a nation, but sin is a reproach to any people" (Prov 14:34; my translation). As much as is conceivably possible, we want our local, state, and national governments to reflect Judeo-Christian morals. If they refuse to do so, then we will pay the price in the long run.

In order to effect change, pastors, educators, and each and every parishioner, who believes that the Bible is God's authoritative Word and is our rule of faith for sexual ethics and morality, must begin speaking up and instructing and educating those in our immediate context of what has been the historic church tradition on same-sex activity and what the Bible teaches. Will we change the laws of the land regarding same-sex activity? If the battle over *Roe v. Wade* is any indicator, probably not any time soon. Nevertheless, what we as the people of God do now in informing our children and our congregations may effect change in the generations to come as they become more attuned to the dangers of sexual deviancy.

In light of these concerns, I will devote the first portion of this chapter to an examination of how the same-sex issue has affected and changed the church in the past sixty years. In the last half of this chapter I will

---

1. Gushee, *Changing Our Mind*, 10.
2. So, the position of Gushee, *Changing Our Mind*, 19.

look at the scholarly approaches to biblical teaching on the topic with an overview of how Christians should understand the Bible on this issue.

Homosexuality and the Church

For 2000 years, the historic Christian tradition has been consistent on what constitutes a biblical sexual ethic when dealing with same-sex activity: it has declared it to be unholy, ungodly, and not reflective of the biblical witness.[3] Church Creeds and Articles of Confession attest to the fact that orthodoxy was consistent across denominations and traditions (Catholic and Protestant) on the issue of same-sex activity. While the world has always been prone to sexual proclivities contrary to Scripture, within the church, the shift towards an anti-biblical sexual ethic started only in the mid-twentieth century. In this regard, Todd Wilson offers a stern warning about the church's changing views on sexuality when he says, "... this living tradition is now on life support as it drifts inexorably toward death, at least in the minds of many Christians. The church has forgotten what it has always believed."[4]

As outlined in my opening two chapters, much of the drift within the church can be attributed to the rise of rationalism and historical critical theories that marginalized the authority of Scripture. This began to take hold in European churches in the 1950s and 60s and soon bled over into ecclesial discussions in the US in the 1960s and 70s in a more focused manner. Scanzoni and Mollenkott's book, *Is the Homosexual My Neighbor?* published in 1978, gives an overview of these rumblings, undercurrents, and vocal movements of that era as churches, especially mainline churches, but some evangelical ones as well, moved to accept practicing homosexuals into full communion, and even ordination.

At the heart of these types of books—and there were several coming out at that time—was the push to "rethink" the Bible and the church's position on homosexuality. The agenda to accept same-sex activity within the church was clear as evidenced by the arguments in Scanzoni and Mollenkott's book. They draw their book to a close by commenting, "But as more and more persons become less afraid of the topic and more sensitive to the issues involved, a groundwork is being laid for creative rethinking on the theological/biblical/ethical level and for compassionate

---

3. See the excellent overview by Fortson and Grams, *Unchanging Witness* (2016).
4. Wilson, *Mere Sexuality*, 37.

counsel on the practical/personal level."[5] As I noted in my previous chapter, Mollenkott, as a recent divorcee and lesbian, had a vested interest in this shift. We have certainly had a precipitous fall since this statement was made. Today, most mainline churches fully embrace all aspects of the gay lifestyle for their homosexual congregants. Evangelicals are also quickly losing ground in this regard as a new generation of pastors and elders take the reins of churches. Culture and seminaries have done their work well to acclimate and "educate" people into full acceptance of this alternate lifestyle, which is now mainstream. Indeed, the seeds of division planted in the 1960s and 70s are now taking root and yielding a bountiful crop of church splits and dissension.

A Source of Division

A proper understanding of the biblical teaching regarding homosexuality is important because of what this sexual deviancy is doing to the church. I have already addressed the split within the Episcopal church in 2008, and most people attuned to the church world know that the Presbyterian church has also fractured over the issue.[6] Beyond these cases, in America alone, the same-sex issue has affected the Mennonite, Lutheran, Methodist, and some branches of the Baptist church, just to name a few. Currently, the United Methodist Church is on the verge of splitting, and no doubt will, because of the lack of "compromise" by conservatives about accepting ordained gay ministers and gay marriage. For affirming people, the tolerance again goes in one direction.[7]

While many conservative evangelicals such as Baptists and Pentecostals may think that the agenda of the LGBTQ community will never be a major issue for us, we should heed the warnings of Anglican theologian David W. Virtue who notes that the tactic of "pansexual" Christians is to infiltrate orthodox churches and parishes, flip them to their way of thinking, and then watch them shrivel and die.[8] This is already happening in evangelical churches as the old guard retires or dies off and new "woke" evangelicals take their place. Virtue rightly warns that mere acceptance was never the LGBTQ goal, but rather "total capitulation and control" of

5. Scanzoni and Mollenkott, *Is the Homosexual My Neighbor?* 132.
6. See my discussion in Peterson, "Review," 104–8.
7. Stimson, "United Methodist Church."
8. Virtue, "Pansexual."

The Mandate of Gender Distinctions Part 3

the churches. What started as a call for the *harmless* acceptance of same-sex marriage in the early 2000s—a live-and-let-live mentality—has now turned to outright bullying and lobbying of the government to remove tax-exempt status from churches and colleges who do not *change* their views on same-sex lifestyles and marriage.[9] This is how they plan on punishing any church that refuses to capitulate. The trajectory is obvious. While most Americans erroneously thought that acceptance of same-sex activity and marriage seemed harmless enough, after all, this is the land of liberty and freedom, this was never the end game for the LGBTQ agenda; it was the complete control and overthrow of the "Judeo-Christian heritage and moral framework" of America and the destruction of traditional Christianity as we have always known it.[10] As an Anglican, Virtue poignantly summarizes what has been the outcome of accepting the LGBTQ agenda when he states, "secular homosuperiority has now totally replaced scripture as authoritative for the mainline denominations who see themselves in the vanguard of change, inviting God to change His mind for them. The inconvenient truth of scripture be damned."[11] Evangelicals need to take to heart Virtue's warning especially considering the dire situation in which the church in the West finds itself. I readily agree with Virtue when he concludes, "We are in a do or die moment. We may yet see the persecution of Christians on a scale we have never seen before in this country. As Cardinal Francis George said, 'I expect to die in bed, my successor will die in prison and his successor will die a martyr in the public square. His successor will pick up the shards of a ruined society and slowly help rebuild civilization, as the church has done so often in human history.'"[12]

I am sure that some evangelicals will say that this is excessive and would never happen to us. I hope I am wrong, but for those of us who have watched the rapid cultural shifts during the summer months of 2020, and the rise of militancy and the "cancel culture," it no longer seems so farfetched. Christians in the West will either capitulate or face the full force of governmental and social censure now that LGBTQ groups have forced their views and mandates on society while politicians and administrators of all stripes cower in submission. For example, during the

9. Virtue, "Pansexual."
10. Virtue, "Pansexual."
11. Virtue, "Pansexual."
12. Virtue, "Pansexual."

recent Democratic presidential race, then candidate, Beto O'Rourke, declared that if he were president he would go after the tax-exempt status of churches unless they fell in line with legislation related to LGBTQ rights.[13] Again, how did we get here? It always starts in the church with a compromise on the Bible or a reinterpretation of a problematic passage or two, or, in this case, seven (the seven so-called "clobber passages" see below).

While Virtue is speaking of the radical changes within the Anglican/Episcopal Church over the last two decades, I can speak to these same concerns personally because my wife is an ordained Anglican, and her diocese in Pittsburgh was in the middle of the entire fiasco during the tenure of Bishop Robert Duncan. Once gays could practice their sexual preferences with the sanction of the Episcopal Church, it was only a matter of time before marriage rights were foisted upon the church in the name of equal rights. With only about two percent of the Episcopal Church (laity, clergy, and bishops) identifying as homosexual,[14] that small fraction of the church pushed the rest of the American Episcopal Church to the extreme and brought about a complete split. This was accompanied by civil litigation, which forced the conservative churches, who refused to go along with the charade, to lose their property and denomination-held monetary resources (e.g., pension plans).

I can recall when I first met my wife in 2006 and we began talking about this issue. I told her then that her local church would be better off leaving their property behind and cutting their losses in order to remain faithful to God. While the litigation went on for several more years, the church where she attended, and where we were married, was indeed lost to the Episcopal Church through litigation. What did they do with it? They sold it to a gun range group and banked the money to help fund their dying enterprise for several more decades. They were flushed with cash from the sale of properties of conservative Episcopal churches all over the US. I guess the leadership of the Episcopal Church failed to take Paul's words to heart on not taking a brother or sister to secular courts (1 Cor 6:1). Ah, but they had given up on Paul long ago when they rejected some of the clearest teaching on the whole issue of homosexuality in the Bible! (Rom 1; 1 Cor 6:9; 1 Tim 1:10).

And what happened to conservative churches that tried to stay within the American Episcopal Church and effect positive change? Dissenters

---

13. Brown, *Evangelicals at the Crossroads*, 51.
14. Virtue, "Pansexual."

are now being harshly disciplined and threatened into compliance under the church's new "canon law" on sexual ethics.[15] As I said in 2006, and repeat here, the Enemy will not allow dissent. Bible-believing Christians who try to remain "married" to these godless and lawless churches will be crushed if they push back against the new sexual ethic. Paul's words ring true here, "what fellowship has righteousness with unrighteousness and what communion has light with darkness" (2 Cor 6:14 my paraphrase); the mainline churches have indeed fallen into darkness and are apostate.

Again, I give a stern warning: this can happen to conservative evangelical churches, especially if we do not teach our kids what the Bible clearly teaches. If we fail to do so the next generation will experience chaos if we turn away from the authority of God's Word for "another gospel" pedaled to us from other venues. In this regard, part of the church's response to the LGBTQ issue has been to rely on the professionals in the fields of psychology, sociology, and psychiatry to determine how we should minister to those dealing with same-sex attraction, gender dysphoria (transgenderism), and similar sexual issues. While I am certainly not trying to belittle legitimate Christian counseling and insights of professionals who stay close to the Word of God, I do want to point out the dangers associated with the thinking of many of those working in these fields. It is now common fare to have a lenient approach to those struggling or practicing same-sex sin by elevating the "good" or wellbeing of the person over the authority of God's Word. It bears repeating: God loves all people and Jesus' blood covers all sexual sin. Nevertheless, the ground shift in churches is rooted in the fact that many of today's generation know of someone who is in a same-sex relationship and who views those relationships and lifestyles as "normal" and "good."[16] But we cannot allow personal emotions to supersede God's Word when faced with the heart-wrenching stories of friends and loved ones who are practicing homosexual sin.[17] Remember, Jesus said, "If anyone comes to Me, and does not hate his own father and mother and wife and children and brothers and sisters, yes, and even his own life, he cannot be My disciple" (Luke 14:26; NASB). Therefore, we must seek rightly to divide God's Word. But

---

15. Mouser, "Bishop."

16. See discussion by Wilson, *Mere Sexuality*, 25–31.

17. These are numerous. For example, Scanzoni and Mollenkott (*Is the Homosexual My Neighbor?* 43–45) give a rapid-fire list of personal stories and then conclude that we must act. See my discussion in *Sin of Sodom*, 1–2.

how do we do that with so many contradictory voices on what the Bible "says" about same-sex activity? It is to this concern that I now turn.

Modern Scholarly Approaches to the Same-sex Debate

I have covered the topic of scholarly approaches to this debate at length in a previous work[18] and will therefore only highlight the main approaches that scholars take when addressing this topic from a biblical perspective. The two main sides are what are often termed "affirming" (those who think the Bible teaches or allows same-sex activity) and "non-affirming" (those who insist that the Bible rejects same-sex acts as an acceptable expression of God-ordained sexuality). As a non-affirming scholar, I will be addressing the biblical texts through this lens. However, before addressing these texts, I want to focus on the general affirming scholarly perspective. Due to the intricacies of the debate, I will handle the discussion in broad terms even though there are nuanced perspectives found among scholars.

The marginalization of the biblical witness concerning homosexuality can be found in numerous scholarly works. Generally, affirming authors rehash the same old tired arguments and then conclude that the Bible has nothing much to say on the topic of homosexuality, especially "loving, caring, same-sex relationships." To prove this point, although I could engage dozens of affirming scholars on this topic, I will primarily address the arguments of Scanzoni and Mollenkott, who were instrumental in starting this discussion among American churches back in the 1970s. For those who have read anything on the topic of homosexuality and the Bible from modern authors, you will quickly see the common themes and lines of argumentation. Not much has changed in the arguments since then, although some are a bit more nuanced.

That said, I want to highlight several ways affirming scholars address the biblical teaching on the topic. First, one of the more prominent arguments is the "context" problem. Scholars argue that the church has misunderstood texts on homosexuality because they have been taken out of context, either historically, textually, or covenantally. Second, a common assertion is that the Bible does not speak that much about homosexuality so it must not be that important to God. Third, and one of my favorites (tongue in cheek), is the argument that because Jesus is silent on

---

18. See Peterson, *Sin of Sodom*, xvii–xix.

the topic, it must be okay.[19] Fourth, right now you are probably saying, "Yeah, but what about Sodom and Gomorrah?" Affirming scholars bypass this text with ease by saying that the Sodom text is inadmissible "evidence" because this is dealing with domination or the attempted rape of angels. Moreover, when speaking about Sodom, the prophet Ezekiel (see Ezek 16:49) supposedly does not mention Sodom's sin as being homosexuality. Fifth, the two Leviticus passages dealing with homosexuality are sidelined because they are dealing with cultic matters and ritual cleanliness not "loving, caring, same-sex relationships" as witnessed today.[20] Sixth, in the same way our moral trajectory concerning slavery, women's rights, and the status of Gentiles has changed now that we are in Christ, we should now include homosexuals as just one more example of these marginalized groups. And seventh, in the NT, Paul's teaching on the topic is marginalized for various reasons. Romans 1 could be interpreted in a variety of ways, and Paul's word choices in the vice lists of 1 Corinthians 6:9 and 1 Timothy 1:10 are too confusing to know for certain what Paul meant. Therefore, considering these various arguments, affirming scholars conclude that the Bible really does not address the issue of homosexuality as we see it today. Now to be sure, I am being a little satirical in my overview. Many scholars have offered extensive discussions on these topics. Nevertheless, the conclusions are invariably the same. The Bible is either too ambiguous or there is some "chink" in the biblical armor that allows for same-sex activity to be condoned by God, or at least accepted by the church. I will give one example of the latter case before moving on.

While researching for this book, I was reading a short online article where the author argued that because we cannot possibly hope to know what causes someone to be LGBTQ, we should stop asking and just "listen with acceptance," "instill a sense of self-worth," and "provide unconditional love." He then reinforced this form of acceptance by quoting Paul's words to the Galatians in 6:2 where Paul tells believers to bear one another's burdens. The author says that Paul did not tell the Galatians to try to figure out what the cause of the sin was but simply to bear their burdens.[21] As I read some of the comments readers posted below the article some disagreed with the author but many thought the author's point was valid. After all, Jesus is love and we should just love people and not try to point

---

19. E.g., Collins, *Biblical Values*, 81.

20. This has a long history. See Scanzoni and Mollenkott, *Is the Homosexual My Neighbor?* 59–61.

21. Yaksh, "Born this Way?"

out the sin or its cause, right? This is a typical response in light of Western acceptance of the gay lifestyle and gender dysphoria issues.

As a Bible guy, the biblical interpretation part of my brain kicked into gear and began refuting his point. First, I would want to know what the author means by "accepting" those in this situation. I may be wrong, but I suspect based upon his comment that the church should not try and "fix" them, that he means do not bother trying to effect change in their life for the better, that is, seeking for them to be delivered or motivated to live a chaste life. Second, what the author fails to do is look at the context of Galatians 6. Yes, we should, and are required to, bear the burdens of those caught in a sin, but it is for the purpose of restoration (6:1), not acceptance of a lifestyle counter to the Bible. Paul goes on to say in 6:7–8, "Do not be deceived, God is not mocked; for whatever a man sows, this he will also reap. For the one who sows to his own flesh shall from the flesh reap corruption, but the one who sows to the Spirit shall from the Spirit reap eternal life" (NASB). The proper response should always be to love, but to accept sexual sin as okay is a problem. Applying the author's argument differently, would we say that a believer should bear the burdens of a person who is an adulterer and not try to "fix" or restore them, but rather accept them and allow them to go on in their sin? I hope this is not what he was saying.

I related this story to point out how easy it is to twist the Text into making it seemingly agree with your perspective of accepting sexual sin because it is difficult to figure out how or why someone is dealing with LGBTQ issues. As with any person's sin, the issue is that we are fallen and need to repent, not to be coddled. But if you have already accepted LGBTQ lifestyles as normal and immutable then what other conclusion are you going to reach when you approach the Text? This brings me to my next point.

The problem with the affirming scholarly approach to the issue of homosexuality is that they come to the Text with a preconceived conclusion as to where they want to go with the interpretation. Again, I am reminded of Eve's encounter with the Serpent. The Serpent said, "Did God say . . . ?" When Eve considered the tree, she realized that it was good for food, good to make one wise, and pleasing to the eye. However, despite the three positive aspects of the tree there was one negative: God said, "No!" Today, affirming scholars look at the "positive" aspects of same-sex coupling and note the "good" things about it and conclude that it can help combat loneliness, it is loving, the Spirit seems to be blessing these couples, they make such a happy couple, and the list goes on. As I just noted, the problem is God said, "No!" When faced with this seemingly harsh command from God, affirming scholars do not reevaluate *their* conclusions that elevate the positives over the negative, but rather they ask the same question that the Serpent asked Eve—"Did God say . . . ?"—in order to reimagine what God has said in the Bible. In this case, they go back to the Bible and attempt to reinterpret each text in a manner fitting their perspective. And guess what: if you want the Text to reinforce your point of view you can do it if you try hard enough. The problem is the Bible never supports or affirms sexual deviance as normative. At least the honest affirming scholars note that the Bible is unequivocal on this issue. It does not support same-sex lifestyles. Despite the scriptural clarity, however, some evangelical scholars, and many lay people, still believe the Bible is okay with same-sex activity if it is within the confines of marriage.

Finally, before I get into the biblical texts it bears repeating that the major problem facing the evangelical church is the question of the authority of God's Word, not issues of interpretation as is often asserted. Scriptural authority is often downplayed in favor of interpretative concerns. While affirming scholars are quick to argue that they, too, believe in the authority of God's Word, they feel that for two thousand years the church has misinterpreted the Bible, at least when it comes to homosexuality. Others, evangelical or otherwise, also push for the equal authority of one's experience and the role the Spirit plays in informing their positions. The problem with these latter two methods is that neither are trustworthy. The heart is deceitfully wicked (Jer 17:9) and suggesting that the "Spirit" supposedly tells someone to do something contrary to the written Word, which was inspired by that same Spirit, is problematic on its face.

What the Bible Says about Homosexuality

Before moving to the biblical teaching on homosexuality, I want to deal with the thorny issue of "context," which I touched on above. Context is often touted by affirming scholars as the primary reason for "misunderstandings" related to the biblical teaching on homosexuality. I find it interesting that it is always the texts on homosexuality that the church has "misinterpreted" as opposed to other texts related to incest, adultery, bestiality and the like. What is more, many of the texts dealing with homosexuality fall within the canonical context of other sexual sins thus pointing to the problematic nature of these acts.[22] And when dealing with sexual sins, the cultural, covenantal, and historical contexts are almost never a factor in their modern applicability. For example, Leviticus 18 and 20 deal with sexual laws, homosexuality included (18:22; 20:13), for which both Egypt and Canaan were judged as well. In this one example, the historical, cultural, *and* the covenantal contexts coalesce proving that these sexual prohibitions are incumbent upon all people of all times. This is no less true of the Genesis mandates, which I have been dealing with throughout. The truth is that even though evangelical affirming scholars continue to contort the Scripture to aid in their support of homosexuality, the fact remains that the Scriptures are unequivocal on this point. Many of these scholars reject the biblical teaching and simply opt for their experience and personal decisions and choice on the matter. Finally, even if one were to eliminate the dominant passages that teach against homosexuality, the overall tenor of Scripture makes it clear that only heterosexual activity is condoned. Never does it open the door for same-sex activity in *any* context.[23]

Genesis 1 and 2

In my chapter on marriage redefinition I addressed the opening two chapters of Genesis at length. Human coupling was established as between a man and a woman, not between two men or two women. Despite this clear teaching, as early as the 1970s, several scholars were pushing the erroneous position that homosexuality was just another variation of God's "good" creation.[24] Their arguments were based upon the thinking that same-sex couples could participate in "cohumanity" just like heterosexual people because genital coupling was not the only way this could be attained.[25] The firmly set posts of the Genesis-mandates fence were being wiggled in preparation for an all-out assault on sex and gender distinctions as well as biblical marriage.

---

22. Dallas, *Gay Gospel*, 106.
23. So, too, Sider, *Completely Pro-Life*, 114–15.
24. Joyce Liechenstein, *New York City Presbytery News* (May 1977) 4. As cited by Scanzoni and Mollenkott, *Is the Homosexual My Neighbor?* 41.
25. Scanzoni and Mollenkott, *Is the Homosexual My Neighbor?* 129–32.

The Mandate of Gender Distinctions Part 3

Despite the assertions, there is absolutely no basis for homosexual affirmation within the opening chapters of Genesis. While it is true that there is clear variation within plant life and the animal kingdom, humanity was unique and is clearly defined as being male and female, both of whom were made for heterosexual marriage. And Jesus' reference to male and female as the basis of marriage in Matthew 19 and Mark 10, pushes against trying to find support for homosexuality in the Genesis mandates. Not surprisingly, even some who support homosexual coupling state clearly that Genesis 1 and 2 do not support such a reading.[26]

Genesis 19 and Judges 19

Because these two accounts tell a similar story of visitors to a strange city being set upon by the men of the city, I will handle them together even though I will focus on Genesis 19.[27] These are two of what affirming authors have labelled the seven "clobber passages" used by non-affirming scholars to point out the sinfulness of homosexual sex. While I have devoted an entire book to Genesis 19, here I will point out the major interpretive issues related to this chapter. As noted above, the dominant interpretation of this chapter by affirming scholars is that it has nothing to do with loving same-sex relationships but rather rape, domination, and inhospitality. As such, they conclude that it is meaningless to the discussion.

There are no less than five solid reasons why such a conclusion is too hasty. First, because affirming scholars often scream, "Context!" I will begin there. Genesis 19 must be read in the context of a similar destruction noted earlier in Genesis, namely, the flood of chapters 6–9. There is a distinct pattern to these two accounts: 1) something sexual takes place that causes God to send judgment; 2) God sends judgment by raining down water/fire from heaven; 3) one man and his family survive by God's intervention; and 4) in the immediate aftermath of the judgment, an incestuous sexual encounter happens between a drunken father and a child.[28] The key points I want to address are numbers 1 and 4. While the cryptic interaction of the sons of God and the daughters of men in Genesis 6:1–4 has been variously interpreted, in the broader context of

---

26. Song, *Covenant and Calling*, 62–76.

27. For an extensive handling of this chapter, see Peterson, *Sin of Sodom* (2016).

28. For a more detailed breakdown of the structural patterns, see Peterson, *Sin of Sodom*, 43–45.

Genesis, it seems clear that something sexual is taking place that displeases God. Now whether that was sexual relations between divine beings and human women (the dominant interpretation today), or whether it was the godly leaders/line of Seth indiscriminately marrying whomever they chose creating harems (the position I hold) is not important at this juncture. What is important is that sexual transgressions are in view in both cases *before* judgment came. Not surprisingly, one of the earliest Jewish commentaries on Genesis written around 400 CE, *Genesis Rabbah* (26.5), notes that 6:1–4 describes a period of sexual wantonness where God did not destroy the world "until they had begun writing nuptial hymns for marriages between males or between man and beast."[29] Early interpreters thus recognized some sexual deviance triggered God's judgment. The second part of the context is how both accounts end. Noah and Lot both get drunk (Noah on his own accord and Lot with the help of his daughters) and then a child takes sexual advantage of the father. While there is much debate about what happened between Noah and his son, Ham, the language of the text and the parallels with Genesis 19 seem to point to a sexual act by Ham against his father.[30] Therefore, contextually, sexual sin is in view in the Sodom account.

Second, long before God pronounces and enacts judgment upon Sodom for supposed inhospitality, the author of Genesis notes that the *men* of Sodom were "great sinners against the Lord" (Gen 13:13). The terminology of "sinning against" God is only used to speak of sexual sin in Genesis (see Gen 20:6; 39:9). Again, we can conclude that sexual sin is in view in this account.

Third, I have argued at length elsewhere that Genesis 19 is presenting a narrative commentary, what I have called case law, on the sexual sins of Leviticus 18 and 20, specifically, incest, adultery, and homosexuality.[31] As a narrative commentary addressing these chapters on sexual sin, the reader is shown what the repercussions on a nation/city are when deviant sexual behavior becomes the dominant sexual ethic. Unchecked deviant sexual sin can bring God's wrath and judgment upon a people.

Fourth, the assertion that loving same-sex relationships are okay today because Genesis 19 deals with gang rape or domination fails to consider the fact that often legislation (Genesis is part of the Law/Torah)

---

29. Neusner, *Genesis Rabbah Volume I*, 282.
30. For a more detailed treatment, see Peterson, *Sin of Sodom*, 45–47.
31. See Peterson, *Genesis as Torah*, 85–88.

The Mandate of Gender Distinctions Part 3

gives the worse-case scenario and assumes that supposed lesser acts associated with that law are also forbidden. As an example, the Jewish people of Jesus' day thought that if they did not commit the act of adultery, they were fine to lust after a married woman in their hearts. However, Jesus points out the actual meaning of the law and says that even looking is a sin (Matt 5:27–28). It pushes the bounds of all credulity to assume that God would be fine with same-sex activity if it is not coercive. Finally, in Ezekiel 16, Ezekiel addresses the sin of Sodom and lists several of their sins.[32] Most affirming scholars only cite 16:49, which focuses on social injustice or inhospitality. They fail to go on and give the overall context of Ezekiel 16 and the immediate context of verse 50. Ezekiel 16 is the most graphic sexually explicit chapter in the Bible and verse 50 says that the men of Sodom committed "an abomination" (singular in the Hebrew text) before God. As a priest, Ezekiel consistently quoted Leviticus and the Law. Here Ezekiel is referencing the only place in the Torah where abomination is used in the singular in the context of sexual sin, namely, Leviticus 18:22, which deals with homosexuality.

In light of these numerous concerns, it is problematic to suggest that the Sodom event has nothing to do with sexual sin related to homosexuality. This brings us to the second two "clobber passages" in the Bible, those found in Leviticus.

Leviticus 18:22; 20:13

Both of these passages state plainly that men should not have sex with each other because it is an abomination before God, with 20:13 adding the death penalty for the action. Affirming scholars have tried to downplay these texts in various ways. Four of the dominant interpretations include: that these texts are dealing with crossing forbidden boundaries within a family unit; that they are dealing with cultic issues and only apply to Israel; that they are speaking of domination, such as in war, where a man is made like a woman who is penetrated; or that because Christians accept having sex with a menstruating woman, which is also a part of this sexual law (Lev 20:18), we should accept homosexuality.[33]

Again, several points disprove these assertions. First, Leviticus 18 begins and ends with a comment that Egypt and Canaan had practiced

---

32. See Peterson, "Ezekiel 16:49–50," 307–20.
33. Scanzoni and Mollenkott, *Is the Homosexual My Neighbor?* 112–15.

these types of sexual sins and were punished for them (Lev 18:3; 24–30). This means that the sexual laws of chapters 18 and 20 are incumbent upon all people not just Israel. Second, and closely related to the first point, is the fact that it is ludicrous to assume that if one practices homosexuality outside of a family or "cultic" setting God is fine with it. Leviticus 18 and 20 do not mention cultic activity when speaking of homosexual acts. This conclusion can also be applied to the argument about domination or coercive homosexual sex. My discussion above about forbidding all lesser sins related to the main sin applies here as well. Third, homosexuality is also forbidden in the NT and Paul coins a new term for homosexuality based upon the language in Leviticus 18 and 20 when he rejects homosexual activity (see more below).

Finally, drawing a parallel between sex with a menstruating woman and homosexuality is grossly oversimplified at its best, and downright ridiculous and misleading at its worse. To begin, homosexuality is deviant sexuality, which is strictly against the Genesis mandates, while the other is dealing with mixing blood and semen in an act which is an affront to God in the Old Testament. Second, the punishment for homosexuality was death in Leviticus as opposed to being "cut off" from one's people for those who had coitus during menstruation. The penalties point to a difference in the way God viewed these acts. Third, following this line of argumentation, because incest and bestiality also appear in Leviticus 18 and 20, should we accept these acts as okay? Of course not! Fourth, one could argue that the New Covenant gives some leniency on sexual intercourse during menstruation by not mentioning it, but homosexuality is repeatedly rejected as sinful. Nevertheless, despite what some may suggest, I still do not think that sex during menstruation is something that Christians should be involved in if for no other reason than the Bible frowns upon it.

I would like to end this section by quoting Jewish commentator, Dennis Prager. He notes, "To a world which divided human sexuality between penetrator and penetrated, Judaism said, 'You are wrong—sexuality is to be divided between male and female.' To a world which saw women as baby producers unworthy of romantic and sexual attention, Judaism said, 'You are wrong—women must be the sole focus of men's erotic love.' To a world which said that sensual feelings and physical beauty were life's supreme goods, Judaism said, 'You are wrong—ethics and holiness are the supreme goods.'"³⁴ Thus, the Torah, and the rest of the Old Testament never condone same-sex activity, and neither does the New Testament.

Homosexuality in the NT

The last three "clobber passages" fall within Paul's letters of instruction to the early church (Rom 1:18–30; 1 Cor 6:9; 1 Tim 1:10). Before looking at these passages, however, I want address the moral trajectory argument that abolished slavery, brought about women's rights, and allowed for the inclusion of Gentiles in the church.³⁵ At some point, all of these have been used to argue for the inclusion of practicing homosexuals in the church. I will make two points that discredit such a comparison. First, this is a false analogy, or an apples and oranges comparison. While being a Gentile, slave, or a woman is never pronounced as sinful, the church did take issue with anyone from these groups who committed sin (sexual or otherwise). One need only to read Corinthians to come to this conclusion. Moreover, unrepented sin could exclude a person from entering heaven. In the NT, homosexuality is always presented as sinful. Same-sex oriented people can be included in full fellowship as long as they remain chaste. Second, a close reading of the Bible in its totality reveals that there is a trajectory to liberate each of the three groups in question (Gentiles, slaves, and women), which is stated clearly in Paul's words to the Galatians in 3:28. This trajectory is never stated for anyone practicing sexual sin or same-sex activity. Therefore, when affirming scholars engage in these types of so-called moral-trajectory arguments they are starting out with a wrong premise.

Romans 1:18–30

This portion of Paul's teaching is the clearest denunciation of homosexuality practiced by both men *and* women. Affirming arguments are legion in their attempts to get around this text.³⁶ These include: Paul is speaking about homosexual acts in the context of idolatry; Paul is

---

34. Prager, "Why Judaism."

35. For a more detailed treatment, see Peterson, *Sin of Sodom*, 10–12.

36. See several of these in Scanzoni and Mollenkott, *Is the Homosexual My Neighbor?* 61–66.

speaking about the excess of the Roman emperors; Paul is dealing with heterosexuals who go "against their nature" and experiment in homosexual sex (homosexuals are fine because they are oriented to homosexuality already); we can ignore this text because Paul did not know about sexual orientation as we do today; or that Paul is saying homosexuality is just like any of the other sins noted in the vice list of Romans 1:29–30.

It is impossible to refute here at length every one of these arguments, but a few points need to be made. First, it is preposterous to assert that Paul would have been fine with loving same-sex acts because he is supposedly only referring to heterosexuals going against their "nature" or that he is speaking only to those who practice *abusive* homosexuality as did the Roman emperors.[37] The vice lists in 1 Corinthians and 1 Timothy push against such an assertion (see below). Second, even if homosexuality is listed with other sins, that does not make it any less sinful. Third, living in the Roman Empire we can be assured that Paul knew about homosexual orientation. If Plato's *Symposium* (ca. 385–70 BCE) knew of orientation, Paul surely would have. Fourth, Paul's coupling of idolatry and homosexuality in Romans 1 needs to be understood within his overall argument. Paul isolates homosexuality for special attention *because* it is such an egregious flouting of the creation mandates, which are clearly displayed in our physical bodies as male and female. Placing one's self above God's mandates is the ultimate form of idolatry. Thus, Paul's teaching in Romans 1 is consistent with the Genesis mandates as well as the rest of the Bible's teaching on homosexual activity, a point reinforced in the vice lists.

1 Cor 6:9–10; 1 Tim 1:9–10

The vice lists found in Pauline texts have also been the focus of much attention based upon the ambiguity of the interpretation of certain terms. Is Paul addressing homosexual lifestyles, effeminate men, men who were playboys, young men who sold themselves to older men (pederasty), or some other form of sexual wantonness? Into this interpretive conundrum some have suggested that even if the texts reflect homosexual practices, this does not mean that Paul was against loving same-sex relationships (see above argument). In fact, some have propounded that Paul is simply stating that all people are sinful and in need of Christ's saving grace. Once

---

37. Scanzoni and Mollenkott, *Is the Homosexual My Neighbor?* 65–66.

that grace is applied, because we all still sin, one should not impose on the homosexual the need to deny his or her orientation and lifestyle. Instead, they should live chaste lives before God in committed loving same-sex relationships if they should so choose.[38]

There are so many problems with this line of reasoning that it is hard to know where to begin, but I will address at least a few of the major difficulties. First, while Paul is in fact using the vice lists to give an overview of sins that people in their unsanctified state formerly practiced, this does not mean we should continue doing them after applying Christ's blood to our lives. To suggest that it is fine for homosexuals to continue in their lifestyles simply because it is their orientation is tantamount to saying that the murderer can continue to murder, or that thieves and drunkards can continue to practice their vice as well as long as they are sanctified. Now that is not to say that some may not fall back into the snare of sin, we all know this can happen (Rom 3:23; 1 John 1:9). Christians can, and do, fall short of God's standards and should repent. That is the key, repentance of these sins. But to suggest that practicing same-sex sexual acts regularly is fine as long as you are "sanctified" is to miss Paul's point completely.

Second, in 1 Corinthians 6:9 and 1 Timothy 1:10, Paul coins a term from the Levitical law which clearly points to homosexual sex, namely, *arsenokoitēs* which literally means a "man bedder." This term comes from the sexual laws of Leviticus 18:22 and 20:13 in the Greek Septuagint and clearly refers to homosexuality. And if Paul wanted to address sex between an older man and a boy, he could have used the word pederasty (Gr. *paiderastia*). Paul clearly had an all-encompassing idea in mind by coining this term. Therefore, no matter how hard affirming scholars try to twist the meaning of Paul's words to mean one of the above-stated vices, most modern English translations have indeed captured what Paul was teaching.

Third, affirming scholars suggest that the term "homosexuality," as English translations render *arsenokoitēs*, is a modern designation and therefore should not be applied to ancient contexts. This again is to misunderstand the reality that the sin of sexual deviancy, while perhaps labelled something new today, was just as common and known by ancient audiences. Semantics is not a strong argument.

---

38. So, Scanzoni and Mollenkott, *Is the Homosexual My Neighbor?* 66–71.

Finally, to suggest that because homosexuality is listed beside the sins of greed and lying, which describe the sins of many Christians, we should therefore not focus on homosexuality any more than these other sins is a poor argument. The reality is, while many Christians do struggle with the sins mentioned in the vice lists, no truly Spirit-convicted Christian would simply pass off those sins as being "normal" or acceptable because "God made them that way," a common refrain among "Christian" LGBTQ people when referring to their sexuality. On the contrary, honest, Spirit-led Christians recognize their sins like greed and lying and attempt to overcome them with the Lord's help.[39] On the other hand, those advocating for the normalizing of same-sex activity often do so with "pride" and boldness.

Jesus' Teaching and Finished Work on the Cross

Before finishing this section, I would like to address three arguments often used to support homosexuality from Jesus' instruction. One of the most oft-repeated arguments in favor of homosexuality is that because Jesus himself never mentioned it, homosexuality must not be that important. So why should we be overly concerned about it? This is not only an argument from silence, but it is to miss the power and authority of the rest of the Bible when dealing with sexual ethics, not the least of which is the instruction of Genesis 1 and 2. This also applies to the second argument which is the case for "frequency." Just because homosexuality is only explicitly mentioned in seven places does not mean that it is not that important. The truth is Jesus did not teach directly about pedophilia, incest, and bestiality either, but we certainly do not think these are fine. One must be careful not to create a canon within the canon whereby the NT becomes more authoritative on sexual ethics than the rest of the Bible. [40] This is poor interpretive method.

A more nuanced theological argument for homosexuality and same-sex coupling is based upon Jesus' finished work on the cross. Some assert that Jesus' resurrection initiated a new eschatological order where procreation is supposedly not as important. After all, eventually there will be no death so new life is not needed through procreation.[41] This,

---

39. See similar comments by Longman, *Bible and the Ballot*, 228.
40. See comments by Dallas, *Gay Gospel*, 189–93.
41. So, Song, *Covenant and Calling* (2014).

some argue, is why the NT celebrates celibacy as an acceptable way to serve God (Jesus and Paul were celibate; cf. 1 Cor 7:7). Considering this change in the church's eschatological trajectory where procreation will no longer be needed, some argue that non-procreative same-sex coupling can be pleasing to God because they can devote their relationship to serving God like those who are celibate. I must admit that when I read this argument, I found it completely unconvincing and others have come to this conclusion as well.[42]

I would simply make three points in rebuttal. First, this argument places too much emphasis on a future reality in the eschaton. We are not in that reality yet but rather are under biblical authority, which still forbids homosexuality outright. Second, any sexual activity that flouts the Genesis mandate establishing binary gender for sexual activity, this side of the eschaton, is to go against God's law. Finally, while the NT does not overtly teach on the importance of procreation, as observant Jews, the authors certainly would have supported the family unit and children as both Paul and Jesus do consistently.[43]

Some Final Notes and a Warning

There are common threads within affirming scholars' approaches to the Bible and homosexuality which are dangerous. First, to apply modern sexual ethics and morality to an ancient text is the opposite of what a good interpreter should do. The process is just the opposite. The fact that homosexuality has only *recently* become acceptable because of scientific "evidence" and psychology is already on unstable ground. Second, postmodern interpreters rely too heavily on their own reasoning and rationality, which has also been corrupted by the fall. While modern philosophy and psychology may assert something is logical and acceptable, the Bible is clear that "the heart is more deceitful than all else And is desperately sick; Who can understand it?" (Jer 17:9; NASB). Third, the Genesis mandates make it clear that sexual fulfillment is to be undertaken in the confines of heterosexual unions. Even though some may suggest that the ancients did not understand sexual orientation as we do today, and that we can therefore allow variations of the mandates, this is extremely tenuous. As noted earlier, to add to these clearly stated mandates based upon

---

42. Hill, "Gay Christians," 37–40, 42. Here, Hill critiques Song's assertions.
43. Contra Knust, *Unprotected Texts*, 82–83.

the assertions of modern behavioral science is a dangerous precedent to set, and is one undertaken based upon an argument from silence in the Scripture. Fourth, some affirming scholars note how gay Christians often experience the Spirit's presence and God's favor in their personal lives and in their church services, thus supposedly demonstrating that God is okay with their lives as they are. This is already problematic because God does not contradict his Word. As Joe Dallas rightly notes, who is to say that a person is not experiencing emotions only, or a demonic delusion? Even if "gay Christians" do experience the Spirit and God's blessings is this because God is okay with their sin, or is it because God's gifts are without repentance (Rom 11:29)?[44] Corinth certainly experienced God's blessing and the presence of the Spirit, but their sin was rampant and in need of correction! Fifth, another factor often brought to bear on the discussion is the issue of the feeling of "love" experienced by same-sex couples and recognized by other people around them. If a "gay Christian" says that they love someone of the same sex it must be right. This cannot be sustained any more than an adulterer or a fornicator can argue that they love their partner, which may in fact be true. However, love is not the final arbiter of right and wrong, the Bible is.[45] Sixth, if affirming scholars and behavioral scientists are correct in saying that homosexuals can never change their orientation, then what are we to do with the Joe Dallases, Sy Rogerses (1956–2020),[46] and Rosaria Butterfields of the world not to mention the countless others who have been transformed by the power of Christ?[47] The common denominator in these types of testimonies is the acknowledgment that they needed to stop living their lives for themselves and instead surrender every aspect of their lives to Jesus. Only then did they begin to find healing spiritually, emotionally, and yes, sexually. This seems to be exactly what Paul is referring to in his vice list to the Corinthians when he speaks about the changed lives of the Corinthian believers (1 Cor 6:11).[48] Seventh, and closely connected to the

---

44. Dallas, *Gay Gospel*, 150–52.

45. Dallas, *Gay Gospel*, 152–53.

46. Briggs, "Sy Rogers."

47. See the comments of Satinover, *Homosexuality*, 26. Scanzoni and Mollenkott (*Is the Homosexual My Neighbor?*, 107–8) acknowledge that some people may appear to change but, they argue, these people probably were not really hardcore homosexuals but rather either bisexual or only working through their curiosities. In other words, they had a lower level of homosexual draw or proclivity.

48. For a more detailed treatment of the different steps to transformation which

previous point, is the simple fact that too many affirming scholars are too quick to limit the power of the Spirit to change lives. Indeed, Al Mohler is correct to note that the issue of homosexuality and/or sexual sin is not fixed at the therapy level, it is a spiritual issue and must be handled at that level.[49] While many may struggle with sexual sin all their lives, this does not mean that opening the door to sinful activity is the answer. Even if we accept the premise that some sexual orientation is unalterable, a premise with which I do not agree based upon the power of God to change lives, that does not mean that it is somehow right or should be accepted as God-honoring. As I have noted in an earlier chapter, pedophilia is often asserted to be unalterable, but we still do not accept such lifestyles in our Western society, at least not yet. Finally, as I have noted before, even honest affirming biblical scholars recognize that the Bible is unequivocal on this topic: they just choose to follow their experience instead.[50] This final position is the reason why we as a church are in serious trouble. The authority of the Bible has been rejected in favor of experience.

Now, I offer a final warning, which was also voiced by Al Mohler. If the government can dictate what Christian counselors say to patients, so, too, in the not-too-distant future pastors will be told what they can and cannot teach or preach. Thus, religious liberty (i.e., our first liberty in the Bill of Rights) is in danger of being crowded out by other "stronger interests," namely, the sexual revolution that is trampling over every part of religious liberty at breakneck speed, a movement that will end up beating at, and knocking down, the door of every religious institution and church.[51]

Conclusion

As we have seen, the effects of the LGBTQ movement on the church and biblical interpretation, especially as it relates to homosexuality, have been devastating. Some self-professing (former) evangelical Christians suggest that the culture's acceptance of gay adoption, gays in the military,

combines biblical sexual ethics and ministry to those struggling with same-sex attraction, see Burk and Lambert, *Transforming Homosexuality* (2015). Here they argue for the sinfulness of even same-sex orientation and attraction because it is against God's nature (pp.27–33).

49. Mohler, *The Briefing* (Aug 31, 2016).

50. See for example, Loader, "Homosexuality and the Bible," 17–48; and Johnson, "Homosexuality and the Church."

51. Mohler, *The Briefing* (Aug 31, 2016).

business and media acceptance of gay themes and the like are all positives and a move in the right direction for culture and especially the church.[52] Sadly, all this tells us is that the church and Western culture have taken one more step towards an unholy alignment, which is anything but positive.[53] God is the one who established the prohibitions and put in place the mandates of Genesis 1 and 2, not humans. We have no right to change what is taught clearly in both Testaments of the Bible. This is a path down which we should not go. Can we do the same for those stuck in loveless marriages and who find long-term committed sexual fulfillment in the arms of another person, same-sex or otherwise? Or shall we allow them to leave the marriage because they now realize that they simply were not attracted to their spouse, have fallen out of love, or now recognize their true "orientation"? What about those who claim they are attracted to multiple people at the same time? Or what about those who are only attracted to children? And the list could go on. When you yield to emotions and sentiment, then any number of sins could be legitimated. God's Word must be the final authority.

At the same time, we cannot throw our hands up in the air in defeat and say, "that is just the world being the world." What are we telling our children if we do this? This is nothing more than being equivalent to Pontius Pilate who washed his hands of Jesus' crucifixion even though he allowed it to happen. Christians who think this way will not be able to sidestep being accountable to God for what they accept in the church, how they teach their children, and who they put in office to rule over them. In this regard, I find Longman's conclusion deeply troubling when he says that it is a "happy convergence of values" when the church and the state agree "at least for the moment" on forbidding incest or polygamous marriages.[54] So is he saying that the church should not try to prevent legislation that would allow for polygamous and incestuous marriages?

---

52. E.g., Gushee, *Changing Our Minds*, 28–32.

53. Interestingly, Gushee (*Changing Our Minds*, 57) in his attempt to be more conciliatory to LGBT concerns and in an effort to find a more moderate position, acknowledges the dangers of allowing culture to influence biblical interpretation "because cultures are sometimes quite wrong." Yet, this seems to be what he actually does throughout his transition from "non-affirming" to "affirming." Since his 2014 book, Gushee has admitted there is no middle ground anymore, you are either for LGBT rights and acceptance or you are not. See Al Mohler's assessment of Gushee's changing positions on this topic at Mohler, *The Briefing* (Aug 31, 2016) and Mohler, "A Response to David Gushee."

54. Longman, *Bible and the Ballot*, 230.

We sat by and allowed the LGBTQ movement to change the church; what is next? We need to stand firm for godly morality if we want to see our culture flourish. But if the church is impotent when it comes to setting the standard for sexual ethics and morality, what hope is there for society? The church has dropped the ball on the issue of homosexuality. Back in 1996 Jeffrey Satinover stated plainly that ". . . the hallmark of a society in which all sexual constraints have been set aside is that finally it sanctions homosexuality as well."[55] I believe he was only partly right. Society can sink lower when it denies gender distinctions completely in favor or transgenderism. On this point, the church is once again beginning to fumble the ball.

---

55. Satinover, *Homosexuality*, 17.

Chapter 12

The Mandate of Gender Distinctions Part 4

The Transsexual Revolution

> I shall not today attempt further to define the kinds of material
> I understand to be embraced [as obscene/pornography],...
> but I know it when I see it.

SOME MAY WONDER WHAT this famous quotation of Justice Potter Stewart from the 1964 SCOTUS case, *Jacobellis v. Ohio* dealing with obscenity and pornography, has to do with transgenderism. Put simply, I share Justice Stewart's thought process when it comes to my understanding of modern transgenderism: I may not know all the technical ways transgenderism may be defined, but I know what will cause maximum chaos in a society when I see it. Indeed, Prager is correct to point out that while "The Left has done many destructive things to America. It is quite possible that none will prove to be more destructive than its attempt to obliterate gender-distinctions."[1] And in light of the Genesis mandate on gender distinctions, I readily agree with Branch that "transgenderism is the ultimate rejection of Judeo-Christian sexual ethics."[2]

---

1. Prager, "Feminization." As noted by Brown, *Jezebel's War*, 116.
2. Branch, *Affirming God's Image*, 17.

I can honestly say that of all the broken mandates that we have covered throughout this book, the most destructive attack against them all, and the most heinous attack on God's plan for humanity, is the attack on gender distinctions and the desire to obliterate them and make them of no consequence. While homosexuality warps the use of sexual activity and gender roles in favor of one's "orientation," transgenderism not only blurs the sexual and gender boundaries, it often includes the obliteration of these distinctions by radical hormone and surgical alteration (what some have called "mutilation"[3]) of one's body in order to make it "fit" a perceived gender identification (cf. 1 Cor 6:19–20).[4] In this vein, Denny Burk notes that transgenderism attempts to reshape the body to match the brain's perception of a person's gender as opposed to reshaping the brain to match one's biological gender.[5] What ever happened to the Hippocratic Oath of "do no harm"? We certainly would object to removing a perfectly good arm or leg of someone who suffers from "body integrity disorder," but we are being told it is fine to remove perfectly functioning reproductive organs in the name of moral progress.[6] This in many ways is what makes the push of the trans movement in Western culture so heinous. It is the fundamental and irreversible alteration of God's good creation for the purpose of meeting the psychological "needs" of the individual in question.

At the same time, I want to be clear from the outset that the following discussion is meant to sound a warning of the dangers that radical transgenderism poses to stable culture and for the church. It is not meant as an attack against any individual per se who is struggling with gender dysphoria and who needs our love and understanding. Also, I do recognize there are various shades of transgenderism,[7] but here I will speak in broader categories for the purpose of noting the breach of the Genesis mandate of gender distinctions. In this regard, what has been happening in Western cultures in the past five years is nothing less than absolute chaos and it happened with breakneck speed. When we begin to tear

---

3. Murray, *Madness of Crowds*, 203.

4. For a detailed treatment of what is involved in gender reassignment surgery, see Branch, *Affirming God's Image*, 94–112.

5. Burk, "The Transgender Test," 96. See also Roberts, *Transgender, Talking Points*, 40.

6. Branch, *Affirming God's Image*, 107.

7. For a survey of these, see Branch, *Affirming God's Image*, 23–25. See also Murray, *Madness of Crowds*, 186–87.

down the age-old and time-tested fences and boundaries, we are bound to feel the negative effects. The trans issue is no less the case. In fact, it may be the true marker that we are crossing a threshold from which we may not be able to return barring God's intervention.

Some may suggest that this is the world's issue and not the church's problem. They would be wrong. Transgenderism is not just affecting those outside of the four walls of the church, it is affecting those in the pews *and* the pulpit. For example, Branch details the story of the first transgendered pastor in a Baptist denomination.[8] And recently, a trans woman Baptist pastor in Canada was terminated when she "came out."[9] The madness of gender confusion is not just mainstream, it is in our churches. In one news account, I read about how a Presbyterian pastor's transgendered "son" (who used to be a girl) married a transgender "woman."[10] So, a girl became a man and a man became a girl and they got married: they each switched and took on the role of the opposite gender. Now to be sure, some may argue that this is the exception as opposed to the rule and will not affect us anytime soon. I am not that optimistic, especially if the same-sex debate is any indicator of the trajectory of church policy, it will be here before we know it.

Because I have handled the biblical discussion already in Chapter 9, in this chapter I will note the biblical instruction when needed as a means of reminding the reader of what is at stake. As I have been noting throughout, Scripture must always be our starting point, as opposed to one's feelings and personal opinions about gender and sexuality.[11] This being noted, in this chapter I will examine the current trajectory of Western culture vis-à-vis the trans debate and attempt to point out the overt and latent dangers being posed to both culture and the church. Before beginning, however, it is important to note that transgender-like activity is as old as time, as I noted during the discussion in Chapter 9. From males emasculating themselves in cultic devotion to Ishtar or Cybele, to coerced or uncoerced sterilization for various reasons, there has always been some within society who have struggled with gender dysphoria.[12] However, what the culture and church is dealing with today

8. Branch, *Affirming God's Image*, 38.
9. Parke, "Baptist Pastor."
10. Briggs, "John Ortberg."
11. So, too, Branch, *Affirming God's Image*, 38–39.
12. Branch, *Affirming God's Image*, 7–8, 46. For a brief history of transgenderism, see Branch, 6–19.

is something quite different in its intensity and prevalence. Indeed, what is going on today is not something happening on the fringes of society, it has become mainstream, it is being foisted upon all areas of our society, and it has happened at breakneck speed. How does such a small minority (0.6–0.7 percent of the population[13]) wield so much power? The Enemy has blinded the world and many in the church.

The Effects of Transgenderism on Culture

What took decades to accomplish in the gay movement has happened in record time with the trans movement.[14] Social commentator Douglas Murray in his recent book *The Madness of Crowds* points out that 2015 marked the beginning of the breakout of the trans movement with the transition of former Olympian, Bruce Jenner, to Caitlyn Jenner.[15] In was at this time that the former male Olympian world record setter of Wheaties-cereal-box fame declared he had become his true self as a woman. Murray also points out that one of the first things the freshman congresswoman Alexandria Ocasio-Cortez from New York did once taking office was to have a fundraiser for the British trans group Mermaids, which supports giving hormone therapy to children.[16] But these are not the only things that have happened that are controversial when addressing the transgender "madness" as Murray calls it.

In 2019 the ACLU began to lobby for tampons to be placed in men's restrooms in order to bring "menstrual equity."[17] In this regard, in some regions of Britain, local authorities are issuing guidelines to teachers in primary schools that they should tell all of their students that boys, too, can have periods in order to make trans kids feel more accepted.[18] And now many awards shows are debating on whether to add award categories to include trans or gender non-conforming people.[19] Even the airlines are adapting to the new "woke" culture where trans rights are central, and avoiding offense is a must. One report notes that the EasyJet

---

13. For the stats see Branch, *Affirming God's Image*, 21.
14. Murray, *Madness of Crowds*, 186.
15. Murray, *Madness of Crowds*, 200.
16. Murray, *Madness of Crowds*, 246; and Barr, "Ocasio-Cortez."
17. Dorman, "ACLU."
18. Murray, *Madness of Crowds*, 186.
19. Good Morning Britain, "Piers Debates."

company now wants its employees to stop using the greeting "Ladies and Gentlemen" opting for more gender inclusive language like "welcome everyone." This was spurred by the complaints of one UK professor (Dr. Andi Fugard of the University of London) on social media.[20] The fear with which companies are gripped when threatened by the social media mob is staggering. The report went on to note that several other airlines (e.g., Air Canada, American, United) are also following suit even going so far as offering non-binary booking options (e.g., American Airlines).

We also now have an entire classification of families that identify as "trans" in cases where one or both identify as trans.[21] The confusion of such pairings can be seen in the struggle of trans persons to choose a "title" (father, mother, "mather" etc.) or role when raising their children.[22] New designations for parents are now being adopted such as "male mothers, female fathers, trans men who carry their child."[23] One Canadian study on trans parenting concluded that there is now a need "to degender parenting and to detach motherhood from female-bodied persons, and fatherhood from male-bodied persons, by referring to people according to their reproductive functions."[24] This, of course, is all in an effort to normalize such pairings.

How could Western culture get to the point where we feel that this is normal and good? As I have been pointing out throughout this book, the Enemy does not kick open the door and declare his presence. He is subtle and does it through craft and deception. It is time for Western culture, and especially pastors, parents, educators, and grandparents to wake up and recognize the danger that is now threatening not just America as a nation, but our immediate families as well. We are in danger of being swept into the madness. If you do not believe me, then take note of what has happened in Canada with the passing of legislation demanding that people use the proper pronouns for those in the trans community or face the consequences. The now-famous battle waged by Canadian clinical psychologist Jordan Peterson against the changes to the *Canadian*

---

20. Puhak, "EasyJet."
21. See Petit et al., "Negotiating," 282.
22. Petit et al., "Negotiating," 283.
23. Petit et al., "Negotiating," 294.
24. Petit et al., "Negotiating," 294.

Human Rights Act (Bill C-16) stands as a chilling reminder of where we are heading as a society.[25]

Transgenderism in Media

As I will note below, there is no hiding from this new form of gender redefinition. The "madness" is coming at us from all sides[26] and is bombarding our children wherever they turn. Being "trans" is to the 2000s as gay was to the 90s. It is hip and made popular by trans models (e.g., Laith Ashley)[27] and shows like *I Am Jazz*, a reality show about a boy who identifies as trans and at 18 opts for gender reassignment surgery.[28] The show follows the process detailing how the surgery did not go as planned because of underdeveloped genitals due to the extensive use of hormone blockers for so long.[29] In a separate case, one of the leading transsexuals on YouTube, who began his transition to a female at the age of 22, now at the age of 25 wants to de-transition so he/she can have a child.[30] This will be done through a surrogate because "she" is currently with a man. "She" feels the natural urge to pass on "her" DNA to the next generation. However, a side-effect of hormone therapy for a transitioning male is sterilization.

    Can you think of anything more bizarre and outside of the realm of sane society? Yet here we are in the first half of the twenty-first century being faced with the complete overthrow of sexual ethics and morality all in the name of "progress." But this is not progress. God made creation good, and in that creation, male and female were the genders God chose to perpetuate society. The other day I saw a meme on social media that hit the nail on the head. It said, "ever notice how gender reassignment surgery only offers two genders: male or female?" Now I know that there will be some who, due to biological and genetic issues, or through invasive surgery, choose to be neuter, but for all intents and purposes, the

---

    25. Jordan Peterson is a clinical psychologist from the University of Toronto who came under fire for opposing Bill C-16.

    26. See Murray, *Madness of Crowds*, 183.

    27. Hendricks, "Ashley." Ashley notes the tension of coming out as trans because his mother is a "Pentecostal Christian."

    28. Murray, *Madness of Crowds*, 219.

    29. Spargo, "Jazz."

    30. White, "Detransitioning."

meme is correct. We cannot improve on God's good creation when it comes to gender.

As I noted above, the Enemy has been subtly changing the minds of people about the "goodness" of gender confusion. A few weeks ago, I was watching an episode of the now-ended series *The Mentalist*. Episode 21 from season 4 titled "Ruby Slippers," which originally aired April 26, 2012, presented transgenderism in a very liberating and positive manner. The show has a "heartwarming" ending with one of the main characters of the episode singing *Somewhere Over the Rainbow* as it glorifies transgenderism. That was eight years ago and now here we are changing birth certificates and driver's licenses to match someone's perceived gender.

It goes without saying that Hollywood has jumped on the bandwagon to do everything in its power to promote sexual deviance and perversion as the norm. They have been doing that for years. But something as American as apple pie is now being corrupted, namely, children's superheroes. Along with Captain America, Thor, the Hulk, Iron Man and many other children's favorites, Marvel Comics now has plans to introduce a transgender character.[31]

Another form of media embracing the madness is the magazine *GQ*. Masculinity is no longer depicted as the rugged male of the 1950s, it is the transsexual dressed in flowing gowns and female attire.[32] And *GQ* is not alone or a one-off. There is a move afoot to push fashion designers to make all their clothing lines gender neutral, and to "de-gender beauty."[33] The uniqueness of God's good creation as male and female no longer is the standard: in a gender-confused society, genders are oppressive and to be shunned. This is what our children and wider culture are being faced with daily. This is no longer tangential; it is mainstream. Indeed, children are now being forced to deal with the sexual confusion of others whether they want to or not.

Transgenderism, Schools, and Athletics

President Obama contributed to the increasing madness in May of 2016 when he instructed public schools to allow transgendered people to use the bathrooms and locker rooms of their choice. He based his decision on

---

31. CNN News Source, "Marvel Universe."
32. Welch, "Pharrell"; and Brown, "The New Masculinity."
33. Starr, "De-Gender Beauty."

Title IX, which handles issues of sex discrimination in educational settings.[34] While courts blocked the policy, and the Trump administration repealed this directive,[35] you can be assured that a future administration will not only revert back to this policy but enshrine it in law. Indeed, the Trump administration's decision was met with protests from LGBTQ activists, the same activists who will lobby a new more progressive administration to reimplement the policy. It makes no difference that warnings have been sounded about the dangers to women especially in these types of situations. We were told that we were fearmongering and that this would never happen. Well, those who sounded the warning were indeed correct. Just recently another male was arrested for sexually assaulting a minor in a "gender neutral" bathroom in a school in Wisconsin.[36]

The trans folly is no less tangibly present in the brave new world of trans athletes competing in girls' sports. I find it ironic that most of the trans athletes creating issues are male-to-female trans persons. It makes perfect sense. Males are genetically stronger and more muscular. This sets up not only an uneven playing field, but dangerous conditions for girls and women, especially in contact sports like rugby, boxing, or wrestling.[37] And even after taking hormone blockers, studies have shown that male-to-female trans persons are still stronger than women.[38] It does not take a rocket scientist to realize that the ones who are going to be the most disadvantaged are women. But many female athletes do not dare say anything against the new normal for fear of being labeled transphobic.

In track and field, weightlifting, cycling, you name it, trans male-to-female athletes are not just winning and smashing records, they consistently lead the pack over their biological female counterparts.[39] The concern is real. As Murray notes, a quick Google search reveals numerous accounts of this new phenomenon.[40] As just one example, three Connecticut women are filing suit against the "Connecticut Association of Schools and Connecticut Interscholastic Athletic Conference, as well as the boards of education in Bloomfield, Cromwell, Glastonbury,

---

34. Walsh, "Parents Object."
35. Vitali, et al., "Transgender Bathroom."
36. Montanaro, "Gender Neutral Bathroom."
37. See Brown, "Rugby Players."
38. Brown, "Rugby Players."
39. See discussions by Prager, "Meanwhile"; and Brown, "Rugby Players."
40. Murray, *Madness of Crowds*, 236–38.

Canton and Danbury."[41] The reason? The biological males who identify as female consistently have won track titles causing the women to place behind them robbing them of the opportunity for scholarships.

Many people recognize that this needs to be changed. Despite the push by some sociologists to support trans people in the sports of their choice, former professional female athletes note that the physical differences between men and women is insurmountable.[42] Again, the problem is that all common sense and decency is quashed as being transphobic. The silencing of dissent is becoming more and more pervasive in all walks of life, not just in athletics.

Transphobia: The Crushing of Dissent and the "Cancel Culture"

The silencing of voices opposed to transgender lunacy is not just at the individual level, it can affect entire states. For example, when North Carolina passed legislation (Bill HB2) enforcing the position that people must use the restroom commensurate with their birth gender, the repercussions were immediate. The politically correct NCAA sports association refused to allow any basketball tournaments in the state.[43] Other companies and organizations like the NBA piled on to boycott the state. This was meant to inflict the maximum amount of financial damage as possible unless the state capitulated. Under a newly elected Democrat governor, the controversial bill was reworked.[44]

The silencing of dissent is also being directed at pastors and parents. When a mid-west evangelical pastor preached on the sanctity and immutability of gender as given by God, the local LGBTQ community attacked him and his church and bullied the local art scene into breaking sponsorship ties with the church.[45] There is no compromising on this issue for the LGBTQ community. They do not just want acceptance, they want to coerce and shame Christians to conform so that they can "purge"

---

41. Wallace, "Transgender Athletes."
42. Good Morning Britain, "Transgender Athletes."
43. Branch, *Affirming God's Image*, 3.
44. Levin, "North Carolina,"
45. Blake, "LGBT Activists."

any unacceptable teaching, even sermons, that do not conform to their view of sexual ethics.[46]

The attacks are also directed against the parent-child bond. Recently, two pro-transgender groups (GLSEN and the National Center for Transgender Equality) have produced transgender policies for schools that drive a wedge between parents and their trans children. They urge schools to keep parents in the dark about their divisive plans. For example, they encourage schools to aid trans children in their lifestyle choices by using a preferred identity of the child unbeknownst to the parent.[47] The move is not just to silence the dissent of the parent, it is to separate the child from the unwilling or uncooperative parent by severing the family bond through legal means if necessary.[48] This is nothing less than an outright undermining and attack on God's mandate of the family. As I have been noting, the Enemy wants to undo all the Genesis mandates. They are all intertwined to fulfill God's purpose for a flourishing family and society. When we mess with one, other repercussions naturally follow.

You do not have to be a Bible-believing evangelical to be in the crosshairs of the trans agenda. Even those who are secular, rich, pro-LGBTQ, and famous are not exempt. Author J.K. Rowling, of Harry Potter fame, was attacked for supporting a female scientist who insisted one cannot change their biological sex. The scientist lost her job and a judge refused to side with her because her position was not only indefensible but was bigoted and not acceptable to British society.[49] The entrenched orthodoxy of the Left on LGBTQ issues is not to be toyed with. People are being singled out and made examples of in order to silence dissent. And there is no room for joking about such issues. On the contrary, comedian Ricky Gervais also took heat being called a transphobe for making a joke about transgenderism on Twitter.[50] People are also under fire for writing about the dangers of transgenderism. In this vein, recently a journalist with the Wall Street Journal by the name of Abigail Shrier published a book titled *Irreversible Damage: The Transgender Craze Seducing Our Daughters* (2020). While the author is supportive of adults who are transgendered, in the book she highlights the dangers to adolescent girls who

---

46. Blake, "LGBT Activists."
47. Branch, *Affirming God's Image*, 114.
48. Branch, *Affirming God's Image*, 120.
49. The Associated Press, "JK Rowling."
50. Day, "Rickie Gervais."

may be rushing into irreversible decisions at too young of an age. The response? Much like the Nazi purge, the Left attacked her and called for her book to be burned while some stores removed it from their shelves, at least temporarily.[51]

This has been going on for some time online. The average person now who voices an opinion different than the politically correct position is being silenced. Something as basic as an offense about the use of a wrong pronoun can land one in hot water with the online censorship crowd. People's social media accounts are being suspended for "misgendering" people if they use the wrong pronouns.[52] It is obvious that this is simply the Left's way of silencing any opposition to their gender choices and confusion. Ironically, they denounce any detractors with pejoratives like "Nazi" and "white supremacist" while they themselves are using fascist tactics.

In another recent headline, Pennsylvania's former Health Director and current assistant secretary for Health under the Biden administration, Dr. Rachel Levine, who is a male-to-female transgendered person (I will let the irony of those two concepts just sit there), became irate when a reporter called Levine by the wrong pronoun.[53] While I certainly do not support antagonistic behavior towards any person, as adults we should have thicker skin and take the higher road. But unfortunately, in a world where claims of transphobia and homophobia prevail, those who misgender someone in the gender chaos of Western culture, are immediately belittled and harassed until the appropriate apologies are rendered.

Again, some may simply reply and say this is the extreme. They would be wrong. This is not the extreme, it is becoming mainstream with Christians coming under fire for holding to a sexual ethic commensurate with the Genesis mandates. In one case in Britain, a Christian doctor was fired for not calling a biological male a woman. When the case went to court, the court said, "Belief in Genesis 1:27, lack of belief in transgenderism and conscientious objection to transgenderism in our judgment are incompatible with human dignity and conflict with the fundamental rights of others, specifically here, transgender individuals. [. . .] in so far as those beliefs form part of his [the doctor's] wider faith, his wider faith also does not satisfy the requirement of being worthy of respect in a

---

51. See Shrier, "ACLU"; and https://www.rt.com/usa/506758-uc-berkeley-lavery-book-burning-trans/.

52. Prestigiacomo, "Zuby."

53. Zanotti, "Pennsylvania Health Director."

democratic society, . . ."[54] Note well that the court makes it clear that the Bible is "incompatible with human dignity." God, the creator of humans and the one who gave dignity to his creation through divine mandates to set parameters for human flourishing, now is deemed just the opposite in the eyes of the British court. Again, I am reminded of Isaiah's words, "Woe unto those who call evil good and good evil and replace darkness for light and light for darkness" (Isa 5:20a; my translation).

As part of the LGBTQ movement, the trans agenda has also been accepted at most workplaces in the human resources departments and as such, company policy will inevitably clash with Christians and their beliefs.[55] We need to be aware that this is not an idle threat; it is real and Christians need to be aware of what they will be facing if they refuse to adhere to the new normal, which requires proper deference to the trans community through proper gender and pronoun usage.

The LGBTQ community takes no prisoners on these issues, even if dissent comes from among their own allies. For example, in the early 2000s, when some lesbian feminists began recognizing the problems that men claiming to be women posed for women, they began to push back. They rejected the idea that trans "women" (men to women) were truly women. The result was an attack on these feminists by the trans movement by denouncing such positions as transphobic.[56] As a second example, one of the unintended side effects of gender dysphoria related to transgenderism is that when younger people feel they need to transition to their perceived gender, later they may realize that this is not what they want. Thousands of trans people de-transition when they get older (usually mid-twenties). Not surprisingly, to do so once again is to invite the pejorative accusation that they are transphobic.[57] I suppose the vitriol of the trans community against their own is understandable. Such positions as these latter two undermine their agenda and propaganda that being trans, like being homosexual, is immutable and therefore something to be embraced. As it turns out, this is simply not true. Yet, despite such positions, societal groups of all stripes are lining up to pay homage. And politicians are complicit in this chaos as they pander to this group in order to garner their support.

54. Berrien, "British Court."
55. Branch, *Affirming God's Image*, 133–34.
56. Murray, *Madness of Crowds*, 210–17.
57. Sky News, "Trans People."

Transgenderism in Politics

The transgender chaos affecting Western culture is not lessening, it is getting more intense, especially due to politicians who attempt to show society just how "woke" they are and how in touch they are with "oppressed" groups. For example, former Democrat presidential contender Elizabeth Warren said in a December 19, 2019 presidential debate that if she were elected president she would change the rules on prison admittance and allow trans men or women to choose which prison they go to based upon the gender with which they identify.[58] One can only imagine how this would be abused and the chaos it would create for women's prisons. Indeed, recently a convicted rapist, who now identifies as a woman, was placed in a female prison where "she" sexually assaulted four women![59] This is not a one off. Recently, California followed Rhode Island and Massachusetts in passing legislation that allows inmates to choose the prison in which they are incarcerated based upon gender identification.[60] In this brave new world anarchy reigns. Again, a prime example can be seen in a recent headline. On January 16, 2020, *The Des Moines Register* reported the headline "Convicted of Sex Crimes as a Man, Felon no Longer Deemed Threat because of Gender Change."[61] And this is not the only case of such actions. Some men who are convicted of pedophilia have claimed to be women in order to be moved to women's prisons or to gain early release. The political and legal systems are paralyzed by political correctness and the pressure placed on them from the LGBTQ community.

Instead of trying to mitigate the disaster, governments are reinforcing the chaos with even more troubling legislation. As a case in point, Virginia is in the process of adopting Bill 657 which would allow transgender people to change their birth certificates to match their preferred gender without necessarily having gender reassignment surgery.[62] And in New York, changing your birth certificate to your preferred gender is as easy as taking an affidavit with a notary.[63] The West is on a path that is not just troubling, it is destructive, especially when it is being foisted

---

58. The Fix, "Transcript."
59. Murray, *Madness of Crowds*, 246.
60. Heck, "California."
61. Cullen, "Felon."
62. Robinson, "Birth Certificates."
63. NYC Health, "Birth Certificates." As noted by Brown, *Jezebel's War*, 104.

upon the majority by the medical profession through unproven theories or simply due to pressure from these interest groups.

In this vein, the changes in the APA manual (DSM) are politically driven rather than scientific. When the APA voted to remove homosexuality from its list of disorders in 1973 the handwriting was on the wall for further changes to the DSM when the next "revolution" came along. In this regard, Branch notes that "transgender activist Nicholas Teich says, 'It took until 1973 to rid the DSM of a diagnosis of homosexuality as a mental health disorder, so transgenderism may be following that course, just several decades behind.'"[64] According to many mental health professionals, any mental anguish that transgendered people feel is due to the Judeo-Christian worldview held by Christians.[65] Thus, once again, the die is cast to target Christians as the problem for the world's ills when it comes to the new sexual ethics. No negative judgments are to be made about these new sexual proclivities, and the feeling of shame related to one's sinful desires is the new taboo. We need to be aware of what we are facing, and we need to be praying that God will embolden his people to preach the truth of the Bible. And like my earlier discussion on the LGBTQ's indoctrination of our children concerning homosexuality, we also need to be aware of their insidious plan to indoctrinate our children with this latest attack on the Genesis mandates through the push for transgender acceptance.

Trans Indoctrination

For centuries, society has marginalized sexual deviance, especially those who identified as the opposite gender of their birth. Even in more recent history, although people identified as transgendered, it was never viewed as normal sexual behavior to be celebrated. As such, part of the trans agenda in the recent years has been to desexualize their actions/condition in the public eye so that they can be more acceptable to society. This was the same approach used by the gay lobby. Anybody attempting to offer research or an opinion, which connects this condition to deviant sexual attractions, is labeled "offensive" and "bigoted," and, ironically, quickly attacked and marginalized in the most hateful of manners.[66]

---

64. Branch, *Affirming God's Image*, 31.
65. Branch, *Affirming God's Image*, 32.
66. Murray, *Madness of Crowds*, 197–98.

The truth is the perversion of some aspects of this movement is telling of the degradation of society and our ambivalence to society's rejection of God's mandates. Recently someone posted a short video on Twitter of a drag queen inappropriately dressed and lewdly dancing in front of a seated little girl no more than four or five years old. This took place while numerous adults looked on approvingly and clapped. The look on the little girl's face tells you all you need to know about the inappropriateness of the scene. She stares ahead with a stunned look on her face not knowing how she is to respond.[67] As a father of three little girls I was infuriated at the scene and questioned how any parent could allow their child to be subjected to this display: how much more depraved can people get? You may say you would never allow this to happen to your child but what about those innocent story hours at the public library? Even these are no longer off limits to the trans community's grasp and larger agenda.

In this regard, it is now becoming common fare for drag queens to read to preschoolers as an appropriate means of "educating" children about alternative lifestyles. While on the face of it most Christians may recoil at the inappropriateness of this type of exposure to deviant sexual ideas at these tender ages, this is in no way deterring the trans community from pushing their agenda. When questioned on the topic of public library reading to children, one drag queen admitted that he is grooming children at story hour to think differently about LGBT issues.[68] This happened in a Lafayette, LA public library where children as young as three were in attendance. While he went on to clarify that he wanted the next generation to be more tolerant of homosexuals, in using the term "grooming" he let slip what the true agenda was, even though he insisted that was not the plan. During an interview about the situation, John Ritchie, the director of TFP Student Action, pointed out that, "Instead of protecting the precious innocence of our children with wholesome stories, libraries are misusing our tax-dollars to harm their innocence. [. . .] To attempt to dismantle and destroy the distinction between male and female is not only biologically ridiculous, but also a direct attack against God's plan for us and for the family. Everyone who loves the family should wake up, pray and push back."[69] Another member of the community spoke out

---

67. Walsh, "Drag Queen."
68. Risdon, "Drag Queen." For the video itself, see LifeSiteNews, "Drag Queen."
69. Risdon, "Drag Queen."

and declared that "This is not about tolerance or anti-bullying. [...] It is a direct and intentional effort to create gender confusion and doubt among very young children at the very time they need solid guidance and understanding. The intent is to plant a seed to make children more likely to question their sexuality or gender at a later age."[70] This is indeed the plan.

In one account from Canada, a trans/homosexual activist boldly admitted, "I am here to tell you: All that time I said I wasn't indoctrinating anyone with my beliefs about gay and lesbian and bi and trans and queer people. That was a lie."[71] The piece was written by a long-time Canadian gay activist S. Bear Bergman, a woman who identifies as a transgender man. The article appeared in the Huffington Post "tellingly titled 'I Have Come to Indoctrinate Your Children Into My LGBTQ Agenda (And I'm Not a Bit Sorry).'"[72] She went on to boldly declare that her goal was to make other people's children like her even if doing so goes against the clear teachings of their faith or religion.[73] She also says that she and her activist friends have come to shine the light of "truth and fairness" upon their lifestyle and to dispel the myths and ignorance surrounding LGBTQ people.[74] The "truth" that Bergman fails to point out is the actual truth of the lowered life expectancy of gay and bisexual men (20 years lower), increased STDs, cancer and various other diseases.[75] The heart of the LGBTQ agenda directed at our children became crystal clear when Bergman said she would be "'delighted' if she could convince children to disagree with their parents on homosexuality."[76]

As I have been warning throughout this book, the LGBTQ agenda is evident, and they no longer seek to hide it.[77] They are coming after our children and they are doing it through the schools, curriculum, and now public libraries. A few of their titles which they make available to children are: *Girls Will Be Boys Will Be Girls*; *Sometimes the Spoon Runs Away with Another Spoon*; *The Princess Knight*; *A Girl Named Dan*; *It's Okay to be Different*; *10,000 Dresses*; *My Princess Boy*; *My Mommy is a Boy*;

70. Risdon, "Drag Queen."
71. Baklinski, "Gay Activist."
72. Baklinski, "Gay Activist."
73. Baklinski, "Gay Activist."
74. Baklinski, "Gay Activist."
75. Baklinski, "Gay Activist."
76. Baklinski, "Gay Activist."
77. Bergman, "LGBTQ Agenda."

When Kathy is Keith.[78] Again, some may say this is the extreme, or that I am fearmongering. I wish I were wrong, but the medical statistics show just the opposite. They are showing that the indoctrination is working as younger and younger children are seeking medical help to deal with their gender dysphoria, or, in many cases, to transition to their preferred gender.

The Medical Concerns of Transgenderism

Part of the problem with the rapid changes in Western culture when it comes to the disturbing trend of transsexualism is the complete support many trans people get from the medical community without questioning the legitimacy of the request to transition. To do so is to reject the "true" feelings of a child or a teen. Instead, medical intervention is pushed forward as the only option, accompanied by the gravest threats that failure to do so could result in depression, anxiety, substance abuse, running away from home, or in worse case scenarios, suicide: parents are scared into accepting the decision of the child with the support of the medical field and culture.[79] Some commentators have noted that as of 2017 in the US, children as young as eight were eligible for treatments to transition using hormone blockers followed up by surgical intervention.[80] I cannot help but think that the Enemy is using medical professionals, who in some cases have themselves "transitioned" from one sex to another,[81] to twist and warp young people of today.

Also of concern is what has been labeled "clustering." This is when children who identify as being in the wrong body influence their peers to join in because of the attention and/or novelty of the idea. In the UK alone, from 2014–2019, there was a 700 percent increase in child referrals to gender clinics.[82] Many children are exposed to this in school, on the internet, and in various other forms of media. In many cases without such exposure, most children simply would not move in this direction.[83]

---

78. Baklinski, "Gay Activist."
79. Branch, *Affirming God's Image*, 32–33; and Murray, *Madness of Crowds*, 222.
80. Murray, *Madness of Crowds*, 224.
81. Note the troubling account related by Murray, *Madness of Crowds*, 228–29.
82. Murray, *Madness of Crowds*, 218.
83. Murray, *Madness of Crowds*, 222–23.

Gender clinicians often use the terms "insistent, persistent, and consistent" in order to verify if one is truly trans.[84] This opens a whole Pandora's Box related to hormone therapy and gender reassignment surgery. Many times, this is nothing more than gender dysphoria which they outgrow,[85] a similar phenomenon with same-sex attracted teens.[86] Yet, many in the medical community are moving forward in aiding the trans madness despite the fact that long-term studies of the psychological side effects of hormone therapy and surgical transitioning is not encouraging especially for children. Some of the best studies to date show, negative, not positive results, especially on brain and general growth development in children.[87] For those opting for gender reassignment surgery the procedure is rife with possible medical complications not to mention the scientific fact that the patient will always be the biological sex of their birth regardless of any medical procedure.[88] And the psychological benefit is not as promising as hoped for.[89] In males who transition to female, there is a 51 percent higher mortality rate than the general public due to increased "suicide, AIDS, cardiovascular disease, drug abuse, and other unknown causes."[90] To be sure, while early studies attempted to paint a rosy picture of transitioning, the data shows greater dissatisfaction with life, depression, suicidal ideation, and a disturbing trend of higher rates of death, especially due to actual suicide.[91] Fortunately, some medical professionals are sounding the alarm and pointing out the dangers and long-term harm of hormone blockers and gender reassignment surgery.[92]

In some cases, gender dysphoria is brought on by parental abuse. As a case in point, one sad story involves a man named Nathan Verhelst from Belgium. His mother did not like her when she was born as a girl (named Nancy). She thought she was ugly, and she let her child know it. In an effort to deal with the rejection Nancy transitioned to Nathan

---

84. Murray, *Madness of Crowds*, 221; and Branch, *Affirming God's Image*, 28–33.

85. Branch, *Affirming God's Image*, 88–92, 115–17; Murray, *Madness of Crowds*, 203, 233. Estimates have it that 80 percent of children with gender dysphoria will outgrow it as teens, although, most of them will identify later as gay or lesbian.

86. Satinover, *Homosexuality*, 22.

87. Branch, *Affirming God's Image*, 86–92.

88. Branch, *Affirming God's Image*, 101–6.

89. Branch, *Affirming God's Image*, 103–5.

90. Branch, *Affirming God's Image*, 87, see also 104–5, 121–23.

91. See Dirks, "Transition"; and McKee, "I Want to be a She."

92. Martin, "Gender-Identity Treatment."

and lived a troubled life. It ended when Nathan chose to commit doctor-assisted suicide. Even at that point, his mother refused to care.[93] What has society become? It is exactly where the Enemy wants us, confused, depressed, suicidal, and blind to the abundant life that comes from following God's mandates for flourishing. What could be clearer than our very own gender distinctions?

Conclusion

I hope that this chapter has helped put into perspective the dangers that Western culture and the church are facing in light of the rejection of the mandate of gender distinctions. We need God now more than ever to deal with the downward spiral of society. We must preach the truth that people must be born again. We are all born flawed, but God can help if we submit to him.[94] In this regard, Nathanael Blake from *The Federalist* correctly notes, "Christianity provides an identity based on the divine person of Christ, rather than the contingencies of life or the self-indulgence of desire. Christian moral teaching is thus personal without being arbitrary. Its moral precepts protect human flourishing. Although often difficult, they give healing and wholeness. Instead of wrath, they offer peace to the soul, which we all need."[95] Jesus is indeed the answer to the chaos we face in Western culture today. Without Jesus, the chaos will only increase. You may think that it cannot get any worse. Again, you would be wrong. The rapidity with which Western culture has undone the mandates of Genesis is breathtaking. And the rejection of the mandate of gender distinctions only shows that we are still sliding and freefalling.

When I started this book, I realized that within a few months or even a few short years it would be outdated due to the rapidity of the changes in Western culture. In my Preface, I noted the work of Grudem back in 2010 and how it is already outdated. Others have noted a similar phenomenon when dealing with the trans issue. Bill Muehlenberg states, "I have already written books about how much people have suffered and been abused by the homosexual agenda in full swing. Now it looks like I need to write more books on how the new trans tyranny is destroying everything it touches. If I do, by the time it gets into print it will already be

---

93. Murray, *Madness of Crowds*, 184–85. See also Waterfield, "Belgian."
94. Briggs, "Jesus' Answer."
95. Blake, "LGBT Activists."

out of date. Such is the rate of downward decline in the West."[96] Indeed, this is most evident in the current attack on what I feel is one of the last of the Genesis mandates, namely, the distinction between humans, animals, and inanimate creation.

---

96. Meuhlenberg, "Trans Tyranny."

Chapter 13

The Mandate of Species Distinctions

On September 17, 2019, Union Theological Seminary in New York City held a confession chapel to plants.[1] Regarding this event, a Union Seminary online post read, "Together, we held our grief, joy, regret, hope, guilt and sorrow in prayer; offering them to beings who sustain us but whose gift we too often fail to honor." While the event drew a host of responses, a common, and appropriate, "tweet" in reaction to this chapel "service" was the quotation from Romans 1:25: "For they exchanged the truth of God for a lie, and worshiped and served the creature rather than the Creator, who is blessed forever. Amen" (NASB). Although many were taken aback at the display, I guess one should not be surprised at such an event when the school itself is devoted to a pluralistic faith tradition, which includes Buddhist, Muslim, and a variety of Christian traditions.[2] When challenged, Union's official response was: "The diversity and breadth of our chapel services is a huge part of what makes Union Union. And we wouldn't change it for the world."[3]

Now to be sure, some may say that this is the extreme and that most seminaries are not engaged in such questionable expressions of faith. To a degree this may be true if we are speaking only about conservative seminaries, but in reality, mainline seminaries have been moving in this direction for some time.[4] For example, Vanderbilt allows for their students to

---

1. Parke, "Plants."
2. Parke, "Plants."
3. As cited by Parke, "Plants."
4. See further comments on Union Theological Seminary by Brown, "Confessing

The Mandate of Species Distinctions

observe pagan Wiccan holidays such as Samhain (Halloween) and the Maypole observance of Beltane on May 1.[5] Such policies have the obvious purpose of pulling campuses away from traditional Christianity, which is often viewed in a negative light.[6] Where this becomes relevant for our current discussion is the connection that such policies and actions have in relationship to the Genesis mandates.

Up to this point I have shown how the Enemy has systematically, and with increasing speed, undermined the Genesis mandates as laid out in Genesis 1 and 2. I have also shown how this has worked in a somewhat reverse order beginning with the attack on marriage, the family, children/procreation, and gender distinctions. As I noted at the end of the last chapter, the undermining of gender distinctions is perhaps the most heinous attack on these mandates in that it rejects the very nature of who we are as human beings created by God. But sadly, there is yet another mandate that Western culture is attempting to undo and has already had some success in undermining. This is the mandate of species distinctions. What I mean by this is that God mandated that humans have dominion/control over the animals and inanimate creation (Gen 1:26, 28). Yet here we are now faced with animals and "mother earth" being not only elevated above humanity, but actually replacing God. Again, Paul knew what he was talking about when he spoke of the degradation of humanity in Romans 1, the base level of which is worshipping the creature rather than the Creator (Rom 1:25).

In this penultimate chapter, I will examine Western culture's rapid shift to elevate animals and inanimate creation—often subsumed under the umbrella of environmental concerns—over humanity in general, and human life in particular. I will begin this discussion by looking at what the Bible has to say about humanity's role in earth care and care for the animals.

God's Command to Have Dominion

The Genesis mandate of species distinctions is self-evident in God's command for humans to have dominion over the animals and inanimate creation (Gen 1:26, 28). Even though the exact meaning of "dominion"

---

to Plants."
    5. Ghianni, "Vanderbilt."
    6. Swain, "Vanderbilt's Policies."

(*radah*) has been debated at length,[7] it should not distract us from the overall tenor of Scripture which clearly presents humans as being of the highest value within creation (Gen 9:5–6; Ps 8:3–8; Matt 6:26; 10:31; Luke 12:24; etc.). This being noted, I want to begin by making it clear that I am not a proponent of what has been termed the "raping" of the earth for the benefit of humanity.[8] I think this perspective is a poor understanding of our roles as caretakers of God's good creation. On the other hand, I am also not a proponent of allowing earth care to be elevated to the point of causing human pain and suffering, or even death. It is telling of our degraded state as a culture when we reject the foundational mandate related to the separation of what is of utmost value, namely, humans, who have eternal value, and animals and inanimate creation, which were created for human enjoyment and appropriate use. God mandated the hierarchy within creation and the Psalmist reiterated this in Psalm 8:3–8. I also find it troubling when some want to diminish or resist texts that clearly teach of the superiority of humanity over creation (e.g., Gen 1:26–28) or attempt to show how "unspecial we are" in light of the broader creation.[9] While perhaps not the intention, this can lead in a direction that is theologically dangerous, not to mention it is a direct afront to the work of Christ on the cross to redeem *humanity*, not creation in general. Although it is true that all creation will be redeemed in the eschaton (Rom 8:19–22; Col 1:20), that is not the role of Jesus' finished work of the cross.

With this caveat, I want to begin by noting that one could argue that God was the first environmentalist when he set boundaries on what Israel could and could not do with the land and with animals. The land had to have its Sabbath rests (Lev 25:4; 26:34, 43; 2 Chron 36:21) as were the animals (Exod 20:10; Deut 5:14), and animals could not be abused in farm labor, either physically (Deut 22:10; cf. Prov 12:10) or psychologically (Deut 25:4) or when they were slaughtered for food (Lev 17). On these latter points, perhaps it is time for Christians to take note and get involved in efforts to change industrial farming practices in America that abuse animals for the sole purpose of higher profits.[10] God also cares for the beasts of the field (Gen 8:11; Pss 50:10–11; 104:21; Matt 6:26; 10:29; Luke 12:24; 14:5) and domesticated animals (Jonah 4:11). And God put

---

7. See discussion in Horrell, *Environment*, 23–36.
8. Collins, *Biblical Values*, 107–8.
9. So, Horrell, *Environment*, 129, 128, 137, here 131; and Brady, "Preface," 13.
10. See discussion by Richter, *Stewards of Eden*, 29–47.

restrictions on how wild animals were to be used (Deut 22:4, 6–7). As a type case, Deuteronomy 22:6–7 appears to be setting a precedent that applied to all wild animals: Israel was to practice conservation by not over hunting.[11] And the Chronicler notes that one of the reasons for the exile of Israel was due to Israel's misuse of the land by not giving it its Sabbath rests (2 Chron 36:21). Even though the restrictions and laws exemplified in the above-noted verses are not all-inclusive, they are detailed enough to give us a clear picture of how we are to treat animals and the environment (Gen 8:22; Deut 20:19).

Considering this clear teaching there can be no question that believers should care for the world that God has given to us. At the same time, it is wrong to assume that everything we do to alter the environment for human flourishing is in some way wrong. We are called to tame and have dominion over the environment and in doing so we may have to create dams, levies, and the like or invent pesticides and treatments to kill pests and those things that would kill humans: these are needed in order to aid in human flourishing.[12] We must always remember that we live in a world that is now fallen and tainted by human sin. The pristine world that Adam and Eve inherited is corrupted, although someday it will be renewed (Rom 8:21; Rev 21:1). As such, we need to create methods of living in this new state. Nevertheless, the issue must always be subduing the world in a safe manner, not one that will cause more harm to all involved in the long term. That said, Christians must always keep in mind that Jesus pointed out that the value of humans surpasses that of animals (Matt 6:26; 10:31; 12:12),[13] a far cry from what we are seeing unfold today.

Animal Superiority

One of the more troubling trends related to the rejection of the species distinction mandate is the elevation of animal life over the value of human life. Even though worship of plants (sacred trees; e.g., Exod 34:13; Deut 7:5; 12:1–4; Judg 3:7; 1 Kgs 14:15; 2 Chron 31:1), animals (e.g., Deut 4:17–18; 5:8; Ezek 8:10), and the earth/universe (e.g., sun, moon, stars, rivers, rocks, etc.; e.g., Deut 4:19; 17:3) is as old as time, throughout history people recognized the lower level of animals when it came to using

---

11. Richter, *Stewards of Eden*, 50–57.
12. See Grudem, *Politics*, 322–23.
13. Grudem, *Politics*, 325.

them for food, sacrifice, or clothing. Today this is being challenged as being inhumane by groups such as PETA, ALF, or ARM. I find it telling when environmentalists reject even the idea of using animal furs and leather for clothing when God himself was the first to use animals for this very purpose (Gen 3:21).[14] For some time now there has been a growing trend to see humans and animals as being on the same level and having the same importance.[15] But humans were the pinnacle of God's creation being made a little lower than the angels (Ps 8), whereas animals were subservient to humans with God approving of their use as food for us (Gen 9:3–4).[16]

Even though most may agree with our ability to eat meat, today, radical environmentalist movements are proposing draconian measures that put the environment and animals ahead of human flourishing, and safety in some cases. Christian theologian, Wayne Grudem, notes this well when he states, "Secular environmentalists object to the killing of deer or geese in residential neighborhoods, even when these animals are so numerous they have become a significant public nuisance and even a danger to health (as with the prevalence of ticks that spread Lyme disease). They will object to the killing of mosquitoes with pesticides even when the mosquitoes spread West Nile Virus and (in Africa) spread malaria that kills millions of people."[17]

How is this happening? This goes back to Chapter 3 when I pointed out the rejection of God and the acceptance of a secular humanistic and naturalistic ideal. If humans are just evolved creatures with no souls, then we are no more than animals ourselves and no better than they are. In fact, some educators teach that certain animals are more evolved than us in various ways. In this vein, it is not at all unheard of now for educators and professionals to suggest to those they instruct that we are lower than the apes on the "evolutionary ladder" because we cannot forage in the trees the way they can.[18] From this vantage point, we should not be surprised when some climate scientists insist that whatever response we

---

14. Grudem, *Politics*, 328.
15. See for example the work of Singer, *Animal Liberation* (1975).
16. Sider, *Completely Pro-Life*, 14–15,
17. Grudem, *Politics*, 327.
18. See Watkins, *New Absolutes*, 77.

take to climate change, animal life must be on par with human life.[19] This is troubling to say the least.

The Blurring of Species Distinctions

People identifying as animals is another even more disturbing tendency and growing trend. Recently Twitch, an online video-streaming service for gamers, hired a transgender person, who identifies as "FerociouslySteph," as one of seven people on their Safety Advisory Council.[20] Aside from the troubling power-crazed comments by the individual,[21] the transgendered person identifies as a deer, roams around their backyard eating grass to help be in tune with their deerself, and has "deergasms" on screen when they have their head rubbed.[22] This is not just madness, this is insanity being given a platform online by a mainline gaming platform that young adults, and no doubt children, see daily. You cannot make this up.[23] Again, I can hear people saying that this is the extreme. Although this may be an extreme when it comes to personal behavior, Western culture is going to extremes in other ways when dealing with the value of animals vis-à-vis humans.

Let me demonstrate by giving a few examples as evidence of these extreme positions. If we vilify those who raise or hunt animals for food or call for the deaths of those who trophy hunt game animals, we are no better than the extremists. In an earlier article, I noted the fallout over the killing of Cecil the Lion by a Minnesota dentist in 2015. The vitriol and hate directed at this man was nothing less than insane.[24] This has happened repeatedly to people who post pictures online of their hunting expeditions. Many who do so receive death threats, have their homes and businesses targeted, and in some cases must move to get away from those who would do them harm. News networks have noted the public shaming[25] and even violent attacks against people by animal-rights activists

---

19. See discussion in Ross, *Climate Change*, 46.
20. AMP, "Advisory Council."
21. See Sausage Roll, "Twitch Admin Threatens."
22. Slightly Offensive, "Madness."
23. A simple Google search of "Twitch transgender who identifies as a deer" yields dozens of videos documenting the madness.
24. Peterson, "Genesis Mandates," 137–38.
25. Sahadeo, "Kylie Jenner."

simply because they were wearing a fur coat.[26] Why? Because animals have more value than human life in their minds. And these examples do not take into account those who are now having reconstructive surgery and tattooing their bodies to look like animals, evidence of which can be found by a quick online search.

Christians and Environmental Care

This year marks the fiftieth anniversary of Earth Day. As the global warming and climate change hysteria heats up, no pun intended, new studies are showing that Protestant pastors and congregations are getting onboard with the "settled science." Stephanie Martin notes, "The half-century birthday of Earth Day also brings news of shifting attitudes among U.S. clergy. According to data from LifeWay Research, a majority of America's Protestant pastors now—for the first time—say global warming and climate change are real and human-caused. When asked to respond to the statement 'I believe global warming is real and man-made,' 53 percent say they agree. (Of that total, 34 percent say they 'strongly agree.') For comparison, only 36 percent of surveyed pastors agreed with a similar statement 10 years ago."[27] This shift in sentiment comes primarily from younger pastors who have a college education.

With this rapid change one can understand why there is a growing divide between older and younger believers on the issue of climate change, and how Christians should respond. In this regard, a quick perusal of the literature shows a stark divide on how we as Christians are to care for the environment and how we should view the current climate issues. On one side of the debate you have those who insist that environmental concerns are not hype and on the other side we find complete ambivalence due to an eschatological perspective that assumes that we are going to be "leaving" this world soon and the earth will be destroyed by God's fiery judgment anyway (2 Pet 3:10–13).[28] At the same time, there are those who take a mediating position.[29] I do not intend to solve these issues here. Rather, I want to place this discussion within the context of

---

26. Phillips, "Ohio Woman."
27. Martin, "Climate Change."
28. See discussion in Horrell, *Environment*, 11–20.
29. See Ross, *Weathering Climate Change* (2020); and Richter, *Stewards of Eden* (2020).

my overall thesis that Western culture is embracing a disturbing trend to reject God's mandates and to blur the lines of what is in God's control and what is within human capabilities.

We certainly need to care for the environment but in many ways, it has become cult-like for some. And those not supporting the so-called "settled science" are not necessarily naïve and stupid. Nor are they narrow-minded fundamentalists as some would have us believe.[30] As touched on above, many evangelicals realize that environmental care is an important part of being a Christian; yet, there is a division on how one is to harmonize what the Bible teaches about the dominion and elevation of humanity over creation and the proposed solutions to the climate-change dilemma.[31] As noted above, God clearly cares about the way people treat his creation (cf. Exod 23:10–11; Deut 20:19; 22:4, 7, 10; Prov 12:10; Isa 34:13–15; Jonah 4:11; Rom 8:18–23) especially with Sabbath rests and the Jubilee year.[32] However, it is not anti-science to believe in the Bible when it says that the earth will be remade someday (2 Pet 3:4–7; Rev 21–22). These are certainly not mere myths, and fantasies and the imaginations of ancients as some would propose.[33] Although there may be some level of metaphor in the language,[34] these passages still, nonetheless, seem to be pointing to some great culmination in the eschaton. The truth is many Christians are skeptical of the outlandish claims of the majority due to the "religion" of climate change sweeping Western cultures which favor all things science and environmental over God. It has become a new religious dogma.

Environmental Worship

In the introduction to this chapter I noted that some self-professing Christians are now praying and repenting to plants as an acceptable means of showing their love and care for the earth. In many ways, this is equivalent to neo-paganism which places the earth at the level of God.

30. So, Gushee, *Still Christian*, 93–96.

31. For those in support of environmental care but who reject the strict anthropocentrism found in the Bible, see Horrell, *Environment* (2010); Habel ed., *Readings* (2000); Habel and Wurst eds., *Earth Story* (2000); and White, "Evangelical Declaration," 17–22.

32. See Collins, *Biblical Values*, 112–14.

33. So, Collins, *Biblical Values*, 123–25.

34. Richter, *Stewards of Eden*, 93–100.

Even though people may not literally be bowing to plants in prayer, our actions are in fact betraying our attitudes in this regard. Along with this change in "worship" focus, fear of humanity's impending demise is a side effect which drives the discussion. This focus on fear and doom is telling when considering from whence this new focus has derived. We must remember that God is not the author of fear (2 Tim 1:7).

Most are now familiar with the internet and UN "sensation" Greta Thunberg from Sweden. She epitomizes an entire generation of children who have been raised in fear of the immanent destruction of our planet by global companies and capitalistic countries. Children are having to take antidepressants to get through life because of fear of the earth ending.[35] Thunberg also reflects a growing trend to place environmental care above everything else. And now we have politicians sitting in the halls of America's Congress who are advocating the cessation of having children to "save the world." These same individuals are often a part of, or closely associated with, radical environmentalist movements that push abortion, and abortion related drugs, as the means of controlling the population. Again, I want to be clear. I think that every believer should be a good steward of the planet, but this is different than placing the earth in the position of God and then instilling fear in the hearts of children so that they can no longer enjoy their childhood. This is abuse in my view. And elevating environmental care to the detriment of human existence and life is anti-biblical and should be rejected by Christians.

Overpopulation

It is telling when the environmental issues we are facing are coupled with anti-biblical sexual ethics and a rejection of the biblical mandates. Some radical groups are using the climate change crisis as a means of pushing for the rejection of heterosexual marriage and families in order to save the climate.[36] Understood through the lens of "ecojustice," it is no surprise that homosexual coupling is in vogue and is touted as another acceptable way to control the population. These types of ideas are not just coming from fringe left-leaning organizations, they are becoming more mainstream daily.

---

35. Genovese, "BP Exec."
36. E.g., Berg, "Extinction."

Recently I read about some who have gone so far as to demand that people should reduce the number of children they have due to overpopulation declaring that having a large family makes one guilty of an "eco-crime."[37] Peter J. Smith and Steve Jalsevac in an online article state that "Radical environmentalist, Paul Watson, founder and president of the Sea Shepherd Conservation Society, which tries to increase whale populations, [...] denounced the 'human virus' saying 'We are killing our host the planet Earth.' Watson who has unapologetically called human beings the 'AIDS of the Earth,' declared human beings must reduce the world's population to less than 1 billion people, dwell in communities no larger than '20,000 people and [be] separated from other communities by wilderness areas,' and recognize themselves as 'earthlings' dwelling in a primitive state with other species."[38] Similarly, Patricia MacCormack, a professor of continental philosophy at Anglia Ruskin University in England, in her new book titled *The Ahuman Manifesto* advocates for allowing humans to go extinct by phasing out reproduction.[39] Not only does this type of perspective represent a growing radicalism vis-à-vis climate change, it also goes directly against God's mandate to procreate. In one article MacCormack is quoted as saying, "I arrived at this idea from a couple of directions. I was introduced to philosophy due to my interest in feminism and queer theory, so reproductive rights have long been an interest to me—this led me to learn more about animal rights, which is when I became vegan."[40] The article goes on to note that MacCormack asserts in her book "that humanity has caused mass problems and one of them is creating this hierarchal world where white, male, heterosexual and able-bodied people are succeeding, and people of different races, genders, sexualities and those with disabilities are struggling to get that."[41] At the heart of her thought process is the devaluation of the human species—at least the "white, male, heterosexual and able-bodied people." It also spurns the Genesis mandates.

In response to these types of outlandish claims, Barry Brownstein, professor emeritus of economics and leadership at the University of Baltimore, comments that despite what doomsday predictors are saying,

---

37. Smith and Jalsevac, "Environmentalist."
38. Smith and Jalsevac, "Environmentalist."
39. Ryder, "Climate Change."
40. As quoted by Ryder, "Climate Change."
41. Ryder, "Climate Change."

increased capitalism and freedom is what will lift countries out of poverty and overpopulation. Even though Doomsday organizations like Zero Population Growth seek to undermine procreation, a vital mandate established by God, Brownstein notes that the planet can easily sustain the current population growth because of increased production capabilities that are outpacing population growth.[42] He goes on to note that it is restrictive economies and communistic countries like North Korea that tend to struggle with environmental disasters due to the stifling of human ingenuity. With about 17 percent less land but double the population, South Korea (38,691 square miles and 51.5 million people) easily serves as a case in point when compared with North Korea (46,500 square miles and 25.5 million people). One nation has experienced prosperity and environmental stability while the other suffers in both categories.

Studies from as early as the mid-90s and early 2000s have shown that the earth's land and resources can maintain a population exponentially larger than what we have today while increases in technology and food production have consistently outpaced population growth.[43] God gave humans the ability to solve these problems, but godless societies have quashed this creative ability by their repressive policies.

Many have pointed out the problems with environmental advocates who use scare tactics to stop reasonable progress. An excellent resource is the work done by Bjorn Lomborg[44] and the distillation of Lomborg's work by Wayne Grudem in chapter 10 of his book *Politics According to the Bible*. What both scholars note well is the abundance of natural resources that God included in his good creation. What these types of scholars argue is that despite the cries of the crowd, the earth is not coming to an end environmentally but rather it is just the opposite. We are improving our ability to produce food, to find resources for energy, to improve the quality of living for most people, to lower the poverty levels, to increase life expectancy, and manage the earth. Now to be sure, that does not mean we should turn a blind eye to climate issues that we can help to fix.

---

42. Brownstein, "Overpopulation." See also Grudem, *Politics*, 329–42.

43. See Lomborg, *The Skeptical Environmentalist* (2001); and Watkins, *New Absolutes*, 73.

44. Lomborg, *The Skeptical Environmentalist* (2001).

The Global Warming Crisis

Americans are all too familiar with the ongoing crisis of global warming and the hype Al Gore's movie, *An Inconvenient Truth*, stirred back in 2006. Many informed studies have been done on the topic and I am certainly not claiming to be an expert in this regard. Others have done excellent work in this field and I would direct my reader to their work and source lists.[45] That said, while I may not be a climate-change denier—as is often the label pejoratively affixed to those who in any way disagree with the hype—I do recognize the problems with the "settled science" and the fearmongering that comes with it. The oft-cited "consensus" of scientists is simply not true.[46] There are also good scientific studies showing just the opposite of what is being touted as "fact."[47] What is more, the UN's Intergovernmental Panel on Climate Change (IPCC) has been tarnished by the events now known as "Climategate."[48] Now while other Christians have defended the work of the IPCC,[49] caution is always in order when putting too much faith in science and not enough faith in the power of God to sustain his good creation. God has made the earth resilient enough to handle these fluctuations,[50] but we still need to be mindful of how we can be good stewards of the environment and the earth that God has given to us.[51]

One of the other problems with the environmentalist movement is the loss of freedom through enforced government control over people's lives. Václav Klaus, president of the Czech Republic from 2003–2013 likens the radical environmentalist movement to being under the former communist iron curtain.[52] God's creative mandates endowed humanity with freedoms and autonomy that have been usurped and done away with in a number of societies due to the results of the fall. By restricting

---

45. See Ross, *Weathering Climate Change* (2020).

46. See for example Oregon Institute of Science and Medicine Petition Project at http://www.petitionproject.org/index.php; Solomon, *The Deniers* (2008). As noted by Grudem, *Politics*, 371.

47. See Grudem, *Politics*, 361–83 and the sources noted there.

48. For the list of offenses see Grudem, *Politics*, 375.

49. Ross, *Climate Change*, 20–21.

50. Grudem, *Politics*, 367–70 esp. 367.

51. Ross's perspective in *Weathering Climate Change* is a good balance of this approach.

52. Grudem, *Politics*, 380–81.

freedom to explore and develop earth's resources, radical environmentalist dictates coupled with governmental overreach will continue to enslave many developed countries and pedal a message of fear and doom. This is not something that believers should promote.

Natural Consequences of Elevating the Earth and Animals over Humans

I have already noted that when science becomes the final arbiter of truth, and when naturalistic thinking pushes for the elevation of animals and the earth over the value of humans, several unintended consequences can happen. I like to give people the benefit of the doubt, but I know that the degradation and destruction of God's creation has been the plan of the Enemy all along. A prime example of this degradation of humanity comes in the form of rejecting the value of the human body. A second way is the pushing of godless ideologies like euthanasia.

Human Composting

The first example is best exemplified by a TEDx talk on June 16, 2016, by Katrina Spade.[53] In the talk, Spade rejects conventional burial and cremation in favor of composting human remains. The resulting compost would be used for growing gardens and the heat generated from the process could be harnessed to heat buildings. As of 2016, Spade says that a composting site is coming to Seattle, Washington soon. Spade was correct. In 2019, the governor of Washington signed bill SB5001 into law making Washington the first state to legalize human composting, which took effect May 1, 2020.[54] Planning is now underway for the first human composting site in Washington scheduled for 2020. While the concept is revolutionary and "earth friendly," for those from a conservative Christian perspective, the response may be anything from intrigue to horror. I certainly understand that we all will end up as "dirt" one day (Gen 3:19), but the premise on its face removes the value of the human body in a spiritual sense and lowers it to the level of animals and other compostable objects.

---

53. Spade, "Composting."
54. Kiley, "Composting."

When it comes to issues of proper burial, it is true that the Bible does not give explicit God-mandated instructions on how people should bury their dead. Nevertheless, the Bible is replete with accounts on care for the dead and the importance of family tombs and graves for the remembrance of our ancestors. Even though people may argue for the above-noted types of cutting-edge approaches as a means of improving economic stability and earth care, there is something spiritually troubling behind such plans. It not only lessens a focus on the resurrection of the body it also lowers humanity to the level of other living organisms. Thus, humans are to be viewed only for what value they can offer to humanity in this lifetime, and in this case, the value they can contribute by their death. It also leads to further degradation of the value of humans. One such example is the desire of a Swedish scientist to end the "conservative" taboo against cannibalism to help fight climate change by adding an alternate source of "food" for people.[55] These ideas are certainly extreme, but we must remember that the sexual revolution and the extremes of the 1960s have now become mainstream. Radical changes and rejection of God's mandates begin with ideas that are often extreme and then are slowly implemented as society becomes desensitized and accustomed to these as the norm. I would remind my reader how abortion has become widely accepted and partial-birth abortion and infanticide are now being practiced. This brings me to a second disturbing development of Western culture, the rise of euthanasia.

Euthanasia

If humans have no special place within creation beyond what they contribute in the here and now, what happens when they are no longer deemed a contributor to society? These types of arguments are at the heart of the push to legalize euthanasia. In light of God's mandate of species distinctions, this type of thinking lowers human life to the level of the beasts and the rest of earth's living organisms. At its heart is a rejection of the clear species distinctions that God made in creation. Humans held a special place at the pinnacle of creation because of the eternal nature of their souls. Euthanasia is a devaluing of life in a callous way. Of course, it is not a huge leap to go from killing children at the front end of life to killing people at the end of their lives. States are now moving to pass

---

55. Pluralist, "Cannibalism."

legislation that would allow for doctor-assisted suicide (e.g., Oregon). Although troubling, this makes sense when we are told our entire lives that there is nothing after death and that we are no more than a blob of cells which will make great fertilizer once we are gone. This step is the natural progression. Western countries are racing to legalize euthanasia under the guise of "humane" treatment of those suffering physical and emotional strain.[56] With such thinking now becoming mainstream, there is really not much left for humans to distort.

Conclusion

Back in the 1930s, ethnologist and social anthropologist Joseph Daniel Unwin noted, "If we observe the human organism, we notice that it possesses at least three attributes that appear to be lacking in all other mammals. [. . .] These are the power of reason, the power of creation, and the power of reflecting upon itself."[57] While Unwin did not evaluate humanity from an explicit Judeo-Christian perspective, he did touch on something fundamental to God's good creation. We are indeed different and higher than the animals, and by extension, inanimate creation. This is no longer the view of many in Western societies. Naturalistic thinking and evolutionary theory have dumbed down culture's view on the sanctity of life as evidenced in the proliferation of abortion, euthanasia, and the call for ecojustice. Environmental concerns trump all other concerns and lower humans to the level of brute beasts. One thing that Christians could learn from this new environmental and naturalistic worldview is that they are committed to their cause, which has become their religion. They have a long-term outlook. If we adopted this committed lifestyle and applied it to our Christian worldview we would actually see a changed culture for the better. Now, do not get me wrong, from an earth-care perspective we have come a long way as believers, with many Christians now adopting an appropriate view of care for creation and responsibility for God's gifts to us. But too many are living in fear and adopting a worldview that misses the true value of life.

The undoing of this last mandate, which was really the first mandate given by God to creation and humanity, leaves nothing left for us to degrade, at least as of now. What this means is that with the growing push

---

56. See Hamilton, "Terminally Transsexual."
57. Unwin, *Sex and Culture*, 417.

for environmental and "ecojustice" the value of human life will continue to decrease. If we are all going to be dead in a decade due to climate disasters, as many on the Left are now claiming, why not adopt the ethic of *carpe diem*? This is the exact type of chaos that the Enemy has always desired of God's good creation. The Enemy wants the end of all things that are blessed by God, indeed, the end of Eden. In this vein, perhaps as believers we should be careful about whose "gospel" and "truth" we are imbibing. There is an entire secular and ungodly move to devalue and undermine everything good about the Genesis mandates, and much of this is being pushed now at the political level. It is to this touchy and emotionally charged topic that I turn and conclude my book.

Chapter 14

The Influence of Politics on Morality and Evangelicals

> The increasingly aggressive nature of the pro-choice agenda in the Democratic Party, its hostility toward biblical morals, its elevation of identity politics, and its undermining of religious freedoms is gravely disturbing.[1]

THIS STATEMENT BY THE current Southern Baptist Convention president J.D. Greear highlights the political component related to the changing tide of Western morality and ethics. Generally speaking, the Democrat party has moved in full force to adopt ever-increasing anti-God and anti-Genesis-mandates measures. The vacillation on whether to include God in their platform in 2012 is a prime example of their rejection of God.[2] Conversely, many on the right feel that the Republican party, again, generally speaking, have held to at least some semblance of godly ideals, whether real or through lip service,[3] as laid out in the opening chapters of Genesis.

Truthfully, I struggled with whether to add this chapter dealing with politics in light of the old adage that in polite society you should never talk about politics or religion especially if you want to keep harmony in a

---

1. Martin, "Trump."
2. Tapper and Bingham, "Switch."
3. So, Wallis, *God's Politics*, 56–57.

family or any social setting. But my research has shown that you cannot assess the issue of the undoing of the Genesis mandates in Western culture without laying a good portion of the blame at the feet of the political establishment, and by extension, those who insist on putting certain godless politicians into power for decades. The constant and growing pandering of politicians to left-leaning ideologies is having a direct effect on the direction of Western culture, and unfortunately the church as well.

Before beginning this discussion, I do want to note an important point as a precursor to my comments. Those who advocate for Christian non-involvement in the political process because it is supposedly unbiblical are ceding the direction of our culture to the ungodly, especially the Left.[4] Politics is certainly not the answer for our lost world, Christ is, but that does not mean that we should not be involved in making our country more reflective of Judeo-Christian ideals.[5] Anti-political arguments based upon political conditions in the first-century context of the Roman Empire are not analogous to modern Western democracies, which are based upon a representational model. True, Jesus did not preach politics in his ancient context; that was not his purpose any more than it was to preach to Gentiles (Matt 15:24), yet we know the latter changed with his death, burial, and resurrection. We also need to be careful not to base our entire worldview upon a three-and-a-half-year snapshot of Jesus' ministry. He certainly did and said a lot which was not recorded (John 21:25). As I noted in an earlier chapter, arguments from silence are dangerous and are also used for Jesus' supposed acceptance of homosexuality.

The Bible is replete with examples of individuals who had political influence on, and involvement with, godless kings. These include Joseph, Daniel and his three friends, Mordecai, Esther, and Nehemiah (to name a few). I would also remind those who advocate for a "hands-off" position to politics to consider the prophet Samuel's words to Israel prior to their "election" of a king in 1 Samuel 8. He did not just throw his hands in the air and say, "God will do what God will do." On the contrary, at the leading of God mind you, Samuel pleads with Israel to reconsider their choice for political leadership because of the dangers of the monarchy and the policies which would directly affect them and their children for generations (read 1 Sam 8:9–18). Nevertheless, because of their hardheartedness and godless and uninformed desires, God gave them the king they

---

4. See the heartfelt, although misguided, perspective by Fulp, "Politically Engaged."

5. See a similar argument by Brown, *Evangelicals at the Crossroads*, 197–99.

wanted—Saul—and it ended poorly. This was not God's perfect will for Israel. The lesson is clear: when choosing people to rule over you, know what your choice will mean for you and your family for generations to come. Seek God's direction in these important decisions. And while we should not be divisive, we should be politically engaged not only for our own immediate benefit but for that of our children, grandchildren, and so on. The political climate *we* create as believers by whom we elect, will affect the church and the spreading of the gospel as well.

Finally, this is the same type of argument I would make for those who insist that believers cannot vote for either of the candidates of the two major political parties running for president because of their glaring flaws and sin.[6] When evangelicals choose to stay home and not vote they are in essence giving a vote to the Left and by extension are indirectly endorsing their policies. Or when evangelicals spoil their ballot by opting for a write-in candidate that will never have a chance of winning nationally, they aid in the continuation of the ruination of our country.[7] I can hear the words of Jesus in this regard when he sent his disciples out into the world for ministry. He said, "Be as wise as serpents yet as harmless as doves" (Matt 10:16 my paraphrase). When it comes to standing up to the Left and their godless ideologies, believers must be ready to take the fight to the Enemy both practically (e.g., politically) and spiritually (e.g., prayer and the Gospel). The lives of innocent children—and our own families—are laying in the balance. With God's help, we must do everything in our power to stop the destruction.

The Growing Divide within Evangelicalism

In a recent interview, evangelical pastor Timothy Keller pointed out that much of the divide within the evangelical church is directly related to politics. He noted that liberals have moved away from their old standard of fighting for the working class (blue collar) and have adopted agendas such as sexual issues, which turn off many evangelicals.[8] While Keller is indeed correct about the Democratic party's move to the left,

---

6. I would point my reader to John Piper's stance, a position with which I strongly disagree. See Piper, "Policies."

7. See the excellent rebuttal of Piper's position by Wayne Grudem, "Response" and Mohler's cogent argument for conservative leaders, namely, Trump (Mohler, "2020 Election").

8. Briggs, "Political Polarization."

his assertion that liberals are the main ones to address issues of race and economic justice—the reason why some evangelicals vote liberal—is not accurate especially in more recent years. The reality is that these issues are also important to the conservative Right but perhaps not with the same emphasis or agreement on how best to resolve these concerns. The Left's rejection and outright onslaught against the Genesis mandates of marriage, sexuality and gender, procreation, and species distinctions, not to mention their hostility towards anything religious or of God, is simply a bridge too far for many conservative evangelicals. The foundations of society are under attack by the Left and many evangelicals refuse to sit idly by anymore and watch the further erosion of our culture. However, when conservative evangelicals stand up to this onslaught, the Left attacks them labeling them as haters, homophobic, transphobic, out of touch with society and cultural norms, climate-change deniers, old fashioned—you name it. Left-leaning media companies have also joined the fray and hurl insults at will. But then again this should not surprise us. This has been the plan of the sexual revolutionaries and cultural Marxists all along. The problem is that many evangelicals who identify as liberal choose to stick their heads in the proverbial sand while the radical Left pushes Western culture towards the moral abyss.

The reason for this continued "evangelical" support for godless policies is twofold. Many of these left-leaning evangelicals simply refuse to accept the fact that the Democratic party of J.F.K. no longer exists. On the other hand, others are voting in a manner which reflects *their* changed morality, which aligns with the Left's agenda. In this latter case, I would challenge their use of "evangelical" as an identifier. They may be spreading the "gospel," but it certainly is not the one taught in the Bible.

In this regard, what has been happening within evangelicalism over the past three decades can be directly attributed to the changing political climate within the church, especially the growing divide among self-identifying "evangelicals." To be sure, the 2016 election (and so, too, the 2020 election) did more than cast a spotlight on the country's left and right political poles, it also divided evangelicals. I say "divide" but in reality it caused more of a rift between the minority liberal/left-leaning evangelicals and the majority center-right evangelicals. With 81 percent of white evangelicals voting for Donald Trump in 2016, the truth is that only a minority of white evangelicals did *not* vote for the president unlike the almost even split when it comes to Republicans and Democrats nationwide. And in the 2020 election, 97 percent of conservative

Christians voted a second time for President Trump.[9] Sadly, what used to be a left-right divide based upon mainline churches and evangelicals is now becoming more pronounced among those identifying with the latter category.

Evangelicals of all stripes, especially younger people, are rapidly adopting cultural shifts in sexual ethics and social movements. In his edited volume titled *Still Evangelical?* the president of Fuller Theological Seminary in Pasadena, California, Mark Labberton, notes,

> Until the previous decade, the overwhelming percentage of evangelicals would have reliably and consistently defended a traditional view of marriage as a relationship between a man and a woman, and maintained that homosexual activity is outside of the bounds of biblical ethics. In the last decade, this consensus has eroded in two directions: geographical and generational. As the East and West Coasts of the United States have led the way in the growing affirmation of LGBT people and lifestyles, evangelicals in these regions have quietly done likewise. When the Supreme Court affirmed same-sex marriage, the state debates and votes ceased, and a lot of evangelicals accepted the legal status and legitimacy of same-sex relationships. Perhaps even more noteworthy is the generational divide over the acceptance of LGBT relationships, with affirmation from 47 percent of white evangelicals under the age of thirty, despite their otherwise more traditional views. Their cultural frame led to a recasting of their faith understanding.[10]

I find this statement by Labberton not only telling of the state of evangelicalism, but also troubling. It is clear that raising a family in this environment, and in particular geographical regions of the country, is fraught with spiritual danger. Evangelicals from several denominations (e.g., Pentecostal, Baptist, Presbyterian, Methodist) will have to deal with these ethical issues sooner than later. As a Pentecostal, I have seen this change within my own denomination at several levels including among younger people within the pews and those in, or soon to be in, positions of leadership.

To a certain degree, I think that the account of Daniel and his three friends from the OT speaks to what is happening in Western culture

---

9. Briggs, "Conservative Christians."

10. Labberton, "Introduction," 11. See also comments by Longman, *Bible and the Ballot*, 213–14.

and evangelicalism specifically. Daniel and the rest of the exiles in the early deportation to Babylon faced both the geographical divide from Israel and the issue of the generational divide (they were separated from family) when it came to cultural pressures. The good news is they overcame on both counts. As *young* men in a foreign geographical region (like Labberton's East-West Coast comments) of the ANE, they remained faithful to God because they had a deep-seated tradition and *experience* with God—they knew what they believed in and why. What Labberton states is not a good thing for evangelicalism; it is further evidence of the secularization and acculturalization of our youth. This is a danger that must be taken seriously for the evangelical church to remain the light and salt to the world.

Many younger evangelicals simply assume that being "liberal" is more enlightened than being associated with putative narrow-minded, partisan, and out-of-step conservative evangelicals,[11] as if *only* conservative evangelicals are partisan and entrenched. The truth is both sides can be so. What is more, many who reject conservative beliefs (both scripturally and politically) have no problem with embracing the radicalness of the Left. Conversely, many conservative evangelicals believe that it is not a badge of honor to move away from the authority of Scripture and adopt the instability of cultural norms and accepted dogmas. More often than not, it is telling of liberal biases and a disdain for conservative evangelicals when anything "conservative" or traditional is mocked and reviled.[12] Indeed, to be conservative is to be derided as uninformed and naïve and out of touch with cultural trends, and more importantly, with what left-leaning evangelicals feel is "God's plan" for humanity.

The disdain for those holding traditional values is easily picked up in the writings of left-leaning evangelicals. Most of the time it takes on the tone that social and biblical "liberals" are the "smart" and "informed" group while the rest of conservative Christendom are merely has-beens of a quickly changing and bygone era who are grasping for power while trying to remain relevant. Yes, it is a dangerous coup that conservative evangelicals are planning (with tongue in cheek). They want to take over all parts of Western culture, America especially, with their brand of biblical interpretation and morality as established by God in Genesis 1 and 2.

---

11. See for example the comments of Gushee, *Still Christian*, 79–102.
12. See for example the comments of Gushee, *Still Christian*, 30–31.

The truth is that those who may be well-intentioned in their attempts to thwart what is often pejoratively labeled the "Religious Right"[13] fail to recognize is that the so-called culture wars have not gone in the favor of the Religious Right over the past three decades. On the contrary, just the opposite is true. The plans of the liberal Left to take over culture through media of all types and through the universities has been very successful.[14] What many of the recent books by former or self-professing "elite"[15] (their words) evangelicals tell us is that they were more upset with the political defeat in 2016 (2020's election is another matter in light of the voting irregularities) than they were about the dangerous moral trajectory of the West.[16] They could not handle the loss of power and the threat to their political and social agendas some of which clearly minimize or undermine the authority of Scripture. As noted above, how is it possible that 81 percent of a group of evangelical voters got it so wrong in 2016? I often ask the question, perhaps it is the 19 percent who should ask themselves the questions: Why was I in the minority? Have I missed something? This divide is stark. Now to be sure, some of the 19 percent would include those who did not vote for either candidate but rather wrote in their own candidate.

The rift continued into the 2020 election cycle. In the lead up to the 2020 election, some pastors of conservative evangelical churches resigned their positions because of their congregation's support of the Republican ticket: they concluded that their congregation had refused to heed their teaching on the role of the church as the "conscience" of the state.[17] The truth is that perhaps these congregations were indeed concerned about the "conscience" of the state, but not in the way some myopic pastors view or define "conscience." Many conservative evangelicals recoil at the trajectory of America and their churches, particularly among their youth. They recoil at the Left's consistent attack against the unborn, traditional beliefs, free speech, and the church itself. Perhaps this is the reason they vote the way they do. To be sure, while the religious elite harped about the

---

13. See for example the pejorative nature of the phrase used by Hauerwas, *War and the American Difference*, 9.

14. See the work of Ellis, *Breakdown* (2020).

15. This is language used by Galli, "Unity," 140–41, 147.

16. It is telling that so many books have popped up since the 2016 election of Trump. Many are negative and question the Christian stance of those who voted for Trump. See for example Fea's *Believe Me* (2018).

17. Jackson, "Michigan Pastor."

President's tweets and personality traits, the country was quickly sliding into the moral abyss. It reminds me of an analogy I once heard. It is like they are polishing the handrails of the Titanic while it is plunging to its destruction in the depths of the icy Atlantic Ocean.

Evangelicals against Evangelicals

For those who support a partial political solution to the problem of the cultural takeover by our post-Christian and postmodern culture, Labberton's condescending assertion that the choice for evangelicals is between "bigotry and justice"[18] (with the evangelical right representing the former and the evangelical left the latter) is just another example of the growing divide between the two sides of evangelicalism. Such rhetoric is irresponsible, unhelpful, and elitist. Others like John Fea suggest that the evangelical right is reacting out of a "politics of fear."[19] This may be true to a degree, but at the same time it is laughable when one considers the fearmongering of the Left during the four years of Trump's presidency. The Left insisted that America as we know it would end unless he was removed from office.

While I am sure some evangelicals would fall into the camps propounded by Labberton and Fea, neither of these accusations are completely accurate. The fact is many on the right would simply respond that the authority of the Bible is what is at stake. It is not "bigotry and injustice,"—as if the evangelical right are proponents of the latter in the first place—or "fear" per se, to be concerned about what the Left is doing to our country, especially if you are raising children in today's America. And it must be made clear that not all evangelicals are anti-intellectual because of their rejection of left-leaning elites' arguments; they simply disagree with their premise that conservatism represents all that is wrong with the evangelical right.

The problem is that many evangelicals want to be relevant; they want to be accepted and "cool." Part of the desire and desperation of some evangelicals to be "relevant" and "woke" is to side with cultural shifts (e.g., evangelicals supporting the ideologically problematic Black Lives Matter movement and *Christianity Today's* support of churches

---

18. Labberton, "Introduction," 14.
19. Fea, *Believe Me*, 7–9, 13–41.

paying reparations to African Americans[20]), which are dominated by many who identify as Democrat. This is playing itself out in America in both subtle and not so subtle ways. This is done subtly by innuendo and aspersions about the lack of sophistication of those who support traditional values and Republican candidates. It is done overtly by questionable editorials like those found in "the flagship magazine of anti-Trump white evangelicalism"[21] *Christianity Today* as written by the former editor-in-chief Mark Galli,[22] and doubled down on a few days later by *CT's* president.[23] Galli's perspective is encapsulated in this quote from his *CT* editorial, which Brown labels "The shot heard around the evangelical world."[24] Here Galli says,

> To the many evangelicals who continue to support Mr. Trump in spite of his blackened moral record, we might say this: Remember who you are and whom you serve. Consider how your justification of Mr. Trump influences your witness to your Lord and Savior. Consider what an unbelieving world will say if you continue to brush off Mr. Trump's immoral words and behavior in the cause of political expediency. If we don't reverse course now, will anyone take anything we say about justice and righteousness with any seriousness for decades to come? Can we say with a straight face that abortion is a great evil that cannot be tolerated and, with the same straight face, say that the bent and broken character of our nation's leader doesn't really matter in the end?

This short editorial went viral and was trumpeted by many of the mainstream news outlets, especially the left-leaning ones, as they used it to bludgeon evangelicals and to try and shame them for supporting a pro-life president because of his lack of "morals." They assert that those on the right supported the President for political reasons as opposed to moral reasons. On its face, this is false. Can you please tell me what is any more immoral than the butchering of one's children (or the undoing of every one of the Genesis mandates related to sexual ethics), which is now a dominant platform of the Left?

20. Foust, "Christianity Today."
21. Fea, *Believe Me*, 40.
22. Galli, "Trump."
23. Dalrymple, "Update."
24. Brown, *Evangelicals at the Crossroads*, 135.

I am glad that Rev. Franklin Graham responded to their full-frontal attack on evangelicals who supported Trump in 2016 or who may have supported him in 2020. The truth is Galli's words are not only troubling; they are incorrect biblically. Despite what some polling may suggest, many conservative evangelicals feel that abortion is the greatest blight on the nation of America,[25] and, as I noted in an earlier chapter, it is the liberal Left who continue to push for its full acceptance now to the point of infanticide. Rev. Graham points out the liberal drift to the left in his response to Galli. Graham notes that "Christianity Today said it's time to call a spade a spade. The spade is this—Christianity Today has been used by the left for their political agenda. It's obvious that Christianity Today has moved to the left and is representing the elitist liberal wing of evangelicalism."[26] I am also grateful that evangelicals like Dr. James Dobson,[27] Wayne Grudem,[28] 200 other evangelical leaders,[29] and even non-evangelicals,[30] took the time to write rebuttals to Galli's problematic statement.[31] Conservative evangelicals are listening to the same news and reports but simply do not agree with what Galli and his associates are proposing.[32] Many who identify as conservative evangelicals are not ignorant and nearsighted on this. In fact, most are much more farsighted than Galli and his ilk.[33]

Again, I find it telling that many "liberal evangelicals" tend to fall within the academic elite and those who have been influenced by higher education, which is dominated by liberal ideology. At the heart of this is the influence of the Left's virtue-signaling philosophy, which has crept into evangelicalism in the guise of being inclusive and morally superior to those who hold traditional putative antiquated values. The Scriptures

25. So, too, the findings of Brown, *Evangelicalism at the Crossroads*, 100–109.
26. Warren, "Franklin Graham."
27. Dobson, "Statement."
28. Grudem, "Response."
29. Miles, "Evangelical Leaders"; and Leahy, "Evangelical Leaders."
30. Prager, "Christianity Today."
31. See also Galli's anti-Trump and anti-conservative evangelical remarks in his essay "Unity," 138–52.
32. It seems clear on which side of the political divide Galli is sitting when he says, "So we have done our best to give evangelical Trump supporters their due, to try to understand their point of view, to see the prudential nature of so many political decisions they have made regarding Mr. Trump."
33. Since Galli's article, he has left evangelicalism and now identifies as Catholic. I guess he was not very "evangelical" to begin with. See Stetzer, "Evangelical."

have been misinterpreted we are told. Or have been misunderstood for over two thousand years. Of course, some scholars of the last few decades believe *they* have finally gotten it right. At the least, this is troubling, and at worse, it is downright prideful. Os Guinness gives a stern warning to left-leaning evangelicals, who have become the pawns of the Left's agenda. He notes,

> For a generation now the air has been thick with talk of "changing the world" but who is changing whom? There is no question that the world would like to change the church. In area after area only the church stands between the world and its success over issues such as sexuality . . . Something is rotten in the state of Evangelicalism, and all too often it is impossible to tell who is changing whom . . . Today's Evangelical revisionists should take sober note. Time and again I tremble when I hear or read their flimsy arguments. They may be lionized by the wider advocates for the sexual revolution for fifteen minutes, because they are siding with that wider culture in undermining the clear teaching of Jesus and the Bible that stands in their way . . . But in truth, the sexual revolution has no real interest in such Evangelicals, and they will be left as roadkill as the revolution blitzkrieg gathers speed. But that is nothing compared with the real tragedy of the revisionists. It is no light thing for anyone to set themselves above and against the authority of Jesus and his Scriptures . . . Judas stands as the warning for all who betray Jesus for their personal, sexual or political interests and condemn themselves for their disloyalty (ellipses mine).[34]

Guinness is indeed correct. I would rather stand on the side of the evangelical "Right" and hold to the traditional interpretation of Scripture than to be found wanting on the day of judgment because I accepted teachings counter to the Scriptures. As Paul said in Romans "Let God be true and every person a liar" (Rom 3:4; my paraphrase).

The Limits of Political Activism

The election cycle of 2016 changed many things in the culture wars and elevated the militancy of the Left when they realized that many of their sacred cows were in danger of being rejected (e.g., abortion, same-sex marriage, and radical environmental issues). The truth is many evangelicals

---

34. Guinness, *Impossible People*, 73–74.

may have recoiled at the actions of President Trump but that does not mean they would move to the left and vote for a candidate who stands for everything counter to the Bible. Hillary Clinton's candidacy was more than many could stomach because of her ungodly stances on social issues and sexual ethics.[35] This was no less true of Joe Biden's candidacy. To be sure, gay marriage (an oxymoron from a biblical perspective), transgender confusion, hostility to traditional values, a loss of safety in one's own community or home, the loss of free speech, rising socialistic tendencies, radical abortion laws, and infanticide are just a few of the reasons Christians are standing up and rejecting the liberal Left.

With the election of Donald Trump in 2016, many conservative evangelicals hoped for a halting of the downward slide of Western culture by means of changing the balance of the Supreme Court and district courts nationwide, as well as through favorable policy decisions (e.g., the removal of the provision in "Obama-care" which mandated that every employer pay for questionable reproductive care). While Trump was true to his word to appoint three conservative Supreme Court justices, and he certainly was pro-life and pro-church, recent SCOTUS decisions favoring left-of-center moral policies related to gay and transgender rights prove the dangers of trusting in the courts alone.

Political activism certainly is not the end all nor is it to be used in place of the Gospel to reach the lost.[36] But that does not mean that we should not be involved to effect change in our rapidly evolving culture. And it does not imply that trying to pass godly laws means that evangelicals expect everyone to become "Christian." Basing our sexual morality and ethics upon the Bible is simply the right thing to do in many cases. As I have noted before, the author of Proverbs notes well that "righteousness exalts a nation, but sin is a disgrace to any people" (Prov 14:34; NASB). As individuals, we need to have a "public religion" not just a private faith;[37] if we do not speak out, the Left will fill the void. The cultural Marxists are co-opting the political system and evangelicals need to be aware of where

---

35. The out-of-touch perspective of left-leaning evangelicals was on display when Fea (*Believe Me*, 71) said that Hillary Clinton is "a devout mainline Methodist" while presenting her agenda on immigration, families, women's rights, and of all things, children, in glowing terms while downplaying or failing to point out the extremely anti-God and unbiblical positions she had especially related to abortion, homosexuality, and transgenderism. Of course, Clinton's visible contempt for conservative America came through with her "basket of deplorables" comment.

36. Ashford, "Christian Politics," 450–51.

37. On this point I agree with Wallis, *God's Politics*, 31–40.

this is taking our country. The oft-cited argument—usually made by left-leaning evangelicals—that evangelicals are hurting our witness because of who we vote for and due to the stands we are taking on issues such as abortion, gay marriage, capital punishment, the environment, the Second Amendment, immigration, and politics in general is not something I get too overly concerned about.[38] While these types of arguments are often used as a threat meant to scare conservative evangelicals into changing their positions on key cultural and biblical issues, I encourage believers with these convictions to hold their ground. The world will never love Christians for what they stand for no matter how much we try to appease the crowd.[39]

The Left's Marginalization of Those Holding to Biblical Morality

What left-leaning evangelical writers and pundits often fail to remind their listeners/readers of, or simply do not know—although I find this hard to believe—is that the proponents of anti-Genesis-mandate agendas made it their mission, several decades ago, to propagate the marginalization of conservative Christians in America who hold "atavistic" beliefs—code for biblical ideals—on moral issues such as marriage, abortion, homosexuality, and transgenderism. Our young people have been indoctrinated by secular schools, the media, and left-leaning evangelicals, and have been told that it is not politically correct to hold biblical principles which are out of step with Western culture.

It did not take an election in 2016 to marginalize conservatives, this has been going on for decades lest we forget Obama's quip in 2008 that conservatives are "bitter" and "cling to our guns or religion." The 2016 election only gave the secular Left and left-leaning evangelicals the impetus to voice their displeasure with those on the right who are more conservative on these important issues or who have a differing approach on how to fix them. Again, it is easy to cast aspersions on your opponents when they have already been marginalized by the wider culture and most media sources. Young people are attuned to this marginalization. Gen Z and Millennials are the product of their environment and as such have

---

38. So, Claiborne, "Evangelicalism," 154.

39. See also the pertinent comments by Brown, *Evangelicals at the Crossroads*, 203–6.

been taught to reject any biblical principles that in some way counteract or push against what the culture has deemed "good" and "just" and "virtuous." This is reinforced by a recent survey by George Barna, which shows that Millennials now have radically different views than their parents on "respect for others, interest in faith, and enthusiasm for America."[40] Divisive attitudes, a rejection of orthodox faith and traditions, and a scorning of love of country are the hallmarks of younger generations as they move into positions of authority and power. Such changes are bound to bring the nation to its knees both spiritually and culturally. The work of radical educators and a hyper-left-leaning media have done the Enemy's job well. We have raised a generation of evangelicals, and Americans in general, with a hatred for anything and anyone who voices a traditional stance on morality and culture: we are a nation divided against itself and it surely cannot endure as such (see Matt 12:25). Our job as pastors, educators, parents, and grandparents is not to back down from the pressure of the culture, but rather to face it head on and challenge it through sound biblical principles.

The division of evangelicals on these issues is troubling indeed. But the reality is that most of our youth are "already gone" by the time they graduate secular universities due to the political and cultural pressure from friends and professors. As noted in Chapter 2, across America on college and university campuses one can easily find a hodgepodge of disgruntled groups coming together for the purpose of dislodging those with the "power" and replacing them with their own tyranny of racial, gender, sexual, reproductive, and environmental justice. In the aftermath of the 2020 election, the silencing of conservative voices and the attacks against those who voted for President Trump has already begun. Those who once held the reins of power will pay dearly under the domination of "woke" America. A new day has dawned, and the radicals will show the rest of America how just, woke, and politically correct they are.

One of the newer social movements is the push for socialism where everyone is "equal" and has similar power and equality of outcomes, what is often labeled by the word "equity." Of course, this is a utopian pipedream that will never come to fruition especially when self is on the throne. It is sheer hubris to suggest that fallen humanity can right the proverbial listing ship. Their efforts are doomed to failure because they lack the power of the Gospel and the power of forgiveness that comes

---

40. Martin, "Generation Gap."

with it. And while it is common for some well-intentioned believers to side with these causes and to hold that Jesus would be on their "side" because of the "social oppression" of the current power structures, in reality Jesus would condemn any movement built upon revenge, hatred, and lust for power as opposed to forgiveness. What is more, Jesus would be against any movement that flouted his Father's divine mandates.

Political and Societal Anarchy Follows a Rejection of God and God's Mandates

A natural progression of society's rejection of God's laws for human flourishing is the flouting of civil law. This includes the promotion of illegal acts which ultimately pave the way for general anarchy. I will point out two current trends within America which serve as harbingers of our culture's trajectory towards lawlessness. The first deals with immigration and the second deals with the erasing of history.

First, apart from the political and ideological problems and baggage associated with the idea of "social justice,"[41] left-leaning evangelicals' fight for "justice" for illegal immigrants is troubling. They embrace modern cultural shifts that turn a blind eye to the lawlessness of illegal immigration in their push for open borders or full acceptance of the "undocumented."[42] I find it confusing that members of the evangelical church under the guise of justice and compassion, call out conservative evangelicals, often employing pejoratives such as xenophobia and racism,[43] when immigration laws of the US are enforced but remain silent on the glaring issue of the breaking of the law in the first place by those entering a country illegally. Breaking the laws of a country (or God) can have long reaching and unintended devastating consequences for the innocent within one's own family—the account of Achan in Joshua 7 is a good reminder. The issue of the legal plight of the Dreamers and DACA recipients due to their parents' or guardians' illegal actions is a case in point.

Similarly, I also struggle with an argument that seeks to invoke the biblical laws on immigration drawn from the Torah (e.g., Lev 19:33–34; 23:22; 24:22; Deut 26:12) but rejects legislation in the same legal texts against sexual deviancy, the value of the unborn, or the sovereignty of

---

41. See discussion by Ellis, *Breakdown*, 146–48.
42. E.g., Romero, "Immigration," 66–80.
43. E.g., Opstal, "Remaining to Reform," 120–23, 132.

God to dictate what is morally right. The truth is this confused mentality about what is morally right and wrong, and supposedly scripturally backed,[44] goes hand in hand with the lawlessness of the Enemy par excellence and the lawlessness of the Left (e.g., sanctuary cities, failure to enforce immigration law and federal legislation on the protection of the border and aiding ICE, rejection of immigration reform, refusal to allow voting oversight, refusal to condemn riots in the streets, etc.).[45] I am all for allowing immigrants to come to western countries legally (I am one myself), but you cannot have it both ways. Western democracies are just that, democracies, they are not theocracies like Israel was. If you choose to adopt biblical laws on immigration then you had better be prepared to go further and adopt the entire ethical stance of the Law especially when it comes to morality, sexual ethics, and the protection of the truly unprotected in society, the unborn—to err in one law is to err in them all (James 2:10).

The second point I would like to make deals with our rapid push to erase our history through lawlessness. The old saying that life imitates art is certainly true in Western culture today. A recent Amazon series called *The Man in the High Castle* traces what life would have been like in America had the Nazis and the Axis powers won the Second World War. In one episode, the Nazis destroy the Statue of Liberty in order to erase the past and begin afresh with Jahr Null (year zero) of their new world order. The heroes of the series are black communists who defeat the Nazis. While this series is fictional, the stance of Western postmodernism is not far behind with its removal of historical landmarks, statues, and paintings, many times done illegally in mob actions fueled by Marxist-based groups like Antifa and BLM.

The tearing down of monuments is a symptom of a greater problem of rejecting history and the things of the past. This is done in the name of justice and the removal of "offensive" images. The problem is who decides what is offensive and just? In the Middle East, ISIS was offended by their history under ancient Assyrian rulers as well as the monuments related to Christianity and Judaism. In response, along with the destruction of priceless ancient ruins, they blew up the traditional site of the prophet Jonah's tomb. As an archaeologist I cringed at the senseless destruction. We

---

44. The laws related to the treatment of the foreigner in the OT Law are not a one-to-one parallel with today's immigration policy in the US as is often assumed. See for example the detailed treatment by Hoffmeier, *The Immigration Crisis* (2009).

45. See also Wallace, "Thief."

collectively shook our heads and wagged our fingers at the atrocities they committed in this vein. However, only a few years later here we are with our own version of "ISIS" who are purging all things that are offensive to their "wokeness." The reality is that today's definition of "offensive" art displays and "inappropriate" historical monuments will certainly change, and a new generation will begin to purge the history and monuments of today's "woke" America. Where does it end? I see it clearly heading for an attack on churches, Christians, and the established norms and Judeo-Christian ideals of the Bible. Indeed, since beginning writing this chapter, news stations reported that a Left-wing former BLM leader wants the removal of all imagery of Jesus and the virgin Mary from society including church murals, stain glassed windows, and statues because of their representation of "white supremacy."[46] Already, vandals have desecrated statues in churches due to racial prejudices.[47] And in Portland, Oregon, mobs have burned Bibles.[48]

Some may be asking: what does the removing of statues have to do with sexuality and morality? My response is simple. Back in the 1930s Unwin noted that with the suppression of sexual drives, that is, the elevation of sexual chastity before marriage and monogamy within marriage, cultures will make great advancements and commemorate their history and become more "deistic" (i.e., believing in a higher power).[49] Conversely, societies where sexual liberation is practiced at all levels will in turn undo their history, devolve, eliminate deistic tendencies and rationalistic thinking, and revert to a zoistic (to have a "dead level of conception" and be "entirely self-focused on day-to-day, wants and needs"[50]) state within three generations and collapse.[51] This collapse tends to be "to its lowest state of flourishing" a position which usually is followed by being conquered by a greater culture.[52] What could be more telling of where Western culture is quickly heading? One commentator noted that at this pace Western culture will collapse by the "last third of this

---

46. Betz, "Shaun King."
47. Miles, "Sacred Heart."
48. Vincent, "Protesters."
49. Unwin, *Sex and Culture*, 424–32.
50. As summarized by Durston, "Sexual Morality."
51. Unwin, *Sex and Culture*, 425.
52. Durston, "Sexual Morality."

century."[53] This is why Christians of all stripes must take a stand for established biblical laws and church traditions. These traditions and moral instructions must not be gutted and torn down by such a subjective ideology. Removal of sexual and moral ethics are only the beginning. The end of the anarchy will be a destruction of society and all that God has created as good in Genesis 1 and 2. Evangelicals need to be willing to suffer and resist the pressure and ridicule of culture and sadly even of other evangelicals if they want to effect change.

Conclusion

The links between political and social movements, lawlessness, and the rejection of the Genesis mandates is clear. Any student of history knows that the move to lawlessness in areas of politics, social issues, sexuality, and moral concerns leads in only one direction, a rejection of God and all that he has declared to be good. As I noted in my introduction to this chapter, even though I struggled with including this chapter I knew that it was important to understanding the downward spiral of Western cultures, especially America. A nation, church, society, or whatever, divided against itself will not stand, lest we forget the words of Jesus (Matt 12:25; Mark 3:25), the same words that Abraham Lincoln recited in 1858 just prior to the US Civil War (1861–1865). It is time for a call to repentance and unity under the authority of God, which is to say, the authority of what God has declared in his Word, not the least of which is God's mandates in Genesis 1 and 2. Only a unified people of God will be able to withstand the attacks on our children, grandchildren, and society at large (see John 17). This will not be done at the political level; it will only come about by a repentant church which reaches out to the lost with the Gospel. Nevertheless, our political involvement is important in democratic countries. We can have a voice in the direction of our country and in turn preserve the freedoms enshrined in our Constitution. To fail to get involved is to cede our rights and freedom to the Left and their growing mobs.

---

53. Durston, "Sexual Morality."

Chapter 15

Conclusion

> A lie doesn't become truth, wrong doesn't become right and evil doesn't become good just because it's accepted by the majority.

THIS QUOTATION, OFTEN ATTRIBUTED to Booker T. Washington (1856–1915), captures the reality of what Western culture has become in our postmodern world of enlightened and "woke" sexual ethics and morality. God's clearly mandated order for human flourishing has been rejected at all levels. As I noted in Chapter 3, this began with a rejection of God and an elevation of self. Western culture has accepted the lie that biblical sexual ethics and morality are passé and no longer applicable in a postmodern and post-Christian context. We have been told that science and the medical community knows best. But we must remember that science can never tell us what is good and evil, what is morally right, or what we ought to do, that is the realm of God.[1]

The speed with which these changes have happened, and the reverse order of the attack on the Genesis mandates has left nothing remaining for Western culture to destroy other than allowing more perversion within these deconstructed mandates (e.g., polyamorous marriages, pedophilia, bestiality, infanticide, and euthanasia). The current state of Western culture is precarious to say the least. When every mandate of God is flouted, there is nothing left but chaos, destruction, and ultimately God's judgment,

---

1. Satinover, *Homosexuality*, 126, 146.

although God's judgment may be to allow a country to implode as noted in Joseph Daniel Unwin's observations (see previous chapter).

For the believer who thinks *their* sexual ethic is wiser than God's, I sound a warning. Be careful! I know former pastors and their spouses as well as leading evangelical voices whose lives are now a wreck because they drifted from the historic faith tradition when dealing with sexual ethics. It began with an acceptance of homosexuality as "normal" and quickly progressed to acceptance of same-sex marriage and transgender lifestyles. A lowered sexual ethic in their own personal lives followed. Within a few short years some of their own marriages began to falter as they got caught up in extramarital affairs with many turning to divorce to escape "loveless" marriages. On more than one occasion I have seen these same people, now divorced, remarrying or even finding their "true self" in the arms of someone of the same sex. The downward spiral is insidious, and it affects not just our personal lives but also the wider culture.

As I have been writing this book, the chaos of postmodernism has been wreaking havoc on numerous cities across America. The irony of postmodernism's undoing of God's commands and opting to enthrone "self" instead is that it runs afoul of the cultural Marxism that it endorses. Elevation of self does not cohere with communistic ideology, which crushes individualism and pushes everyone into the same mold. This is exactly what we have been experiencing in Western culture. Those who do not conform to the group think of Western culture's morality and sexual ethics are being overrun by the cultural blitzkrieg and "cancel" culture. What is more, as we have seen, the natural outcome of rejecting God is the rejection of law and order, which leads to even more chaos. God's law goes first—this is what has been happening since the 1960s—and then people turn on each other and begin to fight over whose law will take its place. This is not fearmongering. This is the reality coming to Western societies if we do not change our course.

The chaos of postmodern thinking and cultural Marxism was on full display in June of 2020 when a six-block section of Seattle's capital region was taken over by Antifa and other anarchists. The police were driven out and, in the void, roving bands of armed "enforcement" took their place. In a matter of days, these new "police" began using extortion and strongarm tactics to impose their will. This was followed by reports of two murders in the zone. People never dreamed that sowing chaos in culture by undoing millennia-old moral and ethical fences would reap these results. While some may argue they have nothing to do with each other, they would be wrong. When people feel free to rewrite sexual and moral ethical codes, what do you think they will go after next? They will resist other areas of order that they do not like such as law enforcement, border security, and the autonomy of nations. They will even foment negative race relations. They want chaos because the Enemy is behind it all. While many may reject the interconnectedness of the Genesis mandates with Western culture's downward spiral, the studies are clear that they are all intertwined. Sexual immorality, fatherlessness/a breakdown of the family unit, homosexuality, gender confusion, are all related when it comes to sexual ethics.[2]

God's plan for humanity as established in Genesis 1 and 2 is for the flourishing of society; yet, the current trajectory of Western society is not encouraging, and in fact, is downright frightening. Apart from the moral and ethical concerns, the problem with the rise of social activist movements is that they have become involved with every facet of the power structures within society. No matter how mundane and boring, left-leaning activists have gained control in order to transform these institutions (e.g., local political positions, school boards, community groups, etc.).[3] Meanwhile, evangelicals, and Christians in general, remain on the sidelines wondering why their towns, cities, and states, are being transformed before them. Christians need to take back these smaller battlegrounds and in doing so the larger battles will be won. In light of these concerns, there are two ways Christians can respond to culture's rejection of the Genesis mandates: one spiritual and the other political.

Moving Forward: Our Country and the Evangelical Church

It is no longer an option for Christians who say they love God, his Word, their children, and their country to stand idly by and allow the Enemy to destroy everything we hold dear. We need both a spiritual and a political awakening. When between 30 and 40 million conservative Catholics and evangelicals did not participate in the election cycle of 2016, it is understandable why we are facing the absolute chaos of society and culture

---

2. Brown, *Jezebel's War*, 110.

3. This is also noted by James Lindsay in his interview at American Thought Leaders, "James Lindsay."

as I have noted throughout this book. Many have remained silent and allowed chaos to take over.

While some evangelicals push back against Christians getting involved in politics and attempting to change culture,[4] this is a wrongheaded way of looking at the role of Christians in society.[5] For example, John MacArthur notes that "Using temporal methods to promote legislative and judicial change, and resorting to external efforts of lobbying and intimidation to achieve some sort of 'Christian morality' in society is not our calling—and has no eternal value. Only the gospel rescues sinners from sin, death, and hell."[6] Although I readily agree that the preaching of the Gospel is our primary commission in life as believers, there are multiple avenues of doing that. We must always keep in mind that the author of Proverbs understood this dilemma when he said that righteousness exalts a nation, but sin is a reproach to any people (Prov 14:34). If we allow our nation to become so corrupt morally and so hostile to the Christian faith that the church can no longer function freely, then we are doing a disservice to our children and grandchildren who have to grow up in this moral morass. There is nothing that says we cannot do both: share the gospel *and* petition secular government for a morally acceptable society. The OT prophets certainly understood that these things go hand in hand. One need only read the account of Ahab and Jezebel to realize what can happen to godly principles and instruction, not to mention an entire nation, when evil is allowed to have full reign. Jezebel killed the prophets of Yahweh at will and led the nation into moral and spiritual decline (1 Kgs 18).[7] Is that what we want for America? Canada? I think not. These changes are not going to come about by a few feel-good sermons. Even though change comes through the preaching of the Gospel, if there is no freedom to share the Gospel or to speak in the public square then the Gospel will be greatly hindered and it will be the fault of Christians for not taking a stand when we had the chance.

This can take on more sinister forms than mere corruption of a nation's sexual ethics and morality. It can also lead to a complete change

---

4. Longman states, "we should not try to coerce people into living in conformity with our biblical values" (*Bible and the Ballot*, 65); however, there are many biblical values that we impose on other people simply because they are right and moral.

5. See Ashford, "Christian Politics," 449.

6. MacArthur, *Why Government Can't Save You*, 15, see also, 129–45.

7. For a full treatment of this as it relates to Western culture, see Brown, *Jezebel's War* (2019).

of a culture's value system, unless we have forgotten what happened to Germany in the 1930s. I am sure many would say this would never happen to America, but I would like to give two examples that have grave consequences if left unchecked. First, many have turned a blind eye to the rise of Islam within Western cultures, a position that will certainly have devastating repercussions for Christians if Europe is any litmus test. Already in certain regions of Europe, Islam is so entrenched that these areas have become "no-go" zones for law enforcement and non-Muslims.[8] Shall we stand by silently in our political correctness while liberal activists push for the acceptance of Islam as a viable part of our culture,[9] a religion that is virulently anti-Semitic, and abuses children and women in unimaginable ways? The last time I read Matthew 18, Jesus makes it very clear about the punishments for those who abuse the least of these, that is, children.[10] To be sure, there are those who still advocate for the full acceptance of Islam as a religion of peace when in fact former Muslims are sounding the alarm that it is anything but. It is a religion married to a political ideology that is counter to everything America was founded upon, not to mention the fact that many of its adherents seek the overthrow of the West.[11] We need to be vigilant to protect people of all stripes from this type of oppression.

The second example is even more pressing. It is the rise of socialistic ideology within younger generations. As I noted in Chapters 2 and 3, the educational system has been inundated with Marxists instructors, who seek to overthrow Western culture in favor of a utopian pipedream that will marginalize Christianity and destroy Western culture's Judeo-Christian foundation. America in particular is on the precipice and many Christians are oblivious to the peril because of a complete detachment from what is going on around them. Again, people may say this would never happen to America, but unless believers wake up, spiritual freedom will certainly be curtailed; it is already happening. The increasing power of the government, the increasing militancy of the cultural Marxists, and

---

8. Shaw, "No-Go Zones."

9. Mohammed, *Unveiled*, 266–75. Fea (*Believe Me*, 54) seems to have no problem with the changing religious face of America when he touts the religious demographic changes in America which include Islam as the fastest growing religion in America after the passage of the Hart-Celler Act of 1965.

10. Mohammed, *Unveiled*, 6–12, 46–49, 50–54, 55–61, 72–79.

11. Mohammed, *Unveiled*, 219–21.

the cultural pressure to conform is palpable and real not just in society but now within churches.

As I noted in earlier chapters, Christians have done amazing things by getting involved in the political process and in activism. In the West alone, Christians were instrumental in bringing about the end of slavery through abolitionist movements. This is no less true of the civil rights movement championed by Martin Luther King Jr. But we must keep in mind that these actions were also built upon grassroots movements that focused on building a consensus outside of the political structures as well.[12] Christians, evangelicals in particular, need to continue to stand against the onslaught on our society by the Enemy through bad policies and laws that undermine the Genesis mandates, which are so foundational to society, the family, and human flourishing in general. As it has often been said, "The only thing necessary for evil to triumph is for good men (and women) to do nothing" (John Stuart Mill).[13] As believers it is vitally important we do everything in our power to push for laws that reflect a godly society as mandated by God to *all* creation, not just the Israelites or modern Christians.

Now to be clear, I am in no way advocating for the total reliance on political structures to answer the woes of Western civilization. On the contrary, this must always be coupled with the power of the Gospel to change lives. As the inward lives of people are changed, outward actions will help bring about a more righteous and just society. A word of caution, however, is also in order. For those evangelicals who continue to vote a certain way thinking that social change will be effected by a particular political party that seeks to focus on select social issues—usually for the self-serving benefit of gaining political votes—while that same political party advocates for the undoing of every mandate given by God in Genesis 1 and 2, then perhaps it is time for those evangelicals to reevaluate the "social change" for which they are advocating. As a recent naturalized citizen of the United States, I have witnessed firsthand in Canada, the country of my birth, the dangers of political movements built upon "woke" "social justice," cultural and moral relativism, and supported by the government and many mainline churches and believers: it has destroyed many aspects of the social fabric.[14] We indeed need to

---

12. Wallis, *God's Politics*, 61–64.
13. Robin, "Who Really Said That?"
14. See also Mohammed, *Unveiled*, 76–77.

reach out to the lost, but we also need to get involved to effect change so that culture reflects at least some semblance of a fear of God.

The best solution for Western culture's rejection of Judeo-Christian principles, barring a great awakening of sorts, is for the church to resist conforming to culture. And when people have hit rock bottom and seen the error of their cultural experiment, Christians need to be there ready to offer them the hope of the message of Christ.[15] Of course, that does not mean that we have to wait until such time. On the contrary, we must be actively engaged in the shaping of culture and politics while resisting the urge to conform. It has long been noted by Christians and secularists alike that Western culture was founded upon Judeo-Christian ideals that must remain intact for this culture to flourish.[16] While Western culture certainly has had its issues, Western democracies, whose foundations were built upon Judeo-Christian values and belief in the value and equality of all humans, have been a source of good for the world (e.g., the defeat of Nazism, the rejection of communism, the raising of people out of poverty). Laws and mandates as established by God in Genesis are good and right.

As a father of five, I have come to appreciate the fact that children need boundaries—fences of sorts—to constrain their enthusiasm to be their own person too quickly. Many days they simply refuse to be obedient and hate the enforced rules. Despite these moments of confrontation, I know that what I am saying and doing is best for them and their flourishing. The "laws" of my house hopefully will make them into respectable citizens with a healthy fear of God. Similarly, the dos and don'ts of the Genesis mandates may not seem pleasant to a culture that desires to go its own way, but it will surely come to realize that God's laws are good and bring human flourishing, not death.[17] Yet, more is needed than a mere *recognition* of a Higher Power. People need to come to a saving knowledge of Jesus Christ for without this aspect of change, sooner or later we will drift once again away from the Way, the Truth, and the Life and scriptural authority in the same way generation after generation of Israelites drifted in and out of relationship with their God. This brings me to my second main point: the role of family in effecting change.

---

15. See also Ashford, "Jordan Peterson," 16–17.
16. Peterson, *12 Rules for Life*, 104; and Grudem, *Politics*, 64–65.
17. See also a similar conclusion by Ashford, "Jordan Peterson," 28–29.

Conclusion

Moving Forward: Our Family and Culture

Michael Brown is correct to note how we can remedy the slide among our youth. First, we need to have a deeper relationship and experience with God as opposed to the "lightweight" nature of our faith. Second, we need to teach our kids and grandkids that serving God is going to mean a transformation of our lives, not just something tacked on to everything else. Third, we need to equip our children with a solid apologetic and not pat answers. They need to be taught the Bible by theologically sound teachers. And fourth, we need to teach our kids that the propaganda from the social movements such as the LGBTQ agenda is not the answer even though they may marginalize Christians as bigots and being behind the times.[18] I would add to this list that we need to tell our children and grandchildren our stories of God's love and our spiritual experiences. We need to pass on our faith. Moreover, we can no longer allow our children to be educated by the culture and the secular education system while we say nothing. The Bible is univocal on the fact that parents, and not the state, are to be the primary educators of children.[19] This responsibility is not to be shuffled off to schools and daycares or other government agencies. The biblical law makes it clear that we are to teach our children when they get up, when they lay down, and when they walk along the road (Deut 6:6–7) and elders and pastors are supposed to do the same or be disqualified from service in the church (1 Tim 3:4–5; Titus 1:6).[20] This responsibility is placed upon both parents. As I have said before, someone should be in the home raising their children whether it is the father or mother. More money or a successful career should never be the motivating factor for the abdication of educational responsibilities in the home, especially biblical instruction.[21]

From a cultural perspective, we should never expect unbelievers to behave as believers. And we should never assume that the unbeliever will simply fall into line with the teachings of Scripture. Sinners do what sinners do: they sin. That does not mean that we should throw our hands in the air and allow the Enemy to have free reign in our culture. We

---

18. Brown, "Atheists." There is some good news on this front. Some surveys show that younger generations are becoming less tolerant of the LGBTQ agenda. See Brown, *Evangelicals at the Crossroads*, 179–71.

19. Sider, *Completely Pro-Life*, 115–16.

20. Sider, *Completely Pro-Life*, 115–16.

21. Sider, *Completely Pro-Life*, 116–17.

can, however, pray for a revival in our land whereby the Holy Spirit will change hearts. Perhaps God will be merciful to our land if we pray (2 Chron 7:14). Perhaps God will see fit to unite believers in turning back the laws that are offensive to the Creator. Perhaps we can stave off God's judgment, for if God's Word is any indicator of how he treats sin, judgment is certainly coming. The truth is Christians need to be proactive as opposed to reactive to our out-of-control culture. We need to teach our families what the Bible says about sexuality. We need to teach our children why premarital, extramarital, and distorted forms of sexual unions are wrong and what the natural outcomes of these actions are.[22] We need to bring back a solid teaching of Genesis 1 and 2 and then instruct on the repercussions of the fall. In so doing, our children will have a biblical grid through which to filter post-Christian morality. At the same time Christians can model what true and authentic sexuality looks like.[23]

Moving Forward: Our Local Church

From an ecclesial perspective, for those who repent and seek reconciliation, we must be ready to welcome back into fellowship those who have truly repented of sin (Gal 6:1). At the same time, cultural shifts and the rejection of God's creation mandates need to be exposed for what they are: an attack on God and his commands. As I noted in the Preface, we as believers are responsible for who we sit under for our spiritual sustenance. If your church, denomination, or pastor are in some way vacillating on the issues of sexual morality and the teaching of the Word, it may be time to consider a new church home. Of course, if you feel there is still hope for change then by all means stay the course and pray and push back against cultural encroachment and rejection of the Word. If books like this have helped you and informed you on the correct understanding of God's Word concerning these issues, please tell others and get these types of resources into their hands. Start small groups and women's studies and work through the material. Find conservative, qualified speakers to come and address your congregation about the importance of these issues. We need to do more, however, than merely rejecting the cultural shifts, we need to be willing to act and minister to those who are hurting and are dealing with issues of homosexuality, abortion, divorce, gender

---

22. Balswick and Balswick, *Authentic Human Sexuality*, 324–26.
23. Balswick and Balswick, *Authentic Human Sexuality*, 326.

confusion, and the like.[24] For those who have had firsthand experience with these issues and have been healed or delivered by God, then maybe God is calling you to work with those who are dealing with those things with which you yourself once struggled. These types of ministries can aid those who are looking for someone to listen and pray with them while they navigate the often-hostile environment of our Western culture.

Finally, in the same way the Enemy uses interest groups to push his agenda, we need to follow the words of Jesus when he said to be as wise as serpents but harmless as doves (Matt 10:16), meaning, we need to do all that is within our power to effect a desired outcome. While "confrontation" often carries a negative connotation, we nonetheless must confront sin in the church in whatever form it takes. I end this study by reiterating aspects of the conclusion of William Watkins back in the mid-1990s. In the face of a society that is calling for tolerance at every level, we need to be "intolerant" not of people, but of that which is against God's commands and truth of the Genesis mandates, namely, the role of the nuclear family, the goodness of heterosexual marriage, the beauty and blessings of procreation and children, the goodness and rightness of gender distinctions, and the value of humanity in the mandate of species distinctions. We need to be intolerant of agendas that seek to corrupt our children both culturally and educationally. We need to be intolerant of every force that would seek to marginalize Christians and push an agenda that would remove any godly ideal from the public square. Put simply, we need to be intolerant of anything that takes its stand against God and calls evil good and good evil.[25]

---

24. Dallas, *Gay Gospel*, 227–28.
25. Watkins, *New Absolutes*, 240.

Bibliography

Achtemeier, Mark. *The Bible's Yes to Same-Sex Marriage: An Evangelical's Change of Heart*. Louisville: Westminster John Knox, 2014.

Activist Mommy. "Movie Featuring 'Relationship' between Child Robot and Adult Man Met with Walkouts, Backlash at Film Festival." (Mar 4, 2020) at https://activistmommy.com/movie-featuring-relationship-between-child-robot-and-adult-man-met-with-walkouts-backlash-at-film-festival/?fbclid=IwAR1GlpToyvMZnk6HxKsziXEfQyPPsL4v7-3bE74iKJULAVyv28qvqJTgv1I.

———. "Reboot of 'Clifford the Big Red Dog' Features Character with Lesbian Parents." (Mar 1, 2020) at https://activistmommy.com/reboot-of-clifford-the-big-red-dog-features-character-with-lesbian-parents/?fbclid=IwAR07yUQgRmh7_9uM8jTJXW7DyKoMe9jxOYuME-dG3kJAQPUVTzH3TmxXMZQ.

Adams, John. "Letter to Officers of the First Brigade of the Third Division of the Militia of Massachusetts, October 11, 1798." In vol. 9 of *The Works of John Adams, Second President of the United States*, edited by Charles Francis Adams. Freeport, NY: Books for Libraries, 1969.

Adely, Hannah. "LGBTQ History Lessons Will Soon Be Mandatory In New Jersey Classrooms; 12 Schools to Pilot Program." *USA Today* (Jan 7, 2020) at https://www.usatoday.com/story/news/education/2020/01/07/nj-schools-teach-lgbtq-history-months-before-new-state-law/2830712001/?fbclid=IwAR1QMh3XmXcG6Wafq9XhvUxSahayfVuqtH6jEFEJgDBGAZvJFdn3Bh3Zaac.

Agrawal, Priya. "Maternal Mortality and Morbidity in the United States of America." *BWHO* 93, no.3 (2015) 135.

Allender, Dan B., and Tremper Longman III. *God Loves Sex: An Honest Conversation about Sexual Desire and Holiness*. Grand Rapids: Baker, 2014.

American Thought Leaders. "James Lindsay: Deep Dive into 'Critical Social Justice' & How It Took Over the Humanities." *YouTube* (Mar 24, 2020) at https://www.youtube.com/watch?v=8N55gFjg4yg&feature=youtu.be&fbclid=IwARoje5WUDq5y6DWgwTQenSpi3z06n9zSG2S3iu4vLTIkgHQRdb-qhh2x2R8.

AMP. "Twitch Appoints ADL-Linked 'Trans-Deer-Girl' to Safety Advisory Council." (May 19, 2020) at https://americanpriority.com/news/twitch-appoints-adl-linked-trans-deer-girl-to-safety-advisory-council/.

Ascol, Tom. "Critical Race Theory and Christianity." *Sovereign Nations* (Oct 28, 2020) at https://sovereignnations.com/2020/10/28/critical-race-theory-christianity-tom-ascol/?fbclid=IwAR2mGtlF9te12r1DOyiuaQ9sLNjfxI7c3I1gIRiaCm61IoIIEKaTaWnkuJ8.

Ashford, Bruce Riley. "Jordan Peterson and the Chaos of Our Secular Age." In *Myth and Meaning in Jordan Peterson: A Christian Perspective*, edited by Ron Dart, 7–29. Bellingham, WA: Lexham, 2020.

———. "Tailoring Christian Politics in Our Secular Age." *Them* 42, no. 3 (2017) 446–51.

Associated Press. "Hallmark to Reinstate Zola Commercial Showing Brides Kissing, after Backlash." *Fox News* (Dec 15, 2019) at https://www.foxnews.com/lifestyle/hallmark-zola-commercial-brides-kissing-same-sex-wedding-reinstated.

———. "Virginia Bans Conversion Therapy for Minors." *Fox News* (Mar 4, 2020) at https://www.foxnews.com/us/virginia-bans-conversion-therapy-for-minors.

Bailey, Dean. *Beyond the Shades of Gray: Because Homosexuality is a Symptom Not a Solution*. Bloomington, IN: Westbow, 2011.

Baklinski, Pete. "Ex-Gay Man: 'Homosexuality Is Just Another Human Brokenness.'" *LifeSite News* (Oct 20, 2014) at https://www.lifesitenews.com/news/ex-gay-homosexuality-is-just-another-human-brokenness?utm_content=buffer3a70e&utm_medium=social&utm_source=+lifesitenews%2Bfacebook&utm_campaign=buffer&fbclid=IwAR3cq52He9kvDQpcTEEHvIVVsOcWZb8Edv4oCKCjfGSkLZggUXMWsaVsuwk.

———. "Gay Activist: Of Course Our Goal Is to 'Indoctrinate Children Into the LGBTQ Agenda.'" *LifeSite News* (Mar 13, 2015) at https://www.lifesitenews.com/news/gay-activist-our-goal-is-to-indoctrinate-children-into-lgbtq-agenda.

Balswick, Judith, and Jack Balswick. *Authentic Human Sexuality: An Integrated Christian Approach*. 2nd ed. Downers Grove, IL: IVP, 2008.

Barna. "Atheism Doubles Among Generation Z." (Jan 24, 2018) at https://www.barna.com/research/atheism-doubles-among-generation-z/.

———. "The End of Absolutes: America's New Moral Code." (May 25, 2016) at https://www.barna.com/research/the-end-of-absolutes-americas-new-moral-code/.

Barr, Sabrina. "Alexandria Ocasio-Cortez Helps Raise More than £200,000 for UK Trans Charity Mermaids." *Independent* (Jan 22, 2019) at https://www.independent.co.uk/life-style/alexandria-ocasio-cortez-mermaids-gender-trans-charity-uk-donkey-kong-twitch-a8739866.html.

Barth, Karl. *Church Dogmatics. Vol III.4*, edited by G.W. Bromiley and T.F. Torrance. Edinburgh: T&T Clark, 1961.

Bartholet, Elizabeth. "Homeschooling: Parent Rights Absolutism vs. Child Rights to Education & Protection." *Arizona Law Review* 62 (2019) 1–80.

Bartiromo, Michael. "Couple Says 'Sexually Fluid' Relationship Allows Them to 'Love Infinitely in All Directions.'" *Fox News* (Oct 28, 2019) at https://www.foxnews.com/lifestyle/couple-says-sexually-fluid-relationship-allows-them-to-love-infinitely-in-all-directions.

Benshoff, Harry M., and Sean Griffin. *Queer Images: A History of Gay and Lesbian Film in America*. Lanham, MD: Rowan and Littlefield, 2006.

Berg, Desmond. "Extinction Rebellion's True Target Is Not Climate: It's Idea that Heterosexuality is 'Normal.'" *Sovereign Nations* (Oct 22, 2019) at https://sovereignnations.com/2019/10/22/extinction-rebellion-not-climate-heterosexuality-normal/?fbclid=IwAR3oXYXf35NzSKooFg7wI-7otpGSqbOipEs7tLxWqSUX6V1bbdbGhq6FhgI.

Bergman, S. Bear. "I Have Come to Indoctrinate Your Children into My LGBTQ Agenda (And I'm Not a Bit Sorry)." *Huffpost* (updated Feb 2, 2016) at https://www.huffpost.com/entry/i-have-come-to-indoctrinate-your-children-lgtbq_b_6795152?guccounter=1.

Berrien, Hank. "British Court in Transgender Case: Bible 'Belief is 'Incompatible' with Human Dignity.'" *The Daily Wire* (Oct 2, 2019) at https://www.dailywire.com/news/british-court-in-transgender-case-bible-belief-is-incompatible-with-human-dignity/?fbclid=IwAR1tPQBNBns3ALj7lF4c9nL9jtRmQd84tOlcQxxoFjTsdTZUMYBJ3Dj1js8.

Betz, Bradford. "Iowa Man Who Sets LGBTQ Flag on Fire Gets over 15 Years in Prison." *Fox News* (Dec 20, 2019) at https://www.foxnews.com/us/iowa-lgbtq-flag-fire-church-prison.

———. "Shaun King: Statues of Jesus Christ are 'Form of White Supremacy,' Should be Torn Down." *Fox News* (June 22, 2020) at https://www.foxnews.com/media/shaun-king-jesus-christ-statues-white-supremacy.

———. "Thousands of Fetuses Found in Illinois Home to be Buried in Indiana, Officials Say." *Fox News* (Feb 11, 2020) at https://www.foxnews.com/us/fetuses-found-illinois-home-buried-indiana.

Blake, Judith. "Abortion and Public Opinion: The 1960–970 Decade." *Science* 171, no.3971 (1971) 540–49.

Blake, Nathanael. "LGBT Activists Get Church Banned from Local Arts Scene for Believing the Bible." *The Federalist* (Oct 23, 2019) at https://thefederalist.com/2019/10/23/lgbt-activists-get-church-banned-from-local-arts-scene-for-believing-the-bible/?fbclid=IwAR27yHQjkPCQrW—_yimqws3a7GH6MKp6o6ha9dCYFFEnSwoX3WSbc_ewtw.

Bonhoeffer, Dietrich. *Ethics: Dietrich Bonhoeffer Works, Volume 6*. Minneapolis: Fortress, 2005.

Brady, Veronica. "Preface." In *Readings from the Perspective of the Earth*, edited by Norman C. Habel, 13–17. Sheffield: Sheffield, 2000.

Branch, J. Alan. *Affirming God's Image: Addressing the Transgender Question with Science and Scripture*. Bellingham, WA: Lexham, 2019.

Briggs, Megan. "An Astonishing 99% of Conservative Christians Showed Up to Vote This Year (For Trump)." *ChurchLeaders* (Dec 1, 2020) at https://churchleaders.com/news/386169-an-astonishing-99-of-conservative-christians-showed-up-to-vote-this-year-for-trump.html?utm_source=outreach-cl-daily-nl&utm_medium=email&utm_content=text-link&utm_campaign=cl-daily-nl&maropost_id=&mpweb=256-9192742-742444023.

———. "Jesus' Answer to Transgenderism: You Must Be Born Again." *ChurchLeaders* (Sept 27, 2019) at https://churchleaders.com/pastors/videos-for-pastors/360031-jesus-answer-to-transgenderism-you-must-be-born-again.html?utm_source=outreach-cl-daily-nl&utm_medium=email&utm_content=text-link&utm_campaign=cl-daily-nl&maropost_id=&mpweb=256-8281138-742444023.

———. "John Ortberg Hoping to Regain Trust after 'Poor Judgment' at Menlo Church." *ChurchLeaders* (Feb 4, 2020) at https://churchleaders.com/news/370232-john-ortberg-hoping-to-regain-trust-after-poor-judgment-at-menlo-church.html?utm_source=cl-fridayweeklysend-nl&utm_medium=email&utm_content=text-link&utm_campaign=cl-fridayweeklysend-nl20200207&maropost_id=742444023&mpweb=256-8590775-742444023.

———. "Political Polarization Is the Crisis We Should Be Fighting Right Now." *ChurchLeaders* (April 30, 2020) at https://churchleaders.com/news/375037-political-polarization-is-the-crisis-we-should-be-fighting-right-now.html.

———. "Sy Rogers, Pastor Known for Overcoming Homosexuality, Has Died." *ChurchLeaders* (April 21, 2020) at https://churchleaders.com/news/374623-sy-rogers-pastor-known-for-overcoming-homosexuality-has-died.html?utm_source=outreach-cl-daily-nl&utm_medium=email&utm_content=text-link&utm_campaign=cl-daily-nl&maropost_id=&mpweb=256-8796511-742444023.

Brown, Jon. "California State Senator Fights for Bill That Could Alter Sex Offender Registration for Gay Sex with Minors." *The Daily Wire* (Aug 16, 2020) at https://www.dailywire.com/news/california-state-senator-fights-for-bill-that-could-alter-sex-offender-registration-for-gay-sex-with-minors/?fbclid=IwAR01GD5KqvMbEN86gZlDSJzUBYtJMWoLAlBRb7MnhaKmoE1tt1RkadDSPgk.

Brown, Michael. "Are Schumer's Threats against Conservative Justices a Foretaste of What Is to Come?" *AskDrBrown* (Mar 5, 2020) at https://askdrbrown.org/library/are-schumer%E2%80%99s-threats-against-conservative-justices-foretaste.

———. "As We Mindlessly Careen Our Way Down the Slippery Slope." *AskDrBrown* (Feb 17, 2020) at https://askdrbrown.org/library/we-mindlessly-careen-our-way-down-slippery-slope.

———. "Ask the Female Rugby Players if Biological Sex is the Same as Perceived Gender." *AskDrBrown* (Oct 10, 2019) at https://askdrbrown.org/library/ask-female-rugby-players-if-biological-sex-same-perceived-gender.

———. "Did California Legislators Just Vote to Protect (Gay) Adults Who Have Sex with Minors?" *AskDrBrown* (Sept 3, 2020) at https://askdrbrown.org/library/did-california-legislators-just-vote-protect-gay-adults-who-have.

———. *Evangelicalism at the Crossroads: Will We Pass the Trump Test?* Concord, NC: Equal Time, 2020.

———. "The Ghastly Practices of Planned Parenthood." *AskDrBrown* (Oct 21, 2019) at https://askdrbrown.org/library/ghastly-practices-planned-parenthood.

———. *Jezebel's War with America: The Plot to Destroy Our Country and What We Can Do to Turn the Tide.* Lake Mary, FL: Frontline, 2019.

———. "Killing the Unborn, Confessing to Plants." *AskDrBrown* (Sept 20, 2019) at https://askdrbrown.org/library/killing-unborn-confessing-plants.

———. "Mayor Pete, Stop Fostering the Sexualization of Little Children." *AskDrBrown* (Feb 25, 2020) at https://askdrbrown.org/library/mayor-pete-stop-fostering-sexualization-little-children.

———. "My Message to 'Pro-Life Evangelicals for Biden.'" *AskDrBrown* (Oct 6, 2020) at https://askdrbrown.org/library/my-message-%E2%80%98pro-life-evangelicals-biden%E2%80%99.

———. "The New Masculinity: Turning Men into Women." *AskDrBrown* (Nov 2, 2019) at https://askdrbrown.org/library/new-masculinity-turning-men-women.

———. "Pixar Targets Your Children with Their First Gay Lead Character." *AskDrBrown* (Mar 27, 2020) at https://askdrbrown.org/library/pixar-targets-your-children-their-first-gay-lead-character.

———. "Please Governor Cuomo, Do Not Boast Against God." *The Line of Fire* (April 17, 2020) at https://www.youtube.com/watch?v=-MjhaV1mvUI&feature=youtu.be.

———. "Putting the Culture Wars in a Multigenerational Perspective." *AskDrBrown* (Mar 1, 2020) at https://askdrbrown.org/library/putting-culture-wars-multigenerational-perspective.

———. *A Queer Thing Happened to America: And What a Long, Strange Trip It's Been.* Concord, NC: Equal Time, 2011.

———. "The Shocking Difference between Pentecostal Pastors and 'Mainline' Pastors." *AskDrBrown* (Feb 24, 2020) at https://askdrbrown.org/library/shocking-difference-between-pentecostal-pastors-and-%E2%80%98mainline%E2%80%99.

———. "Why Are There So Many Gen Z Atheists?" *AskDrBrown* (Jan 15, 2020) at https://askdrbrown.org/library/why-are-there-so-many-gen-z-atheists.

Brownson, James V. *Bible, Gender, Sexuality: Reframing the Church's Debate on Same-Sex Relationships*. Grand Rapids: Eerdmans, 2013.

Brownstein, Barry. "The Myth that Our Planet Faces an Overpopulation Crisis." *Foundation for Economic Freedom* (Sept 5, 2019) at https://fee.org/articles/the-myth-that-the-world-is-facing-a-population-crisis/?fbclid=IwARoRxgZKUT1Ts McldQC1Pi1TqjD8J4_CND_HVHwNWVsJRVutbiUoMgZl8g.

Burk, Denny. "The Transgender Test." In *Beauty, Order, and Mystery: A Christian Vision of Human Sexuality*, edited by Gerald Hiestand and Todd Wilson, 87–99. Downers Grove, IL: IVP, 2017.

Burk, Denny, and Heath Lambert. *Transforming Homosexuality*. Phillipsburg, NJ: P&R, 2015.

Burpo, Todd, with Lynn Vincent. *Heaven is For Real: A Little Boy's Astounding Story of His Trip to Heaven and Back*. Nashville: Thomas Nelson, 2010.

Butler, Judith. *Gender Trouble: Feminism and the Subversion of Identity*. 1990, New York: Routledge, reprint 2007.

Carr, David M. *The Erotic Word: Sexuality, Spirituality, and the Bible*. Oxford: Oxford University Press, 2003.

Carson, D.A. *Christ and Culture Revisited*. Grand Rapids: Eerdmans, 2008.

Casanova, Amanda. "Hundreds Gather in Orlando to Celebrate Jesus Delivering Them from LGBT Lifestyle." *Christian Headlines* (Sept 16, 2019) at https://www.christianheadlines.com/blog/hundreds-of-people-gather-in-orlando-to-celebrate-jesus-delivering-them-from-lgbt-lifestyle.html.

CBN News. "Former LGBTQers Testify: If You No Longer Want to Be Gay or Transgender, You Don't Have to Be." *CBNNews.com* (Jan 5, 2020) at https://www1.cbn.com/cbnnews/us/2020/january/former-lgbtqers-testify-if-you-no-longer-want-to-be-gay-or-transgender-you-dont-have-to-be?fbclid=IwAR3DK16dkiO-xwXgK-OYOm5kAybx4QBAi2-svRLvcGNsVVv8MHayoj_5Vto.

CDC. "Infant and Maternal Mortality in the United States: 1900–99." *Population and Development Review* 25, no.4 (December 1999) 821–26.

———. "Sexually Transmitted Diseases." *Gay and Bisexual Men's Health* at https://www.cdc.gov/msmhealth/STD.htm.

Chasmar, Jessica. "Gov. Cuomo: "Pro-Life, Pro-Gun Conservatives 'Have No Place' in New York." *The Washington Times* (Jan 19, 2014) at https://www.washingtontimes.com/news/2014/jan/19/gov-cuomo-pro-life-conservatives-have-no-place-new/.

Chen, Lauren. "VICE Pushes to 'Destigmatize' Pedophilia" 'It Would Be Very, Very, Inhuman to Judge Such a Person.'" *The Blaze* (Sept 3, 2019) at https://www.theblaze.com/lauren-chen/normalizing-pedopilia?utm_content=bufferb8ec8&utm_medium=referral&utm_source=facebook&utm_campaign=fb-theblaze&fbclid=IwAR2LjPSmOmE6-wngqVqNmboDtwbPM9IbRuWUeQjriAY Ak9g8nGynKytf9LM.

Chesterton, G.K. *The Thing*. http://www.gkc.org.uk/gkc/books/The_Thing.txt.

Chung, Gabrielle. "HGTV Features Its First-ever Throuple on *House Hunters*: 'Representation Matters.'" *People* (Feb 13, 2020) at https://people.com/home/hgtv-features-first-throuple-on-house-hunters/?utm_source=twitter.com&utm_medium=social&utm_campaign=social-button-sharing.

Claiborne, Shane. "Evangelicalism must be Born Again." In *Still Evangelical?: Insiders Reconsider Political, Social, and Theological Meaning*, edited by Mark Labberton, 153–72. Downers Grove: IVP, 2018.

CNN News Source. "Transgender Character Coming to Marvel Universe." *News Channel 8* (Jan 1, 2020) at https://www.wfla.com/entertainment-news/transgender-character-coming-to-marvel-universe/?fbclid=IwAR2cT_b7ZJTe9VlWUmgKI7KOt-RTxohKWDyO1yLcJOFvWO9aKcuOlZKZ2EA.

Collins, John J. *What are Biblical Values? What the Bible Says on Key Ethical Issues*. New Haven: Yale University Press, 2019.

Compton, Julie. "'Boy or Girl?' Parents Raising 'Theybies' Let Kids Decide." *NBC News* (July 19, 2018) at https://www.nbcnews.com/feature/nbc-out/boy-or-girl-parents-raising-theybies-let-kids-decide-n891836.

Congdon, Robert N. "Exodus 21:22–25 and the Abortion Debate." *BSac* 146.582 (1989) 132–47.

Congress.Gov. "S.2008-Therapuetic Fraud Prevention Act 2019," at https://www.congress.gov/bill/116th-congress/senate-bill/2008/text.

Coogan, Michael. *God & Sex: What the Bible Really Says*. New York: Hatchet Book Group, 2010.

Copan, Paul. *Is God a Moral Monster? Making Sense of the Old Testament God*. Grand Rapids: Baker, 2011.

Copan, Paul, and Matthew Flannagan. *Did God Really Command Genocide? Coming to Terms with the Justice of God*. Grand Rapids: Baker, 2014.

Cox, Daniel, and Amelia Thomson-DeVeaux. "Millennials Are Leaving Religion and Are Not Coming Back." *FiveThirtyEight* (Dec 12, 2019) at https://fivethirtyeight.com/features/millennials-are-leaving-religion-and-not-coming-back/?fbclid=IwAR0QtakDjYsa4hZ2zDTNglvSMNSxV4DeLiDG03Ef92VQkUf5OxmwWiqqZYo&fbclid=IwAR0QtakDjYsa4hZ2zDTNglvSMNSxV4DeLiDG03Ef92VQkUf5OxmwWiqqZYo&fbclid=IwAR3EhA628OprmQAODcqtGvCBaJs1NRXJ6Wn5A9uWARE1XGNFUthoWvwoKa8&fbclid=IwAR2oLXU905GpFLflt5eR4XQoWaJ2bgYdOBVwrYyno-XN9e7wPBeAuEk2Bu8.

Cox, Harvey. *The Secular City*. New York: Macmillan, 1966.

Coyle, Jake. "With a Gay Protagonist Pixar Short 'Out' Makes History." *Associated Press* (May 28, 2020) at https://www.ksat.com/entertainment/2020/05/28/with-a-gay-protagonist-pixar-short-out-makes-history/.

Crawford, Timothy G. *Blessing and Curse in Syro-Palestinian Inscriptions of the Iron Age*. American University Studies 7. Theology and Religion 120. New York: Peter Lang, 1992.

Cullen, Tom. "Convicted of Sex Crimes as a Man, Felon No Longer Deemed Threat because of Gender Change." *Des Moines Register* (Jan 16, 2020) at https://www.desmoinesregister.com/story/news/crime-and-courts/2020/01/16/felon-no-longer-deemed-threat-after-sex-reassignment-treatment/4479275002/.

Curley, Christine, and Brian Neil Peterson. "Eve's Curse Revisited: An Increase of "Sorrowful Conceptions." *BBR* 26, no.2 (2016) 1–16.

D'Souza, Dinesh. *Illiberal Education: The Politics of Race and Sex on Campus*. 2nd ed. New York: Vintage, 1992.

Dallas, Joe. *The Gay Gospel: How Pro-Gay Advocates Misread the Bible*. 1996, Eugene, OR: Harvest House, reprint 2007.

Dalrymple, Timothy. "The Flag in the Whirlwind: An Update from CT's President." *Christianity Today* (Dec 22, 2019) at https://www.christianitytoday.com/ct/2019/december-web-only/trump-evangelicals-editorial-christianity-today-president.html?fbclid=IwAR2Urw5tb_9vqo3KfKZR4WorKpWGmzYF9-KvoMpgGOBppdf_2R6B_lz8uDM.

Day, Nate. "'Onward' Movie to Feature Disney's First Openly LGBTQ Animated Character, Voiced by Lena Waithe." *Fox News* (Feb 23, 2020) at https://www.foxnews.com/entertainment/onward-movie-feature-lgbtq-animated-character-lena-waithe.

———. "Rickie Gervais Slams Outcry over Transgender Jokes: 'The More People Get Offended . . . the Funnier I find It." *Fox News* (Dec 20, 2019) at https://www.foxnews.com/entertainment/ricky-gervais-slams-outcry-over-transgender-jokes.

DeFranza, Megan. "Journeying from the Bible to Christian Ethics in Search of Common Ground." In *Two Views on Homosexuality, the Bible, and the Church*, edited by Preston Sprinkle, 69–111. Grand Rapids: Zondervan, 2016.

———. *Sex Difference in Christian Theology: Male, Female, and Intersex in the Image of God*. Grand Rapids: Eerdmans, 2015.

Dimock, Michael. "Defining Generations: Where Millennials End and Generation Z Begins." *Pew Research Center* (Jan 17, 2019) at https://www.pewresearch.org/fact-tank/2019/01/17/where-millennials-end-and-generation-z-begins/.

Dirks, Paul. "Transition as Treatment: The Best Studies Show the Worst Outcomes." *Public Discourse The Journal of the Witherspoon Institute* (Feb 16, 2020) at https://www.thepublicdiscourse.com/2020/02/60143/?_hsenc=p2ANqtz-8K-sUqE5lNJia9S8BeO91IE0Rqq7hHw40V6vpYKBsUhxq4kH5gOmruoYN_xcMPhntcCDDkv1SqGWjHAPkcudH7FURjkw&_hsmi=84118592&fbclid=IwAR1XgD7H3ssXiMn9ZbqfSUPg8QFEZWjLmjBHvsIz8Zpp9OTu366Rx-278G8.

Dobson, James. "Dr. James Dobson Issued Today the Following Statement, As a Private Citizen, to the Christian Community." *Openheaven.com* (Dec 21, 2019) at https://www.openheaven.com/2019/12/21/dr-james-dobson-issued-today-the-following-statement-as-a-private-citizen-to-the-christian-community-by-james-dobson-ph-d/?fbclid=IwAR1ujBEzEcMUaKOl_GkdoJMqlxaVCxhmFQwXOHWUnmXpYS4J5D6YHCNKpSo.

Dorman, Sam. "ACLU Calls for Tampons in Men's Rooms in Order to Achieve 'Menstrual Equality." *Fox News* (Dec 18, 2019) at https://www.foxnews.com/us/aclu-tampons-mens-room-menstrual-equity.

———. "Testimony from Planned Parenthood, Tissue Procurer Sheds Light on Babies Born Alive, with Beating Hearts." *Fox News* (July 1, 2020) at https://www.foxnews.com/us/planned-parenthood-tissue-procurer-abortion-clinic-testimony.

Driver, G.R., and John C. Miles. *The Assyrian Laws*. Oxford: Clarendon, 1935.

Dugan, Andrew. "U.S. Divorce Rate Dips, But Moral Acceptability Hits New High." *Gallup* (July 7, 2017) at https://news.gallup.com/poll/213677/divorce-rate-dips-moral-acceptability-hits-new-high.aspx.

Dumas, Breck. "Netflix Accused of Sexualizing Children with Movie about Kids Who Embrace 'Sensual Dance." *The Blaze* (Aug 19, 2020) at https://www.theblaze.com/news/netflix-cuties-accused-sexualizing-children?utm_content=bufferdff90&utm_medium=referral&utm_source=facebook&utm_campaign=fb-glennbeck&fbclid=IwAR3hByIPNnCHkZ-vQYxx5x3GJWKsauvx1Qtshj2HDKgum3Cf_qM4L14Pq74.

Durston Kirk. "Why Sexual Morality May Be Far More Important Than You Ever Thought." *Quest: Thoughts about God, Truth, and Beauty* (Dec 1, 2019) at https://www.kirkdurston.com/blog/unwin?fbclid=IwAR28PsbVhFoivg-TDOc9R-3Ukgd18USh8oat5OhcaQtTMc-dtrbmsSIWC3U.

Eastman, John. "What Does Separation of Church and State Mean?" *PragerU* (May 25, 2020) at https://www.facebook.com/prageru/videos/936990186742707/UzpfSTEyODMzNTg4Mzk6MTAyMjI1NDY1MDgwNzMxMTU/.

Ellis, John M. *The Breakdown of Higher Education: How It Happened, the Damage It Does, & What Can Be Done*. New York: Encounter, 2020.

Ertelt, Steven. "Cecile Richards: You Can't Be a Democrat if You Don't Support Abortion. 'It's Non-Negotiable.'" *LifeNews.com* (Aug 2, 2017) at https://www.lifenews.com/2017/08/02/cecile-richards-you-cant-be-a-democrat-if-you-dont-support-abortion-its-non-negotiable/?fbclid=IwAR1ThX1vqjno4JBtzGmOlsO46hkmipasQH7usAx8DINtcg2_WIsdZWibvII#.XrNMhItge2E.facebook.

Fea, John. *Believe Me: The Evangelical Road to Donald Trump*. Grand Rapids: Eerdmans, 2018.

Feldhahn, Shaunti, and Tally Whitehead. *The Good News about Marriage: Debunking Discouraging Myths about Marriage and Divorce*. Colorado Springs, CO: Multnomah, 2014.

Fingerhut, Hannah. "About Seven-In-Ten Americans Oppose Overturning Roe v. Wade." *Pew Research Center* (Jan 3, 2017) at https://www.pewresearch.org/fact-tank/2017/01/03/about-seven-in-ten-americans-oppose-overturning-roe-v-wade/.

Floyd, Ronnie W. *The Gay Agenda: It's Dividing the Family, the Church, and a Nation*. Green Forest, AR: New Leaf, 2004.

Ford, Adam. "The Leading Cause of Death Globally in 2020 Was Abortion . . . Over 42 Million People Killed." *Not the Bee* (Jan 1, 2021) at https://notthebee.com/article/the-leading-cause-of-death-in-2020-was-abortion.

Fortson III, S. Donald, and Rollin G. Grams. *Unchanging Witness: The Consistent Christian Teaching on Homosexuality in Scripture and Tradition*. Nashville: Broadman & Holman, 2016.

Foust, Michael. "Christianity Today Calls for Reparations from Churches: 'Repentance Is Not Enough.'" *Christian Headlines* (June 11, 2020) at https://www.christianheadlines.com/contributors/michael-foust/christianity-today-calls-for-reparations-from-churches-repentance-is-not-enough.html.

Fox News. "New Jersey Man Allegedly Threatened Farmers Who Denied Him Sex with Animals." *New York Post* (Oct 11, 2019) at https://www.foxnews.com/us/new-jersey-man-allegedly-threatened-farmers-who-denied-him-sex-with-animals.

Fox, Megan. "Exposed: Planned Parenthood's Degenerate 'Comprehensive Sex Education' Lesson Plans." *PJ Media* (Apr 6, 2018) at https://pjmedia.com/parenting/planned-parenthoods-degenerate-comprehensive-sex-education-lesson-plans-exposed/?fbclid=IwAR1pY5l5JupLcYg4aSu5KZCtQlmhDmDMcIiAk2J6xHrIdEUqEYS42DKoTqI.

Franke, John, and Stanley Grenz. *Beyond Foundationalism: Shaping Theology in a Postmodern Context*. Louisville, KY: Westminster John Knox, 2001.

Freiburger, Calvin. "Warren Declares 'Gender-nonconforming' Americans the 'Backbone of Our Democracy.'" *LifeSite News* (Nov 12, 2019) at https://www.lifesitenews.com/news/warren-declares-gender-nonconforming-americans-the-backbone-of-our-democracy.

Fulp, Daryl. "It's Not Our 'Christian Responsibility' to be Politically Engaged." *ChurchLeaders* (Nov 6, 2018) at https://churchleaders.com/pastors/pastor-articles/336986-what-does-the-bble-say-about-politics-its-not-our-christian-responsibility-to-be-politically-engaged.html?utm_source=outreach-cl-daily-nl&utm_medium=email&utm_content=text-link&utm_campaign=cl-daily-nl&maropost_id=&mpweb=256-8998547-742444023.

Gagnon, Robert A.J. *The Bible and Homosexual Practice: Texts and Hermeneutics*. Nashville, TN: Abingdon, 2001.

Gaines, Steve. "An Appeal to Rightly Apply 2 Chronicles 7:14." *ChurchLeaders* (July 4, 2020) at https://churchleaders.com/pastors/pastor-articles/306103-an-appeal-to-rightly-apply-2-chronicles-714-steve-gaines.html?utm_source=outreach-cl-daily-nl&utm_medium=email&utm_content=text-link&utm_campaign=cl-daily-nl&maropost_id=&mpweb=256-8982985-742444023.

Galli, Mark. "Looking for Unity in All the Wrong Places." In *Still Evangelical?: Insiders Reconsider Political, Social, and Theological Meaning*, edited by Mark Labberton, 138–52. Downers Grove: IVP, 2018.

———. "Trump Should Be Removed from Office." *Christianity Today* (Dec 19, 2019) at https://www.christianitytoday.com/ct/2019/december-web-only/trump-should-be-removed-from-office.html.

Gallup. "Gay and Lesbian Rights." at https://news.gallup.com/poll/1651/gay-lesbian-rights.aspx.

Gane, Roy E. *Old Testament Law for Christians: Original Context and Enduring Application*. Grand Rapids: Baker, 2017.

Gardner, R.F.R. *Abortion: The Personal Dilemma*. Grand Rapids: Eerdmans, 1972.

Garrett, Duane. *Proverbs, Ecclesiastes, Song of Songs*. NAC 14. Nashville, TN: Broadman, 1993.

Gaydos, Ryan. "US Women Soccer Stars Ali Krieger and Ashlyn Harris Get Married in Miami." *Fox News* (Dec 29, 2019) at https://www.foxnews.com/sports/us-women-soccer-stars-ali-krieger-ashlyn-harris-married.

Gaynor, Gerren Keith. "Hallmark Pulls Zola Commercial of Brides Kissing after Conservative Group Calls for Boycott." *Fox News* (Dec 14, 2019) at https://www.foxnews.com/lifestyle/hallmark-pulls-zola-commercial-of-brides-kissing.

Gearty, Robert. "Massachusetts Professor Accused of Trying to Kill Faculty Colleague in Christmas Eve Attack." *Fox News* (Jan 5, 2020) at https://www.foxnews.com/us/massachusetts-professor-accused-of-trying-to-kill-faculty-colleague-in-christmas-eve-attack.

Genovese, Daniella. "BP Exec: Climate Change Worries Caused Daughter's Friends to Take Antidepressants." *Fox News* (Dec 30, 2019) at https://www.foxbusiness.com/business-leaders/bp-ceo-bob-dudley-climate-change-antidepressants.

Ghianni, Tim. "Vanderbilt Allows Students to Observe Wiccan Holidays." *Reuters* (Aug 19, 2011) at https://www.reuters.com/article/us-wiccan-religion-tennessee/vanderbilt-allows-students-to-observe-wiccan-holidays-idUSTRE77I4VK20110819.

Ginsberg, Allan. "The Allan Ginsberg Project." (Feb 14, 2016) at https://allenginsberg.org/2016/02/ginsbergpodhoretz/.

Goldingay, John. *Old Testament Theology: Israel's Gospel*. Downers Grove, IL: IVP, 2003.

Good Morning Britain. "Do Transgender Athletes Have an Advantage in Female Sporting Events?" (Mar 4, 2019) at https://www.youtube.com/watch?v=I75kfAVF64A&feature=share&fbclid=IwAR0HVIdDDicJgj6SshAhHeVjshcUFHJ_MvAtV7ppU9-wve03qADNxGNOdoY.

———. "Piers Debates Transgender Activist Over Genderless Acting Awards." (May 9, 2017) at https://www.youtube.com/watch?v=CaO-krc5ZRM&feature=share&fbclid=IwAR0s6XUoNnkIuBzwx4SfWNqrqxgeh_dC9n5hMh7DfxR9BsGBNGdyc_t4CpI.

Grabowski, John S. *Sex and Virtue: An Introduction to Sexual Ethics*. Washington, DC: The Catholic University of America Press, 2003.

Grant, James. "Outrage as Lady Collin Claims Soliciting Sex from minors 'Is Not the Same as Paedophilia' in Good Morning Interview on Prince Andrew." *DailyMail.com* (Nov 18, 2019) at https://www.dailymail.co.uk/news/article-7698157/Lady-Colin-Campbell-claims-soliciting-sex-minors-not-paedophilia.html?fbclid=IwAR0oWdZRDPSsbMiQi-bGDXcuVEcJKPtcOWZQ1vxVo8tvO83_S9QcNeMHzCI.

Gray, Frances. "Original Habitation: Pregnant Flesh as Absolute Hospitality." In *Coming to Life: Philosophies of Pregnancy, Childbirth, and Mothering*, edited by Sarah LaChance Adams and Caroline R. Lundquist, 71–87. New York: Fordham University Press, 2013.

Green, Lisa Cannon. "New Survey: Women Go Silently from Church to Abortion Clinic." *Care Net* (Nov 23, 2015) at www.care-net.org/churches-blog/new-survey-women-go-silently-from-church-to-abortion-clinic.

Grudem, Wayne. *Politics According to the Bible*. Grand Rapids: Zondervan, 2010.

———. "A Respectful Response to My Friend John Piper about Voting for Trump." *Voices: The Christian Post* (Oct 27, 2020) at https://www.christianpost.com/voices/a-response-to-my-friend-john-piper-about-voting-for-trump.html?fbclid=IwAR2iLBQCvlt4dACopLkHZGHpKnvToAN7ganhq5e76WgmY2HSE41uHMuViys.

———. "Trump Should Not Be Removed from Office: A Response to Mark Galli and Christianity Today." *Townhall* (Dec 30, 2019) at https://townhall.com/columnists/waynegrudem/2019/12/30/trump-should-not-be-removed-from-office-a-response-to-mark-galli-and-christianity-today-n2558657?fbclid=IwAR1x-PFH2m2d—A-JV8LbVS6MxrCj1dcAcLewPqAnaFoYHk6aVOjvGnT2tM.

Guinness, Os. *Impossible People: Christian Courage and the Struggle for the Soul of Civilization*. Downers Grove, IL: IVP, 2016.

Gushee, David P. *After Evangelicalism: The Path to a New Christianity*. Louisville, KY: Westminster John Knox, 2020.

———. et al. *Changing Our Mind*. 2nd ed. Canton, MI: Read the Spirit, 2015.

———. *Getting Marriage Right: Realistic Counsel for Saving and Strengthening Relationships*. Grand Rapids: Baker, 2004.

———. *Still Christian: Following Jesus Out of American Evangelicalism*. Louisville, KY: Westminster John Knox, 2017.

———. *The Sacredness of Human Life: Why an Ancient Biblical Vision Is Key to the World's Future*. Grand Rapids: Eerdmans, 2013.

Habel, Norman C. ed. *Readings from the Perspective of the Earth*. Sheffield: Sheffield, 2000.

Habel, Norman C., and Shirley Wurst eds. *The Earth Story in Genesis*. Sheffield: Sheffield, 2000.

Halon, Yael. "Buffalo School Teaching Students to Question Nuclear Family as Part of BLM-integrated Curriculum." *Fox News* (Sept 18, 2020) at https://www.foxnews.com/media/buffalo-public-school-teaching-elementary-students-to-question-nuclear-family-as-part-of-blm-integrated-curriculum-tucker.

Hamilton, Graeme. "Terminally Transsexual: Concerns Raised over Belgian Euthanized after Botched Sex Change." *National Post* (Nov 22, 2013) at https://nationalpost.com/news/canada/terminally-transsexual-concerns-raised-over-belgian-euthanized-after-botched-sex-change.

Hammer, Josh. "Hammer: Remember Those Who Told Us Gay Marriage Would Not Lead to Polyamory: They Were Wrong." *The Daily Wire* (Oct 25, 2019) at https://www.dailywire.com/news/hammer-remember-those-who-told-us-gay-marriage-would-not-lead-to-polyamory-they-were-wrong?utm_source=facebook&utm_medium=social&utm_campaign=mattwalsh&fbclid=IwAR3GIvT39WATgMZ2n340A7ugtN4buiaUWl9ruieEPg7swbYNA_280YCudlk.

Hardin, Garrett. "Abortion or Compulsory Pregnancy." *Journal of Marriage and Family* 30, no.2 (May 1968) 246–51.

Harland, P.J. "Menswear and Womenswear: A Study in Deuteronomy 22:5." *ExpTim* 110, no. 3 (1998) 73–76.

Harper, Lisa Sharon. "Will Evangelicalism Surrender?" In *Still Evangelical?: Insiders Reconsider Political, Social, and Theological Meaning*, edited by Mark Labberton, 19–30. Downers Grove: IVP, 2018.

Hartline, Jennifer. "It's Not Kavanaugh. It's Roe." *The Stream* (Sept 20, 2019) at https://stream.org/not-kavanaugh-roe/.

Hauerwas, Stanley. *War and the American Difference: Theological Reflections on Violence and National Identity*. Grand Rapids: Baker, 2011.

Heck, Peter. "California Will Now House Prisoners according to Gender Identity Instead of Biological Sex." *Disrn* (Sept 28, 2020) at https://disrn.com/news/california-will-now-house-prisoners-according-to-gender-identity-instead-of-biological-sex?fbclid=IwAR3IWNw9yQ8hAsbjx9n3UOPpYoiK1Kd-XgZ37Lh9SP4hgf3_VG1Sxxs8PIU.

Hendricks, Jaclyn. "Hunky In-demand Model Laith Ashley Was Born a Girl." *News.comau* (Mar 22, 2016) at https://www.news.com.au/entertainment/celebrity-life/hunky-indemand-model-laith-ashley-was-born-a-girl/news-story/16b58b33ed889af184ef87903f2d7c7a.

Hiestand, Gerald. "Put Pain Like that Beyond My Power: A Christocentric Theodicy with Respect to the Inequality of Male and Female Power." In *Beauty, Order, and Mystery: A Christian Vision of Human Sexuality*, edited by Gerald Hiestand and Todd Wilson, 101–18. Downers Grove, IL: IVP, 2017.

Hill, Wesley. "How Should Gay Christians Love?" In *Beauty, Order, and Mystery: A Christian Vision of Human Sexuality*, edited by Gerald Hiestand and Todd Wilson, 31–43. Downers Grove, IL: IVP, 2017.

History.com Editors. "Gay Marriage." *History* (June 2, 2020) at https://www.history.com/topics/gay-rights/gay-marriage.

Hodges, Mark. "Homosexuals Face Greater Health Risks than Heterosexuals: Study." *LifeSite News* (June 30, 2016) at https://www.lifesitenews.com/news/homosexuals-face-greater-health-risks-than-heterosexuals-study.

Hoffman, David. "Christians are Being Silenced: Pastor Arrested after Preaching Love in LGBTQ Neighborhood." *Voices: The Christian Post* (June 8, 2019) at https://www.christianpost.com/voice/christians-silenced-pastor-arrested-preaching-love-lgbt-neighborhood.html.

Hoffmeier, James K. "Abortion and the Old Testament Law." In *Abortion: A Christian Understanding and Response,* edited by James K. Hoffmeier, 49–63. Grand Rapids: Baker, 1987.

———. *The Immigration Crisis: Immigrants, Aliens, and the Bible.* Wheaton, IL: Crossway, 2009.

Holmes, David L. *The Faith of the Founding Fathers.* Oxford: Oxford University Press, 2006.

Horrell, David G. *The Bible and the Environment: Towards a Critical Ecological Biblical Theology.* London: Routledge, 2010.

Irvine, Spencer. "Self-Identifying Marxist Professors Outnumber Conservatives as College Professors." *Accuracy in Academia* (June 15, 2016) at https://www.academia.org/self-identifying-marxist-professors-outnumber-conservatives-as-college-professors/.

Isom, Mo. *Sex, Jesus, and the Conversations the Church Forgot.* Grand Rapids: Baker, 2018.

Jackson, Jesse T. "12,000+ Sign Petition to Remove Franklin Graham from Samaritan's Purse." *ChurchLeaders* (Sept 3, 2020) at https://churchleaders.com/news/381710-petition-remove-franklin-graham-samaritans-purse.html?utm_source=cl-sundaysend-nl&utm_medium=email&utm_content=text-link&utm_campaign=cl-sundaysend-nl20200906&maropost_id=742444023&mpweb=256–9073488-742444023.

———. "Tim Keller Sparks Twitter Debate Over Political Comments." *ChurchLeaders* (Sept 22, 2020) at https://churchleaders.com/news/382650-tim-keller-sparks-twitter-debate-over-political-comments.html?utm_source=outreach-cl-daily-nl&utm_medium=email&utm_content=text-link&utm_campaign=cl-daily-nl&maropost_id=&mpweb=256–9099152-742444023.

Jacobs, Emily. "9-year-old Boy Asks Pete Buttigieg for Help Coming Out as Gay at Rally." *New York Post* (Feb 24, 2020) at https://nypost.com/2020/02/24/9-year-old-boy-asks-pete-buttigieg-for-help-coming-out-as-gay-at-rally/.

Jackson, Jesse T. "Michigan Pastor Leaves Church over Congregation's Support of Trump." *ChurchLeaders* (Oct 21, 2020) at https://churchleaders.com/news/384204-michigan-pastor-leaves-church-over-congregations-support-of-trump.html?utm_source=cl-fridayweeklysend-nl&utm_medium=email&utm_content=text-link&utm_campaign=cl-fridayweeklysend-nl20201023&maropost_id=742444023&mpweb=256–9134864-742444023.

Jin, Fengyi, et al. "Trends in Anal Cancer in Australia, 1982–2005." *Vaccine* 29 (2011) 2322–27.

Johnson, Luke Timothy. "Homosexuality and the Church." *Commonweal* (June 11, 2007) at https://www.commonwealmagazine.org/homosexuality-church-0.

Johnson, William Stacy. *A Time to Embrace: Same-Sex Relationships in Religion, Law, and Politics.* 2nd ed. Grand Rapids: Eerdmans, 2012.

Jones, Beth Felker. "Embodied from Creation Through Redemption: Placing Gender and Sexuality in Theological Context." In *Beauty, Order, and Mystery: A Christian Vision of Human Sexuality,* edited by Gerald Hiestand and Todd Wilson, 21–30. Downers Grove, IL: IVP, 2017.

Kaiser, Walter Jr. *Toward Old Testament Ethics.* Grand Rapids: Zondervan, 1991.

Kamitsuka, Margaret D. *Abortion and the Christian Tradition: A Pro-Choice Theological Ethic.* Louisville, KY: Westminster John Knox, 2019.

Kass, Leon R. "Regarding Daughters and Sisters: The Rape of Dinah." *Commentary* 93, no.4 (1992) 29–38.
Kellstedt, Lyman A. "Abortion and the Political Process." In *Abortion: A Christian Understanding and Response*, edited by James K. Hoffmeier, 195–217. Grand Rapids: Baker, 1987.
Kelly, Stewart E., and James K. Dew Jr. *Understanding Postmodernism: A Christian Perspective*. Downers Grove, IL: IVP, 2017.
Kiley, Brendan. "Washington Becomes First State to Legalize Human Composting." *The Seattle Times* (May 21, 2019) at https://www.seattletimes.com/seattle-news/washington-becomes-first-state-to-legalize-human-composting/.
King, L. W. ed. *Babylonian Boundary-Stones and Memorial-Tablets in the British Museum*. London: British Museum, 1912.
Kirk, Marshall, and Hunter Madsen. *After the Ball: How America Will Conquer Its Fear and Hatred of Gays in the '90s*. New York: Doubleday, 1989.
Kline, Meredith G. "Lex Talionis and the Human Fetus." *JETS* 20, no.3 (1977) 193–201.
Knust, Jennifer Wright. *Unprotected Texts: The Bible's Surprising Contradictions about Sex and Desire*. New York: HarperOne, 2011.
Kreider, Rose M. "Increase in Opposite-sex Cohabiting Couples from 2009 to 2010 in the Annual Social and Economic Supplement (ASEC) to the Current Population Survey (CPS)." *Housing and Household Economics Division* (Sept 15, 2010) 1–19 at https://www.census.gov/content/dam/Census/library/working-papers/2010/demo/inc-opp-sex-2009-to-2010.pdf.
Labberton, Mark. "Introduction: Still Evangelical?" In *Still Evangelical?: Insiders Reconsider Political, Social, and Theological Meaning*, edited by Mark Labberton, 1–17. Downers Grove: IVP, 2018.
Lamm, Bri. "New California Bill Would Lower Penalties for Adults Who Have Sex with a Minor." *ChurchLeaders* (Sept 3, 2020) at https://churchleaders.com/news/381746-new-california-bill-would-lower-penalties-for-adults-who-have-sex-with-a-minor.html?utm_source=outreach-cl-daily-nl&utm_medium=email&utm_content=text-link&utm_campaign=cl-daily-nl&maropost_id=&mpweb=256-9072111-742444023.
Lapin, Tamar. "Sports Illustrated Model-Turned History Teacher Accused of Sleeping with Students." *Fox News* (Dec 3, 2019) at https://www.foxnews.com/entertainment/sports-illustrated-model-history-teacher-accused-sexual-misconduct.
Lawrence, Jenna. "AEI Panel: Marxists Outnumber Conservatives in Social Sciences." *Campus Reform* (June 13, 2016) at https://www.campusreform.org/?ID=7678.
Lazar, Shira. "Sologamy: People Who Marry Themselves." (May 15, 2017) at https://www.youtube.com/watch?v=YiOnH4I6CCY.
Leahy, Michael Patrick. "Evangelical Leaders Confront Christianity Today for Magazine's 'Entirely Partisan, Legally Dubious' Support for Trump Impeachment." *Breitbart* (Dec 22, 2019) at https://www.breitbart.com/politics/2019/12/22/evangelical-leaders-confront-christianity-today-for-magazines-entirely-partisan-legally-dubious-support-for-trump-impeachment/?fbclid=IwAR3HkbZZ7l9oRUOI-ZReGtYqnb9RjuPeTjMM3vhUy-XU8lucrqe7Co5CfGs.
Lee, Kurtis. "Here is How the Boy Scouts Has Evolved on Social Issues over the Years." *Los Angeles Times* (Feb 5, 2017) at https://www.latimes.com/nation/la-na-boy-scouts-evolution-2017-story.html.

Levering, Matthew. "Thomas Aquinas on Sexual Ethics." In *Beauty, Order, and Mystery: A Christian Vision of Human Sexuality*, edited by Gerald Hiestand and Todd Wilson, 165–80. Downers Grove, IL: IVP, 2017.

Levin, Dan. "North Carolina Reaches Settlement on 'Bathroom' Bill." *The New York Times* (July 23, 2019) at https://www.nytimes.com/2019/07/23/us/north-carolina-transgender-bathrooms.html.

LifeSiteNews. "Drag Queen on 'Story Hour': 'We're Grooming Next Generation.'" *YouTube* (Nov 27, 2018) at https://www.youtube.com/watch?v=899uwvQE7Ic&feature=youtu.be.

Lindsay, James. "Deep Dive Into 'Critical Social Justice' & How It Took Over the Humanities." *YouTube* (Mar 24, 2020) at https://www.youtube.com/watch?v=8N55gFjg4yg&feature=youtu.be&fbclid=IwARoje5WUDq5y6DWgwTQenSpi3zo6n9zSG2S3iu4vLTIkgHQRdb-qhh2x2R8.

Lindsay, James, and Michael O'Fallon, "Grievance Scholars Expose the Trojan Horse of Social Justice in Faith and Academics." *Sovereign Nations* (Aug 9, 2019) at https://sovereignnations.com/2019/08/09/grievance-scholars-trojan-horse-social-justice-faith-academics/?fbclid=IwAR2Nd7L8sL8VkglzxIJ106le9zRxiY9XXTMn9bP5_G7GlhLDh9PumSikOQw.

Lipka, Michael. "Muslims and Islam: Key Findings in the U.S. and around the World." *Pew Research Center* (Aug 9, 2017) at https://www.pewresearch.org/fact-tank/2017/08/09/muslims-and-islam-key-findings-in-the-u-s-and-around-the-world/.

Loader, William. "Homosexuality and the Bible." In *Two Views on Homosexuality, the Bible, and the Church*, edited by Preston Sprinkle, 17–48. Grand Rapids: Zondervan, 2016.

Loewenstamm, Samuel E. "Exodus 21:22–25." *VT* 27, no.3 (1977) 352–60.

Lomborg, Bjorn. *The Skeptical Environmentalist: Measuring the Real State of the World*. Cambridge: Cambridge University Press, 2001.

Longman III, Tremper. *The Bible and the Ballot: Using Scripture in Political Decisions*. Grand Rapids: Eerdmans, 2020.

MacArthur, John. *Why Government Can't Save You: An Alternative to Political Activism*. Grand Rapids: Zondervan, 2000.

Martin, Stephanie. "Barna: This Is the Largest Generation Gap We've Seen in 7 Decades." *ChurchLeaders* (Sept 23, 2020) at https://churchleaders.com/news/382699-barna-this-is-the-largest-generation-gap-weve-seen-in-7-decades.html?utm_source=cl-fridayweeklysend-nl&utm_medium=email&utm_content=text-link&utm_campaign=cl-fridayweeklysend-nl20200925&maropost_id=742444023&mpweb=256-9100673-742444023.

———. "Evangelical Leaders React to Mohler Supporting Trump." *ChurchLeaders* (April 17, 2020) at https://churchleaders.com/news/374422-evangelical-leaders-react-to-mohler-supporting-trump.html/2.

———. "Heated CRT/I Debate Overshadowing SBC's Reconciliation Sunday." *ChurchLeaders* (Feb 6, 2020) at https://churchleaders.com/news/370437-critical-race-theory-racial-reconciliation-sunday.html.

———. "Majority of Protestant Pastors Believe Climate Change is Human-Caused." *ChurchLeaders* (April 20, 2020) at https://churchleaders.com/news/374687-earth-day-2020-majority-of-protestant-pastors-believe-climate-change-is-man-made.html.

———. "New Conservative Resurgence Seeks to Correct Liberal 'Drift' in SBC." *ChurchLeaders* (Feb 14, 2020) at https://churchleaders.com/news/370997-new-conservative-resurgence-seeks-to-prevent-liberal-drift-in-sbc.html.

———. "UK Launches Review of Controversial Gender-Identity Treatment." *ChurchLeaders* (Sept 25, 2020) at https://churchleaders.com/news/382831-uk-launches-review-of-controversial-gender-identity-treatment.html?utm_source=outreach-cl-daily-nl&utm_medium=email&utm_content=text-link&utm_campaign=cl-daily-nl&maropost_id=&mpweb=256-9102216-742444023.

Mason, Matthew. "The Wounded It Heals: Gender Dysphoria and the Resurrection of the Body." In *Beauty, Order, and Mystery: A Christian Vision of Human Sexuality*, edited by Gerald Hiestand and Todd Wilson, 135–47. Downers Grove, IL: IVP, 2017.

McCarthy, Tyler. "Netflix Comedy Sees 1 Million Petition for its Removal for Offending Christians with Depiction of Jesus as Gay." *Fox News* (Dec 13, 2019) at https://www.foxnews.com/entertainment/netflix-comedy-1-million-petition-removal-offending-christians-jesus-gay.

———. "'Survivor' Contestants Admit They Exaggerated Claims of 'Inappropriate Touching' to Win the Game." *Fox News* (Nov 14, 2019) at https://www.foxnews.com/entertainment/survivor-contestants-exaggerated-inappropriate-touching-win-game.

McKee, Jonathan. "Mom, I Want to be a She." *ChurchLeaders* (Feb 26, 2020) at https://churchleaders.com/youth/youth-leaders-articles/371417-mom-i-want-to-be-a-she.html?utm_source=outreach-cl-daily-nl&utm_medium=email&utm_content=text-link&utm_campaign=cl-daily-nl&maropost_id=&mpweb=256-8639495-742444023.

McLean, Dorothy Cummings. "TEDx Speaker: 'Pedophilia is an Unchangeable Sexual Orientation,' 'Anyone' Could Be Born that Way." *LifeSite News* (July 18, 2018) at https://www.lifesitenews.com/news/ted-speaker-pedophilia-is-an-unchangeable-sexual-orientation-anyone-could-b.

McNeill, John J. *Sex as God Intended: A Reflection on Human Sexuality as Play*. Maple Shade, NJ: Lethe, 2008.

Meacham, John. *American Gospel: God, the Founding Fathers, and the Making of a Nation*. New York: Random House, 2006.

Meuhlenberg, Bill. "The Terrorism of Trans Tyranny." *Culture Watch* (Dec 13, 2018) at http://billmuehlenberg.com/2018/12/13/the-terrorism-of-trans-tyranny/.

Michael, Robert T., John H. Gagnon, Edward O. Laumann, and Gina Kolata. *Sex in America: A Definitive Survey*. Boston, MA: Little, Brown and Co., 1994.

Miles, Frank. "Nearly 200 Evangelical Leaders Condemn Christianity Today Editorial on Trump." *Fox News* (Dec 22, 2019) at https://www.foxnews.com/faith-values/nearly-200-evangelical-leaders-condemned-christianity-today-editorial-on-trump.

———. "Sacred Heart of Jesus Statue in Texas Cathedral Destroyed." *Fox News* (Sept 16, 2020) at https://www.foxnews.com/us/sacred-heart-of-jesus-statue-destroyed-in-texas-cathedral.

Mohammed, Yasmine. *Unveiled: How Western Liberals Empower Radical Islam*. Free Hearts Free Minds, 2019.

Mohler, Al. "Ask Not for Whom the Volcano Erupts; It Erupts for Thee: A Response to David Gushee." *Albert Mohler Articles* (Aug 30, 2016) at https://albertmohler.com/2016/08/30/response-david-gushee/.

———. *The Briefing* (Aug 31, 2016) at https://albertmohler.com/2016/08/31/briefing-08-31-16.

———. *The Briefing* (Dec 6, 2019) at https://albertmohler.com/2019/12/06/briefing-12-16-19/?utm_source=Albert+Mohler&utm_campaign=9dd222fe11-EMAIL_CAMPAIGN_2019_04_08_09_12_COPY_01&utm_medium=email&utm_term=0_b041ba0d12-9dd222fe11-309876509&mc_cid=9dd222fe11&mc_eid=09f79b8502.

———. "Christians, Conscience, and the Looming 2020 Election." *Albert Mohler Articles* (Oct 26, 2020) at https://albertmohler.com/2020/10/26/christians-conscience-and-the-looming-2020-election?fbclid=IwAR3FgGzkY87iYBiLOIOZ3GiSf-L8Y8Imuc6w9WKrXYAkvwXwCj3Oj5at3j8.

Montanaro, Dan. "High School Closes Gender Neutral Bathroom after alleged Sexual Assault." *mrcTV* (Mar 4, 2020) at https://www.mrctv.org/blog/wisconsin-high-school-closes-gender-neutral-bathroom-after-male-student-sexually-assaults?fbclid=IwAR1kjoMzz9wBBpAau9BoHCN5cCRi4Ydq29DIgjbmUvAUZG-4vwOMwrl3aDYc.

Morgan, Robin ed. *Sisterhood is Powerful: An Anthology of Writings from the Women's Liberation Movement.* NY: Random House, 1970.

Moskowitz, Clara. "Same Sex Couples Common in the Wild." *LiveScience* (May 16, 2008) at https://www.livescience.com/2534-sex-couples-common-wild.html.

Mouser, Jessica. "7 Venues in UK Refuse Franklin Graham after LGBTQ Pressure." *ChurchLeaders* (Jan 28, 2020) at https://churchleaders.com/news/369801-lgbtq-franklin-graham-tour-not-u-k.html?utm_source=outreach-cl-daily-nl&utm_medium=email&utm_content=read-more&utm_campaign=cl-daily-nl&maropost_id=&mpweb=256-8600379-742444023.

———. "Barna: More Americans Now Believe in Satan than God." *ChurchLeaders* (April 21, 2020) at http://churchleaders.com/news/374625-barna-americans-satan-god.html?utm_source=cl-fridayweeklysend-nl&utm_medium=email&utm_content=text-link&utm_campaign=cl-fridayweeklysend-nl20200424&maropost_id=742444023&mpweb=256-8801759-742444023.

———. "Bishop Found Guilty for Refusing to Allow Same-Sex Weddings in Diocese." *ChurchLeaders* (Oct 7, 2020) at https://churchleaders.com/news/383513-william-love-same-sex-weddings.html?utm_source=cl-sundaysend-nl&utm_medium=email&utm_content=text-link&utm_campaign=cl-sundaysend-nl20201011&maropost_id=742444023&mpweb=256-9119264-742444023.

———. "Pew Research: 46% of US Evangelicals OK with Premarital Sex in a Committed Relationship." *ChurchLeaders* (Sept 1, 2020) at https://churchleaders.com/news/381586-pew-evangelicals-premarital-sex.html?utm_source=cl-fridayweeklysend-nl&utm_medium=email&utm_content=text-link&utm_campaign=cl-fridayweeklysend-nl20200904&maropost_id=742444023&mpweb=256-9071978-742444023.

———. "Report: 104 of 255 Netflix Shows for Teens have Mature Rating." *ChurchLeaders* (April 29, 2020) at https://churchleaders.com/news/374993-parents-television-council-netflix.html?utm_source=outreach-cl-daily-nl&utm_medium=email&utm_content=text-link&utm_campaign=cl-daily-nl&maropost_id=&mpweb=256-8823647-742444023.

———. "ROE Act Would Remove Need for Parental Consent to Get Abortion." *ChurchLeaders* (Jan 8, 2020) at https://churchleaders.com/news/368647-roe-act-parental-consent-abortion.html?utm_source=outreach-cl-daily-nl&utm_medium=email&utm_content=text-link&utm_campaign=cl-daily-nl&maropost_id=&mpweb=256-8516254-742444023.

Mouw, Richard. "Continuing the Task." In *Beauty, Order, and Mystery: A Christian Vision of Human Sexuality*, edited by Gerald Hiestand and Todd Wilson, 59–70. Downers Grove, IL: IVP, 2017.

Muhammad, Nayirah. "Meet the Theyby Babies: Kids Raised Without Gender." *Advocate* (Nov 25, 2018) at https://www.advocate.com/youth/2018/11/25/meet-theyby-babies-kids-raised-without-gender.

Murray, Douglas. *The Madness of Crowds: Gender, Race and Identity*. London, England: Bloomsbury Continuum, 2019.

Neusner, Jacob. *Genesis Rabbah Volume I: Genesis 1:1 to 8:14*. Brown Judaic Studies 104. Atlanta: Scholars, 1985.

Norman, Greg. "British Woman, 19, could Face Prison after Cyprus Court Finds Her Guilty of Lying about Gang Rape." *Fox News* (Dec 30, 2019) at https://www.foxnews.com/world/british-woman-reportedly-found-guilty-of-lying-about-rape.

North, Anna. "The Controversy around Virginia's New Abortion Bill, Explained." *Vox* (Feb 1, 2019) at https://www.vox.com/2019/2/1/18205428/virginia-abortion-bill-kathy-tran-ralph-northam.

NYC Health. "Health Department Announces New Law Offering Third Gender Category on Birth Certificates Takes Effect on Tuesday." *Recent Press Releases* (Dec 31, 2018) at https://www1.nyc.gov/site/doh/about/press/pr2018/pr104-18.page.

O'Reilly, Matt. "What Makes Sex Beautiful?: Marriage, Aesthetics, and the Image of God in Genesis 1–2 and Revelation 21–22." In *Beauty, Order, and Mystery: A Christian Vision of Human Sexuality*, edited by Gerald Hiestand and Todd Wilson, 197–212. Downers Grove, IL: IVP, 2017.

Office of Adolescent Health. "Adolescent Development and STDs." *US Department of Health & Human Services* (Last reviewed March 28, 2019) at https://www.hhs.gov/ash/oah/adolescent-development/reproductive-health-and-teen-pregnancy/stds/index.html.

Ontario Proud. *Facebook* (Feb 22, 2020) at https://www.facebook.com/OntarioProud/photos/a.1889928757951892/2641823979429029/?type=3&theater.

Opstal, Sandra Maria Van. "Remaining to Reform." In *Still Evangelical?: Insiders Reconsider Political, Social, and Theological Meaning*, edited by Mark Labberton, 120–37. Downers Grove: IVP, 2018.

Osten, Craig, and Alan Sears. *The Homosexual Agenda: Exposing the Principal Threat to Religious Freedom Today*. Nashville: B&H, 2003.

Outnumbered. "Obama Says Women Ruling All Nations Would Improve 'Just about Everything.'" *Fox News* (Dec 16, 2019) at https://video.foxnews.com/v/6116235122001#sp=show-clips.

Pappas, Stephanie. "Was Same-Sex Behavior Hardwired in Animals from the Beginning?" (Nov 22, 2019) at https://www.foxnews.com/science/was-same-sex-behavior-hardwired-in-animals-from-the-beginning.

Parke, Caleb. "Baptist Pastor 'Shocked' after Being Fired for Transgender Reveal." *Fox News* (July 24, 2020) at https://www.foxnews.com/world/church-pastor-transgender-fired-baptist.

———. "Christian Singer Makes Shocking Announcement: 'I No Longer Believe in God.'" *Fox News* (May 26, 2020) at https://www.foxnews.com/entertainment/christian-hawk-nelson-god-faith-instagram.

———. "Franklin Graham Responds after UK Venue Canceled for 'Incompatible' LGBTQ Views." *Fox News* (Jan 28, 2020) at https://www.foxnews.com/world/franklin-graham-uk-event-lgbtq-christian.

———. "Liberal Seminary Students Worship Potted Plants as 'The Beings Who Sustain Us.'" *Fox News* (Sept 19, 2019) at https://www.foxnews.com/faith-values/liberal-seminary-students-worship-plants?fbclid=IwAR1hAvMqZhTPeLsRZjnj16-ncOkurEuhh_NdMn-Bp75quN2EaGkfMkMMFKo.

Patterson, James, and Peter Kim. *The Day America Told the Truth: What People Really Believe About Everything That Really Matters*. New York: Prentice Hall, 1991.

Pavlich, Katie. "Rabid Feminists are Gleefully Writing about Aborting Baby Boys . . . because They're Boys." *TownHall* (Aug 14, 2019) at https://townhall.com/tipsheet/katiepavlich/2019/08/14/feminists-are-gleefully-writing-about-aborting-baby-boysbecause-theyre-boys-n2551609?utm_content=bufferaa203&utm_medium=social&utm_source=facebook.com&utm_campaign=buffer&fbclid=IwAR1bT8qlDn3qzp1p5JOqPjJpz9aLLZITnCIoo-d6NyoonpO3LsyW2qySIsE.

Peetz, Caitlynn. "MCPS Developing First-of-its-kind LGBTQ Class." *Bethesda Beat* (Feb 5, 2020) at https://bethesdamagazine.com/bethesda-beat/schools/mcps-developing-first-of-its-kind-lgbtq-class/?fbclid=IwAR3YMRD-XoTzTMCJ7fSluHrobM_DZ64qmSsGrdsuYU5O3NdmfokZumON2W4.

Peters, Rebecca Todd. *Trust Women: A Progressive Christian Argument for Reproductive Justice*. Boston: Beacon, 2018.

Peterson, Brian Neil. "Does Genesis 2 Support Same-Sex Marriage?: An Evangelical Response." *JETS* 60, no.4 (2017) 681–96.

———. *Genesis as Torah: Reading Narrative as Legal Instruction*. Eugene, OR: Cascade, 2018.

———. "The Gibeonite Revenge of 2 Sam 21:1–14: Another Example of David's Darker Side or a Picture of a Shrewd Monarch?" *JESOT* 1, no.2 (2012) 201–22.

———. "Identifying the Sin of Sodom in Ezekiel 16:49–50." *JETS* 61, no.2 (2018) 307–20.

———. "Male and Female Sexual Exploitation in the Light of the Book of Genesis." *JETS* 62, no.4 (2019) 693–703.

———. "A Possible Scriptural Precedent for Paul's Teaching on Divorce (and Remarriage?) in 1 Corinthians 7:10–15." *TynBul* 69, no.1 (2018) 43–62.

———. "Postmodernism's Deconstruction of the Genesis Mandates." *JETS* 62, no.1 (2019) 125–40.

———. *Qoheleth's Hope: The Message of Ecclesiastes in a Broken World*. Lanham, MD: Lexington/Fortress, 2020.

———. Review of Jack Rogers's "Jesus, the Bible, and Homosexuality: Explode the Myths, Heal the Church (2009)." *JBMW* 20, no. 1 (2016) 104–8.

———. "The Sin of Sodom Revisited: Reading Genesis 19 in Light of Torah." *JETS* 59, no. 1 (2016) 17–31.

———. *What was the Sin of Sodom: Homosexuality, Inhospitality or Something Else?* Eugene, OR: Resource, 2016.

Peterson, Jordan. *12 Rules for Life: An Antidote to Chaos*. Toronto: Random House Canada, 2018.

Petit, Marie-Pier, Danielle Julien, and Line Chamberland. "Negotiating Parental Designations among Trans Parents' Families: An Ecological Model of Parental Identity." *Psychology of Sexual Orientation and Gender Diversity* 4, no.3 (2017) 282–95.

Pew Research Center: Religion and Public Life. "Views about Abortion among Members of the Historically Black Protestant Tradition." At https://www.pewforum.org/religious-landscape-study/religious-tradition/historically-black-protestant/views-about-abortion/.

Phillips, Morgan. "Ohio Woman Wearing Fur is Stabbed by Animal-rights Activist in Church Police Say." *Fox News* (Nov 21, 2019) at https://www.foxnews.com/us/ohio-woman-wearing-fur-is-stabbed-by-animal-rights-activist-in-church-police-say.

Piper, John. "Policies, Persons, and Paths to Ruin: Pondering the Implications of the 2020 Election." *Desiring God* (Oct 22, 2020) at https://www.desiringgod.org/articles/policies-persons-and-paths-to-ruin.

Planned Parenthood. "How Do I Talk with My Preschooler about Identity?" at https://www.plannedparenthood.org/learn/parents/preschool/how-do-i-talk-with-my-preschooler-about-identity.

Pluralist. "Scientist Wants to End 'Conservative' Taboo against Cannibalism to Fight Climate Change." (Sept 8, 2019) at https://pluralist.com/magnus-soderlund-swedish-scientist-cannibalism-climate-change/.

Power of Positivity. "CDC Reveals Teenage Suicide Has Increased 76 Percent in Last Decade." https://www.powerofpositivity.com/teenage-suicide-rates-increase/?fbclid=IwAR2fP-kQLdljeMNahghzjU-zmqJEwAo3ITCcpyzkb7oNGwudL5Cu41CbvdA.

Prager, Dennis. "Feminization of America is Bad for the World." (Nov 14, 2017) at https://www.creators.com/read/dennis-prager/11/17/feminization-of-america-is-bad-for-the-world-de3e7.

———. "Meanwhile, This is What LGBTQ Organizations are Doing to Society." *RealClear Politics* (Aug 13, 2019) at https://www.realclearpolitics.com/articles/2019/08/13/meanwhile_this_is_what_lgbtq_organizations_are_doing_to_society_141002.html?fbclid=IwAR1uAWVgaci4XA8xJtr9vCk6cTu2gwtk9N_wBdonosOb48ySAt71mooNr94.

———. "A Response to the Editor of Christianity Today." *Townhall* (Dec 24, 2019) at: https://townhall.com/columnists/dennisprager/2019/12/24/a-response-to-the-editor-of-christianity-today-n2558477?fbclid=IwARoI-vFRPoS8hcvY4QzLnvrggKr9Euw1voz63K99Q9TZo1C50EmOIz6S_z8.

———. "Why Judaism (and then Christianity) Rejected Homosexuality." *Crisis Magazine* (Feb 1, 2018) at https://www.crisismagazine.com/2018/judaisms-sexual-revolution-judaism-christianity-rejected-homosexuality?fbclid=IwARo-ctZznxYp-IZa2hkt4LvDH-jPFUoax5nGrFDuMNGS2xhVqy1N55tdgHc#.XXPy6036fjA.facebook.

Prestigiacomo, Amanda. "Cuomo Boasts of Low Covid Infections: 'God Did Not Do That.'" *The Daily Wire* (April 14, 2020) at https://www.dailywire.com/news/cuomo-boasts-of-low-covid-infections-god-did-not-do-that.

———. "Lesbian Priest Tapped to Head Major Abortion Group, Calls Abortionists 'Modern-Day Saints.'" *The Daily Wire* (Nov 6, 2019) at https://www.dailywire.com/news/lesbian-priest-tapped-to-head-major-abortion-group-calls-abortionists-modern-day-saints?utm_source=facebook&utm_medium=social&utm_campaign=benshapiro.

———. "'Ok Dude': Rapper Zuby Suspended for 'Misgendering' on Twitter. Trans Activist Celebrates: 'Pronouns Enforce.'" *The Daily Wire* (Feb 27, 2020) at https://www.dailywire.com/news/ok-dude-rapper-zuby-suspended-for-misgendering-on-twitter-trans-activist-celebrates-pronouns-enforced?utm_source=facebook&utm_medium=social&utm_campaign=mattwalsh.

Pro-Life Evangelicals for Biden. At https://www.prolifeevangelicalsforbiden.com/?fbclid=IwAR2KcsOEXarbA3I8yOlblNO1aMNBCXfAur_-XtcFoPruj2Qogzonog1WpKM.

Pruss, Alexander. *One Body: An Essay in Christian Sexual Ethics*. Notre Dame, IN: University of Notre Dame Press, 2013.

Puhak, Janine. "EasyJet Advises Crew to Drop 'Ladies and Gentlemen' from Plane Greeting in Favor of Gender-Inclusive Language." *Fox News* (Dec 30, 2019) at https://www.foxnews.com/travel/easyjet-passengers-greeting-gender-report.

———. "Washington Married Couple, Woman Open Up about 'Throuple' Relationship, Lifestyle." *Fox News* (Oct 19, 2019) at https://www.foxnews.com/lifestyle/washington-throuple-relationship-lifestyle.

Re, Gregg. "Chief Justice Roberts Issues Rare Rebuke of Schumer's 'Dangerous' and 'Irresponsible' Comments; Trump Slams Lawmaker, Says 'Must Pay a Severe Price.'" *Fox News* (Mar 4, 2020) at https://www.foxnews.com/politics/chief-justice-roberts-rare-rebuke-schumer-calling-comments-kavanaugh-gorsuch-dangerous.

Reader, Soran. "Abortion, Killing, and Maternal Moral Authority." *Hypatia* 23, no.1 (2008) 132–49.

Regnerus, Mark. "Can the Church Save Marriage?" *Christianity Today* (July/Aug 2020) 34–41.

Reilly, Robert R. *Making Gay Okay: How Rationalizing Homosexual Behavior is Changing Everything*. San Francisco: Ignatius, 2014.

Religion and Public Life. "One-in-Five U.S. Adults Were Raised in Interfaith Homes." *Pew Research Center* (Oct 26, 2016) at https://www.pewforum.org/2016/10/26/links-between-childhood-religious-upbringing-and-current-religious-identity/.

Richter, Sandra L. *Stewards of Eden: What Scripture Says about Environment and Why It Matters*. Downers Grove, IL: IVP, 2020.

Risdon, James. "Drag Queen Admits He's 'Grooming' Children at Story Hour Events." *LifeSite News* (Nov 27, 2018) at https://www.lifesitenews.com/news/watch-drag-queen-admits-hes-grooming-children-at-story-hour-events.

Roark, Randall. "The Need for Anal Dysplasia Screening and Treatment Programs for HIV-Infected Men Who Have Sex with Men: A Review of the Literature." *Journal of the Association of Nurses in AIDS Care* 22, no.6 (Nov/Dec 2011) 433–43.

Roberto, Melissa. "Former Miss Kentucky Pleads Guilty in Nude Photo Scandal Involving a Teenage Boy." *Fox News* (Dec 19, 2019) at https://www.foxnews.com/entertainment/former-miss-kentucky-pleads-guilty-in-nude-photo-scandal and https://knewz.com/wisconsin-teacher-sex-teen/.

Roberts, Vaughan. *Transgender, Talking Points*. Epsom, UK: The Good Book Company, 2016.

Robin, Corey. "Who Really Said That?" *The Chronicle of Higher Education* (Sept 16, 2013) at https://www.chronicle.com/article/Who-Really-Said-That-/141559.

Robinson, Rodney. "Virginia Senate Passes Bill to Let Transgender People Get New Birth Certificates." *Sovereign Nations* (Jan 27, 2020) at https://sovereignnations.com/2020/01/27/virginia-senate-transgender-birth-certificates/?fbclid=IwAR2m7ScnrJ45v1rmrlAPujgQnwzUHpbgsO7A-2fr74DqtnlYrFyAeLFgS28.

Romero, Robert Chao. "Immigration and the Latina/o Community." In *Still Evangelical?: Insiders Reconsider Political, Social, and Theological Meaning*, edited by Mark Labberton, 66–80. Downers Grove: IVP, 2018.

Ross, Hugh. *Weathering Climate Change: A Fresh Approach*. Covina, CA: Reasons to Believe, 2020.

Rovner, Julie. "'Partial-Birth Abortion': Separating Fact from Spin." *NPR* (Feb 21, 2006) at https://www.npr.org/2006/02/21/5168163/partial-birth-abortion-separating-fact-from-spin.

Roys, Julie. "5 Reasons Socialism is Not Christian." *The Christian Post* (July 12, 2016) at https://www.christianpost.com/news/5-reasons-socialism-is-not-christian-opinion.html?fbclid=IwAR3HaG2D7rTRV-_Acv2Zd43i0O-LR_oT1joJyEHRIJXYxm_CGJbd6GXNcwI.

Rule, Jane. *Lesbian Images*. Garden City, New York: Doubleday, 1975.

Ryder, Alistair. "'The Only Solution for Climate Change Is Letting the Human Race Become Extinct.'" *Cambridge News* (Feb 5, 2020) at https://www.cambridge-news.co.uk/news/cambridge-news/cambridge-professor-thinks-should-human-17684215?fbclid=IwAR1X4xz-WtEt_3_9gs8CRToCSlFfBnxgLplSs78_q9AO5m7VG2FPYnpLnFg.

Sahadeo, Andy. "Kylie Jenner Receives Major Backlash for Wearing Fur Coat: 'When are You Going to Stop Wearing Dead Animals?'" *Fox News* (Dec 30, 2019) at https://www.foxnews.com/entertainment/kylie-jenner-backlash-fur-coat.

Sailhamer, John. *The Pentateuch as Narrative: A Biblical-Theological Commentary*. Grand Rapids: Zondervan, 1992.

Sandlin, P. Andrew. "Cultural Marxism, Simply Explained." *Sovereign Nations* (April 25, 2018) at https://sovereignnations.com/2018/04/25/cultural-marxism-simply-explained/?fbclid=IwAR1_xXGgd1Qj-SDUl5gTcdgqUxBHNWLLQh53aDFEwVkPJ7MNZrpkRVWDWTw.

Sanger, Margaret. *Women and the New Race*. New York: Brentano's, 1920.

Satinover, Jeffrey. *Homosexuality and the Politics of Truth*. Grand Rapids: Baker, 1996.

Sausage Roll. "'You Should Be Afraid of Me': Trans Twitch Admin Threatens Cis-Gender Gamers." *YouTube* (May 17, 2020) at https://www.youtube.com/watch?v=wL_LUy7LItA.

Saylor, Kristin, and Jim O'Hanlon. "What the Bible Says about Homosexuality." *TEDxEdgemontSchool* (Aug 4, 2016) at https://www.youtube.com/watch?v=XGNZQ64xiqo.

Scanzoni, Letha, and Virginia Ramey Mollenkott. *Is the Homosexual My Neighbor? Another Christian View*. San Francisco: Harper & Row, 1978.

Schow, Ashe. "CNN: A Baby Surviving an Abortion and a Newborn Are Not the Same Thing." *The Daily Wire* (Feb 25, 2020) at https://www.dailywire.com/news/cnn-a-baby-surviving-an-abortion-and-a-newborn-arent-the-same-thing?utm_source=facebook&utm_medium=social&utm_campaign=benshapiro.

Schwartz, Ian. "Chuck Todd to Hillary Clinton: 'When, or if, Does an Unborn Child Have Constitutional Rights?'" *RealClear Politics* (Apr 3, 2016) at https://www.realclearpolitics.com/video/2016/04/03/chuck_todd_to_hillary_clinton_when_or_if_does_an_unborn_child_have_constitutional_rights.html.

Schwarzwalder, Rob, and Natasha Tax. "How Fatherlessness Impacts Early Sexual Activity, Teen Pregnancy, and Sexual Abuse." *Family Research Council* (Dec 2015) at https://downloads.frc.org/EF/EF15L32.pdf.

Shaw, Adam. "Angela Merkel Admits that 'No-Go Zones' Exist in Germany." *Fox News* (Mar 1, 2018) at https://www.foxnews.com/world/angela-merkel-admits-that-no-go-zones-exist-in-germany.

Sheldon, Louis P. *The Agenda: The Homosexual Plan to Change America*. Lake Mary, FL: Charisma House, 2005.

Sherwood, Harriet. "US Preacher Franklin Graham Tries to Reverse UK Tour Cancellations." *The Guardian* (Feb 7, 2020) at https://www.theguardian.com/world/2020/feb/07/us-preacher-franklin-graham-will-try-to-reverse-uk-tour-cancellations.

Shinkoskey, Robert Kimball. "Without Law." *The Family in America* 7:1 (January 1993) 4–7.

Shiver, Phil. "Reddit User Brags about Heading to Planned Parenthood to 'Purge the Two Parasites,' 'Goblins' Inside Her." *The Blaze* (Jan 17, 2020) at https://www.theblaze.com/news/woman-brags-about-abortion-reddit.

Shrier, Abigail. "Does the ACLU Want to Ban My Book?" *The Wall Street Journal* (Nov 15, 2020) at https://www.wsj.com/articles/does-the-aclu-want-to-ban-my-book-11605475898.

———. *Irreversible Damage: The Transgender Craze Seducing Our Daughters*. Washington, DC: Regnery, 2020.

Sider, Ronald J. *Completely Pro-Life: Building a Consistent Stance on Abortion, the Family, Nuclear Weapons, the Poor*. Downers Grove, IL: IVP, 1987.

Singer, Peter. *Animal Liberation*. New York: New York Review Book, 1975.

Sky News. "'Hundreds' of Young Trans People Seeking Help to Return to Original Sex." *YouTube* (Oct 25, 2019) at https://www.youtube.com/watch?v=7FRUDwDmkmo&fbclid=IwAR3VGbw7HFcmVIR3uiJgI9aH9G7oC5rOx46fAVUbl1FFOWyavuUeATeWh3k.

Slattery, Juli. *God's Design and Why It Matters: Rethinking Sexuality*. New York: Multnomah, 2018.

Slightly Offensive. "Madness: Transgender who Identifies as a Deer in now in Charge of Twitch Censorship." *The Blaze* (May 20, 2020) at https://www.theblaze.com/slightly-offensve/trans-deer-twitch-moderator?rebelltitem=1#rebelltitem1.

Smith, Peter J., and Steve Jalsevac. "Environmentalist Extremists Call Humanity 'Virus' a 'Cancer'; Large Families Guilty of 'Eco-Crime.'" *LifeSite News* (May 8, 2007) at https://www.lifesitenews.com/news/environmentalist-extremists-call-humanity-virus-a-cancer-large-families-gui.

Snibbe, Kris. "A Warning on Homeschooling." *The Harvard Gazette* (2019) at https://news.harvard.edu/gazette/story/2020/05/law-school-professor-says-there-may-be-a-dark-side-of-homeschooling/.

Solomon, Lawrence. *The Deniers: The World-Renowned Scientists Who Stood Up against Global Warming Hysteria, Political Persecution, and Fraud*. Minneapolis: Richard Vigilante, 2008.

Song, Robert. *Covenant and Calling: Towards a Theology of Same-Sex Relationships*. London: SCM, 2014.

Sorace, Stephen. "Massachusetts City Recognized Polyamorous Relationships in New Domestic Partnership Ordinance." *Fox News* (July 2, 2020) at https://www.foxnews.com/us/massachusetts-city-polyamorous-relationships-domestic-partnership-ordinance.

Southern Baptist Convention. "On Critical Race Theory and Intersectionality." Birmingham, AL (2019) at http://www.sbc.net/resolutions/2308/resolution-9—on-critical-race-theory-and-intersectionality.

Spade, Katrina. "Let's Talk about Human Composting." *TEDxOrcasIsland* (June 16, 2016) at https://www.youtube.com/watch?v=PRsopS7yTG8.

Spargo, Chris. "Transgender Teen Jazz Jennings Opens Up about Gender Affirmation Surgery and Reveals She Needed Second Procedure after Unexpected Complications from Genital Overhaul." *DailyMail.com* (Oct 16, 2018) at https://www.dailymail.co.uk/news/article-6282045/Trans-teen-Jazz-Jennings-needed-second-procedure-complications-genital-overhaul.html.

Starr, Penny. "Designer Calls on Fashion Industry to End Male/Female Clothing, De-Gender Beauty." *Sovereign Nations* (Feb 4, 2020) at https://sovereignnations.com/2020/02/04/designer-fashion-industry-end-male-female-clothing-beauty/?fbclid=IwAR2wlsyRJGNvmFijl7Uqzwgiza8s_A5vT1cn6RCrm5ny37TV6Wkt6a17p30.

Stein, Sam. "Obama Backs Gay Marriage." *HuffPost* (May 12, 2012) at https://www.huffpost.com/entry/obama-gay-marriage_n_1503245.

Stetzer, Ed. "Evangelicals Becoming Catholics: Former CT Editor Mark Galli." *ChurchLeaders* (Sept 28, 2020) at https://churchleaders.com/outreach-missions/outreach-missions-articles/382902-evangelicals-becoming-catholics-former-ct-editor-mark-galli.html?utm_source=outreach-cl-daily-nl&utm_medium=email&utm_content=text-link&utm_campaign=cl-daily-nl&maropost_id=&mpweb=256-9104860-742444023.

Stimson, Brie. "United Methodist Church Announces Proposal to Split Over LGBTQ Rights." *Fox News* (Jan 4, 2020) at https://www.foxnews.com/us/united-methodist-church-split-lgbtq-rights.

St. John, Paige. "Kamala Harris' Support for Planned Parenthood Draws Fire after Raid on Anti-Abortion Activist." *Los Angeles Times* (April 7. 2016) at https://www.latimes.com/politics/la-pol-kamala-harris-planned-parenthood-20160407-story.html.

Strand, Paul. "The Founders Meant to Keep Government out of the Church, Not God Out of the Government." *CBN News* (July 3, 2020) at https://www1.cbn.com/cbnnews/us/2020/july/the-founders-meant-to-keep-government-out-of-the-church-not-god-out-of-the-government?cpid=socclub-f&fbclid=IwAR34cU4FUaGTQc8tzrrVSH7ppH5M1J3y5uQTdY8SDqYzjfhzIfLvgEiXE7M.

Swain, Carol. "Vanderbilt's Policies Pull Campus away from Christianity." *Tennessean* (May 26, 2016) at https://www.tennessean.com/story/opinion/contributors/2016/05/26/vanderbilts-policies-pull-campus-away-christianity/84955614/.

Tapper, Jake, and Amy Bingham. "Dems Quickly Switch to Include 'God', 'Jerusalem'." *ABC News* (Sept 5, 2012) at https://abcnews.go.com/Politics/OTUS/democrats-rapidly-revise-platform-include-god/story?id=17164108.

TFP Student Action. "Pro-Life vs. Pro-Abortion: Amazing Contrast of Two Marches." (Jan 25, 2020) at https://www.facebook.com/TFPStudentAction/videos/2837825239613387/UzpfSTUyMTE2NzkzMzoxMDE1NzEwODY5OTQ3NzkzNA/.

The Associated Press. "Author JK Rowling Draws Criticism for Transgender Comments." *News Channel 8* (Dec 20, 2019) at https://www.wfla.com/entertainment-news/author-jk-rowling-draws-criticism-for-transgender-comments-2/?fbclid=IwAR3f8ouMaubpqozHOKIGNcpqEEGrIR3_nMKRHxtIjhrJsCYG9OKM7GIZW58.

The Fix Team. "Transcript: The December Democratic Debate." *The Washington Post* (Dec 20, 2019) at https://www.washingtonpost.com/politics/2019/12/20/transcript-december-democratic-debate/.

The Reformation Project. "Dr. David Gushee: Ending the Teaching of Contempt against the Church's Sexual Minorities." *YouTube* (Nov 14, 2014) at https://www.youtube.com/watch?v=G2o3ZGwzZvk.

The Rubin Report. "Ex Muslim Exposes the Reality of Islam in the West." *YouTube* (Dec 22, 2019) at https://www.youtube.com/watch?v=_PXfMY6YqBY&feature=share&fbclid=IwAR3HKrn9ogYqzx8ML3QnE8w8famDfVnHfTMBs_n44ntYwe8g6vUOsy5S-Vg.

Toi Staff. "Jewish Divorces in Israel Up 5% in 2018, with 86% Increase in One Town." *The Times of Israel* (June 12, 2019) at https://www.timesofisrael.com/jewish-divorces-in-israel-up-5-in-2018-with-86-increase-in-one-central-town/#:~:text=The%20divorce%20rate%20among%20Israeli,five%20years%2C%20the%20data%20showed.

Tracy, Katre. "Wheaton Students Protest 'Train Wreck Conversion' Speaker's Ex-Gay Testimony." *Christianity Today* (Feb 21, 2014) at https://www.christianitytoday.com/news/2014/february/wheaton-students-protest-exgay-chapel-rosaria-butterfield.html.

Treat, Jeremy. "Sexuality and the Church: How Pastoral Ministry Shapes a Theology of Sexuality." In *Beauty, Order, and Mystery: A Christian Vision of Human Sexuality*, edited by Gerald Hiestand and Todd Wilson, 45–57. Downers Grove, IL: IVP, 2017.

Trible, Phyllis. "Eve and Adam: Genesis 2–3 Reread." *Andover Newton Quarterly* 13 (1973) 74–81.

Tucker Carlson Tonight. "Planned Parenthood: Teach Your Preschoolers 'Their Genitals Do Not Determine Their Gender.'" *Fox News* (Aug 4, 2017) at https://www.foxnews.com/us/planned-parenthood-teach-your-preschoolers-their-genitals-dont-determine-their-gender?fbclid=IwAR1gAatXh0Ai-J5w0fh7mxgq5wRD-vq8VnmBFlkujooxK8UoqWLDYOik1s4.

Unwin, Joseph Daniel. *Sex and Culture*. Oxford: Oxford University Press, 1934 electronic archive https://archive.org/details/b20442580/page/n7.

Vest, Lamar. "Most Americans Own a Bible, So Why Aren't We Reading It?" *Fox News* (Nov 8, 2011) at https://www.foxnews.com/opinion/most-americans-own-a-bible-so-why-arent-they-reading-it.

Vice News. "The Men Who Call Themselves Non-Offending Pedophiles." (Aug 26, 2019) at https://www.vice.com/en_us/article/j5y8zy/the-men-who-call-themselves-non-offending-pedophiles.

Vincent, Isabel. "Protesters Burn Bible, American Flag as Tensions Rise in Portland." *New York Post* (Aug 1, 2020) at https://nypost.com/2020/08/01/protestors-burn-bible-american-flag-as-tensions-rise-in-portland/.

Virtue, David W. "Progressive Pansexual 'Christians' Have Declared War on Orthodox Believers." *Sovereign Nations* (Dec 30, 2019) at https://sovereignnations.com/2019/12/30/progressive-pansexualist-christians-declared-war-orthodox-believers/?fbclid=IwARoqy1DtElYhGTWPLt5oGc7sVHcQ_K1JDqvBr2pic1p5k_oY_JygXuFSC_M.

Vitali, Ali, Pete Williams, and Mary Emily O'Hara. "White House Reverses Obama-era Transgender Bathroom Protections." *NBC News* (Feb 22, 2017) at https://www.nbcnews.com/politics/white-house/white-house-reverses-obama-era-transgender-bathroom-protections-n724426.

Bibliography

Wallace, Chris. "Pete Buttigieg on Expectations for Nevada Caucuses and South Carolina Primary." *Fox News Sunday* (Feb 16, 2020) at https://video.foxnews.com/v/6132969452001#sp=show-clips.

Wallace, Daniella. "Conn. High School Girls File Lawsuit Arguing that Allowing Transgender Athletes to Compete Is Sex Discrimination." *Fox News* (Feb 13, 2020) at https://www.foxnews.com/us/connecticut-high-school-girls-lawsuit-transgender-athletes-sex-discrimination.

———. "NYC Subway Thief Thanks Democrats after His 139th Arrest, Release: 'Bail Reform, It's Lit.'" *Fox News* (Feb 16, 2020) at https://www.foxnews.com/us/new-york-bail-reform-law-nyc-subway-thief-thanks-democrats-139th-arrest.

Wallis, Jim. *God's Politics: Why the Right Gets It Wrong and the Left Doesn't Get It*. New York: HarperSanFrancisco, 2005.

Walsh, Matt. "Drag Queen." *Twitter* (Feb 28, 2020) at https://twitter.com/MattWalshBlog/status/1233355261622063104.

———. "A School Allows Boys into the Girls Room. Parents Object but Still Send Their Kids to Class. This is the Problem." *The Daily Wire* (Nov 21, 2019) at https://www.dailywire.com/news/walsh-a-school-allows-boys-into-the-girls-room-parents-object-but-still-send-their-kids-to-class-this-is-the-problem?utm_source=facebook&utm_medium=social&utm_campaign=mattwalsh.

Waltke, Bruce. "Reflections from the Old Testament on Abortion." *JETS* 19, no.1 (1976) 3–13.

Walton, John. *The Lost World of the Torah: Law as Covenant and Wisdom in Ancient Context*. Downers Grove, IL: IVP, 2019.

Warren, Mary Ann. "On the Moral and Legal Status of Abortion." *The Monist* 57, no.1 (1973) 43–61.

Warren, Steve. "'My Father Would Have Been Disappointed': Franklin Graham Fires Back at Christianity Today's 'Elitist Liberal' Call for Trump's Removal." *CBNNews.com* (Dec 20, 2019) at https://www1.cbn.com/cbnnews/2019/december/my-father-would-have-been-disappointed-rsquo-franklin-graham-fires-back-at-christianity-todays-lsquo-elitist-liberal-rsquo-call-for-president-trumps-removal?fbclid=IwAR3NgjKCZVa93M54iMLg5O4YRxmmwCQgz8KtLr9lJFXOC5nddOy5JKnbHuM.

Waterfield, Bruno. "Mother of Sex-Change Belgian: 'I Don't Care about His Euthanasia Death.'" *The Telegraph* (June 23, 2020) at https://www.telegraph.co.uk/news/worldnews/europe/belgium/10349159/Mother-of-sex-change-Belgian-I-dont-care-about-his-euthanasia-death.html.

Watkins, William D. *The New Absolutes: How They are Being Imposed on Us How They are Eroding Our Moral Landscape*. Minneapolis, MN: Bethany House, 1996.

Welch, Will. "Introducing GQ's New Masculinity Issue, Starring Pharrell." *GQ* (Oct 15, 2019) at https://www.gq.com/story/masculinity-is-changing-editors-letter-november-2019.

White, Blaire. "I'm Detransitioning." *YouTube* (Nov 21, 2018) at https://www.youtube.com/watch?v=FZnAsk5vWzE.

White, Heath. *Postmodernism 101: A First Course for the Curious Christian*. Grand Rapids: Brazos, 2006.

White, Lynn Jr., "An Evangelical Declaration on the Care of Creation." In *The Care of Creation: Focusing Concern and Action*, edited by R.J. Berry, 17–22. England: Inter-Varsity, 2000.

Wilson, Todd. *Mere Sexuality*. Grand Rapids: Zondervan, 2017.
Yaksh, Mitchell. "Born this Way? Why the Answer Doesn't (and Shouldn't) Matter to Christians." *LeadThemHome* at https://www.leadthemhome.org/2018/05/born-this-way-why-the-answer-doesnt-and-shouldnt-matter-to-christians.html#.XrLfQKhKjIU.
Yeh, Allen. "Theology and Orthopraxis in Global Evangelicalism." In *Still Evangelical?: Insiders Reconsider Political, Social, and Theological Meaning*, edited by Mark Labberton, 97–119. Downers Grove: IVP, 2018.
York, Marilyn. "What Representing Men in Divorce Taught Me about Fatherhood." *TEDxUniversityofNevada* (May 20, 2020) at https://www.youtube.com/watch?v=RlSwsE22nX0&fbclid=IwAR3xXhdJ9k5zWZmD5hPZabITAn1iRlrs3QKtmJtYz8SvVNyv4IuJsCZbjF8.
Zanotti, Emily. "Transgender Pennsylvania Health Director Melts Down in Press Conference after Reporter Uses the Wrong Pronoun." *The Daily Wire* (May 14, 2020) at https://www.dailywire.com/news/transgender-pennsylvania-health-director-melts-down-in-press-conference-after-reporter-uses-wrong-pronoun?utm_source=facebook&utm_medium=social&utm_campaign=benshapiro.

Scripture Index

OLD TESTAMENT

Genesis

1	2, 5–6, 13, 27, 29, 39, 53, 55–56, 82–83, 150, 159–61, 214–15, 222, 226, 249, 269, 281, 284, 287, 290
1:21	85
1:22	90, 158
1:24	85
1:25	85
1:26	85, 249
1:26–27	48
1:26–28	xv, 3, 83, 159, 250
1:27	7, 135, 157–58, 238
1:27–28	53, 82
1:28	85, 90, 113, 137, 249
1:30	85
2	2, 5–6, 10, 13, 27, 29, 39, 53–56, 72, 81–86, 159–61, 214–15, 222, 226, 249, 269, 281, 284, 287, 290
2:15	3n6
2:18	57–58, 82, 82n45, 84, 155
2:20	84
2:21	159
2:22	55
2:22–23	157, 159
2:23	159
2:24	3, 5, 7, 53, 55, 58, 82, 113, 137, 159
2:24–25	55
2:25	61
3	4–7, 36, 53, 82–83
3:1	17
3:16b	53
3:7	61
3:19	260
3:21	252
4:1	90, 121
4:17–22	90
5:1–32	90
5:2	158
6–9	37, 215
6:1–4	92, 215–16
6:5	92
6:19	158
7:3	158
7:9	158
7:16	158
8:11	250
8:17	90
8:22	251
9:1	90, 137
9:3–4	252
9:5–6	250
9:6	122, 135–36
9:7	90, 137
9:20–25	9

Genesis (*cont.*)

10:1–32	90
11:10–32	90
11:30	90
12:2	90
12:10–20	9
13:13	216
15:13	91
16:1–4	9
19	37, 215–16
19:4–11	9
19:8	9
19:33	9
19:35	9
20:1–7	9
20:6	216
21:9	9
21:12–14	65
24:2	141
24:9	141
25:21	90
25:23	137
26:6–11	9
29:23–25	9
29:31	90, 121
30:3–8	9
30:9–10	9
30:14–16	9
30:22	121
31:38	140
34:2	9
34:29	57
35:18	153
35:22	9
38:8	57
38:14–19	10
39:7–20	10
39:9	216
46:26	141
47:29	141

Exodus

1	91
1:5	141
1:22	130
4:24–26	65
12	130
20–23	150
20:2–5	134
20:6	91
20:9–11	94
20:10	250
20:13	132
20:14	59
21	139, 143
21:10	57
21:13	139
21:22	139
21:22–25	139
22:16–17	86
23:7	132
23:26	140
34:13	251

Leviticus

17	250
18	173, 214, 216–18
18:3	218
18:3–18	55
18:21	134
18:22	80, 214, 217, 221
18:24–30	218
18:27–30	55
19:10	149
19:33–34	278
20	173, 214, 216, 218
20:10	59
20:13	80, 214, 217, 221
20:18	217
23:10–11	255
23:22	149, 278
24:22	278
25:4	250
26:34	250
26:43	250

Numbers

5:11–31	140
5:21	141
5:22	141
12:1	65
35:9–15	139
35:22–29	139

Deuteronomy

4:17–18	251
4:19	251
5–26	150
5:8	251
5:13–15	94
5:14	250
5:18	59
6:6–7	289
7:5	251
10:18	111, 149
12:1–4	251
14:29	111, 149
17:3	251
20:19	251, 255
21:10–17	57
22:4	251, 255
22:5	160
22:6–7	251
22:7	255
22:10	250, 255
22:30//23:1	55
23:1//2	160–61
23:17//18	161
24:1	7
24:1–3	65
24:5	54
24:14	149
24:17	149
24:19–21	149
25:4	250
26:12	278

Joshua

7	278

Judges

3:7	251
8:30	57, 141
19	215

Ruth

3	59
3:11–14	59

1 Samuel

1:1–2	57
8	265
8:9–18	265

2 Samuel

5:13	57
12:8	57
19:12–13	54
21:1–14	90

1 Kings

14:15	251
18	285
21	102

2 Kings

21:16	143
23:10	134
24:4	143

2 Chronicles

7:13	38
7:14	38, 110, 290
11:21	58
13:21	58
31:1	251
36:21	250–51

Job

3:16	140
10:11	137
21:10	140

Psalms

8	252
8:3–8	250
50:10–11	250
58:8//9	140
71:6	137
104:21	250
106:34–40	112, 149
119:73	137
127:3	102

Psalms (*cont.*)

139:13	137
139:16	137

Proverbs

12:10	250, 255
14:34	204, 275, 285

Ecclesiastes

3:11	136
6:3	140, 141n24
6:3–5	141
11:5	142, 144

Song of Solomon

2:7	59
2:16	59
3:5	59
6:3	59
7:2	141
7:11	59
8:4	59

Isaiah

1:17	111
5:20	43, 131, 239
13–23	37
16:11	111
16:14	111
34:13–15	255
44:24	137
49:1	137
56:4–5	164

Jeremiah

1:5	137–38
2–3	58
2:11	14
7:6	111, 149
17:9	147, 213, 223
18:5–10	38
19:4	143
22:3	111, 143, 149
22:17	143
32:35	134
46–51	37

Ezekiel

8:10	251
16	58, 130, 217
16:49	211, 217
16:50	217
20:33	37
	23 58
25–32	37

Daniel

4:30	44
10:13	xiii
10:20	xiii

Hosea

1–3	58
4:6a	32, 39
9:14	140

Amos

1–2	37, 149
1:13	142–43, 149
1:14–15	142
7:14	32

Jonah

4:11	250, 255

Micah

6	149
6:8	148

Zephaniah

2	37

Zechariah

7:10	111

Malachi

3:5	111

NEW TESTAMENT

Matthew

4:3–10	34
5:27–28	217
5:32	65
6:26	250–51
7:13	204
7:13–14	138
7:15	xiv
7:16	146
10:14–15	147
10:16	266, 291
10:28	136
10:29	250
10:31	250–51
11:23–24	147
12:12	251
12:25	277, 281
15:24	265
18:6	132, 151, 157
18:6–7	6
18:7	132
19	7, 215
19:1–9	54
19:3–6	55
19:3–12	34
19:4	162
19:8	58
19:12	161–63
19:14	132
19:18	59
25:31–46	148
26:39	34
26:42	34
28:19	138

Mark

3:25	281
6:17–18	55
9:42	151
10	7, 215
10:1–12	65
10:6	162
16:15	138

Luke

1:15	138
1:41	137–38
1:41–44	143
10:11–12	147
12:13–15	102
12:24	250
12:48	6, 144
14:5	250
14:26	38, 209
16:31	124
18:15	143
19:13	xi

John

2	55
3:16	138
14:6	26
17	34, 281
18:38	17
19:11	147
20:29b	48
21:25	265

Acts

8	162

Romans

1	5, 136, 165, 208, 211, 220
1:18–30	219
1:25	248, 249
1:25–28	162
1:26–28	80
1:29–30	220
2:22	59
3:4	17, 274
3:23	10, 221
6:1	147
8:18–23	255
8:19–22	250
8:21	251

Romans (*cont.*)

9	137
11:29	224
12:2	196
13:1–3	122
13:9	59

1 Corinthians

1:18	xi
1:27	31
5:1–8	55
5:6–7	xiv
6:1	208
6:1–6	187
6:9	80, 162, 208, 211, 219, 221
6:9–10	220
6:11	224
6:19–20	229
7	56
7:7	223
7:12–15	65
12	150
14:33	150
15:28	34

Galatians

1:15	137
3:28	162, 219
5:19–20	93
6	212
6:1	212, 290
6:2	211
6:7–8	212

Ephesians

2:2	xiii
5	58
5:3–20	146
9	54

Philippians

3:3–7	33

Colossians

1:20	250
2:8	131
3	54
3:5	93

1 Thessalonians

3:6	xiv
3:14–15	xiv
4:6	13
5:23	136

1 Timothy

1:9–10	220
1:10	80, 162, 208, 211, 219, 221
3:4–5	289
4:2	125

2 Timothy

1:7	256
3:15	143
3:16	39

Titus

1:6	289

James

2:10	279
2:11	59
3:1	132

1 Peter

2:13–15	122
5:8	6

2 Peter

1:21	39
3:4–7	255
3:10–13	254

1 John

1:9	221
5:19	4

Revelation

2:20–22	xiv
21	58
21:1	251
21–22	54, 255

MISHNAH

Gittin

9:10	65

Ohalot

7:6	153

GENESIS RABBAH

26.5	216

www.ingramcontent.com/pod-product-compliance
Lightning Source LLC
Chambersburg PA
CBHW070229230426
43664CB00014B/2252